SECURITY, DEMOCRACY AND DEVELOPMENT

INTERDISCIPLINARY STUDIES
ON CENTRAL AND EASTERN EUROPE

Vol. 14

Edited by
Christian Giordano, Nicolas Hayoz & Jens Herlth

PETER LANG
Bern · Berlin · Bruxelles · Frankfurt am Main · New York · Oxford · Wien

GHIA NODIA AND
CHRISTOPH H. STEFES (EDS)

SECURITY, DEMOCRACY AND DEVELOPMENT

In the Southern Caucasus and the Black Sea Region

PETER LANG
Bern • Berlin • Bruxelles • Frankfurt am Main • New York • Oxford • Wien

Bibliographic information published by die Deutsche Nationalbibliothek
Die Deutsche Nationalbibliothek lists this publication in the Deutsche Nationalbibliografie; detailed bibliographic data is available on the Internet at ‹http://dnb.d-nb.de›.

British Library Cataloguing-in-Publication Data: A catalogue record for this book is available from The British Library, Great Britain

Library of Congress Control Number: 2015938488

Cover illustration: Batumi from iStockphoto.com © by suc

ISSN 1661-1349 pb.
ISBN 978-3-0343-1300-1 pb.

ISSN 2235-7025 eBook
ISBN 978-3-0351-0836-1 eBook

This publication has been peer reviewed.

Hochfeldstrasse 32, CH-3012 Bern, Switzerland
info@peterlang.com, www.peterlang.com

Printed in Hungary

Contents

Ghia Nodia and Christoph H. Stefes

Introduction

This is a book about a very difficult though diverse and fascinating region, the Southern Caucasus. This part of the world is also viewed as part of the larger Black Sea area. Why would we consider it a "difficult" region? Do not all countries or regions, including those that are usually considered relatively successful and orderly, face critical problems? For instance, do not the European Union's multiple crises of recent years make Europe a "difficult region"?

Undoubtedly. Yet the Southern Caucasus, which emerged as a region in its own right in the early 1990's from the debris of the Soviet Union, stands out for the variety and intensity of conflicts (including violent conflicts), instability, and economic hardship. The rest of the world therefore often sees the South Caucasus as a source of disorder and problems that sometimes require urgent intervention (as, for instance, in August 2008, when a war broke out between Georgia and Russia). It is a region that always needs attention, support and preventive action so that problems do not get out of hand and spill over into neighbouring countries and regions. There are, of course, other, more positive reasons to be interested in the South Caucasus. One can easily be attracted by its diverse cultures, ancient history, spectacular landscapes, rich cuisine, heart-warming hospitality, and even sometimes economic opportunity. Nevertheless, for people outside of and unfamiliar with the region, conflict and disorder are usually the first things that come to mind when they hear the word "Caucasus".

For inquisitive minds, which social scientists are supposed to have, there is also good news: the Caucasus may be a difficult region, but it is never a boring one. Its extremely deep and painful social, political and economic transformations require careful analyses and understanding, both in order to relieve the pain and increase chances of success for those countries and peoples but also for increasing our general knowledge about deep transformations, how they fail and succeed, how conflicts flare up and are (sometimes) resolved. This is what this is book is about.

Young social scientists from both within and outside the region are the contributors. One of the multiple problems of the Southern Caucasus (should it be considered among the key ones?) was that it was isolated from the intellectual mainstream of the contemporary world. The myths of salvation inherent in dogmatic Soviet Marxism were replaced with romantic mythology of national awakenings intertwined with an extremely simplistic understanding of popular sovereignty and free-market mechanisms. Only relatively recently have young scholars from countries in the Caucasus started to conceptualize complex processes of development in their own countries through the prism of contemporary theories and methodologies – however imperfect the latter may be. On the other hand, an increasing number of researchers in leading universities around the globe have become interested in the region. Transformative processes that take place there become a source of intellectual inspiration for their research projects. The result is that local and foreign scholars engage in a much wider and richer scholarly conversation. Its results may be fruitful and interesting for those people who do not necessarily specialize in those countries but may draw lessons from work on these countries for comparative research. This book presents a glimpse of the state of that conversation, and of what the global social science community can learn from developments in the Caucasus.

This collection includes the best papers from a conference "Security, Democracy and Development in the Southern Caucasus and the Black Sea Region", financed and organized by the Academic Swiss Caucasus Net (ASCN) in October 2012 in Istanbul. ASCN is funded by Gebert Rüf Stiftung and has been working for several years to increase the quality of social research on the Southern Caucasus and provide new forums for a lively and professional debate on genuinely fascinating topics related to developments in these countries. The present publication has been made possible thanks to the generous support of Gebert Rüf Stiftung and its ASCN programme.

***

The table of contents of this book is in itself a source of information about the region. By choosing topics for their research, the community of scholars prioritizes events and developments. That judgment, like any other, may be contested, and there is always an element of contingency here. Still, what does this table of content tell us about the issues that the Southern Caucasus faces?

In a nutshell, there were several basic and deeply interconnected problems that the new states of the Caucasus (and they are new even though many of them boast of very ancient history) faced in the early 1990's, when the seemingly stable Soviet order abruptly collapsed. These nations had to define what they are, which meant determining on what basis their polities had to be kept together, along which lines their spatial borders had to be drawn, and where they belonged in the contemporary international political order. Having at least notionally rejected the Communist system, they had to build new formal or informal institutions of governance. And, having left the unified and rigidly regulated world of Soviet economics, they had to figure out how they were going to sustain themselves in an increasingly competitive world economy.

Arguably, none of those problems can be considered "solved": borders, political regimes, international alliances are still contested. However, enough time has passed for us to discern major trends of development: who the major actors are and what their interests, visions and strategies are; what structural problems, advantages and disadvantages they have to deal with; what are the lasting outcomes of supposedly "temporary" solutions; how the region fits in the changing world of international relations.

Territorial conflicts are the most conspicuous expressions of the unfinished state of the national projects in the South Caucasus. Whatever theories of state formation or international relations each of us may prefer, we – at least those who live outside of the boundaries of the European Union – still find ourselves in a Westphalian world of nation states. Certainty about state boundaries is the most basic starting point for formulating and solving problems of political, social or economic development and those borders remain the most potent factors of social construction. Yet this is exactly the issue that has remained unresolved in the Southern Caucasus.

The simplest question – "what are the countries that constitute the Southern Caucasus?" – defies clear answers. A politically correct answer that most of international community is willing to accept reads: Armenia, Azerbaijan and Georgia (to stay out of trouble, alphabetical order is used). We also encounter so-called "unrecognized" or "de facto" states of Abkhazia, South Ossetia and Nagorno-Karabakh. They have been around since the early 1990's with the more-or-less stable institutional frameworks that states are supposed to have. Nevertheless, it would also be rather misleading to say that those are genuine states that only lack international recognition in order to be considered "normal". Certainly, they are genuinely independent, and increasingly sealed, from those states of which they are supposed to be integral parts by international law: Azerbaijan in case of Nagorno-Karabakh, and Georgia for Abkhazia and South Ossetia. Yet their independence from what can be called their patron states (Armenia for Nagorno-Karabakh, Russia for Abkhazia and South Ossetia) is rather questionable, and it is quite difficult to imagine their existence beyond that patronage.

Whatever happens with and within the unrecognized states, there is a divergence between the mental maps of their own countries that citizens carry in their heads and the real though not internationally legitimate boundaries that regulate movements of people and goods in effect. These boundaries have emerged based on supposedly temporary ceasefire agreements after wars (signed in 1992 in the case of South Ossetia, 1994 in the cases of Abkhazia and Nagorno-Karabakh, and then 2008 again for South Ossetia and Abkhazia), but they have become the most stable feature of the political geography of the region. This divergence – and recognition of this divergence as something temporary and abnormal – has become a stable feature of political, social and mental lives of these countries.

It may be a symptomatic feature of this volume that none of the articles presented deal with the core reasons of these conflicts, or prospects for their solution. Important as those issues are, a certain fatigue surrounds them: a lot has been said and written on this already, and there is certain fatalistic recognition that there is no improvement in sight. Quite the opposite, in each of the cases risks of deterioration appear to be greater. So, it appears more promising to research what the lasting and apparently insurmountable divergences between legal and effective boundaries do to the institutions and lives of people.

One of the most important of permanently temporary solutions for the South Caucasus conflicts is the fate of internally displaced persons (IDPs) and refugees: people who lost their homes and livelihoods as a result of ethnic cleansings that constitute part and parcel of postcommunist ethno-territorial conflicts. The experience of forceful expulsion (that occurred between 1989 and 1994 for the most, or as recently as in 2008 for some) is tragic enough; but in addition, these people have become hostage to those quasi-temporary solutions. Because solutions are temporary, the IDPs and refugees are supposed to return – and this is something many of them really aspire to – but this prevents them from putting their tragic experiences behind them and integrating into those communities in which they were forced to start their new lives.

There are two articles in this volume that deal with this issue, both focused on the Georgian case. Kabachnik, Mitchneck and Regulska, using the Foucaultian concept of "governmentality", deal with the implications of the status of "internally displaced persons". For a long time, the Georgian government emphasized the temporary character of this displacement: it assumed that full and successful integration of IDPs in the places of their new settlement could be interpreted as an indication that they were not going to return to the areas from which they had been expelled. This expressed itself in limiting electoral rights of IDPs in local elections, keeping them in temporary dwellings, and so forth. The policy changed quite significantly after the 2008 war, when the Georgian government took steps towards "normalizing" the status of IDPs in that they were granted full ownership rights on their lodgings just like other citizens – but the authors also discuss the shortcomings of these new policies. Minna Lundgren zooms in the movements of people across the ABL (administrative boundary line) between Abkhazia and Georgia proper. People on the both sides of it belong to the same (Georgian) ethnic community, and habitual crossings between the Gali district (an almost fully Georgian-populated region within Abkhazia) and Zugdidi on the Georgian side become part of their way of life. However, while this boundary is not an internationally recognized border (and these people do not consider it legitimate either), it certainly feels and works like one.

The existence of effective borders that nevertheless do not enjoy legitimate status has identifiable economic consequences: they hamper economic cooperation and development of the border regions but they can also be considered an economic opportunity, especially for those entrepreneurs who are ready to use illicit methods and benefit from the grey zones created by unrecognized borders and polities. The latter may constitute an interest group that wants conflicts to remain unresolved: but does the existence of such groups actually explain why their solutions have not been achieved yet? People interested in this issue may find it useful to read the chapter by Giulia Prelz Oltramonti in this volume.

The existence of "unrecognized states" is a source of one more paradox. Lack of recognition means *not* being accepted as part of international community; can such political units have any foreign policies still? If yes, what would that look like? Clearly, the unrecognized states strive to have some kind of foreign policies. Hanna Shelest studies this issue based on cases from the region, adding the Transnistrian region of Moldova to her analysis.

***

While undefined – or improperly defined – borders may be the most painful and dramatic problem that the new states of the Caucasus face, the new borders (recognized and unrecognized) have also had the greatest impact on the process of reconstruction of identities within these societies. But while state borders are usually drawn and redrawn at specific turning points in history and then stay fairly stable, the process of identity reconstruction is continuous and never final.

For the benefit of specific research projects, the Soviet legacy may be imagined to constitute some kind of a starting point in this multifaceted process of identity reconstruction – even though nations and societies have much deeper pasts and richer collective memories that transcend seven decades of the Soviet rule. Paradoxically enough, an ethnic rather than a civic understanding of national identity is a notable legacy of Soviet rule (Brubaker, 1996). This can be called a paradox because propagating "proletarian internationalism" and predicting the vanishing of national identities was part of Soviet ideology (Slezkine, 1994). The government tried to instil loyalty to the Soviet state – something that Western scholars might have called a version of civic nationalism. Many Western analysts believed that at least in solving the "national question", the Soviet rule was fairly successful. What happened, however, was that as soon as the rigid control by the communist leadership loosened, Soviet ideology was replaced by nationalism of the most ethnic and exclusivist, and thus destructive, variety (Suny, 1993). It was the prevalence of this type of nationalism that was directly responsible for the ethno-territorial conflicts mentioned above.

Does that domination of ethnic nationalism change? Do states try to base their policies on less exclusivist visions of the nation? Does new openness created by the greater opportunities to travel, or a push to migrations created by economic hardships, cause people to redefine their identities? Would greater contact with a postnational entity like the European Union through instruments like the European Neighbourhood Policy and European Partnership, also alter the ways in which people in the Southern Caucasus perceive themselves? Arguably, if more inclusive civic identities develop among peoples of these countries, this may not help solving existing territorial conflicts (though it can transform people's attitudes to them), but it will prevent new ones, thus making this region more secure and increase chances of building more stable and effective democratic institutions. In this volume, Kevork Oskanian carefully analyses the policies of the Georgian government under Mikheil Saakashvili to redefine Georgian identity, making it more civic in nature.

While ethno-national belonging may be the most consequential in the Caucasus, there are other identities that are transformed in the changing political and societal landscape of the Southern Caucasus. This includes attitudes to gender. The Soviet regime espoused gender equality and, indeed, did a lot in terms of enabling women to get education and jobs: using these formal criteria, the Soviet Union was actually more progressive than many Western democracies. However – and this may be another paradox of communist modernization – the communist legacy left behind relatively conservative attitudes to gender roles in the Caucasus, which include the assumption that the man is the primary breadwinner and head of family. Conversely, economic realities of the postcommunist economy, which is notable for high levels of poverty and unemployment, may have contributed to undermining traditional distribution of gender roles. In particular, labour migration has become main survival strategy for many families, and many of them have started to depend on women who go abroad in search of jobs. In her contribution to this volume, Maroussia Ferry analyses the changing role of Georgian women. Surprisingly, as Ferry points out, while Georgian women often assume the role of the breadwinner and even travel abroad for extensive periods, norms and values change only slowly. In a way, her contribution therefore attests to the power of culture over structure.

***

Having rejected Soviet communism, the new states of the Southern Caucasus had to develop new political systems. In all of them, nationalist elites declared their commitment to democratic institutions and, at least initially, one could believe in the sincerity of that choice. However, in none of Southern Caucasus states did this democratic opening lead to an eventual consolidation of democracy. With the possible exception of Azerbaijan, the political regimes that were created cannot be called autocracies, as they are usually described in the scientific literature. It would be misleading to define them as countries in "democratic transition" either, because their political systems have displayed quite stable characteristics over a couple of decades and, while things *are* changing, one cannot be sure at all that regimes are becoming more democratic rather than otherwise (Carothers, 2002). This uncertainty is not specific to the Caucasus countries, and the classification of such political regimes has become a problem for comparative political studies. Quite a number of concepts emerged in the literature such as "grey zone", "hybrid regimes", "competitive authoritarianism" and "defective democracy" (Carothers, 2002; Diamond, 2002; Levitsky and Way, 2002; Merkel, 2004; Bogaards, 2009). The word "hybrid" may be the most popular and convincing part of those definitions: in such countries, some features of democracy and some features of autocracy are mixed up, but each mixture varies from country to country.

Georgia is usually considered the closest to democracy but its political life is also the most unstable and unpredictable in the region (one may find a research question here: does more democracy correlate with more instability in the Caucasus?). It went through four regime changes since 1990, some relatively orderly (1990 and 2012), some violent (1991–92), and some revolutionary but nonviolent (2003). Each of them promised a new beginning for the Georgian state and democracy but each ended up in recreating what we can call a dominant power system (Carothers, 2002): a single political party or coalition usually consolidated around strong charismatic leaders that control all major levers of political power, but this power is openly and genuinely contested by the divided but militant opposition, fairly free and critical media, a small but vibrant civil society sector and so forth. The system is stable while the government is relatively popular but, once credibility is lost, governments find it difficult to survive for long. At the time of writing it is too early to tell conclusively whether the latest change of power that occurred through fairly orderly elections for the first time in October 2012 will lead to the same outcome.

Azerbaijan occupies the opposite extreme: most analysts categorize it as an autocratic rather than a "hybrid" regime. Since 1993, after a brief interlude with the anticommunist National Front in power, it has been ruled by a single Aliev dynasty: father Heydar, a seasoned Soviet apparatchik, and his son Ilham, who in 2003 succeeded his father and in October 2013 started his third term in the office of presidency. Officially, Azerbaijan also claims to be a democracy, therefore it has some opposition, some independent media and some NGOs, but their freedom and chances to actually influence the situation are rather slim, so the regime has never been seriously challenged. One widely discussed explanation of this autocratic stability may be found in the oil riches of the country (Karl, 1997): in the

2000s, when Azerbaijani oil started to flow to its consumers in the global economy (we will return to this topic in the moment) Azerbaijan enjoyed one of the highest economic growth rates in the world. While the revenues are unfairly distributed, something does trickle down; the ruling elite has enough resources to pay for the security apparatus and ensure that all potential contestants are either co-opted or repressed.

Armenia's political regime is closer to Georgia in being somewhat competitive but not really democratic. It is also an obvious specimen of a "dominant power system" and has been ruled by the same elite since the early 1990's, although personalities at the top did change. Actors outside the ruling elite have some freedom to challenge the regime but are unable to defeat it. The fact that Armenia is the only country in the Southern Caucasus that has emerged victorious in the ethno-territorial wars of the early 1990s might partially explain this stability. Hence, it is no coincidence that it has been ruled by the same elite whose legitimacy is ultimately based on that victory, although there are different clans within it that compete for influence. The only contested change within the state power happened in the parliamentary coup of 1998, when President LevonTer-Petrosian, an erstwhile leader of the Karabakh movement, lost support due to his intention to compromise on the territorial issue with Azerbaijan and wisely chose to resign. The subsequent leaders of Armenia actually came from Nagorno-Karabakh, and in the last years even the most influential opposition party is linked to the Karabakh elite.

The latter example shows that while failure of the Southern Caucasian states to consolidate democratic institutions may be explained by a number of structural factors, unresolved territorial conflicts remain an important one. Whether for victors or losers, the unresolved territorial issue remains an important ground for nationalist mobilization, and contributes to "securitization" (Buzan *et al.*, 1998) of internal political issues. This is not conducive to embracing stable democratic pluralism.

***

It is notable that several authors in this volume choose to focus on the impact of external actors, in particular Western countries and organizations, on political developments in the South Caucasus. Promotion of democracy is one of the proclaimed goals of Western governments and international organizations, and they dedicate certain funds and political capital towards this goal. But what is the effect of such efforts? Or, to look from another perspective, do external factors explain variances in the level of democratic freedom between countries of the Southern Caucasus?

As democracy promotion becomes increasingly salient, while, on the other hand, "hybrid regimes" proliferate, more and more scholars study the role of external actors in democratization (or lack thereof). In their frequently cited book on hybrid regimes that they call "competitive authoritarian" systems, Levitsky and Way (2010) claim that, for such countries, closeness to Europe is the most potent variable explaining their degree of freedom (strength of the repressive apparatus of the regime is another major factor). While internal resources for the establishment of democratic system of check and balances are insufficient (whatever such resources may be), external forces may compensate, at least in part, for such a deficit and induce power elites within a given country to behave in a more democratic way. In Levitsky and Way's terms, such influence may be explained by linkage to and leverage of the West: on the one hand, through different international institutions and other frameworks, local ruling elites develop deep linkages to Western institutions and this leads to transforming their behaviour; on the other hand, Western governments, who presumably wish to spread democratic values and institutions, should have leverage over governments and, generally speaking, political elites of the semi-authoritarian countries.

But what are the factors on which the degree of linkage and leverage depends? The European Union is generally considered the most successful democratizing actor, but not because Europeans have discovered some secret methods that work better than others. The EU is believed to contribute a lot to the consolidation of democracy in the formerly communist countries that have become its members in the 2000s, or are on the way to being admitted. In such cases, a firm promise of EU membership is the most powerful incentive that induces governments and political elites to accept and follow norms and procedures that they might otherwise have evaded. But it is also widely believed that absence of such an incentive significantly reduces leverage of the democratic countries to transform institutions and political practices of nondemocratic countries.

All states of the Southern Caucasus are members of European Neighbourhood Policy (ENP) and, later, European Partnership (EaP). EU calls these policies "instruments" serving to spread its norms and institutions (including those of democracy) in the neighbouring countries. None of those mechanisms, however, implies promise of eventual membership. But, in lieu of such promise, can those mechanisms provide sufficient linkage and leverage to cause significant change in the partner countries?

Most analysts are sceptical and it is indeed difficult to find any "Europeanization" happening in Belarus or Azerbaijan. Georgia may represent a partial exception. It may be no coincidence that, in this volume, all three articles that discuss the influence of external actors on internal political processes focus on Georgia. This is the only country in the Southern Caucasus that has been fairly consistent in its pro-European orientation: despite very confrontational internal politics, all major political forces, as well as a sizeable majority of the public, support joining NATO and the European Union as Georgia's strategic goal. That gives Western powers, in particular, European institutions and the US government some leverage over its ruling elites. This Western leverage might partly compensate for the lack of domestic checks and balances.

Azerbaijan and Armenia are different. Both of them try to complement cooperation with the West (including NATO and European Union) with good relations with Russia. None of them has expressed a wish to actually join those two organizations. Moreover, Armenia, despite the declared foreign policy of "complementarity", is more dependent on Russia for its security, and its decision to join Russia-dominated Eurasian Union, announced in the fall of 2013, may imply the end of "complementarity". This implies that Western actors have much weaker leverage over the ruling elites of those countries. Moreover, the natural riches of Azerbaijan reduce that leverage even more, because Europe is interested in Azerbaijani oil and gas for diversifying its energy supplies, while Western companies want to guard and enlarge their shares in exploiting those resources. This gives Azerbaijan leverage over the West. This explains why it is that young scholars find the Georgian case the most interesting for their research on the role of external factors in democratic development.

***

The birth of the three states in the Southern Caucasus was accompanied by dire economic hardships, due in part to the break-up of the unified and bureaucratically controlled Soviet economic system, and exacerbated by territorial wars. This stage of economic crisis is now overcome and at times all the countries have achieved quite respectable (in the case of Azerbaijan, quite spectacular) rates of economic growth. However, overall, the region (and it includes many parts of oil-rich Azerbaijan) remains poor. It is also very weakly integrated into the global economy. So far, the only important factor that puts it on the global economic map is the oil and gas riches of the Caspian basin to which Azerbaijan has primary access. This book therefore dedicates a section to the issue of energy policies and politics.

Energy and its transportation routes create a set of issues that are economic and political (or geoeconomic and geopolitical) at the same time. While it is often said that politicizing energy problems is wrong, in reality energy has become a deeply divisive political issue, and, in a contested region like Caucasus, it could hardly be otherwise. Since the 1990s, competition between different routes for transporting Caspian hydrocarbon resources was often described as a new "Great Game", and there was a reason for that. Russia made no secret of the fact that it considered the Southern Caucasus to be its backyard and resented outsiders doing business there without its consent. Were Caspian oil and gas being transported exclusively through its own territory, Russia could effectively dominate the region. On the other hand, had Azerbaijan managed to get its resources to the outside consumers circumventing Russia, this success would have implied its economic self-sufficiency that would also underpin chances of genuine political independence. Moreover, if major Western powers, both Americans and Europeans, developed a sufficiently strong interest in gaining access to the resources of the Caspian, they would also have a stake in security and stability of the region, and grow more politically supportive of it.

While its conflict with Armenia was unresolved, and Iran was unavailable for the Americans, the only non-Russian route for Azerbaijani oil and gas could be through Georgia and Turkey. For Georgia, the political benefits of this arrangement much exceeded interest in transit fees (which is why Georgia eventually accepted very low ones): the pipeline, so Georgians believed, would cement its alliance with both Azerbaijan and Turkey, and firmly tie Western interest to Georgia, thus underpinning Georgia's true sovereignty. Turkey had both political and economic interests in this oil and gas transportation project: it needed Caspian energy for developing its north-eastern region, and a network of pipelines running through its territory could turn this country into an energy hub. The latter, apart from obvious economic benefits, improved its negotiating positions in relations with the European Union. The negative element of this scheme was that it expelled Armenia thus increasing its sense of isolation – and of being ultimately dependent on Russia.

Thus, contest for energy transportation routes strongly correlated with the map of geopolitical rivalries. Linkage between Azerbaijan, Georgia, and

Turkey developed a sense of inevitability and was supported by Western powers, especially the United States. This was opposed by Russia, with Armenia being its chief ally in the region and Iran was also less than friendly to the projects of hydrocarbon transportation routes going through Georgia and Turkey.

While the 1990s saw contentious debates and negotiations, chiefly around the project of the Baku–Tbilisi–Ceyhan oil pipeline, the first decade of the new millennium brought important developments on the ground – or, rather, underneath. Baku–Tbilisi–Ceyhan was built in 2002–5, followed by the South Caucasus or the Baku–Tbilisi–Erzurum gas pipeline later in 2006. The third important transportation project is the Baku–Tbilisi–Kars railway, scheduled for completion in 2015. These three projects have significantly redrawn the geopolitical and geoeconomic map of the region. They did cement the strong sense of common interest between Azerbaijan, Georgia, and Turkey (which survived partial reorientation of Turkish foreign policy after under Recep Tayyip Erdoğan and his foreign minister, Ahmed Davutoğlu), turned Azerbaijan into major economic powerhouse in the region, gained Georgia energy independence and a better negotiation positions towards Russia, and turned Turkey into an important energy hub.

But this is not the end of the saga. In the recent years, the greatest interest is towards linking Caspian gas resources to Europe. Here, EU and Turkey and, indirectly, Russia are the main actors. Azerbaijan and Georgia are important stakeholders and beneficiaries, although their interest is less dramatic than in the three projects mentioned above, as pipelines through their territories have already been built. Therefore, at this point energy transportation issues are focused not so much on the Southern Caucasus but, broader, on the Black Sea area.

The key problem here is that EU feels too dependent on Russian gas and fears that Russia may abuse its position. It is therefore interested in diversifying its energy supplies. For that end, it has supported the Nabucco pipeline project that would bring Caspian gas to several European countries. Russia considered this project to be unfavourable to its interests. However, apart from Nabucco, there were also other competing pipeline projects discussed. In 2013, following lengthy and complicated negotiations, it appears that most stakeholders, Azerbaijan and Turkey first of all, gave preference to the Trans-Anatolian Pipeline project (TANAP) that would bring Caspian gas to Southern Europe but would have less impact on energy supplies in the EU than Nabucco. However, this is an ongoing story in which politics and economics continue to be intertwined.

It should also be noted that hydrocarbon resources of the Caspian basin are not only interesting for the European consumers: the growing economies of China and India, as well as other countries, are increasingly becoming stakeholders too.

The authors of this volume focus on different parts of this fascinating story. Sybilla Wege provides the big picture: she gives an overview of the interests of main stakeholders and how they are reflected in different competing transportation projects. Oana Poiană links energy competition to the not-very-encouraging story of attempts to build regional cooperation frameworks in the Black Sea region. Fabio Indeo focuses on the interests and strategic gains of Azerbaijan, and Slawomir Raszewski discusses the Turkish position and divergence of its interests from those of the European Union. Nikoloz Sumbadze brings a completely new perspective: whether and how the advent of shale gas, a newcomer to the global energy market, will change the terms of energy competition globally and in the region.

References

Bogaards, M. (2009) How to classify hybrid regimes? Defective democracy and electoral authoritarianism. *Democratization* 16(2), 399–423.

Brubaker, R. (1996) *Nationalism Reframed: Nationalism and the National Question in the New Europe,* Cambridge University Press, Cambridge.

Buzan, B., Wæver, O. and de Wilde, J. (1998) *Security: A New Framework for Analysis,* Lynne Rienner, Boulder, CO.

Carothers, T. (2002) The end of the transition paradigm. *Journal of Democracy* 13(1), 5–21.

Diamond, L. (2002) Thinking about hybrid regimes. *Journal of Democracy* 13(2), 21–35.

Karl, T. L. (1997) *The Paradox of Plenty,* University of California Press, Berkeley, CA.

Levitsky, S. and Way, L. A. (2002) *Journal of Democracy* 13(2), 51–65.

Levitsky, S. and Way, L. A. (2010) *Competitive Authoritarianism: Hybrid Regimes After the Cold War,* Cambridge University Press, New York.

Merkel, W. (2004) Embedded and defective democracies. *Democratization* 11(5), 33–58.

Slezkine, Y. (1994) The USSR as a communal apartment, or how a socialist state promoted ethnic particularism. *Slavic Review* 53(2), 414–452.

Suny, R. G. (1993) *The Revenge of the Past: Nationalism, Revolution, and the Collapse of the Soviet Union*, Stanford University Press, Stanford, CA.

Part I
Elections, Revolutions and Policies

David Sichinava

Cleavage Theory and the Electoral Geographies of Georgia

ABSTRACT: Georgia has held several important elections from the beginning of 2008, culminating in the fall of 2012 when an opposition political group defeated the ruling party. As competitive elections are relatively new to Georgia, a substantial amount of literature is dedicated to the problems of voting in that country. This chapter investigates how particular theories of voting, especially the cleavage model of Seymour M. Lipset and Stein Rokkan (1967), may be applied to the case of Georgia. The main argument is that political cleavages can be identified; however, their origins differ from those suggested by Lipset and Rokkan. It is argued that the political cleavages in Georgia are the products of the country's recent historical experience – urbanization and ethnic alienation.

KEYWORDS: Georgia, elections, geography, cleavage model, democracy, Saakashvili

Introduction

Unlike most western European countries, Georgia has a relatively short history of free and competitive elections. Little research has therefore been done in the field that would deal with the explanation of voting behaviour and, in particular, its spatial aspects. Cleavage theory, originally suggested by Seymour M. Lipset and Stein Rokkan (1967), cannot be completely applied to Georgian elections, as it is not relevant to this case. This chapter will show the existence of electoral cleavages other than those mentioned by Lipset and Rokkan. It will develop a theoretical model of voting behaviour in nascent democracies, examine the election results of the three national elections held in Georgia since 2008, and try to build a quantitative voting model as well as identify additional important aspects of voting behaviour in Georgia. Centre-periphery and urban-rural political cleavages are relevant in the voting context of Georgia. We argue that these cleavages are the legacies of the communist and precommunist era, which crystallized into voting behaviour.

Theoretical Insights of Electoral Cleavage Formation in Postcommunist Space

Cleavage theory, as suggested by Seymour M. Lipset and Stein Rokkan, refers to the major debate of electoral geography – formation of particular voting behaviour in a given territorial context. Generally, it deals with the process of cleavage formation and its transformation into party systems. Parties are defined as "agents of conflict and instruments of integration", thus mobilizing populations to strengthen their national identities (Lipset and Rokkan, 1967: 3). Conflicts of interests among different societal groups inside the political systems are articulated in terms of political parties. Parties by themselves are instruments of expression in elections representing corresponding population groups (Lipset and Rokkan, 1967). As their analysis mostly covered the politics of established Western democracies, Lipset and Rokkan identified four major dimensions of political cleavages that have long dominated West European politics: centre–periphery, state–Church, land–industry and owner–worker. They also list the corresponding critical revolutions contributing to the formation of dichotomies: the Reformation and Counter-Reformation of the sixteenth and seventeenth centuries, national revolutions after 1789, the Industrial Revolution of the nineteenth century and the Russian Revolution.

At least two political cleavages bear distinct spatial characteristics representing respectively: (i) conflict between a nation-building "centre" and an ethnically, religiously and culturally different "periphery" and (ii) contest between conservative rural areas with an agricultural economy and urban areas with a large proportion of the population being employed in the secondary and tertiary sectors. These political cleavages have greatly influenced the electoral geographies and longtime voting allegiances of the population in Western democracies by forming spatial characteristics of voting behaviour – for example, the establishment of agrarian parties in Nordic states and the emergence of the Scottish National Party (Taylor and Johnston, 1979).

However, there is an argument whether this theory applies to the modern political situation. Several factors, including the emergence of so called "postmaterial" values contribute to the loss of importance of traditional cleavages, which in the past played an important role for voter allegiance. Moreover, Fukuyama's widely discussed idea about the end of ideology questions the overall concept of cleavages as the basis for societal divisions (Johnston and Pattie, 2003).

As we move geographically from western Europe to the east and southeast, numerous questions arise about whether the four dimensions of political cleavages influence the process of party formation and, consequently, electoral behaviour. The region's historical past is quite different from those of west European democracies. Consequently, accounts of emerging social cleavages suggested by Lipset and Rokkan are arguably insufficient. It is worth mentioning that communist regimes, which for decades dominated the region's political scene, caused the violent deterioration of previous political systems.

Formation of political cleavages in postcommunist polities have quite distinct relations to their historical past, depending on the type of communist regime. Herbert Kitschelt (1995) draws three different categories of communist regimes according to their type of policy making and bureaucratic involvement: patrimonial communist, bureaucratic-authoritarian communism, and national/national consensus communism. Most countries of the former Soviet Union, including Georgia, belong to the group of patrimonial communist regimes, which had "low opportunities for intra-elite contestation and institutionalization". The author also stresses that the newly formed urban population, which consisted of workers and white-collar intelligentsia, became "indebted to the communist regime (and successor former Communist leaders) for the dramatic improvements in the standards of life" (Kitschelt, 1995: 455). Here the regime was not contested as there was no independent stratum of intellectuals with precommunism heritage able to challenge the communist regime (as they were physically and morally annihilated) (Kitschelt, 1995). Here the cleavage is defined as the result of the communist past, the so-called "Leninist legacy" and is measured on a liberal–authoritarian axis (Whitefield, 2002).

Evans and Whitefield argue that despite a long period of communist rule, which almost eradicated and structurally changed national political landscapes of the region, ex-communist nations developed several of their own political cleavages based on local factors and their historical past

(Evans and Whitefield, 2000). In a later study, Whitefield identifies several factors that form cleavages in postcommunist polities: precommunist cultural legacies, variations of communist rule and democratic transition, institutions and elite factors, social experiences and identities (Whitefield, 2002).

The theories described above show that communist and precommunist legacies and socio-demographic peculiarities explain the emergence of electoral cleavages; alternatively, all these factors are translated into spatial context (ethnic, religious, economic patterns, formation of historical regions, and so forth).

Historical regionalization is another factor largely contributing to the formation of electoral geographies in East European societies. Historical regions are spatial units that are formed under certain historical, socioeconomic and geographic circumstances. Hence, demographic and religious factors, precommunist heritage as well as identities and the type of economic activities can be conceptualized as historical geographical divisions. Notably, several authors identify historical regionalism and, consequently, geographic variables as crucial determinants of voting behaviour in postcommunist states. Perepechko *et al.* (2007) argue that presocialist political cleavages possess a regional dimension in Russia's electoral geography. Zaricky analyzes the role of historical regionalism in Poland – more specifically, partition of the country and "Prussian heritage" (Zarycki, 2002). Habsburg's historical legacy is important for explaining voting behaviour in Ukraine and Romania (Roper and Fesnic, 2003). And finally, several studies on elections in Ukraine point towards distinct regional and historical-geographic background to explain the country's electoral peculiarities (Clem and Craumer, 2008; Mykhnenko, 2009).

In conclusion, political cleavages in postcommunist societies are products of relatively recent events rather than long-term socioeconomic developments and cultural changes. This conclusion should hold especially for the case of Georgia, which was at the periphery of European industrialization and thus was less affected by the process. We might, however, argue that in addition to communist legacies and socioeconomic peculiarities, precommunist cultural heritage – namely, the historical regionalization of the country – could potentially have a significant effect on the formation of political cleavages and electoral geographies of the country.

Dimensions of Electoral Cleavages in Georgia

Continuous allegations of electoral fraud and undemocratic electoral campaigns have affected Georgian elections since independence. Since 1990, almost all elections have been dominated by single political groups (Gamsakhurdia's Round Table; Shevardnadze's Union of Georgian Citizens; Saakashvili's United National Movement) and candidates having administrative and material resources for the manipulation of the election results. Moreover, in many cases, incumbent candidates did not have strong political opponents and thus their decisive victory was assured. However, from 2008 the situation changed. Until 2012, there was no precedent for power transition using the voting process, excluding the1990 legislative elections held in the Soviet Socialist Republic of Georgia, formally part of the Soviet Union.

Two crucial events in 2008 had a significant impact on Georgia's political developments. After cracking down on protestors in November 2007, President Mikheil Saakashvili called for snap presidential elections in January and announced that he would seek re-election. Levan Gachechiladze, leader of the United Opposition group, which was formed by several political organizations, was the only serious opposition candidate. The incumbent President narrowly managed to avoid the run-off elections by winning 53% of votes. The political configuration was diametrically different for the parliamentary elections, which was held 5 months afterwards. The ruling party, the United National Movement (UNM), gained a landslide victory, managing to gather 60% of the vote and win 72 out of 76 single-member electoral districts, which led to a comfortable constitutional majority in the legislature.

Voter polarization characterized both elections and significantly affected the election results. The events that preceded the January elections, including brutal suppression of a large protest rally, the shutdown of major national broadcaster "Imedi", and the declaration of a state of emergency, split the voters into "pro-government" and "antigovernment" camps. This polarization was especially accentuated in Tbilisi and other major cities where the incumbent President failed to secure much support and sometimes even lost to his rivals. However, parliamentary elections were way more successful for the ruling UNM despite significant levels of voter polarization.

Political groups suggested different political agenda to the voters. Yet they did not differ all that much between the presidential and the parliamentary elections. Levan Gachechiladze, the presidential candidate of the United Opposition group, announced that after his victory there would be a shift from super-presidentialism to a parliamentary system (Civil Georgia, 2007), whereas the whole campaign of Saakashvili and the UNM was focused on social programmes, promising the introduction of free health insurance, the building of new hospitals, higher pensions and more subsidies to the agricultural sector (Corso, 2008).

On 1 October 2012, the parliamentary elections marked an important milestone in Georgia's political history. The Georgian Dream Coalition (GDC) defeated the UNM which had ruled the country since 2004. The main characteristics of the parliamentary elections were its high polarization – except for the GDC and the UNM, no other party was able to collect even 5% of votes in any voting district in the country or win a single-member seat in the parliament. The electoral campaigns were turbulent and sometimes even violent. Both sides blamed each other and claimed that the other was in violation of electoral rules, relying on illegal funds and administrative resources, restrictions on media broadcasting, suppression of party activists, and so forth. The process was significantly affected by the publication of scandalous videotapes allegedly depicting the torture of inmates by the members of penitential system employees. Oppositional Georgian Dream Coalition managed to gather 55% of the proportional vote. In contrast, the United National Movement was able to receive just 40.3% of the votes. The share of votes in the single-member districts was similar. GDP accordingly appointed 85 MPs in the 150 legislative body of the country. The elections also were marked with very high voter turnout – almost 61% of all voters participated in the voting process in difference with 55% in the presidential elections and 52% in the parliamentary elections held back in 2008.

Outcomes of the last three national elections displayed several important spatial patterns, which can also be identified as electoral cleavages. The urban-rural dichotomy of voting was a major one. Rural areas expressed loyalty to Saakashvili and the UNM whereas in the municipal centres, opposition candidates and political parties were doing better. The difference was evident even among urban and rural areas of the same voting districts. Several factors contributed to the emerging pattern of voting behaviour. First, urban areas, especially the capital city, are the main battlegrounds in Georgian politics. In fact, the most important events that led to fundamental political changes had their origins in the streets of Tbilisi and, to a lesser extent, in other urban settlements. Urban residents suffered from unemployment and other economic problems as much as their counterparts in the rural areas. Consequently, we cannot explain the emergence of such a cleavage in terms of socioeconomic hardships. Access to the media and the availability of a wide range of information were other important factors. In comparison to residents of rural settlements, citizens of urban areas enjoyed more diverse sources of information about politics and current events. Opinion polls suggest that television is the main source of information for Georgians (National Democratic Institute, 2011, 2012a, 2012b, 2012c), on the other hand, before 2012, only a limited number of TV broadcasters had nationwide coverage (OSCE/ODIHR Election Observation Mission, 2008). They were often accused of being state controlled (Mikashavidze, 2010) – for example, Imedi TV, which was taken off air on 7 November 2007, resumed its broadcasting only after a year.

The voting behaviour of the ethnic minorities forms another dimension of political cleavages revealed during the national elections of 2008 and 2012. It is a long-established trend that the representatives of ethnic minorities in Georgia, especially those residing in Kvemo Kartli, Javakheti and Kakheti regions, overwhelmingly vote for the incumbent government (Nodia, 2006). In different times these areas were strongholds for the Communists, the Georgian Citizens' Union of Eduard Shevardnadze and the United National Movement. Not surprisingly, the tendency was maintained in the 2008 and 2012 national elections. For example, in the 2008 presidential elections, in the Ninotsminda voting district, which is populated by Armenians, Saakashvili was able to receive about 90% of the votes. In the Azerbaijani-inhabited Marneuli district, 88% of the voters supported the government candidate. In the 2008 parliamentary elections, despite being strong in other areas of the country, the United National Movement largely secured its victory with votes from minority representatives. Finally, in the 2012 parliamentary elections, more than quarter of votes received by the UNM came from the seven districts primarily inhabited by the minorities – Gardabani, Marneuli, Bolnisi, Dmanisi, Tsalka, Akhalkalaki and Ninotsminda).

Electoral turnout is an important factor that can measure the strength of political engagement and voter mobilization around important issues. Lipset and Rokkan argue that political parties serve as "instruments of conflict and mobilization", as they try to translate political support into votes. High turnout in 2008 elections indicated higher support for the government, whereas the situation was different prior to the 2012 elections. In 2008, the local mobilization of the UNM supporters can be explained by active party grassroots organizations (and *allegedly,* use of administrative resources), especially in rural areas. However, the situation was altered prior to the 2012 parliamentary elections, when the Georgian Dream Coalition, which had plentiful resources, established strong network of party activists and local organizations what enabled them to contest the UNM. Another motif of including electoral turnout in the model is the control for the electoral fraud. Higher turnout could indicate not only the mobilization of voters but also vote rigging. Especially in 2008 presidential elections, there were allegations of ballot stuffing and other manipulations supporting the candidate of ruling political group. Interestingly enough, in the 2008 presidential elections, votes cast for Saakashvili and voter turnout correlated highly with each other ($r=0.6308$, $n=76$, $p<0.001$), which also throws the whole process of voting into doubt.

To summarize, there are at least two general electoral cleavages in Georgia that were important for all national elections held in and after 2008. Although political cleavages barely affect party formation in Georgia, there is proof that cleavage structures affect voting behaviour.

Cleavage Model of Voting – Data and Discussion

We have already identified the two crucial electoral cleavages that were important during the national elections of 2008 and 2012. Urban–rural and centre–periphery divisions have had an important impact on the formation of spatial patterns of electoral outcomes. The next step is to prove whether those factors are statistically significant. Our model investigates how the urban–rural dichotomy, ethnic minority population, and the level of political mobilization influenced voting preferences during the 2008 presidential election, and the May 2008 and October 2012 parliamentary elections. More precisely, we want to find out how vote shares for the incumbents reflected the identified political cleavages.

In our model, the votes cast for Saakashvili and the UNM are taken as dependent variables in three submodels for the presidential and parliamentary elections. The urban–rural cleavage is operationalized with the share of city/town population inside the voting district whereas the central–periphery cleavage is represented by the share of ethnic Georgian population in the municipalities (administrative municipalities in Georgia in almost all cases reflect the boundaries of electoral districts). The model employs another independent variable, overall turnout in order to measure the level of political mobilization and control for potential electoral fraud. For the 2012 elections submodel we have 73 cases, as the elections were not held inside Liakhvi, Akhalgori and Upper Abkhazia voting districts, which were out of Georgian jurisdiction and control.

In a generalized form, the following formula describes our model:

Vote share for the UNM candidate = $\beta_0 + \beta_1$ *urban population* + β_2 *Georgian population* + β_3 *turnout*

We used voting district level data from the presidential and parliamentary elections. As there was not a significant time threshold (only 5 months) between the two events, the model assumed that the proportion of urban and ethnic Georgian population would not change significantly and thus used the same data. There are two electoral districts (Liakhvi and Upper Abkhazia) that have no urban type settlement and ten electoral districts of Tbilisi where, despite the incorporation of several rural settlements within their boundaries, the rural share of the population is negligible relative to the whole number of voters in the unit (in fact, there are other objective factors, especially economic activities and administration, which strongly tie the population of these villages to the metropolitan city centre). As the last population census in Georgia was conducted in 2002, the figure representing the share of the urban population on the municipality level is based on 2006 estimates published by the government of Georgia (Government of Georgia, 2007a, Government of Georgia, 2007b, Government of Georgia, 2007c, Government of Georgia, 2007d, Government of Georgia, 2007e, Government of Georgia, 2007f, Government of Georgia, 2007g, Government of Georgia, 2007h, Government of Georgia, 2007i, Government of Georgia, 2007j).

The data is logged into the ordinary least squares (OLS) model in order to reveal the effect of independent variables on the dependent variable.

The model underwent different statistical tests on relevancy. The results are summarized in Table 1.

Table 1: Cleavage model of voting in Georgia.

	2008 presidential elections	*2008 parliamentary elections*	*2012 parliamentary elections*
	Votes cast for Saakashvili	*Votes cast for the UNM*	*Votes cast for the UNM*
Share of urban population (2006)	−0.191 (−4.330)**	−0.201 (−6.560)**	−0.225 (−5.580)**
Share of ethnic Georgian population	−0.218 (−3.990)**	−0.245 (−6.170)**	−0.213 (−3.560)**
Electoral turnout	0.696 (4.660)**	0.418 (4.470)**	−0.351 (−1.770)
Intercept	0.417 (3.750)**	0.674 (10.210)**	0.941 (8.480)**
R^2	0.59	0.67	0.49
N	76	76	73

Notes: * $p < 0.05$; ** $p < 0.01$.

Overall, the suggested equation explains 59% of variation in the 2008 presidential elections, 67% in the 2008 parliamentary elections and 49% of variations in the dependent variable in the 2012 parliamentary elections submodel. We have a steady pattern when looking at the coefficients for the urban–rural cleavage. They are all negative and cause about the same decrease in vote shares for the UNM and Saakashvili. Similarly, the coefficient for the share of Georgian population is also negative for all sub-models; however, they vary significantly – a decrease in the case of the 2008 parliamentary elections and an increase in the 2012 parliamentary elections submodel. To summarize, the two independent variables measuring the major electoral cleavages in the country, cause more-or-less similar negative change in the United National Movement's and Saakashvili's votes. Despite the fact that the elections in 2008 and 2012 differed hugely by both political context and actors as well, the two main cleavages had about the same effect on electoral outcomes.

Lipset and Rokkan argue that the origins of the urban–rural dichotomy lie in deepening societal conflicts that were caused by the Industrial Revolution. In some cases the political cleavage could translate into political parties, for example, in Nordic states, where urban areas dominated political life, "the struggle for democracy and parliamentary rule was triggered off through a broad process of mobilization within the peasantry" (Lipset and Rokkan, 1967: 20). However, it is hard to prove whether the Industrial Revolution could have an impact on the societal division in the country, which is located in the periphery of Europe, where the main developments of the shift occurred. It seems that the urban–rural dichotomy (as well as the centre–periphery political cleavage) arose due to more recent events.

Peculiarities of Georgian urbanization could be an important reason for urban–rural political cleavages. Like other countries of the Soviet Union, Georgia underwent a very rapid process of urbanization. Whitefield (2002) argues, that the urban–rural dichotomy in voting could be traced to the occupational class – indeed, mass urbanization in the Soviet Union was directly defined by increasing industrialization. Occupational classes were formed during the Soviet rule. The mentioned dichotomy still has an influence on formation of voting behaviour and its spatial patterns. On the other hand, as Kitschelt suggests, urban areas were home to large numbers of "white-collar" workers and the intelligentsia, contributing to the strength of urban–rural dichotomy.

Kitschelt's idea sheds light on another important dimension of voting behaviour observed in Tbilisi. The two elections in 2008 revealed a strong difference in the electoral patterns between "prestigious" and "working-class" neighbourhoods of Tbilisi. The opposition candidates (and parties) with radical political demands enjoyed higher political support in well-off areas whereas less prestigious neighbourhoods preferred to vote for the UNM with its focus on social programmes. We can argue that this particular pattern could have the same origin as the urban–rural electoral dichotomy.

City neighbourhoods, especially in Tbilisi, experienced a significant level of social segregation. The central, prestigious areas of the cities were allocated to "white-collar" workers and the intelligentsia, who formed a distinct social landscape. Their economic situation and status greatly improved during the Soviet era. Consequently, it had large impact on their loyalty towards the communist system. The first years of independence were marked with turbulent and violent political events, which caused the ousting of Gamsakhurdia and the return to Georgia, and appointment as Speaker of Parliament, of the long-time leader of Soviet Georgia, Eduard Shevardnadze. The latter spent more than 10 years as the president of independent Georgia until the Rose Revolution in 2003. It is worth mentioning that during Shevardnadze's "second era" many Soviet-time Communist Party members and apparatchiks found their way into various political and public positions. We can argue that the Rose Revolution, which removed the old system, left the old elite and people benefiting from it dissatisfied. However, the popularity of the President and his party, which was maintained until 2007, did not contribute to the emergence of political cleavages.

According to Lipset and Rokkan (1967), the centre–periphery political cleavage is defined as the struggle of peripheral culture and groups against the central, assimilating force. However, the strategies of struggle vary in different countries. As some research argues, ethnic minorities in Georgia have several important obstacles in order to be equally represented in the mainstream political activities. Nodia (2006) lists several areas of concerns: language-related problems, information issues and lower levels of political representation and participation. Thus during all post-Soviet elections, the representatives of ethnic minorities voted for the incumbents (Nodia, 2006). Due to the nonexistence of minority political parties, the representatives of minorities align with the incumbents. Moreover, as recent research by Zollinger and Bochsler (2012) shows, "central" oppositional political parties could also be used as a proxy by minority elites in order to be represented in local and regional parliaments. For instance, both the UNM and the GDC named former and current members of the Javakhk Union as their candidates for single- member districts in the Akhalkalaki region, which is primarily inhabited by ethnic Armenians (Armenia News - NEWS.am, 2012). Yet in Georgia there are few signs of political cleavages that reinforce ethnic divisions. However, it is conceivable that minorities chose political self-exclusion by voting for the government and showing their loyalty to the incumbents in order to defend their own lifestyle and relative stability and security in their local communities.

Another important pattern is the extreme fluctuation of the coefficient for the electoral turnout. It has the largest positive effect in 2008 presidential elections submodel, decreases for the parliamentary elections and becomes insignificant in the 2012 parliamentary elections. As mentioned above, we measure both electoral fraud and voter mobilization using the value of electoral turnout. A large positive coefficient for the 2008 presidential elections suggests that higher turnout led to more support for Saakashvili. However, the situation changed dramatically in 2012. During the parliamentary elections, higher electoral turnout played a strong role in the victory of the GDC which supposedly was able to form strong local organizations and trigger huge public interest in the elections.

By looking at the map of residual distribution by voting districts (Figure 1) some interesting spatial peculiarities could be identified. Initially, we can argue that higher fluctuations in residuals could indicate the existence of additional "hidden" factors that contribute to the formation of particular voting behaviour in a district, which cannot easily be explained by the given model. In the submodel of presidential elections, in Javakheti, Shida Kartli, Racha-Lechkhumi and Upper Imereti the predicted results are quite similar to the observed values, whereas coefficients in Samegrelo, Kvemo Kartli and Guria suggest the most extreme fluctuations. For the 2008 parliamentary elections submodel, the regional discrepancies are present as well – similar to the presidential elections, Samegrelo and Kvemo Kartli show extreme values of residuals. As for the new patterns, Shida Kartli has a high value of residuals. However, in the whole territory of Kakheti, mountainous areas of Eastern Georgia, Tbilisi and surrounding municipalities the model perfectly explains the patterns of voting behaviour. Finally, in the 2012 parliamentary elections model, regional patterns are also maintained. Like the previous parliamentary elections, the model explains the variation inside the Kakheti region. In the mountainous areas of Western Georgia, Upper Imereti and Shida Kartli, the model offers a convincing explanation as well. What is worth mentioning, here, are the two hotspots with the extreme fluctuations in the residuals – Sashkhere municipality, a native area of Georgian Dream Coalition leader and Akhaltsikhe/Aspindza – homeland of the candidate for prime minister, Vano Merabishvili from the UNM. The latter areas also had the highest residual values in previous models as well. In the country, where personal factor in the politics is still decisive and ties to native places are strong, supposedly, this fact could be an important contributor to electoral behaviour.

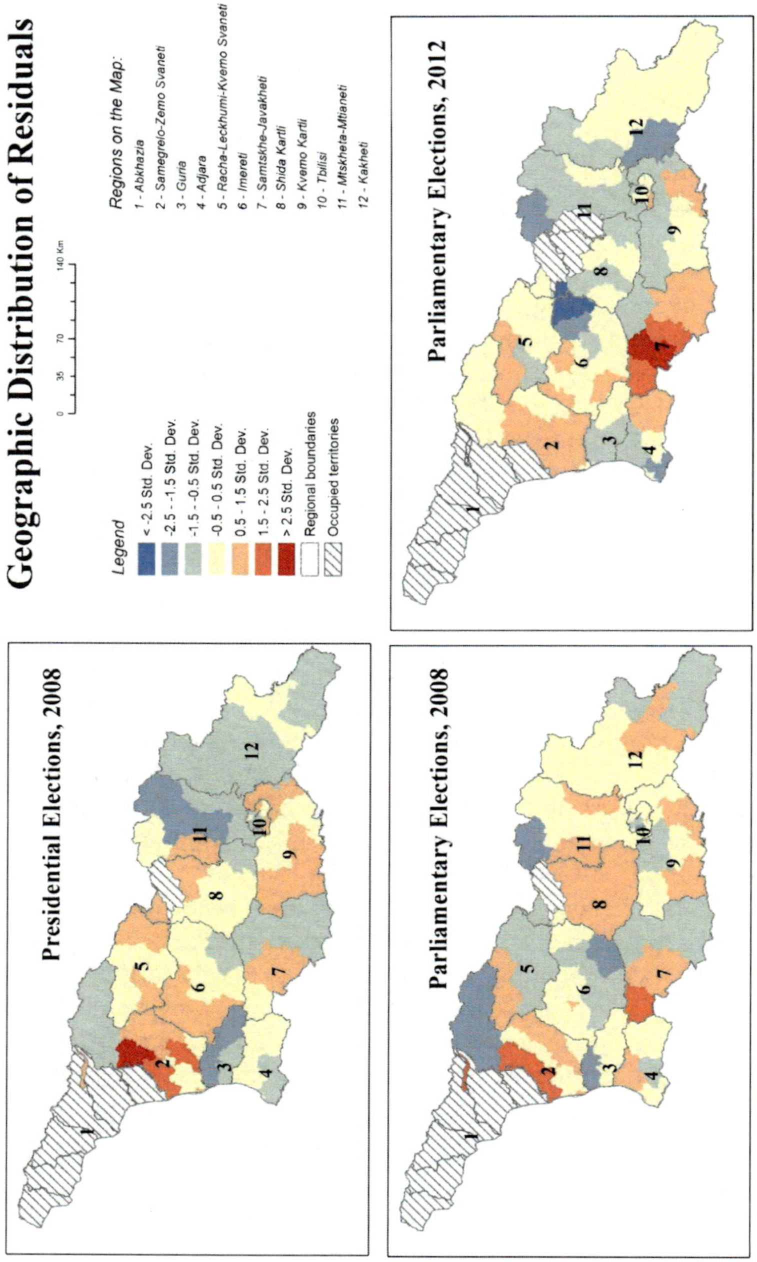

Figure 1: Geographic distribution of residuals.

To conclude, the model suggests that there are two political cleavages contributing to the formation of voting behaviour in Georgia. The analysis shows, that the coefficients are statistically significant for all submodels. The factors contributing to the formation of the electoral cleavages are persistent, which allows us to say that the tendency could be maintained for other elections as well. Territorial distribution of the residuals shows strong regional patterns that indicate local "hidden" factors contributing to the formation of particular voting behaviour in a given area. Despite the fact that the cleavages exist, they are the results of more recent developments, unlike in West European societies.

Conclusion

The cleavage voting model presented in this chapter proposes that electoral dichotomies were important for recent presidential and parliamentary elections in Georgia. However, the electoral cleavages were not formed according to the factors given by Lipset and Rokkan. Urban–rural and centre–periphery electoral cleavages can either be dated back to the Soviet era or the early 1990s when Georgia suffered from violent ethno-territorial conflicts. If we take the urban–rural political dichotomy, the process of urbanization during the Soviet period and changing social structures of urban settlements in Georgia have affected today's electoral developments. Additionally, the "hidden cleavage" of ethnic minorities, which is partly expressed by their lack of integration into the political system, can be explained by more recent events. We can argue that there could be other factors that will be important for explanation of voting behaviour, which are missing from the model; however, the statistical tests do not indicate this. Interestingly enough, the spatial distribution of residuals has significant regional characteristics, which means that there are some other hidden factors that also affect the formation of voting behaviour. As subethnic and regional patterns in Georgia were always quite strong, it is not a surprise that this situation is crystallized in voting behaviour.

References

Civil Georgia (2007) Nine-Party Presidential Hopeful Lays Out Key Priorities, <http://www.civil.ge/eng/article.php?id=16483> (accessed 18 October 2014)>.

Clem, R., and Craumer, P. (2008) Orange, blue and white, and blonde: the electoral geography of Ukraine's 2006 and 2007 Rada elections. *Eurasian Geography and Economics* 49(2), 127–151.

Corso, M. (2008) *Georgia Declares War on Poverty,* <http://www.eurasianet.org/departments/insight/articles/eav020608c.shtml> (accessed 18 October 2014).

Evans, G., and Whitefield, S. (2000) Explaining the formation of electoral cleavages in post-communist democracies. in, *H.-D., Mochmann, E., & Berlin Conference on Comparative Political Research in Central and Eastern Europe. (2000). Elections in Central and Eastern Europe: The first wave. Berlin: Edition Sigma.*

Johnston, R., and Pattie, C. (2003) Representative democracy and electoral geography. In *Agnew, J. A., Mitchell, K., & Toal, G. (2011). A companion to political geography.* Malden, Mass: Blackwell Publishers.

Kitschelt, H. (1995) Formation of party cleavages in post-communist democracies. *Party Politics* 1(4), 447–472.

Lipset, S., and Rokkan, S. (1967) *Party Systems and Voter Alignments, Free Press,* New York, NY.

Mikashavidze, M. (2010) *Media Landscape: Georgia,* <http://ejc.net/media_landscapes/georgia> (accessed 31 December 2014).

Mykhnenko, V. (2009) Class voting and the orange revolution: a cultural political economy perspective on Ukraine's electoral geography. *Journal of Communist Studies and Transition Politics* 25(2–3), 278–296.

National Democratic Institute (2011) *Public Attitudes in Georgia: Results of March 2011 Survey Carried Out for NDI by CRRC,* <http://www.ndi.org/files/Georgia-Survey-Results-0411.pdf> (accessed 18 October 2014).

National Democratic Institute (2012a) *Public Attitudes in Georgia: Results of February 2012 Survey Carried Out for NDI by CRRC,* <http://www.ndi.org/files/Georgia-Survey-Results-0212.pdf> (accessed 18 October 2014).

National Democratic Institute (2012b) *Public Attitudes in Georgia: Results of June 2012 Survey Carried Out for NDI by CRRC*, <http://www.ndi.org/files/Georgia-NDI-survey-update-June2012-ENG.pdf> (accessed 18 October 2014).

National Democratic Institute (2012c) *Public Attitudes in Georgia: Results of August 2012 Survey Carried Out for NDI by CRRC*, <http://www.ndi.org/files/Georgia-Aug-2012-Survey.pdf> (accessed 18 October 2014).

Armenia News – NEWS.am (2012) *Georgian Opposition's Chances High in Parliamentary Elections.*, <http://www.news.am/eng/news/117953.html> (accessed 18 October 2014).

Nodia, G. (2006) *The Political Landscape of Georgia: Political Parties: Achievements, Challenges and Prospects*, Eburon Publishers, Delft.

OSCE/ODIHR Election Observation Mission (2008) *Georgia, Parliamentary Elections 21 May 2008. Final Report*, <http://www.osce.org/odihr/elections/georgia/33301> (accessed 18 October 2014).

Government of Georgia (2007a) *Ach'aris avtonomiuri respublika, pasporti (Autonomous Republic of Adjara, passport)*. Tbilisi: Government of Georgia. Retrieved from <http://government.gov.ge/files/53_74_110944_achara.pdf>.

Government of Georgia (2007b) *Guriis mkhare, pasporti (Guria Region, passport)*. Tbilisi: Government of Georgia. Retrieved from <http://www.government.gov.ge/files/53_74_588492_guria.pdf>.

Government of Georgia (2007c) *Imeret'is mkhare, pasporti (Imereti Region, passport)*. Tbilisi: Government of Georgia. Retrieved from <http://government.gov.ge/files/53_74_482125_imereti.pdf>.

Government of Georgia (2007d) *Kakhet'is mkhare, pasporti (Kakheti Region, passport)*. Tbilisi: Government of Georgia. Retrieved from <http://government.gov.ge/files/53_74_288375_kaxeti.pdf>.

Government of Georgia (2007e) *Kvemo Kart'lis mkhare, pasporti (Kvemo Kartli Region, passport)*. Tbilisi: Government of Georgia. Retrieved from <http://government.gov.ge/files/53_74_757653_kvemo_qartli.pdf>.

Government of Georgia (2007f) *Mtskhet'a-mt'ianet'is mkhare, pasporti (Mtskheta-Mtianeti Region, passport)*. Tbilisi: Government of Georgia. Retrieved from <http://www.government.gov.ge/files/53_74_327991_mtskheta-mtianeti.pdf>.

Government of Georgia (2007g) *Rach'a-lechkhum-kvemo svanet'is mkhare, pasporti (Racha-Lechkhumi-Kvemo Svaneti Region, passport*. Tbilisi:

Government of Georgia. Retrieved from <http://www.government.gov.ge/files/53_74_847928_racha-lechkhumi.pdf>.

Government of Georgia (2007h) *Samegrelo-zemo svanet'is mkhare, pasporti (Samegrelo-Zemo Svaneti Region, passport)*. Tbilisi: Government of Georgia. Retrieved from <http://government.gov.ge/files/53_74_909908_samegrelo-zemo_svaneti.pdf>.

Government of Georgia (2007i) *Samtskhe-javakhet'is mkhare, pasporti (Samtskhe-Javakheti Region, passport)*. Tbilisi: Government of Georgia. Retrieved from <http://www.government.gov.ge/old/files/53_74_736482_samckhe-javakheti.pdf>.

Government of Georgia (2007j) *Shida Kart'lis mkhare, pasporti (Shida Kartli Region, passport)*. Tbilisi: Government of Georgia. Retrieved from <http://www.government.gov.ge/files/53_74_168558_shida_qartli.pdf>.

Perepechko, A., Kolossov, V. and ZumBrunnen, C. (2007) Remeasuring and rethinking social cleavages in Russia: continuity and changes in electoral geography 1917–1995. *Political Geography* 26(2), 179–208.

Roper, S., and Fesnic, F. (2003) Historical legacies and their impact on post-Communist voting behaviour. *Europe-Asia Studies* 55(1), 119–131.

Taylor, P., and Johnston, R. (1979). *Geography of Elections*, Croom Helm, London.

Whitefield, S. (2002) Political cleavages and post-communist politics. *Annual Review of Political Science* 5(1), 181–200.

Zarycki, T. (2002) Four dimensions of center periphery conflict in the Polish electoral geography. In *Klonowicz, T., Wieczorkowska, G. (2002). Social change: Adaptation and resistance. Warsaw: Warsaw University, Institute for Social Studies Press.*

Zollinger, D., and Bochsler, D. (2012) Minority representation in a semi-democratic regime: the Georgian case. *Democratization* 19(4), 611–641.

Anvar Rahmetov

Structural Causes of "Colour Revolutions": Postelectoral Mobilization and Outcomes in the South Caucasus

ABSTRACT: This chapter compares postelectoral protest mobilization in Azerbaijan in 2003 and in 2005, Georgia in 2003 and Armenia in 2008, to examine causes and dynamics of popular mobilization and the breakdown of authoritarian regimes. Structural explanations are tested on the three cases using several indicators of regimes' structural weaknesses. Evidence from the cases suggests that incumbent capacity, including availability of rents, regime type and media freedom, plays a significant role, while high levels of property privatization, vibrant civil society and anti-incumbent regional identity do not. The findings call into question some of the previous findings. However, for greater confidence in the results further research is needed using a larger and more diverse sample of cases.

KEYWORDS: South Caucasus, authoritarianism, protest, colour revolutions, structural causes, incumbent capacity

Introduction: Fraudulent Elections, Legitimacy Crises and Fates of Regimes

If authoritarian regimes are most vulnerable during leadership succession (Hale, 2005), Eduard Shevardnadze was safe in his seat in 2003. Unlike Ilham Aliev or Robert Kocharyan in neighbouring Azerbaijan and Armenia, respectively, Shevardnadze was not a lame duck during the controversial elections of 2003 because presidential elections were scheduled only for early 2005. Moreover, after parliamentary elections of 2003, protesters initially demanded a rerun of the elections, not Shevardnadze's resignation. So why did the regime collapse in 2003? Was it because of irreconcilable divisions inside elites during the succession crises or the unity and strength of the opposition?

The elite schisms were certainly evident in Georgia, but various levels of elite disagreement were also present in the other two countries. In Azerbaijan before the 2003 elections, elite clans were also jockeying for power, not all the elites supported the heir apparency of Ilham Aliev and quite a few worried about his lack of charisma and political experience. The party of power, Yeni Azerbaijan, blatantly nominated his father, Heydar Aliev, for the presidency, not Ilham. Elite divisions became even more apparent after Ilham had come to power, replacing old-guard communists and regional clans with representatives of younger, Baku-based elites and relatives of his wife.

In Armenia around 2008, elite alliances were also unstable. The Kocharyan–Sargsyan succession seemed a safe bet until the first President Ter-Petrossian emerged out of political obscurity to run for presidency. Surprisingly, many people appeared to support him and took to the streets, preferring Ter-Petrossian's presidential record in the war-torn 1990s to the relatively better off years under President Kocharyan. Several deputy ministers and elites also defected to his side. The brutal crackdown and seven deaths that resulted from the postelectoral standoff could also have led to a profound political crisis with society refusing to lend legitimacy to the Sargsyan presidency. However, neither elite divisions nor the crisis led to breakdown of authoritarianism in Armenia.

Of course, elite divisions and legitimacy crises are just two of many ingredients of a revolutionary cocktail. Among the myriad others identified in the literature are economic hardships, relative deprivation, failed states and challengers' ability to mobilize resources, to name a few. This contribution seeks to clarify and identify the configurations of various factors that breed protest and authoritarian breakdown using cases from the South Caucasus.

The chapter proceeds as follows. First, I will briefly sketch out the electoral and postelection dynamics in the three countries during crucial elections. Second, I will review the relevant literature and single out structural explanations and their indicators for further analysis. Third, I will present data from the three countries for the indicators identified above. Fourth, I will discuss which explanations were lent support by the South Caucasus cases. Fifth, in the concluding section, I will discuss findings in view of existing literature and I will propose further research.

Elections and Protests: A Brief Introduction to South Caucasus Electoral Dynamics in the Mid-2000s

The years of early independence in all three South Caucasus states brought instability and conflict. In Azerbaijan and Georgia, civil wars raged between nationalist forces that came to power after the break up of the Soviet Union and members of the former nomenklatura. Armenia and Azerbaijan were in the state of war over Nagorno-Karabakh, an autonomous republic, formerly under Azeri rule, which succeeded from Azerbaijan with the help of Armenian ruling elites. By the end of the 1990s, nationalist forces were subdued by nomenklatura forces that returned to power in Azerbaijan and Georgia, while the Karabakh war turned into a frozen conflict. By the mid-2000s, leaders in all three states were up for re-election and some of them completed their constitutionally sanctioned second terms and had to transfer power. It is against this background that the main succession and election struggles were set.

Azerbaijan could have made a step away from authoritarianism when Heydar Aliev passed the presidency to his son Ilham in 2003 or with Ilham's first parliamentary elections as President in 2005. Both elections passed in a heated atmosphere with international observers highlighting numerous violations. In both cases, alleged violations draw crowds of protesters. In 2005 there were especially notable protests, attracting as many as 15 000 participants (British Broadcasting Corporation, 2005). Many hoped, in the wake of the Serbian, Georgian and Ukrainian revolutions, that there would be a "Baku Spring" in November 2005. However, nothing of this sort occurred. The authorities responded with a harsh crackdown on the protesters, although the "manageable" number of protesters and their peaceful behaviour made the use of firearms and subsequent human victims unnecessary.

In 2003 presidential elections, the heir apparent and the election favourite, Ilham, was running against Isa Gambar, a veteran Azeri opposition figure and a leader of Musavat at the time. Gambar only secured 15% of the vote against Aliev's 75%. The OSCE called elections "generally well administered", but part of the OSCE mission, called by International Institute for Democracy in Eastern Europe (IDEE) issued a Votum Separatum condemning the elections (Institute for Democracy in Eastern Europe, 2003).

In the 2005 parliamentary elections, Aliev's ruling Yeni Azerbaijan party was pitted against Azadliq electoral bloc of three parties (Musavat, Popular Front Party and Democratic Party). According to official results, YAP won 61 seats (out of 125), while the bloc secured only six seats. Alternative polls by international private firms forecast different results and the opposition hoped to stage a Ukrainian- or Georgian-type revolution in Baku. However, administrative pressure and police crackdowns on protesters led the electoral discontent to fizzle out, causing one local observer to call the elections "frustrating" (Alieva, 2006).

In Armenia in 2008, Robert Kocharyan was finishing his second term and was widely expected to help his handpicked successor and longtime ally, Serzh Sargsyan, win the elections. It seemed like Sargsyan was heading for an easy victory, being a clear favourite, when Levon Ter-Petrossian, first President of post-Soviet Armenia, forced into resignation by Kocharyan, entered the electoral campaign in October 2007, with a public speech criticizing the existing "institutionalized mafia-type regime" (Radio Free Europe/Radio Liberty, 2007).

The official results gave Petrossian 22% of all votes against Sargsyan's 53%, with the third candidate, Arthur Bagdasaryan, securing 17%. International observers noted a number of serious violations but were generally positive about the elections.

The opposition refused to recognize the results of elections and called on its supporters to come out and demand honest elections. Protesters gathered on Freedom Square for more than ten days, peaking 150 000 according to some reports (Radio Free Europe/Radio Liberty, 2008). On 1 March, protest actions met aggressive action by the police, which led to ten civilian deaths the following night. Sargsyan called a state of emergency and imposed a 20-day curfew, but the results of the elections were not changed or cancelled.

The Georgian case is the "positive outcome" case among the three, where electoral protests following the parliamentary elections of 2004 grew into the Rose Revolution and when President Shevardnadze's system of managed democracy fell in the face of people-power revolution (Nodia, 2005). Interestingly, Shevardnadze was ousted, even though his presidential term would only finish in 2005. In the Georgian case, although the electoral fraud concerned parliamentary elections, mass indignation swept away the presidency as well, just like in the Kyrgyz Republic.

Voter registration lists appeared to have omitted entire neighbourhoods, especially in areas where opposition was expected to have an upper hand. On election day, there were numerous allegations of voter intimidation, ballot stuffing and violence, leading the OSCE to state that the elections do not qualify under its standards (OSCE, 2003).

The resulting protests continued for some 20 days, reaching about 100 000 participants at their peak. On 22 November the protesters stormed the parliament building and pushed Shevarnadze out of the building, forcing him to sign a resignation letter the next day, after his call for the state of emergency was not obeyed by the military.

State of the Field: Fragile Regimes or Strong Challengers?

A review the of academic literature on the so-called colour revolutions[1] shows that most contributions fall into either of two broad approaches that, for the lack of a better term, I will call "state fragility" and "actor tactics" approaches. It is within these two approaches that the 12 main comparative theories of colour revolutions fall. This chapter is devoted to the analysis of structural conditions, so I will concentrate mainly on structure-centred explanations. I will start with a brief discussion of actor-centric approaches though.

Contributions from the actor-centric approach highlight the importance of actor learning and diffusion of knowhow about how to break authoritarian regimes. The best example of this approach is work done by Bunce and Wolchik (2011) who claim that it is electoral strategies deployed by challengers that have played a crucial role and have acted as a main

1 "Colour revolutions" is a popular phrase used among journalists, pundits and, increasingly, academics to refer to the Serbian "Bulldozer" Revolution of 2000, the Georgian "Rose" Revolution of 2003, the Ukrainian "Orange" Revolution of 2004 and the Kyrgyz "Tulip" Revolution of 2005, which resulted in the overthrow of the respective leaders as a result of mass postelection protests. In some instances, several other popular protests are also included in the group of colour revolutions – for example Moldovan 2009 election protests, Lebanon's 2005 protest against the presence of Syrian troops, Belarusian and Russian postelection protests and others. The latter instances did not end up with the overthrow of existing leaders or elites.

variable differentiating success cases from failures. They state that success strategies make up an "electoral model" of political change that was used to topple autocrats in Serbia, Georgia and Ukraine. These authors explain cases of unsuccessful mobilization (e.g. Armenia in 2008, Azerbaijan in 2005) by limitations put on the implementation of the electoral model.

Scholars belonging to the structure-centric approach prioritize structural weaknesses of authoritarian systems over strategic action by opposition challengers when explaining divergent outcomes of colour revolution attempts. For them, the strength of the opposition and size and influence of protests are mediated by such structural factors as strength of the ruling party and state administration (Way, 2009: 91, 94) and are therefore of secondary importance, although they cannot be ignored. Structural weaknesses could be of a political or economic nature. For example, Hale (2005) stresses political vulnerabilities when he maintains that regimes are especially prone to instability during periods of political succession. He contends that all colour revolutions happened in patrimonial regimes where a lame-duck incumbent attempted to pass power on to his unpopular successor.

While Hale concentrates on political structures, Radnitz and Melnykovska explain how economic structures weigh in. According to Radnitz (2010), the extensive privatization and independent capitalist class it created were the moving force behind colour revolutions. Melnykovska (2007) explains diverging fates of authoritarian capitalism in Russia and Ukraine through characteristics of business groupings and their involvement in politics.

Way (2009) stresses both economic and political structures. On the economic side, he argues that regimes with strong economic linkage to the West are more prone to democratize. Among those with weak linkage, it is those with low authoritarian capacity that are prone to fall to colour revolutions. Authoritarian capacity for Way is a combination of (i) an institutionalized ruling party, (ii) an "extensive and well-funded" security apparatus, and (iii) an autocrat's control over the economy, direct or through dominant natural resource sector. In an earlier paper, Way (2005) has also shown how a salient regional identity prevents a capital-based autocrat from consolidating authoritarian power.

In some contributions, explanatory narrative borrows from both approaches. For example, McFaul (2005) in the analysis of the four "electoral breakthroughs" identified seven commonalities that are necessary although not sufficient for a colour revolution to happen. First of all, the regime had to be a *semi-authoritarian* one, because it was very hard to stage a successful electoral protest in a hardcore dictatorship. Second, an *unpopular incumbent* had to be pitted against a *strong and united opposition* that was *capable of mobilizing masses* by *spreading information about electoral fraud* through *independent media* that a semi-authoritarian regime had tolerated. The resulting political crisis also featured *division within coercive forces* that eliminates the possibility that a political standoff would be resolved by force.

In the remainder of the chapter, I will test the structural approach in light of recent political developments in the South Caucasus. More specifically, I will answer why, given the common political, cultural and administrative legacy of the Soviet Union, conflicts and political instability in the early 1990s, similar windows of opportunity and opposition protests demanding the rerun of elections, the Georgian crisis ended with the fall of Shevarnadze whereas Armenian and Azerbaijani incumbents survived the protests. This is a study using *most similar systems design*, i.e. comparing cases with similar conditions and divergent outcome with a view of explaining divergent outcomes by the few conditions that are not the same between cases.

Cases and Indicators

Armenia

The Armenian presidential elections of February 2008 featured massive postelectoral protest mobilization. Although OSCE observers largely endorsed the poll, the political opposition dismissed it as fraudulent and took its supporters to the street. Before the elections, the outgoing "lame-duck" President Robert Kocharyan endorsed his Prime Minister, Serzh Sargsyan, for the presidential post and the elites entered the crucial elections as a united bloc, despite a lack of a unifying dominant "ruling party". A potential rival from among the business elites, Gagik Tsarukyan and his "Prosperous Armenia" Party endorsed Sargsyan.

The opposition, on the other hand, was divided; not all opposition candidates endorsed the main contender, ex-President Levon Ter-Petrossian. For example, Artur Bagdasarian of Orinats Yerkir Party ran separately, as did several other less important challengers. Moreover, Bagdasarian and his party entered government coalition after the elections.

Regarding incumbent capacity, even though the situation was dire when President Ter-Petrossian stepped down in 1998, things started improving in the 2000s, with state revenue and overall economic wellbeing improving by the critical elections of 2008. Armenia's GDP per capita rose 6.3 times between 2000 and 2008, from USD 621 to 3916. This is impressive given that income per capita did not rise above USD 636 in the previous decade (World Bank Group, 2013). Unlike Ter-Petrossian, both Kocharyan and Sargsyan were spared regional alliances opposing them.[2] Both hailed from Nagorno-Karabakh, the region that is a standard-bearer of Armenian nationalism, and worked together in Soviet Komsomol and the Karabakh Movement (Cheterian, 2008).

Leaked diplomatic cables show that Prime Minister Sargsyan was so confident he would win the elections that he was favouring exit polls (WikiLeaks, 2008). However, exit polls were not conducted, primarily due to opposition from the presidency and challengers themselves who were concerned that a local polling partner, the Armenian Sociological Association, was not impartial. Unable to forge a consensus among key parties, the traditional exit-poll conductors, USAID and International Republican Institute decided not to run polls (Panarmenian, 2008).

In the financial sphere, Armenia was still dependent on outside financing under both Kocharyan and Sargsyan, even though the situation improved considerably by the time Sargsyan took over, as tax collection and the economy had significantly improved. The IMF played an important role in providing for financial stability and the IMF Poverty Reduction and Growth Facility financed government programmes to increase spending on health and education as well as infrastructural investment and public wages (Economist Intelligence Unit, 2008). Gross Domestic Product grew more than 13% each year between 2005 and 2008 (World Bank Group, 2013), per capita spending on health increased more than

2 There are reports, however, of an identity division in Armenia between Hayastantsi and Karabakhtsi Armenians with the majority Hayastantsi feeling that Karabakhtsi have captured national politics and imposed their own narrow regional agenda (International Crisis Group, 2004: 7).

50% between 2002 and 2007, mainly due to GDP growth (World Health Organization, 2013).

Regarding privatization, three-quarters of Armenian GDP came from the private sector in 2007, putting the country among the top privatizers in the former Soviet Union. The country had good scores on EBRD indices of small-scale (4)[3] and large-scale (3.7) privatizations (European Bank for Reconstruction and Development, 2011).

The regime was considered a mildly authoritarian one. Freedom House scores indicate that, since 2003, the country moved from an authoritarian-leaning hybrid regime to "semi-consolidated authoritarianism". Although authoritarian, Armenian political system was much more liberal and less repressive than Central Asian states or even neighbouring Azerbaijan.

With regards to independent media, Armenia again qualifies as having media typical of semi-consolidated authoritarianism. Armenian media scores from Freedom House have deteriorated, rising from 5 starting 2003, but have, nevertheless, stayed below 6 until the notorious elections of 2008 (higher scores mean less media freedom). Authors of another Freedom House report, Freedom of the Press, rated Armenian media as not free in 2007 (Freedom House, 2007b). According to indicators from another index, the Media Sustainability Index by the International Research and Exchange Board (IREX), the Armenian media were rated as an "unsustainable, mixed system", which is characteristic of a country that "minimally meets objectives, with segments of the legal system and government opposed to a free media system. Evident progress in free-press advocacy, increased professionalism, and new media businesses may be too recent to judge sustainability" (International Research and Exchange Board, 2007).

In terms of rentier resources, Armenia's options were limited. The country did not boast rich oil and gas resources, nor did it export electricity. Armenia's main export has been precious stones and metals but these did not become a source of sufficiently vast rentier inflows to buy off and repress the population. Armenia is often mentioned as beneficiary of extensive Russian aid but Russian help is often reported to be limited to reduced prices on imported arms.

3 The scores range from 1 to 4+ (4.33): 1 stands for a centrally planned economy and 4+ signifies a full market economy.

Civil society has been the most developed part of the Armenian political system. The country scored 3.5 on the civil society dimension on Freedom House indicators, putting it only second to postrevolution Ukraine in the former Soviet Union. This score is peculiar to semiconsolidated democracies, so it would be fair to say that Armenian civil society was one of the most developed and vibrant in the post-Soviet space.

Lucan Way has stated that anti-incumbent national identity in four Eastern European nondemocracies might help maintain pockets of autonomy that prevented consolidation of authoritarianism. For example, in the case of Ukraine, anti-Kuchma and anti-Yushchenko Western Ukrainian identity and regionalism has prevented them from gaining firm control there and might have acted as a pocket of democratic potential. Looking at Armenia, Karabakh nationalism certainly prevented Ter-Petrossian from building up his authoritarian machine in the early 1990s but, after he was forced to resign in February 1998, the new leaders were representatives of this regionalism and therefore, anti-authoritarian nationalism became pro-authoritarian when Kocharyan and Sargsyan came to power.

Table 1: Structural conditions in Armenia.

Variable	*Armenia 2008*
Lame duck	Yes
IMF dependence	Yes
Ruling party	No
Privatization	High
Private GDP	*75*
Large scale	*3.7/4*
Small scale	*4/4*
System	Semiconsolidated authoritarian
Democracy score	*5.2/7*
FH political rights	*5/7*
FH civil liberties	*4/7*
FH status	*Partly free*
Media score CT	5.75/7
Media FoP	*Not free*
IREX MSI	*Unsustainable mixed*
Rentier resources	Some

Variable	*Armenia 2008*
Civil society	3.5/7 (sem.cons.dem)
Strong and rich security apparatus	Yes

Somewhat related to the previous several variables is the notion of authoritarian capacity, which Lucan Way operationalizes, for the analysis of colour revolutions, as "at least one of the following ... 1) a single highly institutionalized ruling party with a salient ideology or revolutionary tradition; 2) an extensive and well-funded coercive apparatus that has won a major violent conflict; or 3) state discretionary control over the economy, generated either by the failure to privatize or by reliance on easily captured energy revenues" (Way, 2009: 92).

In the Armenian case, even though the Republican Party has been around as a "ruling party", there were some other partners in the coalition and the recent popularity of Prosperous Armenian precludes one from maintaining that RPA is "the party of power" like Nur Otan in Kazakhstan or United Russia in the Russian Federation.

Regarding the coercive apparatus, Armenians have an army that has "won" the Karabakh conflict and due to Russian support and recent economic growth, the Armenian security apparatus has been well equipped and financed. Moreover, the former Prime Minister and the current President, Serzh Sargsyan, has a military-security background himself and therefore the *siloviki* (literally "strong guys," i.e. people in "power" ministries – Internal Affairs, Defence and State Security) have put their weight largely behind Kocharyan and Sargsyan. Based on the fact that financing of the military and security apparatus was a priority for Armenia and one that the general public also supported, Armenia is coded here as having a strong and well-financed security apparatus.

Third, as already mentioned, Armenian incumbents are relatively cash strapped and do not enjoy the same level of discretionary control over the economy as the regimes in Russia, Belarus and Turkmenistan. Even though officials can pressure individual firms into submission through bullying, unjustified and frequent inspections by tax collectors and raids by prosecutors, government control over the economy overall is comparatively low.

Azerbaijan

During the handover of power in 2003, the outgoing President, Heydar Aliev, was a lame duck due to failing health and the heir apparency of his son, Ilham. His collapse during a televised speech caused wild speculations about his failing health. Aliev's visit to United States for a heart operation in August 2003 added to the speculation. Before returning to the clinic, Aliev appointed his son as the Prime Minister, in a move that was widely seen to guarantee his election using all administrative and financial resources. The succession, however, raised many concerns, especially among the elites who thought of Ilham as lacking charisma and leadership skills. A number of observers had concerns that Aliev junior would not be able to secure the support of significant parts of the elites in 2002 (Economist Intelligence Unit, 2002: 16).

Regarding privatization, Azerbaijan's leadership privatized small businesses, earning a score of 3.67 in EBRD Index, but had less advanced privatization scores on large-scale privatization, with a score of 2 in 2002 and 2004. In 2004, 60% of Azerbaijan's GDP came from the private sector (European Bank for Reconstruction and Development, 2011).

However, unlike Armenia, which only had modest to small rents available from resource exports, Azerbaijan had extensive oil and gas reserves, attracting foreign direct investment cash that was used to cover budget deficits. Moreover, once the oil windfall started coming at the beginning of the 2000s, Azerbaijan State Oil Fund, SOFAZ, was put up to accumulate excess cash. Therefore, it would be fair to conclude that Azerbaijan, unlike neighbouring Armenia, had rentier resources that could possibly be used to buy off and placate the population. Indeed, part of that resource has been spend to improve infrastructure and wages in the budget sector, as well keep the urban intelligentsia employed and happy in the oil sector and accompanying industries.

Table 2: Structural variables in Azerbaijan.

Variable	*Azerbaijan 2003 and 2005*
Lame duck	Yes (2003), no (2005)
IMF dependence	No
Ruling party	Yes
Privatization	Medium

Variable	*Azerbaijan 2003 and 2005*
Private GDP	60
Large scale	2
Small scale	3.67
System	
Democracy score	autocracy
FH political rights	6
FH civil liberties	5
FH status	Not free
Media score CT	5.5 (2003), 6.75 (2004)
Media FoP	Not free
IREX MSI	Unsustainable mixed
Rentier resources	Yes
Civil society	4.25 (2003), 4.5 (2004) (hybrid)
Strong and rich security apparatus	Yes

In terms of the political regime, Azerbaijan was categorized by the Freedom House as an autocracy in 2002 and 2004 with an average score of 5.5 for political and civil rights, highest (i.e. most autocratic) among the three South Caucasus states (Freedom House, 2012). Therefore, unlike Armenia, Azerbaijan was not a soft authoritarian regime.

Regarding independent media, the Azerbaijani media environment has been rated by Freedom House as "not free" in its Freedom of the Press 2002 report and its Independent Media for 2003 score in the Nations in Transit report was 5.5 and declined to 6.75 the following year (Freedom House, 2012). The IREX Media Sustainability Index painted a more favourable picture of the Azerbaijani media in 2002 and 2004, putting it in the same category as Armenia – an unsustainable mixed system of media, with the situation worsening slightly by 2004.

In terms of civil society, Azerbaijan's score was 4.25 in 2003 and 4.5 in 2004, putting it in the category of hybrid regimes in terms of civil society, as defined by Freedom House's Nations in Transit report.

Regarding the anti-incumbent national identity in Azerbaijan, Ilham Aliev's father Heydar hails from Nakhichevan, an autonomous region and an exclave in Armenia, while Ilham's wife is from the Baku-based Pashayev clan. Thus in 2003, during the power transfer, there were certain former

Communist elites and Nakhichevanis that might have had reservations about the family rule but did not show visible signs of it. Once in power, Ilham started replacing Nakhichevani notables in the ruling party and government positions with his own people from the Baku-based technocracy but the opposition to this has been personality-based and did not translate into regional animosity (Economist Intelligence Unit, 2006).

Regarding authoritarian capacity, Azerbaijan, unlike Armenia, has a ruling party. New Azerbaijan has controlled the majority of seats since the 1995 elections, the second largest majority being (largely pro-regime) independents. Other parties, such as ANIP, Musavat and Popular Front are largely marginalized. The NAP has been around for more than a decade and was the launching organization of Aliev senior (Economist Intelligence Unit, 2001). The elite was organized enough to ensure that Aliev junior succeeded without major divisions within itself and without internal fights spilling out into the streets.

Intraparty politics was taken seriously – Aliev junior was a deputy head of YAP/NAP, a position seen as a further guarantee that the party (i.e. elites) would nominate him for presidency. Soon after coming to power, Aliev junior sidelined a number of prominent individuals who could have posed a threat (Economist Intelligence Unit, 2005). After the dynastic succession, the struggle went on within the ruling elites. Aliev arrested a number of ministers for an alleged coup in 2005, including Farhad Aliev, Minister for Economic Development. Mehriban Alieva's clan, the Pashaevs, came to occupy key positions (Economist Intelligence Unit, 2006).

Azerbaijan's military has been engaged in combat missions during the Karabakh conflict. The military apparatus therefore has war experience. Moreover, the country can afford an extensive and well equipped interior ministry and secret police. Even though there is some information that the State Security Ministry might have had leaders whose loyalty to the President was questionable, structural reorganization of the Ministry before Aliev's death probably changed the balance of power in favour of the President (Agentura.Ru, 2011). Due to an oil windfall, Azerbaijan has enough money to spend on beefing up its security apparatus. Moreover, there is some information about the arms race and espionage hysteria between Armenia and Azerbaijan, therefore it would be fair to assume that both countries have an extensive and well equipped military apparatus and Azerbaijan also has strong domestic intelligence component with ties to Turkish intelligence, the MIT and Israel's Mossad (Agentura.Ru, 2011). In the mid-2000s there was enough money in the state budget to massively increase spending on the military (Economist Intelligence Unit, 2006).

Regarding the third component of authoritarian capacity, Azerbaijan's economy is less privatized than that of Armenia and the country has natural resource rents available to consolidate authoritarian capacity. The government depends on oil for fiscal stability (Economist Intelligence Unit, 2002). Starting in July 2001, Azerbaijan was to receive US 100 million in 3 years in poverty reduction grants from the International Monetary Fund (IMF) and received USD 10 million in July 2001 and February 2002; the third tranche was frozen due to disagreement over unified energy prices (Economist Intelligence Unit, 2002). Its revenue stream depends on the energy sector (which accounted for one-third of fiscal revenue and 7% of GDP in 2002 (Economist Intelligence Unit, 2002: 22). Foreign currency coming in as foreign direct investment (FDI) helped pay for the country's trade deficit, with Azeri budget deficit of just 1.2% of GDP by 2003. The oil sector covers budget deficits in the non-oil sector, but there still were wage payment arrears as of 2005 (Economist Intelligence Unit, 2005). An oil windfall was expected at the end of 2005 as money from oil and gas fields had started flowing strongly (Economist Intelligence Unit, 2005: 27).

Georgia

Even though Shevardnadze comfortably won the 2000 presidential elections against a stalwart communist holdover, Jumber Patiashvili, he was seen as a lame-duck President since Citizen's Union lost municipal elections in 2002.[4] He was however, ousted a year before his legitimate second term was over.

Georgia's economy was privatized more thoroughly than that of neighbouring Azerbaijan. The country's EBRD privatization score was 3.33 for large-scale privatization and 4 for small-scale privatization in the 3 years preceding the Rose Revolution and, in 2004, 65% of its GDP came from the private sector (European Bank for Reconstruction and Development, 2011).

4 Some political scientists, e.g. Ghia Nodia, however, think that Shevardnadze became a lame duck even earlier, in November 2001, during the political crisis around the Rustavi-2 TV station (personal conversation).

Having very few natural resources to extract rents from and limited inflow of FDI due to corruption, obsolete infrastructure and a bad business environment, the Georgian authorities had to borrow extensively from abroad, predominantly the IMF, the World Bank, and the International Financial Corporation. The private Paris Club of creditors was also lending to Georgia.

The Georgian political system was the least repressive of the three Caucasian states before their respective political crises. Freedom House's democratization score, though declining, was 4.44 in 2002, which would qualify Georgia as a hybrid or transforming regime (Freedom House, 2002c). The country scored 4 on political and civil rights the same year and qualified as a partially free regime (Freedom House, 2002a).

Georgia's Freedom House score on the media was 2.75 in 2002, a score characteristic of semiconsolidated democracies, while IREX rated its media system as unsustainable, just like Armenia's and Azerbaijan's. Another Freedom House report, Freedom of the Press, indicated that Georgia's media was partly free in its 2002 report, setting it apart from the other two countries, whose media has been labelled as not free before the respective political crises. Anecdotal evidence supports these ratings. Although Armenia's media environment might have been more liberal than the Azeri one, neither had an independent/anti-government TV station, whereas the Georgian opposition had a mouthpiece at Rustavi-2, a station that had the largest viewership in Georgia – 86% reported watching it in a May 2003 survey by IRI (International Republican Institute, 2003).

In terms of civil society, Georgia consistently scored 4 on Freedom House's civil society scores. This score put Georgia, in 2002, ahead of Azerbaijan in 2002 and 2004, but worse than Armenia in 2007 (Freedom House, 2002c, 2007c).

Table 3: Structural conditions in Georgia.

Name of the variable	*Georgia 2003*
Lame duck	Not until the 2005 elections
IMF dependence	Yes
Ruling party	No
Privatization	High
Private GDP	65
Large Scale	3.33

Name of the variable	*Georgia 2003*
Small Scale	4
System	4.4
Democracy score	Hybrid
FH political rights	4
FH civil liberties	4
FH status	Partly free
Media score CT	2.75
Media FoP	Partly free
IREX MSI	Unsustainable mixed
Rentier resources	No
Civil society	4 (hybrid)
Strong and rich security apparatus	No

President Shevardnadze had to deal with regional opposition to his own regime, for example from Aslan Abashidze and his Union of Democratic Revival party. Moreover, until early 2001 there were pockets of unrest created by supporters of the deceased President Zviad Gamsakhurdia. Moreover, Abkhazia and South Ossetia have opposed Shevarnadze's rule and Georgian sovereignty over their territories in general. It is necessary to note, however, that unlike western Ukrainian opposition to President Kuchma, Georgian anti-Shevardnadze regional identity has no prodemocracy spirit to it whatsoever. All three regional groupings opposing Shevarnadze's rule – Abkhazians, Adzharans and South Ossetians – are run by strongmen themselves and do oppose Shevardnadze out of personal, rather than ideological reasons.

Regarding the three pillars of authoritarian capacity, Shevardnadze's Citizens' Union declined in popularity after the 1999 elections. Then the party gained 40% of the votes, an unusually low share for a post-Soviet party of power. Moreover, unlike the Armenian Republican Party, for example, the Citizens' Union was suffering from a serious internal rift, between the pro-Western reformist wing, led by Zurab Zhvania, and a conservative wing, comprising former red directors and communists from Soviet times. The split was finalized when Zhvania and other young reformers left the party in 2002.

Georgia also lacked an extensive and well-established security apparatus. The Georgian military was very weak and ill-equipped, as was spectacularly demonstrated by the military campaign against Russia in 2008. The internal security apparatus was also weak For instance, kidnappings were observed in Georgia as late as 2001 and there were several attempts on President Shevardnadze's life, which both the internal affairs and state security apparatuses failed to prevent. In a dire financial and fiscal situation, the Shevardnadze regime could not afford to spend much on its security and internal repression machine. It might be one of the reasons that he ruled by manipulation and fraud, rather than outright repression.

The Shevardnadze regime also lacked economic power, as it had neither rents from natural resources, nor extensive control of the economy through viable state enterprises. The government had to constantly apply for outside lending to cover fiscal spending excesses and the money always came with strings attached: the IMF would typically ask to streamline revenue by clamping down on corruption, enforcing tax payments, raising some taxes and cutting spending. All conditions were undermining the regime, since Shevarnadze's patronage system depended on unclear rules and selective enforcement, while raising taxes and cutting spending was a politically damaging strategy.

Summary and Discussion

Factual data gathered and summarized in Table 3.4 suggest a number of interesting observations. The first is that "privatization-mobilization-breakdown" is not lent support by the three cases, at least not when measured using the methods employed in this chapter. Levels of privatization do not correlate either with absence/presence of mobilization or with authoritarian breakdown/survival. It might be necessary to refine the argument, but such an exercise would require further research on a bigger sample of cases.

Table 4: Summary of main structural variables.

Structural variables	*Armenia 2008*	*Azerbaijan 2003 and 2005*	*Georgia 2003*	*Good predictor of authoritarian breakdown*
Privatization	High	Medium	High	No
Regime type	Semiconsolidated authoritarian	Semiconsolidated authoritarian	Hybrid	Yes
Media	Not free	Not free	Partly free	Yes
Natural resource rents	Some (diaspora, diamonds)	Yes (oil)	No	Yes
Civil society score	3.5, just like semiconsolidated democracies[c]	4.25 (2003), 4.5 (2004), typical of hybrid regimes	4,typical of hybrid regimes	No
Anti-incumbent identity	No	No[b]	No[a]	No
Incumbent capacity	Medium-low	High	Low	Yes

Notes: [a]Anti-Shevarnadze regionalism of Abashidze was also directed against the opposition, while South Ossetian and Abkhazian regionalism did not translate into specific anti-Shevarnadze policies *in Georgia.* [b]There are distinct clans and interest groups in Azerbaijan, e.g. Yeraz, Nakhichevan and Baku-Shirvan clans, but competing clans were more or less consolidated around Ilham Aliev during the transfer of power from father to son and first parliamentary elections under Ilham Aliev's rule. [c]The civil society scores are juxtaposed with categorization of regimes from Nations in Transit Report (Freedom House, 2007c).

Second, the type of regime in which fraudulent elections take place matters for the outcome of antifraud mobilization. In the three South Caucasus cases Georgia was designated as a hybrid regime, whereas its two neighbours were described as semiconsolidated authoritarian regimes (with Freedom House democracy scores being 4.6 for Georgia, 5.2 for Armenia and 5.5 and 5.6 for Azerbaijan in the 2 years under consideration). Georgia had an average of 4 on its civil and political rights score, Armenia followed with 4.5 and Azerbaijan had 5.5. Thus, in hybrid regimes protest mobilization has a higher chance of success with authoritarian breakdown.

The independent media also played a key role in the success of protest mobilization. All three countries experienced protest mobilizations, despite the fact that Armenian and Azerbaijani opposition lacked a strong mouthpiece like Georgian Rustavi-2. The differences lie in the outcome of mobilization. The Georgian system was rated as partially free by Freedom House's Freedom of the Press report team, with a score of 3.75, whereas its neighbours were both rated nonfree with scores above 5.5. Thus patterns of media freedom coincide with the pattern of authoritarian breakdown.

The countries have diverging luck with rentier resources as well. The Azerbaijani government was well-endowed with oil and now gas resources and started exploiting them once Heydar Aliev came to power and political stability was ensured. Oil incomes skyrocketed in the mid-2000s, providing the country with extra cash that was accumulated at SOFAZ, the Azeri sovereign fund. But even before than FDI inflows helped finance government spending. Unlike Azerbaijan, Georgia had no rentier resource and, until fiscal reforms initiated by the Saakashvili government, the leadership was barely making ends meet with credits and loans from Paris Club and intergovernmental organizations. Armenia is somewhere in between, although closer to Georgia. While it is true that Armenians had few natural resources, except for semiprecious metals and diamond ores, the country had benefited greatly from financial transfers and remittances of the Armenian diaspora. Based on these differences one can conclude that availability of financial rents does play a role in the survival of authoritarianism.

The available data suggest that free and strong civil society does not play a significant role in authoritarian breakdown. Armenia had the best score for civil society before its 2008 electoral crisis, yet there was no demise of authoritarianism there, whereas "revolutionary" Georgia and Azerbaijan, where authoritarianism survived and consolidated, had similar civil society scores of 4.5 and 4.

Furthermore, the available evidence supports the thesis about security apparatus. All three countries witnessed war: Armenia had experienced international conflict, Georgia had a civil war, whereas Azerbaijan had seen both. These conflicts gave useful combat and repression experience to military-security apparatuses in all three countries. However, in terms of financing, the Georgian military and security apparatus was far behind the better financed, equipped and trained Azerbaijani and Armenian servicemen. This hints that financing the security apparatus might prolong the tenure of authoritarians and help them survive political crises.

Anti-incumbent regional identity, identified by Lucan Way (2005) as one factor that prevented consolidation of authoritarianism in Eastern European post-Soviet countries, did not play an important role in the South

Caucasus with the existing regional groups colluding behind an incumbent for tactical reasons.

Finally, regarding incumbent capacity the picture is vague. On the one hand, it is clear that the Shevardnadze regime had extremely low incumbent capacity around 2003, having neither a ruling party, rents nor economic control and not having control over the security apparatus, nor finance for it. Azerbaijan is a total opposite: the country had a ruling party, petrodollar income soaring, a battle-experienced military apparatus and unity in the security apparatus. As a result, the Georgian regime crumbled in the face of popular challenge whereas the Azeri one withstood with some effort.

The Armenian case is somewhere in the middle. On the one hand, the Kocharyan-Sargsyan regime did not have the dominance in party politics that the Aliev regime enjoyed in Azerbaijan. While it is true that the Republican Party is the strongest party in the country and is at the centre of any coalition, it cannot and does not rule alone and the Armenian party landscape features a number of other functioning parties. In addition to not having a party that monopolizes the parliament, the Kocharyan-Sargsyan group did not have any cash available through natural resource rents, unlike Azerbaijan. There was some money from remittances and charity of the Diaspora, but only a fraction of those monies went directly to the regime. However, the Armenian security apparatus stood united and was well financed and maintained despite the overall economic poverty and especially as the economy started picking up. Its unity was significantly helped by the fact that the heir to President Kocharyan, Serzh Sargsyan, was the head of all three main power ministries at some point of his career. The financing of the army increased in reaction to Azerbaijan's boost in military spending in the mid-2000s. Based on these considerations, the incumbent capacity in Armenia is rated as medium.

To sum up, low incumbent capacity plays an important role in regime failure. Georgia did lack high incumbent capacity and, as a result, ended with a breakdown of authoritarianism, while its neighbours had medium to high levels of incumbent capacity, which allowed them to weather political crises more confidently.

Conclusion

In this chapter, I analyzed the importance of structural weaknesses for authoritarian breakdown. Comparing the structural conditions in the three countries, I find that incumbent capacity, including availability of rents, regime type and media freedom play a significant role.

A theoretically unexpected finding, however, was that high privatization, vibrant civil society and anti-incumbent regional identity do not help distinguish cases of mobilization that ended with authoritarian survival from the case of popular mobilization that brought authoritarian breakdown. The finding is theoretically surprising because a number of scholars have identified privatization (Radnitz, 2010) and civil society (Diuk, 2005; McFaul, 2005) as conducive to "colour revolution", whereas anti-incumbent regional identity was found to have a negative effect on authoritarian consolidation (Way, 2005).

The findings have to be taken with a grain of salt, however, since a more convincing theoretical account of the interplay of structural conditions and authoritarian dynamic calls for a wider study, which would bridge the advantages of small N case studies and large N quantitative surveys.

Nevertheless, even this small study proposes two conclusions. The first is that there are cases where established causal links do not play out. It might as well be that this cases falsify the available theoretical propositions and act as "paradoxical cases" that might lead to new theoretical insights. One such example might be Armenia, a country with high levels of privatization, where the authoritarian regime nevertheless survived. The second conclusion is that the accepted methods of operationalizing and measuring theoretical variables might be in need of improvement. Using the same example, Armenian privatization might look good when share of private sector in GDP or various indices are utilized. Yet a closer look might reveal an economy that is informally monopolized by proxies and families of government officials. Closer case studies and alternative measurement techniques might help solve "paradoxes" stemming from imperfect methodology.

References

Agentura.Ru. (2011) *Spetslujby Azerbaidjana* <http://agentura.ru/dossier/azer/> (accessed 19 October 2014).

Alieva, L. (2006) Azerbaijan's frustrating elections. *Journal of Democracy* 17(2), 147–160.

British Broadcasting Corporation (2005) Thousands Join Azerbaijan Protest. *BBC News*, 9 November, <http://news.bbc.co.uk/2/hi/europe/4420604.stm> (accessed 19 October 2014).

Bunce, V. and Wolchik, S. (2011) *Defeating Authoritarian Leaders in Post-communist Countries*, Cambridge University Press, Cambridge.

Cheterian, V. (2008) Armenian election: the waiting game. *Open Democracy*, 19 February, <https://www.opendemocracy.net/article/democracy_power/caucasus_fractures/armenia_election> (accessed 16 January 2015).

D'Anieri, P. (2006) Explaining the success and failure of post-communist revolutions. *Communist and Post-Communist Studies* 39(3), 331–350.

Diuk, N. (2005) The triumph of civil society, in *Revolution in Orange: The Origins of Ukraine's Democratic Breakthrough* (eds. A. Åslund and M. McFaul), Carnegie Endowment, Washington.

Economist Intelligence Unit (2001) *Country Profiles*, <http://country.eiu.com/AllCountries.aspx> (accessed 16 January 2015).

Economist Intelligence Unit (2002) *Country Profiles*, <http://country.eiu.com/AllCountries.aspx> (accessed 16 January 2015).

Economist Intelligence Unit (2003) *Country Profiles*, <http://country.eiu.com/AllCountries.aspx> (accessed 16 January 2015).

Economist Intelligence Unit (2004) *Country Profiles*, <http://country.eiu.com/AllCountries.aspx> (accessed 16 January 2015).

Economist Intelligence Unit (2005) *Country Profiles*, <http://country.eiu.com/AllCountries.aspx> (accessed 16 January 2015).

Economist Intelligence Unit (2006) *Country Profiles*, <http://country.eiu.com/AllCountries.aspx> (accessed 16 January 2015).

Economist Intelligence Unit (2007) *Country Profiles*, <http://country.eiu.com/AllCountries.aspx> (accessed 16 January 2015).

Economist Intelligence Unit (2008) *Country Profiles*, <http://country.eiu.com/AllCountries.aspx> (accessed 16 January 2015).

European Bank for Reconstruction and Development (2011) *Transition Indicators by Country,* <http://www.ebrd.com/pages/research/economics/data/macro.shtml> (accessed 19 October 2014).

Freedom House (2002a) *Freedom in the World Survey*, Freedom House, New York, NY.

Freedom House (2002b) *Freedom of the Press Survey*, Freedom House, New York, NY.

Freedom House (2002c) *Nations in Transit*, Freedom House, New York, NY.

Freedom House (2004a) *Freedom in the World Survey*, Freedom House, New York, NY.

Freedom House (2004b) *Freedom of the Press Survey*, Freedom House, New York, NY.

Freedom House (2004c) *Nations in Transit*, Freedom House, New York, NY.

Freedom House (2007a) *Freedom in the World Survey*, Freedom House, New York, NY.

Freedom House (2007b) *Freedom of the Press Survey*, Freedom House, New York, NY.

Freedom House (2007c) *Nations in Transit*, Freedom House, New York, NY.

Freedom House (2012) *Nations in Transit,* Freedom House, New York, NY.

Hale, E. H. (2005) Regime cycles: democracy, autocracy, and revolution in post-Soviet Eurasia. *World Politics* 58(1), 133.

Institute for Democracy in Eastern Europe (2003) *The Azerbaijan "Elections"*, press release, 21 October, 2003. <http://www.idee.org/azerbaijanelections.html> (accessed 19 October 2014).

International Crisis Group (2004) Armenia: internal instability ahead. *Europe Report* No.158, <http://www.crisisgroup.org/en/regions/europe/south-caucasus/armenia/158-armenia-internal-instability-ahead.aspx> (accessed January 16, 2015).

International Republican Institute (2003) *Georgian National Voter Study*, May 2003, <http://www.iri.org/sites/default/files/2003%20May%20Survey%20of%20Georgian%20Public%20Opinion,%20May%202003.pdf> (accessed January 16, 2015).

International Research and Exchange Board (2007) *Media Sustainability Index 2009/2007*, IREX, Washington, DC.

Lane, D. (2009) "Coloured revolution" as a political phenomenon. *Journal of Communist Studies and Transition Politics* 25(2–3), 113–135.

McFaul, M. (2005) Transitions from postcommunism. *Journal of Democracy* 16(3), 5–19.

Melnykovska, I. (2007) Colour Revolution or Soft Authoritarianism? Different Ways to Cope with Similar Challenges in the Globalised World. Paper prepared for presentation at CEELBAS Workshop "The Coloured Revolutions," 30 April 2008, <http://www.academia.edu/3126006/Colour_Revolution_or_Soft_Authoritarianism_Different_Ways_to_Cope_with_Similar_Challenges_in_the_Globalised_World> (accessed January 16, 2005).

Nodia, G. (2005) The dynamics and sustainability of the Rose Revolution, in *Democratisation in the European Neighbourhood* (ed. M. Emerson), CEPS Paperback Series, Brussels.

Organization for Security and Cooperation in Europe. (2003) Georgia Parliamentary Elections. OSCE/ODIHR Election Observation Mission Report, Part 1.

Panarmenian (2008) *Ekzit pollov vo vremya prezidentskih vyborov Armenii ne budet,* <http://www.panarmenian.net/rus/politics/news/24506/> (accessed 19 October 2014).

Radio Free Europe/Radio Liberty (2007) *Armenia: Former President Lambasts "Criminal Regime",* <www.rferl.org/content/article/1078774.html> (accessed 19 October 2014).

Radio Free Europe/Radio Liberty (2008) Yerevan Protests Resume Despite Government Crackdown, <www.azatutyun.am/content/article/1593545.html> (accessed 19 October 2014).

Radnitz, S. (2010) *Weapons of the Wealthy: Predatory Regimes and Elite-Led Protests in Central Asia*, Cornell University Press, Ithaca, NY.

Way, L. A. (2005) Authoritarian state building and the sources of regime competitiveness in the Fourth Wave: the cases of Belarus, Moldova, Russia, and Ukraine. *World Politics* 57(2), 231.

Way, L. (2009) A reply to my critics. *Journal of Democracy* 20(1), 90–97.

WikiLeaks.Com (2008) *Armenian PM Contradicts Presidency: Exit Poll Still Alive,* <www.wikileaks.org/plusd/cables/08YEREVAN16_a.html>.

World Bank Group (2013) *World Economic Indicators,* <http://data.worldbank.org/indicator/NY.GDP.PCAP.CD> (accessed 19 October 2014).

World Health Organization (2013) *Global Health Observatory Data Repository*, <http://apps.who.int/gho/data/node.country> (accessed 19 October 2014).

Marcy E. McCullaugh

Typical Tin-Pots: Wealth without Welfare in Azerbaijan

ABSTRACT: This chapter provides a theory of redistributive social spending in mineral-rich authoritarian regimes, using the case of Azerbaijan. I analyse health, education and social security spending from 2000 to the present. Under Heidar Aliev (1995–2003) and Ilham Aliev (2003–present) there is little evidence of desire on the part of the government to engage in redistribution. I find that in the absence of potential challenges from within Azerbaijan's cohesive elite structure, the Alievs have not depended on societal allies to maintain their rule, so welfare spending remains low. Due to the empirical and theoretical significance of redistribution under authoritarianism, this explanatory approach makes both substantive and theoretical contributions to the study of authoritarianism and the "resource curse" both within and beyond the former Soviet Union.

KEYWORDS: authoritarianism, resource curse, welfare spending, redistribution, elites, Azerbaijan.

Introduction

In May 2012, Azerbaijan hosted the Eurovision Song Contest, an annual competition held among many active members of the European Broadcasting Division. In preparation for this event and the influx of foreign media, competitors and spectators, the Azerbaijani government embarked on a massive construction campaign to renovate parts of downtown Baku and build Crystal Hall, the site of the contest. A *Transitions Online* investigative report found that this was the most expensive Eurovision in history, where the state spent upwards of 550 million manat ($720 million) on costs directly and "indirectly" related to the song contest (Sultanova, 2012). By comparison, Russia, Norway and Germany, the respective 2009, 2010 and 2011 Eurovision hosts, each spent approximately $40 million in preparation for the contest. In addition, the report found that funds previously allocated for pensions and improving the country's water and sanitation systems were diverted in order to construct Crystal Hall. One Cabinet order specifically earmarked 50 million manat ($62.5 million) to be diverted from a project aimed at renovating the country's decaying network of water pipes for Crystal Hall; another order moved 50 million manat from the pension fund for Eurovision-related costs.

Diverting money from social welfare projects and pensions to stage the Eurovision contest is one of many examples that would lead us to classify Azerbaijan as a predatory "petro-state". Since the mid-2000s, there has been little evidence of desire on the part of the government to engage in redistribution under the Alievs (father and son). Health, education and social security expenditures have remained consistently low as a percentage of GDP and decreased drastically over time as a percentage of total government spending. Yet, in a comparative context, welfare spending trends in Azerbaijan warrant further explanation. Throughout the post-Soviet region, welfare expenditures decreased significantly amidst wrenching budgetary and institutional crises in the 1990s. Then, starting in the early 2000s, the economic picture changed dramatically for the petroleum-rich Soviet successor states – Azerbaijan, Kazakhstan, Russia, Uzbekistan and Turkmenistan – as a result of sustained high oil prices. Even with the significant resources available to them since the early 2000s, however, the commitment to reinvigorate welfare spending has diverged markedly across these cases. Azerbaijan and Turkmenistan have emerged as the lowest spenders but welfare expenditure in Russia under Vladimir Putin (2000–present) has increased substantially since the early 2000s. Kazakhstan and Uzbekistan fall roughly in the middle between these two extremes.

The variation within the post-Soviet region remains consistent after enlarging the universe of mineral-rich authoritarian regimes to include countries in the Middle East, north and sub-Saharan Africa and Latin America (Table 1). While Russia stands out as one of the highest spenders, Azerbaijan rivals Saddam Hussein's Iraq for the place of lowest spender, and devotes less money to welfare (in GDP percentage terms) than both Equatorial Guinea and Gabon. The observed variation in social spending across 25 mineral-rich authoritarian countries allows us to rule out certain alternative explanations that could potentially account for cross-national differences in social spending, including formal institutions (political parties and party systems), regime type, openness to trade (economic freedom), mineral wealth, levels of economic development and modernization and corruption (Table 2).

Table 1: Average health spending in mineral-rich countries (% GDP), 2000–10.

Country	*Average health spending*
Bolivia	3.5
Russia	**3.4**
Algeria	3.3
Saudi Arabia	2.9
Bahrain	2.7
Uzbekistan	**2.4**
Venezuela	2.4
Brunei Darussalam	2.3
Oman	2.3
Angola	2.3
Iran	2.2
Kazakhstan	**2.2**
Kuwait	2.2
Qatar	2.2
Libya	2.1
United Arab Emirates	2.1
Ecuador	2.0
Turkmenistan	**1.9**
Nigeria	1.7
Equatorial Guinea	1.6
Republic of Congo	1.4
Cameroon	1.3
Gabon	1.2
Azerbaijan	**0.9**
Iraq[a]	0.7

Note: [a]This figure is for 2000–2 under Hussein.
Sources: World Bank *World Development Indicators*, available at <http://databank.worldbank.org/data/home.aspx;> Federal'noe Kaznacheistvo Rossiiskoi Federatsii (Federal Treasury of Russia), "Otchetnost' ob ispolnenii konsolidirovannogo biudzheta RF," 2000–11, available at http://roskazna.ru/konsolidirovannogo-byudzheta-rf/; Ministerstvo Finansov Respubliki Kazakhstan (Ministry of Finance of the Republic of Kazakhstan), "Statisticheskii Biulleten", 2000–5, available at <http://www.minfin.gov.kz/irj/portal/anonymous?NavigationTarget=ROLES://portal_content/mf/kz.ecc.roles/kz.ecc.anonymous/kz.ecc.anonymous/kz.ecc.anonym_budgeting/budgeting/reports_fldr> ; Ministerstvo Finansov Respubliki Kazakhstan (Ministry of Finance of the Republic of Kazakhstan), "Dannye ob ispol'nenii biudzhetov", 2006–11, available at http://www.minfin.gov.kz/irj/portal/anonymous?NavigationTarget=ROLES://portal_content/prototype_mf/roles/com.saprun.mf_anonymous_roles/com.saprun.mf_anonymous_ru/BudgetExecutionAndStatistics_Folder/StateBudgetRK_Folder/ConsolidatedBudget_Folder ; Budget AZ, "Azərbaycan Respublikasının dövlət büdcəsinin icrası haqqında", 2000–11, previously available at http://www.budget.az/budget/.

Table 2: Political and socioeconomic indicators in mineral-rich states.

Country	*Mean health spending (% GDP), 2000–10*	*VA score*	*Economic Freedom score*	*Fuel rents (% GDP), 2008*	*GDP per capita, 2008 (PPP, US$ 2005)*	*HDI score, 2008*	*TI score, 2008*
Bolivia	3.5	−0.02	53.2	34	$4172	0.65	3.0
Russia	**3.4**	**−0.97**	**49.9**	**29**	**$14 767**	**0.75**	**2.1**
Algeria	3.3	−1.05	55.7	42	$7367	0.69	3.2
Saudi Arabia	2.9	−1.74	62.8	70	$20 564	0.76	3.5
Bahrain	2.7	−0.82	72.2	40	$23 755	0.81	5.4
Uzbekistan	**2.4**	**−1.9**	**52.3**	**80**	**$2455**	**0.62**	**1.8**
Venezuela	2.4	−0.62	45.0	30	$11 877	0.73	1.9
Brunei	2.3	−1.00	–	63	$46 820	0.83	–
Oman	2.3	−1.07	67.4	51	$24 646	0.70	5.5
Angola	2.3	−1.07	47.1	67	$5166	0.48	1.9
Iran	2.2	−1.48	44.0	49	$10 397	0.70	2.3
Kazakhstan	**2.2**	**−1.01**	**60.5**	**33**	**$10 468**	**0.73**	**2.2**
Kuwait	2.2	−0.53	68.3	64	$49 952	0.76	4.3
Qatar	2.2	−0.77	62.2	49	$67 334	0.83	6.5
Libya	2.1	−1.9	38.7	62	$15 321	0.76	2.6
UAE	2.1	−0.98	62.8	30	$51 361	0.84	5.9
Ecuador	2.0	−0.22	55.4	30	$7127	0.71	2.0
Turkmenistan	**1.9**	**−2.06**	**43.4**	**–**	**$6566**	**0.67**	**1.8**
Nigeria	1.7	−0.60	55.5	35	$1945	0.45	2.7
Equatorial Guinea	1.6	−1.89	52.5	62	$30 988	0.54	1.7
Congo	1.4	−1.16	45.2	69	$3433	0.52	1.9

Country	*Mean health spending (% GDP), 2000–10*	*VA score*	*Economic Freedom score*	*Fuel rents (% GDP), 2008*	*GDP per capita, 2008 (PPP, US$ 2005)*	*HDI score, 2008*	*TI score, 2008*
Cameroon	1.3	-1.02	54.0	12	$2042	0.47	2.3
Gabon	1.2	-0.84	53.6	47	$13 441	0.66	3.1
Azerbaijan	**0.9**	**-1.23**	**55.3**	**65**	**$8023**	**0.70**	**1.9**
Iraq[a]	0.7	-2.03	–	82	$3777	0.55	–

Note: [a]Where available, figures for Iraq are from 2002.
Sources: World Bank *World Development Indicators*, available at <http://databank.worldbank.org/ddp/home.do?Step=12&id=4&CNO=2> (accessed 21 October 2014); Heritage Foundation Index of Economic Freedom 2008, available at <http://www.heritage.org/index/download> (accessed 21 October 2014); Transparency International, Corruption Perception Index 2008, available at http://www.transparency.org/research/cpi/cpi_2008/0/.

The political economy literature on regime type and redistribution suggests that democratic governments redistribute wealth in response to electoral and societal pressures, whereas authoritarian leaders prefer to direct state resources toward a narrow group of supporters, as opposed to the broader public, in order to maintain power (e.g. Bueno de Mesquita *et al.*, 2003). Several cross-national studies have established that democracies, on average, exhibit higher social spending than their authoritarian counterparts (e.g. Brown and Hunter, 1999; Rudra and Haggard, 2005; Orenstein, 2008) but the existing literature does not rigorously explore welfare spending variation *among* authoritarian regimes. While scholars of the rentier state have argued that rulers with access to large revenue streams engage in massive welfare spending programmes to depoliticize society in an effort to dampen popular pressure for democratization (e.g. Anderson, 1995; Vandewalle, 1998), these studies are often based on single country cases and do not account for variation among mineral-rich states. The consensus in the comparative literature on energy-rich states is that they raise social welfare expenditures during boom periods, but the empirical evidence from the former Soviet Union, sub-Saharan Africa and beyond reveals that not all states respond with the same policies. In sum, conflicting theoretical expectations generated by the existing literature on social spending in nondemocratic regimes and resource-rich states currently leave us wondering how authoritarian leaders balance the costs and benefits of distributing wealth beyond elites to the wider population.

In this chapter, I show that a unified political and economic elite in Azerbaijan is the key factor contributing to low levels of welfare spending. Different degrees of unity and conflict among political and economic elites, which I identify as high officials in the regime and wealthy capitalists, affect the autocrat's perceived level of threat and sense of security about his position. When elites are unified, the autocrat's perceived level of threat is minimized. In the absence of potential challenges from within the elite, the autocrat does not depend on societal allies to ensure the continued stability of his position, so welfare spending remains low.

This chapter proceeds in three sections. The next section presents data and evidence to establish that social spending has not been a top policy priority in Azerbaijan since oil resources came online in the early 2000s. In the third section, I show that Azerbaijan has had a unified ruling and business elite under the Aliev dynasty, which has guaranteed a low level of conflict and a minimal probability of challenges to the Alievs' authority from within. By comparing longitudinal changes in welfare spending in Azerbaijan with domestic politics events, I demonstrate that the Azerbaijani rulers have had no perceived need for widespread popular support, which is why welfare spending has remained low. The concluding section summarizes my empirical findings and discusses the broader implication of this study.

Welfare Spending in Azerbaijan

Investing in welfare is a necessary part of what governments can do to develop the human capital base of their societies and improve the quality of life of their citizens. In mineral-rich authoritarian regimes, I argue that welfare spending serves an additional purpose: it is a form of mass rent redistribution. In addition to doling out money to supporters in the ruling coalition, some autocrats direct a portion of this revenue to the larger citizenry. The total size of the buyoff indicates the extent to which an autocrat actively seeks popular support beyond the narrow group of elite supporters. In order to assess the extent of rent redistribution in society, this study looks specifically at public spending on health, education and social security (pensions and nonpension benefits). Taken together, these policy areas capture accurately "the emphasis governments place on social programs" (Brown and Hunter, 1999: 782).

These welfare policy areas are especially important to consider in post-Soviet Azerbaijan. First, the Soviet Union provided far more social benefits to its citizens than other authoritarian regimes (Cook, 2007). Old-age pensions and disability, sickness and other benefits took on a particular significance for the population of Azerbaijan, which carried over to the postcommunist era. As a result, even though this type of welfare spending targets a narrower constituency than society at large, a much higher than average number of people in Azerbaijan rely on pensions and/or other benefits to subsidize all or part of their income. Second, the vast majority of citizens still rely on public health and education systems in Azerbaijan. Private healthcare and education options, while available, are prohibitively expensive for most people. Therefore, state spending in these sectors benefits almost the entire population. In addition, over 50% of public health and education spending in Azerbaijan is devoted to salaries for doctors, teachers and other workers in these sectors, who make up approximately 20% of the labour force. Thus, overall health and education spending levels reflect not only governments' commitment to long-term human capital development but also a subsidy to a significant portion of the population that is actively employed.

Table 3 displays aggregate trends in social spending levels in Azerbaijan in terms of percentage of GDP, as percentage of government spending and per capita from 2000–11. Three measures are presented because each specification captures a different kind of welfare effort. Social expenditures as a percentage of GDP indicate redistributive priorities within the national economy as a whole, whereas budget shares reflect priorities set within the public sector (Kaufman and Segura-Ubiergo, 2001). Welfare spending per capita reflects the actual value of resources directed toward the population (Brown and Hunter, 1999). Table 4 shows health, education and social security spending levels as a percentage of GDP, percentage of government spending and in terms of Azerbaijan New Manat (AZN) per capita from 2000–11. The data presented illustrate that, for the time period under investigation, total social spending as a percentage of GDP and as a percentage of government spending decreased. Total social spending declined by 1.6% of GDP between 2000–7, and then increased by approximately 1% in the midst of the global financial crisis between 2008–9 and thereafter. Total social spending as a percentage of budgetary expenditures decreased by over 20% between 2000–11. These trends are more-or-less mirrored when we examine disaggregated expenditures on health, education and social security. As a share of GDP, education expenditures in Azerbaijan have decreased over time, and health and social security spending in Azerbaijan have not fluctuated significantly but they remain extremely low in light of the country's level of development (World Bank, 2010). Heath, education and social security spending have all declined as a percentage of government spending.

Table 3: Total public expenditures on welfare in Azerbaijan, 2000–11.

Indicator	*2000*	*2001*	*2002*	*2003*	*2004*	*2005*	*2006*	*2007*	*2008*	*2009*	*2010*	*2011*	*Mean*
GDP (%)	6.9	6.2	6.3	6.2	6.3	5.6	5.3	5.4	5.3	6.2	6.4	6.4	6.1
Total budget	42.9	41.0	40.9	35.9	35.7	33.0	25.6	25.6	20.0	24.6	23.2	21.2	30.8
(%) Expenditures per capita (constant 2005 US$)	57	54	57	64	72	88	117	166	195	233	231	257	132

Source: Budget AZ, "Azərbaycan Respublikasının dövlət büdcəsinin icrası haqqında", 2000–11, previously available at <http://www.budget.az/budget/>.>

Table 4: Total public expenditures on health, education and social security in Azerbaijan, 2000–11.

Sector	*Indicator*	*2000*	*2001*	*2002*	*2003*	*2004*	*2005*	*2006*	*2007*	*2008*	*2009*	*2010*	*2011*
Health	GDP (%)	0.9	0.8	0.7	0.8	0.9	0.9	0.9	0.9	0.9	1.1	1.0	1.0
	Total budget	5.4	5.2	4.8	4.5	4.9	5.4	4.3	4.2	3.2	3.8	3.6	3.2
	expenditures (%) Real AZN per capita[a]	5	5	5	7	9	14	19	30	39	45	48	54
Edu-cation	GDP (%)	3.8	3.5	3.2	3.3	3.4	3.0	2.6	2.5	2.4	2.7	2.8	2.5
	Total budget	23.8	23.1	20.5	19.0	19.6	17.4	12.6	11.9	9.1	10.9	10.0	8.2
	expenditures (%) Real AZN per capita	23	23	23	28	35	44	56	83	112	129	131	139
Social pro-tection	GDP (%)	2.2	1.9	2.4	2.1	2.0	1.7	1.8	2.0	2.0	2.4	2.6	2.9
	Total budget	13.7	12.8	15.6	12.4	11.2	10.2	8.7	9.5	7.7	9.9	9.5	9.7
	expenditures (%) Real AZN per capita	13	13	18	19	20	26	39	67	94	116	125	164

Note: [a]1 AZN = $0.8.
Sources: Budget AZ, "Azərbaycan Respublikasının dövlət büdcəsinin icrası haqqında", 2000–11, previously available at <http://www.budget.az/budget/;> World Bank, *Balancing Protection and Opportunity: A Strategy for Social Protection in Transitional Economies* (Washington, D.C.: World Bank, May 3, 2000), available at http://web.worldbank.org/WBSITE/EXTERNAL/COUNTRIES/ECAEXT/0,,contentMDK:20219326~isCURL:Y~pagePK:146736~piPK:146830~theSitePK:258599,00.html (accessed 21 October 2014)>.

In addition to overall spending levels, salaries for medical and education workers as well as pensions have remained stagnant in Azerbaijan. In real terms, doctors' and teachers' salaries are less now than they were in the Soviet period, and "are barely enough to support a family with one dependent" (World Bank, 2010: 65). The government has not introduced or implemented any new social programmes in the last decade that increase the amount of resources directed toward society and, in addition, "side" payments and bribes for services are more prevalent in Azerbaijan than other countries in the region. For example, out-of-pocket health expenses are estimated to be double those in other post-Soviet countries (World Bank, 2010). In short, official spending levels coupled with rampant corruption in service delivery indicate that the public is not included in rent redistribution in Azerbaijan. In addition, public expenditure behaviour in Azerbaijan does not conform to the rentier state thesis, which states that autocrats in resource-rich states increase public spending (including welfare spending) in periods of high export growth and international petroleum prices in an effort to buy off the populace and minimize societal pressure for democratization (Ross, 2001).

Authoritarian Redistribution

The point of departure for my theory of redistributive social spending in mineral-rich authoritarian countries is that power in these regimes is concentrated in the hands of the autocrat and individuals who make up a country's political and economic elites. Political elites, for my purposes, are defined as high officials of the regime who directly or indirectly play a regular part in determining national political outcomes (Putnam, 1976; Higley and Burton, 1989). In these countries, they include senior officials in the presidential administration, members of the government and houses of parliament, regional leaders and other officials depending on the structure of the bureaucracy in each case. Economic elites are economic actors who control a disproportionate amount of a country's wealth. In keeping with Tullock (1987), Wintrobe (1998), Bueno de Mesquita *et al.* (2003) and others, I assume that dictators' primary preference is to stay in power and that the main source of potential threat to their survival in office comes from political and economic elites who have the political capital, economic resources or both to unseat them. Since it is understood that autocrats will consistently behave in such a way as to minimize threats by potential opponents, as discussed above, this undoubtedly involves the distribution of patronage in the form of money and political positions to keep their elite supporters satisfied. My approach presupposes that this behaviour extends into the policy-making arena and that political pressures originating within elite circles condition autocrats' policy decisions and strategies, including those concerning social welfare. Based on my fieldwork in Azerbaijan, Russia and Kazakhstan, as well as additional research on mineral-rich authoritarian regimes in north and sub-Saharan Africa and the Middle East, I can confirm that public policy decisions in these countries are made *de facto* by the autocrat, who may receive input from small top-level elites in the country's executive administration, such as the presidential apparatus or ruling council, but ultimately makes the final budgetary decisions. Thus, the autocrat's preferences have a profound influence on public policy outcomes.

My study proposes that welfare spending variation in mineral-rich authoritarian regimes results primarily from the presence or absence of divisions within a country's political and economic elite hierarchy. The autocrat perceives divided elites as threatening and destabilizing, in which case he attempts to guarantee popular support for himself through generous welfare provisions. A loyal citizenry counterbalances the threat posed from within the elite, as any potential opponent would be loath to unseat a popular leader. On the other hand, unified elites generate a low level of perceived threat to the autocrat, who therefore minimizes welfare spending because he does not need societal allies to maintain his hold on power. In Azerbaijan, a unified political and economic elite is the key factor contributing to low levels of welfare spending.

Elite Cohesion

I argue that elite cohesion (or fragmentation) varies in two ways according to (i) the extent of factionalization among political elites and (ii) the level of overlap between political and economic elites. Elite factionalization refers to *competing* independent power groupings within the regime's ruling coalition that are involved in sustained conflict with one another.

Extensive factionalization increases the likelihood of elite defection from the autocrat for several reasons. First, the autocrat may be a member of one particular faction or clan by virtue of kinship, regional or other ties, placing the other group(s) in opposition to the autocrat. Second, even if the autocrat is not a member of a particular faction or clan but an arbiter of elite conflict, he is constantly in the position of having to manage conflict and balance groups that are opposed to one another. This means he inevitably has to take sides and favour one group over the other, which increases the risk that certain factions will turn against him or defect. In addition, depending on factional composition and ties within a particular group, members may feel greater allegiance to the faction's leader than the autocrat, thereby shrinking the autocrat's base of support. In cases of high factionalization, then, the autocrat is never immune to competition between rival elite groups. In cases of low factionalization among political elites, the autocrat is much less likely to be opposed by those in the ruling coalition.

The second component of elite fragmentation or cohesion is the level of overlap between political and economic elites. This refers to the extent to which economic power and political power are concentrated in the same individuals. When there is minimal overlap between political and economic elites, there is greater dispersion of economic assets among a class of wealthy capitalists who are independent of the state and wield enough financial power to fund opposition to the autocrat. Conversely, extensive overlap implies that the majority of individuals wielding significant financial means are dependent on the state for access to resources, and that the number of economic elites autonomous from the state is small or nonexistent. Thus, elites in this case are less likely to defect from the ruler and "abandon the certainty of access" to these economic resources (Radnitz, 2010: 132). I consider political and economic elites to be divided when ruling coalition factionalization is extensive and the level of political-economic elite overlap is minimal. Conversely, elites are unified when ruling coalition factionalization is low and there is near total overlap of political and economic elites.

In Azerbaijan, elites under the Aliev dynasty are united as a result of low ruling coalition factionalization and near total overlap of politicians and oligarchs. Other than a brief respite from 1987–93, Heidar Aliev ruled Azerbaijan for nearly 30 years, first as the First Secretary of the Communist Party from 1969–87 and then as President of the independent republic from 1993–2003. Following his death in December 2003, Heidar's son,

Ilham, succeeded him and has been in office ever since. Upon assuming the presidency in 1993, Heidar Aliev "utilized the informal networks he had cultivated" for nearly 40 years prior to the Soviet collapse as a KGB officer and leader (1944–69) and then as First Secretary of the Azerbaijani SSR (1969–87) to surround himself with loyal ministers, state agency directors, presidential administration staff and advisors (Radnitz, 2012). Similar to Syria's Bashar al-Assad, when Ilham Aliev became President following his father's death, the majority of top-level elites who had been installed in the 1990s "continued to toe the Aliev line" by remaining in their posts and insulating the new President (Hale, 2005: 149). In addition, Heidar and Ilham Aliev drew extensively from their family network to fill political positions (including, most obviously, the presidential succession from father to son). A significant number of high-level elites are close relatives of the Aliev family or other top-ranking officials. In a survey conducted in 2006 of 89 prominent elite members, Alieva and Torjesen (2007) found that 10% were close relatives of the Aliev family and 19% were related to another top-ranking official.

The Aliev family's political dominance in Azerbaijan for over 40 years, coupled with extensive kinship ties among political elites, has served to minimize factionalization. Several scholars have differentiated between two regional groupings with which Heidar Aliev was associated: the Nakhchivan clan and the Yeraz clan. The Nakhchivan clan refers to Azerbaijanis from the Nakhchivan Autonomous Republic; the Yeraz clan refers to Azerbaijanis who were born in Soviet Armenia.[1] Members of these two clans were integrated and promoted equally by Heidar Aliev in both the Soviet and post-Soviet period, however, and few instances of conflict have emerged between them (Alieva and Torjesen, 2007). While certain ministers and presidential staff members are rumoured to compete with one another for access to power and wealth, few significant internal rivalries exist between them (International Crisis Group, 2010).

Azerbaijan is also a case in which there is near total overlap of political elites and oligarchs because economic resources and political power are concentrated in the same hands. An independent business class failed to emerge in Azerbaijan due to limited privatization in the 1990s and the adoption of state ownership of the petroleum sector (Jones Luong and

1 Heidar Aliev was born in Soviet Armenia but relocated to Nakhchivan.

Weinthal, 2010).[2] This enabled the regime "to pocket significant wealth without making major concessions to reformers" (Radnitz, 2010: 139). The country's oligarchs "mostly consist of ministers who have been promoted by and are allied to the President because of close business interests" (International Crisis Group, 2010: 8). They include Kamaladdin Heydarov, the Minister of Emergency Situations (2006–present) and former Head of the Customs Committee (1995–2006). He is rumoured to be the wealthiest person in Azerbaijan after the Alievs and the Pashaevs, the President's in-laws. The oligarchs also include Ziya Mammadov, the Minister of Transportation (2002–present), and Rovnag Abdullaev, the President of the State Oil Company of Azerbaijan (2005–present). Together, the extended Aliev, Pashaev, Abdullaev, Heydarov and Mammadov families control almost the entire Azerbaijani economy through state and proxy companies, including: the petroleum, construction, agricultural, tourism, insurance and banking sectors; food production, supply and imports; and passenger transport and cargo shipments (International Crisis Group, 2010). Thus, no wealthy business elites independent of the state exist, which greatly reduces the possibility of challenges to the President.

Low Threat to the Alievs' Rule

The literature on authoritarian regime dynamics suggests that threats to autocratic rule are more likely to arise from divisions within the ruling, business or military elites than from foreign intervention or popular uprising (e.g. Geddes, 1999; Bueno de Mesquita *et al.*, 2003). United elites are much less likely than fragmented elites to become involved in conflicts that could threaten the autocrat. In the case of Azerbaijan, key elites, including Ilham Aliev, have a shared goal to reap financial spoils from the state. The regime's main players do not have opposing ideological or policy preferences, so neither Aliev has had to appeal to a wide range of viewpoints. Competition among members of the Azerbaijani elite is certainly present but disputes that emerge are typically of a personal nature and are resolved by the President. In addition, the family and patronage networks surrounding the Alievs and Pashaevs, as well as Kamaladdin Heidarov, Ziya

2 The 1994 "contract of the century" enabled the state to maintain ownership of the country's oilfields while allowing foreign companies to help develop them.

Mammadov and Ramiz Mehtiyev, present a formidable force to contend with for any outsider who might emerge as a challenger.

The only major conflict that transpired during Heidar Aliev's decade as President was a coup attempt in 1995. Soon after the armistice with Armenia over Nagorno-Karabakh, Aliev learned that the OMON (Special Forces) commander, Rovshan Javadov, planned to stage a coup. Troops from Nakhchivan, which formed a type of "praetorian guard", were called up to defend the President, which ended in a shootout that killed Javadov (Radnitz, 2012: 63). It remains unclear, however, whether or not Javadov actually did want to topple the President, or if Heidar Aliev initiated a pre-emptive strike against him for other reasons. Aliev brooked no other serious challenges to his rule before relinquishing power 2 months before his death in 2003.

A potential opening for members of the elite to challenge the Alievs' authority came in 2003 with the transfer of power from father to son. In the October 2003 election, established elites coalesced around Ilham and remained loyal to the Aliev family for several reasons. First, Heidar Aliev, who remained popular among his subordinates, deliberately passed the torch to this son, which signalled to established elites that the *status quo ante* coalition and patronage system would remain in place. Second, Heidar announced that he was stepping down – and that Ilham would be named acting President – just 2 weeks before the election, which left too little time for elites to unite around a potential rival candidate (Hale, 2005). Third, Ilham Aliev "reputedly gave personal assurances to his father's officials that he would leave them in their posts and refrain from disrupting their informal power centers" (Radnitz, 2012: 66). As I show in the previous section, the principal actors on Heidar Aliev's team retained their positions (or obtained better ones) after Ilham survived the succession election in 2003 and fraudulent parliamentary elections in 2005.

The only major instance of intraelite conflict that erupted since Ilham Aliev took power involved the dismissals and arrests of two prominent Yeraz ministers and the marginalization of two of Ilham Aliev's family members in 2005. Ali Insanov, who was Minister of Health from 1996 until 2005, and Farhad Aliev (no relation), who was Minister of Economic Development from 2001 until 2005, were arrested in 2005 and officially charged with conspiring with an exiled opposition leader to stage a coup against Ilham Aliev. What is known about Insanov and Farhad Aliev's insubordination is that they questioned Ilham's inheritance. Some scholars (e.g. Radnitz, 2012) have painted this as an example of factional conflict between Nakhchivanis and Yerazis but the available evidence suggests that these two ministers were forcibly removed because they threatened the domains of more powerful members of the ruling coalition. The feud also involved Ilham Aliev's close blood relatives – his sister Sevil and uncle Jalal (who grew up with Heidar in Nakhchivan) – suggesting that this was not a "clash" between Yerazis and Nakhchivanis. Second, Ali Insanov and Farhad Aliev did not jointly challenge Ilham's authority. Ali Insanov and Jalal Aliev came up against Ramiz Mehtiyev in wanting to exert control over Ilham as opposed to challenging his authority as President (International Crisis Group, 2010), and Farhad Aliev's demise is primarily due to the fact that he came up against Kamaladdin Heidarov. Ilham Aliev's uncle Jalal and sister Sevil were not arrested because family members are considered "untouchables" (International Crisis Group, 2010: 9), but Jalal lost his position as a Member of Parliament and Sevil currently resides out of the country. In short, this was neither a case of factional conflict nor a serious challenge to Ilham Aliev himself but a potential incursion into Mehtiyev and Heidarov's zones of political and economic control.

No Need for Popular Support

To ensure dictatorial survival, autocrats must distribute patronage to political elites in the form of money and positions in an attempt to keep them satisfied. Under certain conditions, however, this strategy is not sufficient to maintain power. In cases of high threat generated by a divided elite, the autocrat is in a much more precarious position. He must pre-emptively limit threats posed by potential opponents, as well as respond to them when they occur. Genuine, widespread popular support for the ruler is an effective deterrent to potential elite opponents. If an autocrat enjoys widespread popular support then the scales will always be tipped in his favour. If potential challengers do not have the "audience" – or the public – on their side, then they will not "start a fight if they are certain that they are going to be severely penalized for their efforts" (Schattschneider, 1960: 8). By contrast, in cases of low threat, as in Azerbaijan, autocrats do not need societal allies, and can more easily sustain their rule without genuine support from the masses.

The Alievs' strategy of doling out money and political positions to members of the elite is sufficient for maintaining power in Azerbaijan. The above discussion reveals that there have been few serious challenges to the Alievs' authority since the early 1990s, and that the primary conflict that did occur in 2005 was partly personal in nature. In addition, the absence of wealthy economic elites who are capable of funding opposition movements or formally challenging the Aliev dynasty has further guaranteed regime stability. Since neither Aliev – especially Ilham – has had any reason to fear reverberations from intraelite conflict, there is no need for society to serve as a counterweight to potential rivals. The Alievs' welfare spending response (or more often their "nonresponse") to domestic events referenced in the previous section, as well as the global economic crisis, reveals their security vis-à-vis members of the elite.

After the drop in welfare expenditure from 14% to 6.6% of GDP between 1990 and 1995, expenditure increased slightly and hovered between 7 and 8% of GDP between 1996 and 2000. The highest expenditure increase occurred between 1995 and 1997, following the March 1995 attempted coup against Heidar Aliev, when expenditure jumped from 6.6% to 8.4%. Expenditure in 1997 represents the highest welfare spending in Azerbaijan since the mid-1990s. However, after Aliev successfully consolidated power in the 1998 presidential elections, in which he won 70% of the vote, expenditure began to decline steadily. From 2000 to 2003, welfare spending declined from 6.9% to 6.2% of GDP, which suggests that there was no pre-emptive move to shore up a societal support base in the lead-up to the presidential succession in 2003. Following Ilham Aliev's rise to power, expenditure experienced its most significant decline in all three welfare sectors, dropping from a combined total of 6.3% in 2004 to 5.3% in 2008. In addition, while the share of total budget expenditures on welfare had also been declining steadily since the late 1990s, it experienced its most substantial drop to date in this time period – from 35.7% in 2004 to 20% in 2008. Notably, following the arrests of Ali Insanov and Farhad Aliev in October 2005, total spending as a percentage of GDP dropped from 5.6% in 2005 to 5.3% in 2006, and the share of budgetary expenditures experienced the largest year-to-year decrease, from 33% in 2005 to 25.6% in 2006.

This trend demonstrates that Ilham Aliev did not need to build up and maintain a societal support base upon assuming and consolidating power, nor did he feel threatened by the one major instance of intraelite conflict that shook his Cabinet in 2005. This is a clear illustration of

Ilham's perception of a secure power base among members of the elite. At the same time, a very modest increase in welfare expenditure trends during the global financial crisis suggests that Ilham Aliev may have responded to fears of potential elite challenges because his patronage system relies almost exclusively on oil revenues. Real GDP growth fell from 25% in 2007 to 5% in 2010 and 0.1% in 2011. Aggregate welfare spending then increased from 5.3% of GDP in 2008 to 6.4% of GDP in 2010 and 2011. In per capita terms, salaries and social transfer payouts experienced their largest year-to-year increase between 2008 and 2009; pensions, for example, increased by a third, from 56 to 74 real AZN ($70 to $92). While this could be called a case of pre-emptive populism, it was very short lived because economic growth began to recover in 2010. After 2009, salaries for public sector employees in the health and education sectors, pensions and all other social transfer payments began to stagnate in real terms. In short, Ilham Aliev has been completely insulated from societal demands and has no need to appeal to the masses through welfare provision to ward off potential rivals.

Conclusion

This chapter tests the theoretical argument that the degree of unity among ruling and business elites in mineral-rich authoritarian regimes affects leaders' decisions about how much to spend on their citizens' welfare. Specifically, it explores the causal link between a small and unified ruling and business elite and low health, education and social-security expenditures in Azerbaijan from 2000 until the present under Heidar and Ilham Aliev. It demonstrates that autocrats who are not threatened by those in ruling and business elite circles do not have to engage in populist redistribution to stay in power and can therefore siphon off the proceeds from oil exports for personal gain – and divert funds from pensions for Eurovision events – rather than investing in social welfare. The Alievs did not believe that they needed societal allies to sustain their rule; instead, they have relied primarily on the loyalty of those in the ruling coalition.

While elites are cohesive under the Aliev regime, an implication of this argument is that Azerbaijan may be more vulnerable to civil unrest compared with other mineral-rich authoritarian regimes within and outside of the former Soviet Union, which devote more resources to social welfare. Poverty and unemployment rates are quite high in Azerbaijan, which may indicate widespread societal dissatisfaction. A disgruntled populace increases the probability that scattered acts of resistance could escalate into full-blown revolution (Kuran, 1991). Perhaps similar to the younger al-Assad, who also succeeded his father, the current Aliev believes he is invulnerable to losing power due to elite cohesion; therefore, he does not have an incentive to invest in social programmes because he does not think that he needs popular support. By poorly subsidizing the masses, however, he is creating a situation whereby disaffection could potentially grow to the point where there is a popular uprising. Indeed, compared with other oil-rich Soviet successor states, Azerbaijan exhibited more acts of civil unrest and detained more activists in spring 2011 in the midst of revolutions in north Africa and the Middle East.[3]

References

Alieva, L. and Torjesen, S. (2007) The Insignificance of Clan in Kazakhstan and Azerbaijan. Unpublished manuscript.

Anderson, L. (1995) Peace and Democracy in the Middle East: the Constraints of Soft Budgets. *Journal of International Affairs* 49, 25–44.

Brown, D. S. and Hunter, W. (1999) Democracy and Social Spending in Latin America, 1980–1992. American Political Science Review 93 (4), 779–790.

Bueno de Mesquita, B., Smith, A., Siverson, R.M. and Morrow, J.D. (2003) The logic of political survival. The MIT Press, Cambridge, MA.

Cook, L. J. (2007) *Postcommunist Welfare States: Reform Politics in Russia and Eastern Europe,* Cornell University Press, Ithaca, NY.

Desai, R. M., Olofsgard, A., Yousef, T. M. (2009) The Logic of Authoritarian Bargains. *Economics and Politics* 21(1), 93–125.

Geddes, B. (1999) Authoritarian Breakdown: Empirical Test of a Game-theoretic Argument. Unpublished manuscript. Available at

3 This assessment is based on online news research using Radio Free Europe/Radio Liberty (see <www.rferl.org>), EurasiaNet (<www.eurasia.net>) and other sources.

<http://eppam.weebly.com/uploads/5/5/6/2/5562069/authoritarian-breakdown_geddes.pdf>.

Hale, H. E. (2005) Regime Cycles: Democracy, Autocracy and Revolution in Post-Soviet Eurasia. *World Politics* 58(1), 133–165.

Higley, J. and Burton, M. G. (1989) The Elite Variable in Democratic Transitions and Breakdowns. *American Sociological Review* 54, 17–32.

International Crisis Group. (2010) *Azerbaijan: Vulnerable Sustainability,* Europe Report No. 207, <http://www.crisisgroup.org/~/media/Files/europe/caucasus/azerbaijan/207%20Azerbaijan%20-%20Vulnerable%20Stability.pdf> (accessed 20 October 2014).

Jones Luong, P. and Weinthal, E. (2010) Oil is Not a Curse: Ownership Structure and Institutions in Soviet Successor States, Cambridge University Press, New York, NY.

Kaufman, R.R. and Segura-Ubiergo, A. (2001) Globalization, Domestic Politics, and Social Spending in Latin America: a Time-series Cross-section Analysis. *World Politics* 53, 553–587.

Kuran, T. (1991) Now out of Never: the Element of Surprise in the East European Revolution of 1989. *World Politics* 44(1), 7–48.

Magaloni, B. and Wallace, J. (2008) Citizen Loyalty, Mass Protest and Authoritarian Survival. Unpublished manuscript. Available at <http://www.princeton.edu/~piirs/Dictatorships042508/Magaloni%20&%20Wallace%20-%20Loyalty,%20Protest,%20&%20Authoritarian%20Survival.pdf>.

Orenstein, M. (2008) Postcommunist welfare states. *Journal of Democracy* 19 (4), 80–94.

Przeworski, A., Alvarez, M., Cheibub, J. and Limongi, F. (2000) Democracy and Development: Political Institutions and Well-Being in the World, 1950–1990, Cambridge University Press, New York, NY.

Putnam, R. D. (1976) *The Comparative Study of Elites,* Prentice Hall, Englewood Cliffs, NJ.

Radnitz, S. (2010) The Color of Money: Privatization, Economic Dispersion, and Post-Soviet "Revolutions". *Comparative Politics* 42 (2), 127–146.

Radnitz, S. (2012) Oil in the Family: Managing Presidential Succession in Azerbaijan. *Democratization* 19 (1), 60–77.

Ross, M. L. (2001) Does Oil Hinder Democracy? *World Politics* 53 (3), 325–361.

Rudra, N. and Haggard, S. (2005) Globalization, Democracy and Effective Welfare Spending in the Developing World. *Comparative Political Studies* 38 (9), 115–149.

Schattscheider, E. E. (1960) *The Semi-Sovereign People: A Realist's View of Democracy in America,* Holt, Rinehart & Winston, New York, NY.

Sultanova, S. (2012) *In Eurovision Spending, Azerbaijan is a Clear Winner,* <http://www.tol.org/client/article/23107-in-eurovision-spending-azerbaijan-is-a-clear-winner.html (accessed 20 October 2014)>.

Tullock, G. (1987) *Autocracy,* Kluwer Academic Publishers, Boston, MA.

Vandewalle, D. (1998) *Libya since Independence: Oil and State Building,* Cornell University Press, Ithaca, NY.

Wintrobe, R. (1998) *The Political Economy of Dictatorship,* Cambridge, New York, NY.

World Bank (2010) *Azerbaijan Living Conditions Assessment Report.* Report No. 52801-AZ. World Bank, Washington, DC.

World Bank (2012) *World Development Indicators,* <http://data.worldbank.org/data-catalog/world-development-indicators> (accessed 20 October 2014).

Part II
External Actors: Do They Help to Democratize?

Povilas Žielys

Guarding or Retarding? US Democracy-Assistance Programmes in Post-Rose Revolution Georgia

ABSTRACT: The 2003 Rose Revolution failed to skyrocket Georgia into the ranks of consolidated democracies. This chapter focuses on the US role in post-revolution Georgia, testing a hypothesis that US-funded democracy assistance programmes were burdened by US security interests and, therefore, detrimental to democratization goals. The chapter examines five groups of US programmes (constitutional assistance, electoral aid, political party development, NGO development and media strengthening) implemented in Georgia in 2004–2008, and reveals some retarding aspects of US democracy assistance. The findings suggest, however, that not only US security interests but also bureaucratic miscalculation by US donor organizations accounted for the flawed democracy assistance effort in Georgia.

KEYWORDS: democratization, democracy assistance, United States, Georgia, Rose Revolution

Despite much enthusiasm and hope associated with the 2003 Rose Revolution, the following years were marked by some doubts whether Georgia was really progressing along the path of democratic development. President Mikheil Saakashvili and his government focused their postrevolution reforms on strengthening the state. They passed constitutional amendments producing a superpresidential regime. Contrary to the principle of a constitutional division of power, the parliament and judiciary were subordinated to the executive. Saakashvili's United National Movement (UNM) secured its continued dominance in the parliament by manipulating electoral legislation (Lanskoy and Areshidze, 2008: 160–162). In addition, Georgia's state authorities largely neglected accountability, political pluralism and the protection of human rights.

In their effort to explain the relatively disappointing outcomes of the Rose Revolution, scholars mainly analysed the role of internal factors, including the ruling elite (Cheterian, 2008; Kalandadze and Orenstein, 2009), opposition (Tatum, 2009), civil society (Tudoroiu, 2007; Laverty, 2008) and institutional legacy (Jones, 2006). Some authors have examined the negative impact of some external actors, namely Russia and the European Union (Tolstrup, 2009; Jonavicius, 2009).

A few authors focused their research on the United States and its influence on democratic consolidation in Georgia. Mitchell (2006, 2009) argued that the George W. Bush administration made a mistake by putting too much trust in the democratic intentions of the Saakashvili government and by redirecting US assistance from "nongovernmental aspects of democracy" (elections, political parties and media) to Georgian state institutions. This argument was echoed by Omelicheva (2010) who blamed the United States for turning a blind eye to human rights violations in Georgia and supporting the Saakashvili government in its goal of rebuilding the state prior to democratizing it. Muskhelishvili and Jorjoliani (2009) also observed that in the wake of the Rose Revolution, the United States stripped funding for watchdog organizations that had previously been the best funded nongovernmental organizations (NGOs) in Georgia. Finally, Lazarus (2010) criticized the United States' unconditional political support for the Saakashvili government and its implicit preference for pro-government NGOs. According to him, such "unprincipled democracy promotion" undermined democratic prospects in Georgia by instilling a sense of impunity within the government and provoking anti-Western resentment amongst the nonparliamentary opposition.

All of the researchers mentioned above assumed that it was the close alignment of the Saakashvili government to US security interests that accounted for flaws and inconsistencies in US democracy assistance to Georgia. However, this hypothesis has two different sides. One can look at the diplomatic level of democracy assistance, i.e. US efforts to dissuade the Georgian government from non-democratic actions by means of public criticism, backstage diplomatic pressure, or economic sanctions. Alternatively, one can examine the programmatic level of democracy assistance, which includes US-funded programmes aimed at levelling Georgia's playing field for political competition and enabling civil society to control government's activities. This analytical distinction has been missing in previous research although it is of utmost importance. At the diplomatic level, the hypothesis of security-burdened democracy assistance is almost obvious because diplomacy reflects the changing priority order of foreign-policy goals. By contrast, this hypothesis sounds much more controversial if applied to the programmatic level. Democracy assistance programs are designed to serve the specific goal of democratization and are implemented by governmental and nongovernmental organizations (agencies, foundations, institutes, and so forth) that are regarded as autonomous and immune to political bias. Accordingly, such programmes should be analysed separately from diplomatic actions of a donor country in order to confirm or refute the link between donor's security interests and outcomes of its democracy assistance programmes.

Unlike the previous research, this chapter respects the analytical distinction between the diplomatic and the programmatic level of democracy assistance. It focuses exclusively on the programmatic level and looks into US democracy assistance programmes implemented in Georgia between the 2003 Rose Revolution and the 2008 Georgian–Russian military conflict. The chapter begins with discussing the theoretical link between security interests of a donor country and its democracy assistance strategies. Based on theoretical insights, it is hypothesized that US security interests distorted US-funded programmes so that they became limited to serving the interests of Georgia's US-friendly leadership. To test this hypothesis, the following five groups of democracy assistance programmes are examined: constitutional assistance, electoral aid, political party development, NGO development and independent media strengthening. The research draws on a series of interviews with US aid providers and recipients that I conducted in Georgia in autumn 2010. The chapter concludes by contextualizing the findings and discovering factors that, along with US security interests, likely accounted for inconsistent US democracy assistance in postrevolution Georgia.

Democratization Goals and Security Interests

Democratization can never be the sole foreign policy objective of any donor country. Even in the United States, which tends to promote democracy with a missionary zeal, democratization must coexist with other objectives and interests: curbing the spread of weapons of mass destruction, combating terrorism, dampening regional rivalries and developing better economic relations (Lowenkron, 2007: 202). Unavoidably, these foreign policy goals not only coexist but also conflict with each other.

Most situations when the democratization goal conflicts with other security interests can be described as one of two interrelated dilemmas. The first dilemma occurs if donor's efforts to promote democracy may lead to destabilization in the recipient country. In this case, the donor country must choose between promoting more democratic or more efficient governance (Spanger and Wolff, 2005). Consequently, the donor country may prefer a stronger executive branch at the expense of political competition. The second dilemma occurs if the democratic process in the recipient country may bring to power political groups that are perceived by the donor country as hostile to its interests. In this case, the donor country may intervene by supporting political allies or by inhibiting the ascent of those forces that oppose the influence and interests of the donor country (Boudreau, 2007). Consequently, democracy assistance programmes may become politically biased.

In post-Rose Revolution Georgia, the United States pursued a multifaceted policy agenda. Apart from being advertised as the only success story of democratic transformation in the region ("beacon of liberty"), Georgia was also important for the United States as a means to demonopolize the access to Caspian energy resources and ensure the cargo transit to US-led military missions in Afghanistan and Iraq (Cornell, 2007: 5–14). In addition, the Bush administration attempted to alter the balance in the geopolitical competition with Russia and bring Georgia into NATO. To achieve those goals, the United States needed a strong state and a staunchly pro-Western leadership in Georgia. The post-Rose Revolution Georgia under President Saakashvili seemed to meet both criteria. For this reason one could assume that the United States government should have welcomed Saakashvili's entrenchment in power and may have bent US-funded democracy assistance programmes in favour of Georgia's leadership.

What democracy assistance programs should be examined? This chapter focuses on the following five sectors that were prioritized by US donors before the Rose Revolution: constitutional assistance, electoral aid, political party development, NGO development and independent media strengthening. It is hypothesized that US-funded legal experts may have advised concentrating powers in the executive because the United States wanted to remove any obstacles for Saakashvili's reform agenda. It is further assumed that the United States' attention to the free and fair electoral process in Georgia should have decreased, as it already had its favourite leaders in power. It is also hypothesized that US-funded organizations should have discriminated Saakashvili's political rivals when providing training for Georgian political parties. Finally, it is assumed that US governmental donors should have cut funding for watchdog NGOs and independent media as the US no longer deemed it necessary to scrutinize the activities of the incumbent government. It is important to note that only programmes funded by US governmental donors are considered because privately funded democracy assistance programmes cannot be analysed as part of state-implemented foreign policy.

Constitutional Assistance

Following the Rose Revolution and Saakashvili's landslide victory in the presidential elections, the Georgian Parliament passed constitutional amendments that were later criticized as the unfortunate expansion of executive power (Areshidze, 2004). It is hypothesized in this section that US-funded programmes provided poor advice to Georgians endorsing a strong presidency, so that a US-favoured leader could comfortably implement his domestic and foreign agenda.

The constitutional reform was carried out in a rush, leaving little room for deliberation and critique. The proposed amendments were briefly discussed in the President-led Constitutional Commission (CC), then submitted to the Parliament on 3 February 2004 and passed only 3 days later. As one of the CC members recalled, neither the CC nor the Parliament had consulted any foreign bodies (telephone interview by the author with a member of the 2002–4 Constitutional Commission, 19 October 2010).

Nevertheless, there was at least one US-funded programme, namely the Georgia Rule of Law Project, aiming to feed into the process of the 2004 constitutional reform. This project was funded by US Agency for International Development (USAID) and implemented by the IRIS Center of the University of Maryland. In the final report of the project it is claimed that it has contributed to the constitutional reform by providing analyses and recommendations on pending constitutional amendments (IRIS Center, 2006). Indeed, when the draft constitutional amendments became available, IRIS Georgia stepped up with the initiative to gather legal experts and government officials at the roundtable in order to discuss the proposed amendments. However, according to an interviewee who worked for IRIS Georgia at that time, they faced unexpected difficulties in obtaining USAID's sanction for such roundtable. After several days of consultations between the Georgian branch of USAID and the US Embassy in Georgia, USAID/Georgia officers came back to IRIS Georgia expressing their doubts with regard to the proposed roundtable. They told that they did not want to impose problems for the new Georgian government in light of US Secretary of State Collin Powel's recent visit to Tbilisi and his strong support for the Rose Revolution. Eventually, IRIS Georgia persuaded its donors and the roundtable was organized. Although most participants criticized the draft constitutional amendments, this event could not have had any impact, as it took place only one day before the Parliament passed the discussed amendments (interview by the author with a former IRIS Georgia representative, Tbilisi, 20 October 2010).

Because of the hurried pace of the constitutional reform, the comprehensive analysis of the amendments was produced by IRIS Georgia only post factum. Legal experts of IRIS Georgia provided a very critical assessment. According to it, the new constitution "considerably violated the principles of division of power" by weakening the Parliament and granting "additional important tools" to the President. The President's right to act as a chairman of a political party was especially criticized as undermining political competition and politicizing the civil service (IRIS Georgia, 2004). It should be noted that this assessment has never been made available to the public. According to the IRIS Georgia representative, this NGO was meant to provide expert advice to the Georgian and US governments and did not have the right to publish its products without a prior consent of its US donors (interview by the author with a former IRIS Georgia representative).

The collected evidence suggests that US-funded constitutional assistance programs were affected by the US government's reluctance to criticize President Saakashvili and his team. As an interviewed then high-ranking Georgian official recalled, foreign partners, including Americans, were not happy about the constitutional changes, as they understood the problems that they might cause. However, foreign partners took no actions because they could not predict that President Saakashvili might abuse his vast powers (interview by the author with a former high-ranking Georgian official, Tbilisi, 21 October 2010). Ultimately, political considerations at the diplomatic level prevailed over impartial judgment at the programmatic level.

Electoral Aid

In 2008, President Saakashvili and his party, UNM, ensured their continuous stay in power by winning presidential and parliamentary elections. According to some assessments, those elections were unfair as the government was abusing its resources (Lazarus, 2010). It is hypothesized in this section that, following the Rose Revolution, United States governmental donors either abandoned election-related programmes or pursued programmes that were biased in favour of Saakashvili and his team.

The assumption of a possible US donors' retreat from the sector of electoral aid was rejected by both US assistance providers and recipients. The interviewed representatives of the USAID mission in Georgia (USAID/Georgia) described the electoral aid as the only type of assistance that depends on *ad hoc* political decisions rather than long-term bureaucratic planning. According to them, USAID provided electoral aid to Georgia on demand and its level remained high after the Rose Revolution. In every pre-election period, USAID used to increase support to watchdog organizations and allocate more funds to election monitoring (interview by the author with USAID/Georgia representatives, Tbilisi, 13 October 2010). Representatives of two major Georgian election-monitoring NGOs, International Society for Elections and Democracy (ISFED) and Union 'new Generation – new Initiative (nGnI), confirmed that there was no dramatic decrease in US funding after the Rose Revolution. The ISFED representative said that it was always relatively easy to find election-related funding (interview by the author with an ISFED representative, Tbilisi, 15 October 2010). The nGnI representatives admitted that nGnI budget was always bigger in a year of national elections (interview by the author with nGnI representatives, Tbilisi, 20 October 2010).

Likewise, the collected evidence does not support the assumption that US electoral aid programmes may have been politically biased. Those critics, who doubted the transparency of Saakashvili's and UNM's electoral victories in 2008, usually cited election-monitoring reports published by the Organization of Security and Cooperation in Europe (OSCE). The question is whether US-funded election monitoring missions came up with less critical reports. If so, one could reasonably argue that the US turned a blind eye to violations committed by the favoured "Rose" leadership. However, the comparative analysis of respective OSCE and National Democratic

Institute (NDI) reports did not reveal any significant differences in this respect. Following the January 2008 early presidential elections, both OSCE and NDI reports contained the same critical remarks on the use of state resources to Saakashvili's benefit; intimidation and pressure on opposition activists, state employees and local observers; unbalanced media coverage; and slow and chaotic vote counting (NDI, 2008a; OSCE, 2008a). Following the May 2008 parliamentary elections, findings of OSCE and NDI missions were very similar again, both referring to the late amendments of electoral code; use of state resources to UNM's advantage; intimidation and pressure on opposition candidates, state employees and local observers; unbalanced media coverage; domination of UNM representatives at all levels of election commissions; and postelection assaults on opposition activists (NDI, 2008b; OSCE, 2008b).

Political Party Development

After the Rose Revolution, Saakashvili's UNM emerged as a dominant political force in Georgian politics. The party secured a strong majority in the parliament turning this institution to a mere "notary public" that rubber stamped President Saakashvili's decisions (International Crisis Group, 2007: 18). It is hypothesized in this section that US governmental donors compromised political pluralism in Georgia by either withdrawing from the sector of political party assistance or giving preferential treatment to the ruling UNM.

Before the Rose Revolution, two US organizations – NDI and the International Republican Institute (IRI) – were working with all relevant Georgian political parties. The situation has changed since 2004. While the IRI continued to assist parties inside and outside the parliament, NDI signed a new contract with USAID and shifted its focus almost entirely towards legislative strengthening. This shift reflected the heightened interest that the US government took in supporting Georgian state institutions, as opposed to civil society organizations (Bader, 2010: 111). The Georgian opposition criticized the NDI's post-2004 focus on parties with parliamentary representation, claiming that the NDI's assistance to parliament, which is controlled by the UNM, merely strengthens the UNM's political monopoly. The then head of the NDI branch in Georgia (NDI/Georgia), Mary O'Hagen, accepted the criticism. She said that NDI/Georgia did not want to be engaged exclusively with parliament but its cooperation with parties outside the parliament was restricted by the contract with USAID (McGlinchey, 2007).

While the NDI was locked in the cooperation with a few parties in parliament, the local IRI branch (IRI/Georgia) continued to offer training to all interested Georgian parties. Nonetheless, the ruling UNM received a disproportionate share of party assistance by IRI because it was more advanced and better coordinated than all other parties (Bader, 2010: 129). In general, IRI provided demand-based assistance so it was up to the parties themselves to come to IRI/Georgia and identify the type of assistance they claim to need (interview by the author with an IRI/Georgia representative, Tbilisi, 18 October 2010). Therefore, it is no wonder that the best organized party – in this case, UNM – was able to secure most support. An interviewed IRI/Georgia representative claimed they had never refused assistance to any Georgian party. The only relevant Georgian party which did not cooperate with IRI was Shalva Natelashvili's Labour Party. According to the interviewee, the Labour Party avoided cooperation with IRI because ideologically Natelashvili was "less engaged with the American crowd than the other people" (interview by the author with an IRI/Georgia representative). Indeed, Natelashvili has repeatedly criticized the US government for financing the Rose Revolution and bringing Saakashvili to power. In one of his speeches, he described IRI as a "gang of Saakashvili's supporters" (Civil Georgia, 2008). Nonetheless, IRI/Georgia worked with the youth wing of the Labour Party (interview by the author with an IRI/Georgia representative).

To summarize, US donors reframed their post-2004 party assistance in a way that did not help to level the playing field in Georgia. Although US-funded programs did not discriminate against Saakashvili's political rivals, they were instrumental in consolidating the ruling party and not the opposition. In 2007, the situation was ripe for the re-evaluation of US donors' strategy, as indicated by a call in the USAID-ordered study to direct future party assistance "at providing democratic alternatives to the UNM" (Democracy International, 2007: 25).

NGO Development

In the period 2004–6, USAID support for the "Democratic Reforms" programme in Georgia decreased from $10.4 million to $8.7 million (US Department of State, 2010). Surprisingly, cuts in funding for civil society occurred at a time when the Georgian third sector, according to the US-AID-developed NGO Sustainability Index, was weakening (USAID, 2011: 217). It is hypothesized in this section that the US government sought to save its favoured leadership in Georgia from public criticism by depriving watchdog NGOs of previously generous funding and by supporting only pro-government NGOs.

All interviewed representatives of Georgian NGOs confirmed that they felt a drop in US funding after the Rose Revolution. According to a Civil Society Institute representative, many NGOs were almost exclusively reliant on foreign grants so they had to suspend or even terminate their activities (interview by the author with a Civil Society Institute representative, Tbilisi, 18 October 2010). The Executive Director of the Human Rights Center, Ucha Nanuashvili, added that post-2004 cuts in US funding most severely affected NGOs outside the largest cities and left some regions of the country without NGO presence at all (interview by the author with U. Nanuashvili, Tbilisi, 15 October 2010).

The representatives of USAID/Georgia admitted there was a shift in assistance priorities of the "Democracy and Governance" programme after of the Rose Revolution. USAID increased its support for Georgian state institutions ("governance") partly at the expense of the support for civil society ("democracy"). This shift took place because many former NGO leaders joined the new government and the government seemed to be result oriented and eager to act (interview by the author with USAID/Georgia representatives). The interviewed NGO representatives acknowledged that US donors' support for the new government was rational and well justified. However, they criticized the relative abandonment of watchdog NGOs that were supposed to hold the government accountable. A representative of the watchdog NGO Former Political Prisoners for Human Rights described the attitude of foreign donors as follows: "If democrats came to power one needs to fund them and not the organisations that criticise those democrats. In fact, nobody was interested in what kind of democrats they really are, how they perceive democracy and how they protect human rights" (interview by the author with a Former Political Prisoners for Human Rights representative, Tbilisi, 12 October 2010).

It took around three years until US government donors revisited their assistance priorities and started re-engaging with Georgian civil society. A USAID performance report of the fiscal year 2007 (October 2006–September 2007) already noted the need of "reversing the decline of civil society organisations' impact since the Rose Revolution and the concomitant expansion of executive branch power" (USAID, 2007). The November 2007 crackdown on opposition protests in Tbilisi served as a final argument for US donors that the post-2004 assistance strategy did not justify itself. For example, USAID/Georgia representatives admitted that they believed in the group of NGO leaders who entered the government. USAID applauded market reforms and the anticorruption measures they implemented and did not notice their insufficient attention to democratic institutions. However, in 2007, the Georgian government made some mistakes and its commitment to democratic principles was cast into doubt (interview by the author with USAID/Georgia representatives). The majority of interviewed NGO representatives confirmed that US donors re-engaged with Georgia's civil society around 2007–8.

Coming back to the period of 2004–6, one has to address the question of pro-government NGOs (so-called GONGOs). Did US governmental donors divert their already reduced funding from watchdog NGOs to less critical GONGOs? In the wake of the Rose Revolution, USAID indeed promoted a close cooperation between NGOs and the new government. The old approach of supporting the organizational development of many NGOs (a "thousand flowers blooming throughout the country") was replaced by the new approach of focusing funds on a few NGOs and implementation of specific projects (interview by the author with USAID/Georgia representatives). However, even when promoting the joint work of NGOs and the government, US donors did not abandon critical watchdogs. According to the representative of one of the watchdog NGOs, the proportion of US funding for watchdog activities on the one hand and for joint projects with the government on the other has changed since 2004, but US donors have never financed exclusively pro-government NGOs (interview by the author with a Civil Society Institute representative).

What may have frustrated some Georgian NGOs was their increased dependency on the Georgian government compared to the pre-Rose Revolution period. As the Executive Director of the Georgian Young Lawyers'

Association, Giorgi Chkheidze, pointed out, US donors continued to refer to the involvement of civil society in the reform process but now it became a duty of the Georgian government to involve NGOs (interview by the author with G. Chkheidze, Tbilisi, 15 October 2010). This opened a way for Georgian authorities to select which NGOs they want to work with while excluding others. As a result, the selected NGOs were labelled as GONGOs – the outcome of which was not surprising in the politically polarized Georgian society.

Independent Media Strengthening

In the period following the Rose Revolution, the Georgian mass media faced a number of challenges, including a shutdown of political talk shows and harassment of independent media outlets by state authorities (Kokashvili, 2005: 226–227). It is hypothesized in this section that US governmental donors turned a blind eye to worrying developments and reduced their support for the media sector because the US government no longer deemed it necessary to scrutinize the activities of the Georgian leadership, which the US now trusted.

Before and during the Rose Revolution, the US channelled most of its media assistance through the USAID-funded Media Innovations Program, which was designed for the 2002–6 period and implemented by the International Research and Exchanges Board (IREX). In 2005, however, USAID refused to extend its flagship media program. Bob Evans, the then IREX Chief of Party in Georgia, has provided a very blunt comment on that: "We were told many times to fully support the new regime and not point out the shortcomings of the new government. 'Watchdog' became 'bad dog' in anticipation of some sort of counter-revolution. USAID seemed to almost simultaneously announce that we ran the best media program they had ever seen and that they had no intention of offering a media program again" (Mitchell, 2009: 130). An interviewed Georgian media expert who was contracted by IREX to work in the Media Innovations Program provided a more moderate assessment. According to this expert, USAID and other US donors suspended direct assistance to independent media because they "assumed prematurely that the Georgian government was so interested in developing democracy that there would be not that much need for outside support" (interview by the author with a Georgian media expert, Tbilisi, 13 October 2010). If that was the case, the postrevolution euphoria of US governmental donors must have been particularly overwhelming. It should be noted that USAID dismissed the advice of its own experts. In the joint IREX and USAID mid-term assessment published in September 2004, it was highlighted in capital letters that the authors of the assessment did not recommend USAID to close its media assistance program (McClear and Koenig, 2004: 8).

The closure of USAID's flagship media programme did not mean that US donors withdrew from the Georgian media sector altogether. According to the same Georgian media expert, USAID diminished its direct support to independent media but it continued to provide assistance indirectly: "All USAID projects had a media component and the money was flowing to media through thematic interventions." In addition, the US embassy in Georgia still had a media assistance program. However, this kind of assistance was not large scale and not systematic (interview by the author with a Georgian media expert, Tbilisi, 13 October 2010).

Some of media-related Georgian NGOs that were previously reliant on US funding managed to find alternative donors, such as the EU or small private foundations. Unfortunately, many media outlets could not diversify their sources of funding. According to the Development Director of the local NGO, Internews Georgia, Tamuna Kakulia, many television channels, radio stations and newspapers were not ready for "financial independence" and "they were forced to attach themselves to the funding from the local government". Consequently, this resulted in self-censorship, decreased diversity of their programming and lower quality of their news programmes (telephone interview by the author with T. Kakulia, 17 May 2011).

Apart from reducing the funds for media-related programmes in Georgia, the United States repeated the same mistake it made when designing the assistance strategy towards the NGO sector. Again, US donors delegated the right to distribute US grants to the Georgian government. Dave Bloss, the Academic Director at the Caucasus School of Journalism and Media Management in Tbilisi, criticized the situation when USAID money went first to the Georgian ministries and then local NGOs had to compete among themselves for a piece of the pie: "There's no way that giving the government control over the purse strings for media development is a good strategy for strengthening either democratic government or free media. It totally distorts the relationship between government and media" (Anable, 2006: 32). This post-2004 model of media assistance likely accounted for the increased level of self-censorship among Georgian media outlets.

Putting Findings into Context

The findings presented in this chapter reveal that, in the wake of the 2003 Rose Revolution, the US government had redirected its assistance to Georgia in a way that benefited the incumbent Saakashvili administration and sidelined opposition and civil society groups. However, these findings are only a snapshot of the period 2003–8 and one needs to put them into broader political context in order to determine their explanatory value.

On the eve of the Rose Revolution, the US allocated significant funds to both the Georgian government and the opposition. By doing so, the US government could hedge its bets and retain its influence over both opposing camps (Mitchell, 2009: 126). One has to admit, however, that the United States' support for President Eduard Shevardnadze had become rather lukewarm by that time. In the months preceding the Rose Revolution, the US government indicated its growing concern over an apparent pro-Russian twist in Georgia's policies (Žielys, 2010: 889). Therefore, the United States wholeheartedly applauded the rise to power of younger, Western-educated reformers. For US policy makers, President Saakashvili embodied a promise to transform the façade democracy and pro-Western rhetoric of the Shevardnaze regime into an established democracy and pro-Western policies. In short, the US government sensed that it was the right moment for putting all its eggs in a single basket. As a result, the Bush administration lent almost unconditional political support to the Saakashvili government. The findings of this chapter show that US governmental donors adopted a similar strategy. Donors believed it was sufficient to assist their longstanding colleagues – Saakashvili government officials who emerged from the NGO sector – and help them to complete Georgia's democratic transition.

As mentioned in the previous sections, the US government has again diversified its aid to Georgia since the end of 2007. The November 2007 imposition of a state of emergency by President Saakashvili forcefully brought a goal of democratization back to the top of the United States' agenda in Georgia. The US media called for US sanctions against Saakashvili (*Washington Post*, 2007) and some members of the US Congress warned of a threat to Georgia's democratic progress (US Senate Resolution 391, 2007). Consequently, the US government had to restore funding for watchdog activities in Georgia. At the same time, the US did not deprive the Georgian government of political and financial support, as Saakashvili remained closely aligned with US security interests. For example, Georgia still declared its intent to join NATO, it was the largest non-NATO contributor of troops to Afghanistan and it continued to oppose Russia's influence in the Caucasus.

In general, such a strategy of the US – supporting both the Georgian government and its critics – has persisted into 2013. The change of government in Georgia following the October 2012 parliamentary elections did not have any bigger impact in this regard. The rise to power of Bidzina Ivanishvili and his Georgian Dream coalition did not take place along the patterns of the Rose Revolution. Firstly, Ivanishvili did not have the image of a devoted democrat and bold Westernizer, something that Saakashvili clearly enjoyed among US policy makers back in 2003. Secondly, US democracy assistance did not play a role in bringing Ivanishvili to power. Unlike Saakashvili's team in 2003, the Georgian Dream led by billionaire Ivanishvili could afford to hire American private consultants and did not much need technical support offered by US-funded NGOs (Mitchell, 2013). In fact, criticism of IRI and NDI became a part of Georgian Dream's election campaign (DFWatch, 2012). Against this background, the Barack Obama administration did not have the incentive to lend exclusive support to the Ivanishvili government. United States' donors did not maintain a special relationship with the Georgian Dream and did not have high expectations with regard to democratic consolidation in Georgia. Therefore, in the post-2012 period there were no preconditions for US donors to repeat the mistakes identified in this chapter.

Conclusion

The general question posed in this chapter was whether US democracy assistance programmes in post-Rose Revolution Georgia helped to guard the nascent democracy or rather retarded its consolidation. It was hypothesized that US security interests affected its democracy assistance, making US-funded programmes politically biased and detrimental to democratization goals. The research revealed some retarding aspects of US democracy-assistance programmes but it did not prove their exclusive link with US security interests.

The assumption of the security-burdened democracy assistance was completely refuted in the elections sector. After the Rose Revolution, US donors continued to provide electoral aid to Georgia at sufficient levels. This finding is in line with a common understanding that US democracy assistance always concentrates on the fairness of electoral process. By contrast, the constitutional assistance was the only type of US assistance that was clearly burdened by security considerations. As documented in this chapter, US authorities preferred to mute a critical expert assessment of the constitutional reform carried out by the US-supported Saakashvili government.

In the sectors of political party, NGO and media assistance, US donors introduced new postrevolution assistance strategies that failed to promote political competition and to strengthen civil society. However, there is no reliable evidence that would prove US security interests being the driving force behind the mentioned strategy change. After the Rose Revolution, US donors shifted their focus from opposition parties to parties with parliamentary representation. At the same time, US donors encouraged NGOs and media outlets to become involved in joint projects with Georgian ministries, as opposed to the previous emphasis on monitoring the government activities. The driving force behind these changes was the unconditional trust put by the US in Saakashvili's democratic reform agenda. Surely, Saakashvili's support for the US war on terror, his pronounced NATO aspirations and resistance to Russian influence fuelled and sustained that trust. However, the security aspect is not the only and sufficient explanation.

As documented in this chapter, some flaws and inconsistencies in US democracy assistance resulted from purely bureaucratic miscalculation. USAID and other governmental donors prematurely tailored their democracy-assistance programmes in Georgia to meet the requirements of the final stage of democratic transition. This miscalculation could be best seen in the political party, NGO and media assistance sectors. The new assistance strategies overestimated the extent of political competition, government accountability and pluralism that could be found in the post-revolution Georgian state and society. In fact, US democracy-assistance programmes became retarding as they were aiming to guard something that had not yet been established.

References

Anable, D. (2006) The role of Georgia's media – and Western aid – in the Rose Revolution. *The Harvard International Journal of Press/Politics* 11(3), 7–43.

Areshidze, I. (2004) *An Opportunity Lost? Constitutional Changes in Georgia at the Start of the Saakashvili Presidency*, <http://www.cipe.org/sites/default/files/publication-docs/areshidze.pdf> (accessed 22 October 2014).

Bader, M. (2010) *Against All Odds: Aiding Political Parties in Georgia and Ukraine*, Amsterdam University Press, Amsterdam.

Boudreau, V. (2007) Security and democracy: process and outcome in a new policy context. *Democratization* 14(2), 313–330.

Cheterian, V. (2008) Georgia's Rose Revolution: change or repetition? Tension between state-building and modernization projects. *Nationalities Papers* 36(4), 689–712.

Civil Georgia (2008) *Natelashvili Lambastes Foreign Observers*, <http://www.civil.ge/eng/article.php?id=18302> (accessed 22 October 2014).

Cornell, S. E. (2007) *Georgia after the Rose Revolution: Geopolitical Predicament and Implications for US Policy*, <http://www.strategicstudiesinstitute.army.mil/pdffiles/PUB757.pdf> (accessed 22 October 2014).

Democracy International (2007) *A Study of Political Party Assistance in Eastern Europe and Eurasia*, <http://pdf.usaid.gov/pdf_docs/PNADK586.pdf> (accessed 22 October 2014).

DFWatch (2012) *Fearing the Bandwagon Effect: Georgia's Opinion Poll Wars,* <http://dfwatch.net/fearing-the-bandwagon-effect-georgias-opinion-poll-wars-79539> (accessed 22 October 2014).

International Crisis Group (2007) *Georgia: Sliding towards Authoritarianism?* Europe Report No. 189, <http://www.crisisgroup.org/~/media/Files/europe/189_georgia___sliding_towards_authoritarianism.ashx> (accessed 22 October 2014).

IRIS Center (2006) *Final Report on Georgia Rule of Law Project,* <http://pdf.usaid.gov/pdf_docs/PDACG559.pdf> (accessed 14 October 2014).

IRIS Georgia (2004) The Model of State Governance in Georgia after the Constitutional Amendments of February 2004. Unpublished research paper (obtained by the author from a former IRIS Georgia representative).

Jonavicius, L. (2009) *Why Ukraine and Georgia have not used the "'Window of Opportunity"? Neo-institutional Analysis of Transformational Stagnation in Georgia and Ukraine.* UNISCI Discussion Papers, No. 19, 12–37.

Jones, S. F. (2006) The Rose Revolution: a revolution without revolutionaries? *Cambridge Review of International Affairs* 19(1), 33–48.

Kalandadze, K. and Orenstein, M. A. (2009) Electoral protests and democratization: Beyond the color revolutions. *Comparative Political Studies* 42(11), 1403–1425.

Kokashvili, M. (2005) The role of the media in Georgia's transition to democracy, in *From Revolution to Reform: Georgia's Struggle with Democratic Institution Building and Security Sector Reform* (eds. P. H. Fluri and E. Cole). Vienna and Geneva: Bureau for Security Policy at the Austrian Ministry of Defence and Geneva Centre for the Democratic Control of Armed Forces, 209–229.

Lanskoy, M. and Areshidze, G. (2008) Georgia's year of turmoil. *Journal of Democracy* 19(4), 154–168.

Laverty, N. (2008) The problem of lasting change: civil society and the colored revolutions in Georgia and Ukraine. *Demokratizatsiya* 16(2): 143–162.

Lazarus, J. (2010) *Neo-Liberal State Building and Western "Democracy Promotion": The Case of Georgia.* Paper presented at the SGIR Seventh Pan-European Conference, Stockholm, 9–11 September.

Lowenkron, B. F. (2007) Realism: why democracy promotion matters. *American Foreign Policy Interests* 29(3), 201–206.

McClear, R. and M. Koenig (2004) *Mid-Term Assessment of IREX Media Innovations Program*, <http://pdf.usaid.gov/pdf_docs/pdacf799.pdf> (accessed 22 October 2014).

McGlinchey, E. (2007) *Foreign Assistance and Domestic Power: Aiding Political Parties in Central Asia and the Caucasus.* Paper presented at the 48th Annual Convention of the International Studies Association, Chicago, 28 February–3 March.

Mitchell, L. A. (2006) Democracy in Georgia since the Rose Revolution. *Orbis* 50(4), 669–676.

Mitchell, L. A. (2009) *Uncertain Democracy: US Foreign Policy and Georgia's Rose Revolution*, University of Pennsylvania Press, Philadelphia, PA.

Mitchell, L. A. (2013) *The Rose Revolution through a Funhouse Mirror*, <http://www.the-american-interest.com/article.cfm?piece=1421> (accessed 22 October 2014).

Muskhelishvili, M. and Jorjoliani, G. (2009) Georgia's ongoing struggle for a better future continued: democracy promotion through civil society development. *Democratization* 16(4), 682–708.

NDI (2008a) *Statement of the NDI Election Observer Delegation to Georgia's 2008 Presidential Election*, <http://www.ndi.org/files/2258_ge_statement_elections_010708.pdf> (accessed 22 October 2014).

NDI (2008b) *NDI Long-term Observation Mission Report Concerning Georgia's 2008 Parliamentary Elections*, <http://www.ndi.org/files/Georgia_LTO_Statement_060408_ENG.pdf> (accessed 22 October 2014).

Omelicheva, M. Y. (2010) Between commitment and pragmatism: assessing international influence on human rights practices in Georgia. *Journal of Human Rights* 9(4), 445–466.

OSCE (2008a) *Georgia. Extraordinary Presidential Election, 5 January 2008. OSCE/ODIHR Election Observation Mission Final Report*, <http://www.osce.org/odihr/elections/georgia/30959> (accessed 22 October 2014).

OSCE (2008b) *Georgia. Parliamentary Election, 21 May 2008. OSCE/ODIHR Election Observation Mission Final Report*, <http://www.osce.org/odihr/elections/georgia/33301> (accessed 22 October 2014).

Spanger, H.-J. and Wolff, J. (2005) *Complementary Objectives, Conflicting Actions? Democracy Promotion as Risk Management.* Paper presented at the annual meeting of the International Studies Association, Honolulu, March 5.

Tatum, J. D. (2009) Democratic transition in Georgia: post-Rose Revolution internal pressures on leadership. *Caucasian Review of International Affairs* 3(2), 156–171.

Tolstrup, J. (2009) Studying a negative external actor: Russia's management of stability and instability in the "near abroad". *Democratization* 16(5), 922–944.

Tudoroiu, T. (2007) Rose, orange, and tulip: the failed post-Soviet revolutions. *Communist and Post-Communist Studies* 40(3), 315–342.

USAID (2007) *Georgia 2007 Performance Report,* <http://pdf.usaid.gov/pdf_docs/pdacl047.pdf> (accessed 28 December 2014).

USAID (2011) *2010 NGO Sustainability Index for Central and Eastern Europe and Eurasia,* <http://www.usaid.gov/sites/default/files/documents/1863/2010complete_document.pdf> (accessed 22 October 2014).

US Department of State (2010) *US Government Assistance to and Cooperative Activities with Eurasia,* <http://www.state.gov/p/eur/rls/rpt/> (accessed 22 October 2014).

US Senate Resolution 391 (2007) *Calling on the President of the United States to Engage in an Open Discussion with the Leaders of the Republic of Georgia to Express Support for the Planned Presidential Elections and the Expectation that Such Elections Will Be Held in a Manner Consistent with Democratic Principles,* <http://www.gpo.gov/fdsys/pkg/CREC-2007-12-06/pdf/CREC-2007-12-06-pt1-PgS14856-2.pdf> (accessed 22 October 2014).

Washington Post (2007) Crisis in Georgia, <http://www.washingtonpost.com/wp-dyn/content/article/2007/11/12/AR2007111201549.html> (accessed 22 October 2014).

Žielys, P. (2010) New version of the Kirkpatrick doctrine in the post-Soviet space. *Democratization* 17(5), 878–898.

Thijs Rommens

Spreading Democratic Governance? NGOs in the Eastern Partnership: The Case of Georgia

ABSTRACT: This chapter applies an external-governance approach to the prospects of the EU's support for democracy in its Eastern neighbourhood and considers the Eastern Partnership as a way for the EU to expand its characteristic model of governance outside its own borders. One of the key elements in the EU's claims to effective and democratic governance comes from the inclusion of non-state actors such as NGOs. This chapter focuses on the case of Georgia and analyses how and to what extent Georgian NGOs have been integrated in the EU's external policies. It addresses the issue of whether NGO inclusion into the Eastern Partnership has ultimately led to increased democratic governance both at the level of relations with the EU and at the Georgian domestic level.

KEYWORDS: civil society, Europeanization, democratization, democracy promotion, Eastern Partnership, European Union, Georgia

Introduction

Through the introduction of the European Neighbourhood Policy (ENP) and the subsequent Eastern Partnership (EaP) the European Union has attempted to strengthen and rationalize its relations with its Eastern neighbours. Amongst a wide array of objectives in the fields of politics, economy and security these policies aim to strengthen democracy in the countries concerned. Compared with earlier rounds of enlargement, the EU has less clout to induce democratization in its neighbourhood. However, this does not inevitably lead to the conclusion that the EU has no other tools or facilities at its disposal to do so.

Applying an external governance approach to the prospects of the EU's democracy support offers room to look at the ENP and EaP as ways for the EU to expand its characteristic model of governance outside its own borders (Kohler-Koch and Eising, 1999). As a *sui generis* polity, the

EU cannot rely on traditional representative channels of democracy alone; one of the key elements in the EU's claims to effective and democratic governance comes from the inclusion of non-state actors such as NGOs. The case of Georgia is used to analyse how and to which extent NGOs have been integrated in the EU's external policies. The inclusion of NGOs into both the ENP and EaP could be considered as a characteristic of the EU's attempts to export its typical form of governance outside its borders. This also touches upon the EU's democracy-promotion efforts through these policies, which only have limited means to induce change through conditionality (Schimmelfennig and Scholtz, 2008). Compared to the accession process, the EU has lost most of its bargaining power and no longer can offset the costs domestic governments experience if they implement democratic reforms. In addition or as an alternative to this direct hierarchical mode, the use of a network mode of governance may be used to strengthen democracy promotion. Although results may be less direct and tangible, applying this framework may reveal that despite drawbacks, the EU's ENP and EaP are still capable of inducing democratic change in the neighbourhood (Börzel, 2010).

In order to assess the potential and actual incidence of this alternative mode of democracy promotion, the argument is developed in four steps. First, the general scene is set upon which the specific topic of this research is taking place. This offers readers not familiar with the subject a short introduction to the topic. Second, the theoretical framework is offered; this research applies an external governance model to analyse the democracy promotion of the EU. In the third part, the efforts and policies of the EU are examined and the question is answered if there is a clear tendency towards a typical EU mode of network governance. In the fourth part, attentions shifts away from EU institutions towards why and how non-state actors make use of these institutions. The inclusion and active participation of these actors is crucial in order to be able to speak of a truly network mode of governance.

Setting the Scene

On paper the European Union (EU) and Georgia appear to be a perfect match. Since it came to power after the Rose Revolution in 2003, the Georgian government has continuously stressed its commitment towards Euro Atlantic integration while the introduction of the European Neighbourhood Policy (ENP) and the subsequent Eastern Partnership (EaP) have provided the EU with a coherent policy towards the region. In reality, relations between the two actors have proven to be less than perfect (Pardo Sierra, 2011). The EU, for its part, has been struggling to reach an internal agreement on what the ENP and EaP exactly are and it has been confronted with the deepest financial crisis in its existence. The Georgian government has been rather reluctant to implement changes set out within the framework of the ENP and EaP. Politically, power has been increasingly concentrated around the presidency. Economically, tendencies opting for a stronger libertarian approach have been conflicting with EU demands (De Waal, 2011). While enjoying strong Western support, Saakashvili has managed to introduce sweeping political and economic reforms of which critics argue that they only serve to introduce a neoliberal economic agenda managed by an authoritarian regime (Lazarus, 2010). Many of these reforms, such as abolishing the food safety agency, clash with EU demands, which shows that the reform agenda is certainly not driven by the desire for European integration. Put briefly, there appears to be a tremendous gap between what is and what could have been.

This applies, in particular, to the field of democratization. Since the outset of the ENP, democracy has been at the centre of the EU's policies. In the 2004 ENP Strategy Paper "commitment to specific actions which confirm or reinforce adherence to shared values" was stated as the number one priority area and, further on, the text specifies "strengthening democracy, respect for human rights and support for the development of civil society" as central amongst these values (European Commission, 2004). Despite these lofty goals, the stress on democratization and democracy promotion fades away once reports and plans were made on a more technical and policy-related level (Rommens, 2008). Added to this, the ENP did not entail dedicated funding for democracy promotion. Nor could it offset the costs of democratization through conditionality as used during EU enlargement. Inevitably, introducing liberal changes such as fair elections, the rule of law or fighting corruption will lessen the autonomy of the actors in power. By balancing these short term losses with the promise of long term gains such as economic growth or financial assistance, actors may be more inclined to pursue a democratization agenda (Schimmelfennig and Scholtz, 2008). As a result the EU has been perceived as a weak actor in the field of democracy promotion (Vachudova, 2005; Sasse, 2008) in cases where it did not offer membership perspectives.

This has severely limited the potential for the EU to influence the pursued policies of the Georgian government. After the Rose Revolution, president Saakashvili was quick to implement a number of sweeping changes that created an instant image of reform and modernization. The most famous example of this agenda was the dismissal of the complete force of the traffic police in 2004 on the grounds that this was the best way to deal with its ingrained corruption. The fact that exactly this feat is still often quoted as one of the main achievements of Saakashvili's reform agenda touches upon two issues. First, it shows that since the frantic beginnings during the first year the new government came to power, similar fundamental reforms have not been implemented. Second, most of these reforms have focused on economic reform and state-building initiatives while efforts to democratize the political system have been less vigorous in comparison (Mitchell, 2009). This is reflected in the ranking of Georgia on several governance indicators: in the field of the fight against corruption and the investment climate Georgia has performed well in recent years, while in the field of political or media freedom its performance stagnated or decreased between 2006 and 2011, as illustrated in Figure 1.

With the EU only disposing of limited means to promote democracy through the ENP and EaP and the Georgian government focusing on state building and economic reform, prospects for democratization appear slim. This research looks into whether there are other ways and mechanisms through which the EU might pursue democracy promotion within Georgia. Other actors apart from the EU and Georgian government like nongovernmental organizations (NGOs) may use the ENP and EaP. which would mean the EU indirectly promotes democratization through these policies.

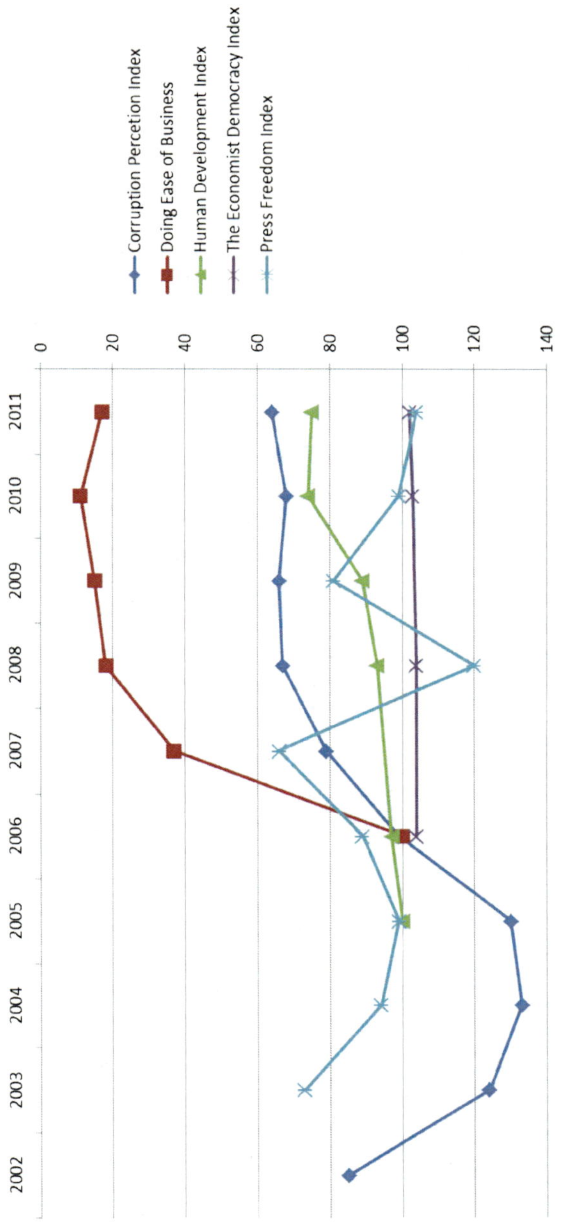

Figure 1: Georgia: rankings on selected governance indicators.

Sources: Transparency International (2011), World Bank (2012), Freedom House (2012), Reporters Sans Frontières (2011).

Theoretical Framework

Instead of the often-applied conditionality based framework for analysing the EU's performance in inducing change in third countries, this research fits in the growing strand of literature that applies a governance approach to the analysis of the ENP. Moving away from the accession-through-conditionality and foreign policy frameworks, the governance approach considers the ENP as an expanding system of functional regional integration bringing together different policy fields and actors (Lavenex, 2008). This goes beyond a set of clear hierarchical goals and relations to more horizontal, process-oriented modes of network governance. Governance entails the engagement of a number of actors, state as well as non-state, on several levels and in a multitude of fields leading to a certain degree of institutionalization, legalization and socialization. In the specific case of the EU's ENP, this implies a high degree of institutionalization and the existence of shared rules beyond the EU and its strictly formal competences (Lavenex and Schimmelfennig, 2009). The notion of governance contrasts with the more conventional concept of government. It reflects a transition from hierarchical to horizontal relations, focusing on processes rather than output, emphasizing voluntary agreements instead of legally binding obligations, and the inclusion of multiple actors apart from the state (Héritier, 2007). The term has been introduced in international relations to address the emergence of political order at the international level in the absence of a global political regime (Rosenau, 1992). The external relations of the EU within the ENP framework have led to a widening of EU policies and rules beyond formal membership. Instead of the hierarchical use of conditionality that urges third countries to adapt to the pressure of the EU, this form of network governance is more horizontal and the result of a more participatory relation between the EU and the partner countries (Freyburg *et al.*, 2009). These characteristics distinguish it from more conventional modes such as hierarchical and market governance. Although full membership is no longer an option under the ENP, the policy still entails a certain degree of boundary shift on the regulatory and organizational level (Youngs, 2009). The extension of EU rules, norms or policies to non-EU member states brings about an expansion of the EU regulatory space whereas the inclusion of these states into certain EU organizations and agencies does the same on the organizational level. This opens up room for actors outside the conventional EU-national government dichotomy such as non-state actors. The ENP has only limited capabilities to influence democratization in third countries directly. However, it may assist democratization more in indirect and unintended ways. In this model democracy support may take place unintended through functional cooperation between the EU and actors in third countries, creating a "back door" for democracy promotion by the EU (Freyburg *et al.*, 2009).

EU Policies

Since Georgia's declaration of independence in 1991, relations between the EU and Georgia have been incrementally intensified. The first relations were developed by the European Parliament through the creation of a European Parliament Delegation for the South Caucasus and election monitoring missions. In 1996 relations were institutionalized when the EU and the Georgian government signed the Partnership and Cooperation Agreement (PCA). Until today it still serves as the legal basis for EU-Georgia relations. The PCA relies on a traditional bilateral format as it created a number of commissions and committees made out of officials from EU institutions and the Georgian government and a parliamentary cooperation committee (European Council and Commission, 1999). The first stage of EU–Georgia relations thus did not introduce any novel mode of governance and did not provide for any opportunities for NGOs to be incorporated in any way into the PCA institutional framework.

After the events of the Rose Revolution, Georgia was included in the ENP in 2004. Although the Commission stressed that the ENP was not related to the previous enlargement processes, it did borrow heavily from it in the fields of processes and design. A Country Report assesses the political and economic situation of the partner country upon which an Action Plan is based that sets out the priorities for the policy. The implementation of these Action Plans is subsequently monitored by yearly Progress Reports. All this is driven by EU institutions and their Georgian counterparts. Although the ENP states that strengthening democratic institutions is one of its key objectives (European Commission, 2006) there is remarkably little potential for input from political or societal actors. The ENP did not entail a specific programme for democracy promotion or civil society support, nor did it explicitly mention civil society as a partner in the policy. Although the ENP may be perceived as an intensification of the existing ties between the EU and Georgia, on the institutional level it continued to work within the existing framework of the PCA.

Increasing demands for upgrading or expanding the ENP grew both among a number of member states of the EU and among the eastern neighbours of the EU. In 2009, the Eastern Partnership was introduced to reinvigorate the relations between the EU and the six former Soviet Union republics in the East. In addition to the already existing bilateral relations between the EU and the national governments of the six Eastern partners, a multilateral component was created (European Commission, 2008). This dual structure makes it possible to formulate an individual approach for each country as well as a coherent regional approach spanning all six countries (Gromadzki, 2010). A second innovation is the explicit incorporation of civil society into the EaP's policies and institutions. Through the creation of a dedicated Civil Society Forum (CSF) and National Platforms (NP), civil society organizations acquire the possibility to formulate input and conduct monitoring activities. The CSF aims to promote contacts among civil society organizations and facilitate dialogue with public authorities and to facilitate the sharing of information and experience on the partner countries' steps toward transition, reform and modernization. The forum holds annual meetings for its over 200 members and it can be invited to governmental meetings on an *ad hoc* basis. This multilateral track is supplemented by NPs on the domestic level. In every EaP partner country a network of civil society actors is created that prepares input for the CSF and provides expertise and knowledge about domestic issues and events. Another initiative is EURONEST: joint parliamentary sessions of European Parliament members and members of parliaments from the six EaP countries. This shows that the EaP clearly steps away from mere bilateral EU-government relations and truly is developing in the direction of a multi-actor constellation (Delcour, 2011), an illustration of the Europeanized system of governance as put forward in the theoretical framework.

This incremental inclusion of civil society actors into the different institutions of the EU's policies has been supported by increased financial means, with money specifically earmarked for civil society being introduced since the introduction of the EaP. During the first years of Georgia–EU relations funding for Georgia fell under the Technical Assistance to the

CIS (TACIS) programme, which was designed to offer the countries from the former Soviet Union assistance during transition. Specific funding for non-state actors was available under the Phare and TACIS Democracy Programme (PTDP) via macro and micro projects and *ad hoc* support for NGOs. TACIS countries accounted for 31 million euro of the PTDP, with Georgia receiving a share of approximate 7%, making it the recipient with the highest funding-to-population ration of all CIS countries (Kaldor and Wilke, 1997). Funding allocated for development for NGOs counted for 46% of the total PTDP budget, which made it the number one priority out of the eight areas of activity of the programme. From 1999, the European Initiative (later Instrument) for Democracy and Human Rights (EIDHR) supplemented the PTDP through promotion of human rights, democratization and conflict prevention, often implemented in partnership with NGOs and international organizations.

The implementation of the ENP corresponded with a change in funding instrument: TACIS was replaced by the ENP Instrument. Despite the first thematic budget line entailing democratic development, there is no specific budget line within ENP funding for NGO support or inclusion. As a result, the ENP entailed a *de facto* loss of funding opportunities for NGOs, with only the EIDHR still available to them. This situation was partly addressed by the introduction of the EaP, although in general the means through which the EU policies were financed remained the same. Two initiatives offered new possibilities for funding specifically for NGOs: the Civil Society Facility and the European Endowment for Democracy. The first initiative provides funding for non-state actors in the Neighbourhood Partners, with €22 million between 2011 and 2013, targeted at reinforcing the role of civil society across the region (ENPI Info Centre, 2011). The second is envisaged to be an independent trust fund focusing on supporting democratization by delivering support to a range of different non-state actors. The idea was launched in February 2011 by the then Polish presidency of the EU Council but talks about the exact nature and financing of the project remain ongoing for the moment (Kostanyan and Nasienak, 2012).

Relations between the EU and Georgia have noticeably gone through a process of intensification. A first phase was characterized by mainly bilateral meetings whereas the introduction of the EaP led to the establishment of various multilateral institutions. The EU appears to have managed to create an institutional set up that would allow for a network mode of governance. Moving beyond the bilateral framework typical of earlier enlargement through a hierarchical mode of governance, the ENP and EaP have led to the creation of institutions that aim to include actors such as parliaments or NGOs. With some delay, financing instruments are following the same evolution.

Georgian NGOs and the EU

International support for NGOs has been the topic of a lively debate during the last years. The colour revolutions have been heralded by proponents of democracy assistance as democratic transformations while opponents have denounced them as foreign-ordained regime overthrow (Wilson, 2010). Authoritarian governments have been actively curtailing the freedom of NGOs: only recently, for example, the Russian government made international funding for NGOs excruciatingly financially demanding (President of Russia, 2012). These extreme positions on the matter seem to dominate the debate and little research is available about how NGOs and international institutions interact in reality. This research offers some insights on how Georgian NGOs have made use of the different EU policies made available to them. By doing so it aims to bring some facts into this highly politicized debate.

The highly politicized nature of this debate entails that critical thinking about this topic risks being incorporated into a political agenda. This does not reduce the need for inquiring into some of the conceptual issues behind the topic of international support for NGOs – on the contrary. Western actors active in democracy assistance often draw a rosy and unproblematic account of international actors who support local NGOs that are representing domestic civil society (Herd, 2005). This raises a number of potential issues. What do we understand under civil society in non-Western societies? Are NGOs indeed representatives of civil society? Does international support limit or rule out the independence of NGOs? There is insufficient space here to allow for an in-depth elaboration of these crucial questions but by using the example of how Georgian NGOs have reacted to the ENP and EaP it tries to offer insights on the interaction between international assistance and domestic NGOs. More specifically, this paper looks into the organizations that are involved in the Georgian

NP within the EaP.[1] The Georgian NP was established in 2010 and at the time of this research consisted out of 80 organizations such as NGOs, think tanks and labour organizations.

Civil society in postcommunist countries is relatively weak compared to other regions, exactly because of the specific nature of the communist political project (Howard, 2002). Not only was there no room for independent pluralist organizations – the state actively supplanted civil society with state-controlled organizations. This typical postcommunist heritage was further exacerbated in the case of Georgia. During and after the fall of the Soviet Union Georgia experienced ethnic conflict and was on the brink of civil war. Under the presidency of Shevardnadze Georgia's political and economic situation stabilized, partly because of Shevardnadze's skilful use of international support for his regime. In order to secure Western support, Shevardnadze introduced democratic legislation, although the execution sometimes remained problematic and allowed the establishment of NGOs and international support for their development. Although Shevardnadze took a harsher stance towards international support for NGOs in the later years of his presidency, NGOs had become important actors within the Georgian political context, as witnessed in their crucial role during the Rose Revolution (Areshidze, 2007). Critics argued that these organizations did not have any link with civil society and were merely "grant gobblers" (Broers, 2005): experts in applying for funding from international donors while not implementing any other programmes or policy advice.

The creation of the multilateral CSF and of the NP on the domestic level has lead to the inclusion of NGOs within the EU's relations with Georgia. This allows for a network mode of governance where NGOs are an important partner. In order to assess whether this could be considered an alternative form of democracy promotion, the democratic credentials of these NGOs need to be analysed. Therefore we turn to look at the organizations that are involved in the NP. Within the NP, three quarters of the respondents classified their organization as a domestic Georgian organization. The remaining quarter described their organization as international or as a local branch of an international organization. This shows that these organizations are not merely imported from abroad but that they have their roots within the country. Most staff is Georgian, which was noticeable

1 An electronic survey held in June–September 2011 among the members of the NP; 44 out of 77 organizations contacted participated (a 57% response rate) and 34 handed in completed surveys. Three organizations could not be contacted.

in the preference by the respondents to fill in the survey in Georgian rather than English: over 60% of the surveys were filled in in Georgian. The fact that two-thirds of the respondents only had offices in Tbilisi affirms the assertion that civil society organizations are professional organizations rather than grass-root organizations. Instead of being bottom-up organizations that cater for needs of the population, many are professionally run organizations managed by what one could consider members of the political elite. Most of them have extensive international professional experience, have studied abroad and have a good command of English. These numbers show a mixed result regarding the nature of the member organizations. They cannot be considered as just transplanted from the West, but they are professionally managed by members of the political elite. This is the nature of Georgian civil-society organizations, and the EU can only work with the organizations that are available. These organizations may not be the representatives of an ideal type of bottom-up self-organization, but rather political actors in their own right (Nodia, 2005).

Another often-voiced criticism is that NGOs are highly dependent on funding from the EU. This contradicts the idea of civil society being independent from political actors and would limit the scope for an independent and critical position for NGOs. Less than half of the members of the NP, however, have received funding by the EU during the 6 years prior to answering the survey, which puts the EU in the middle bracket of international donors for NP members. Only 12% of them claimed that they had not received any international funding at all, which does validate the criticism that Georgian NGOs extensively look to international financial support. However, this is not limited to the NP, nor is it specific for the Georgian case; it is rather typical for post-Soviet civil society. In a way, the weakness of the EU, being a late arrival on the NGO support scene, may be blessing in disguise. It precludes the possibility that the organizations that are active within the NP are on EU "life support" and that their membership is only a formality to preserve their funding.

The first efforts from NGOs within Georgia to monitor the implementation of the ENP Action Plan were set up and organized without support from the EU (Open Society Georgia Foundation/For Transparency of Public Finances, 2007). After the implementation of the ENP Action Plan in 2006, a consortium was created that brought local civil society organizations and international organizations together to observe the implementation of the ENP. Three international NGOs – Open Society, the Heinrich

Böll Stiftung and the Eurasia Foundation – played a central role in the creation of the network. They appear to have filled the void created through the EU's lack of financing or institutional involvement of civil society. This also explains why this initiative did not manage to create a lasting impact. Without interest or support from the EU, these NGOs operated in a vacuum where they felt their initiative was not treated with the attention it deserved (author's interview with NGO official; Tbilisi, June 2011). The incorporation of NGOs into the NP and CSF of the EaP has addressed this lacuna and within these institutions NGOs have a defined role and partners they can address.

This shows that finding the proper way to include civil society organizations in policy making remains a precarious effort. In the first phase of the ENP, NGOs were completely shut out of the political process and, as a result, they did not manage to play a proper role. Through the incorporation of NGOs in the NP and CSF, civil society organizations have become acknowledged actors for the EU. This does entail the risk that these organizations would be usurped by the EU, which would rob them of their independent nature. This would clash with their fundamental identity of being independent, and as their abbreviation implies, non- governmental. The key issue for the EU, then, is to strike the right balance between involving NGOs in an efficient matter while at the same time acknowledging their independent character (Eastern Partnership Civil Society Forum, 2011). By finding the right balance between support and policy-inclusion the EU may contribute to the sustainable development of NGOs in its neighbourhood. The creation of the CSF and the NP signal a shift towards a network governance approach and allow NGOs to make use of the opportunities of the ENP and EaP. This lends extra credibility to the EU's own democratic claims but remains a sterile exercise if it does not have any impact within Georgia itself.

Georgian politics are characterized by high polarization between government and oppositional forces and by the concentration of power in the presidency (Mitchell, 2009). This has also impacted NGO capacity. During the Rose Revolution NGOs had successfully challenged the regime but ended up sternly weakened themselves. A number of former activists have held positions in government, parliament or local councils, making open criticism harder for their former colleagues who stayed in NGOs. Furthermore, this has led to a brain drain of a number of NGOs who have lost their staff with most experience (Nodia, 2005). In general, civil society and

NGOs in particular have partially lost credibility as an autonomous force. This goes to the core of their *raison d'être*: offering a voice for demands from society at large. To do this civil society does not have to capture the state itself but must ensure that certain rights are respected and that political dialogue remains possible (Edwards, 2004).

Are these trends visible within the NP and has the NP provided NGOs with the possibility to change this situation? Relations with domestic political actors indeed seem strained: none of the respondents considered their relations with political parties to be functional, whereas only two of them said the same about relations with the Georgian government. Clearly contacts between political actors and NGOs are far from constructive; the only exception are local governments, with which 10 respondents claimed to have constructive relations. Relations with international actors are scored far better by respondents. This shows that Georgian NGOs consider to have better ties with international partners than that they have with partners that are embedded within the domestic Georgian socio-political setting. A vast majority of the respondents considered the NP as a way to force government to interact with them. Their idea is that, with the EU involved, the Georgian government will have to take their input into account. Asked about their current involvement in policy making, most respondents indicated that they were only marginally involved and that they were limited to monitoring functions. There is a noticeable gap between the expectations of the member organizations and their actual role regarding their involvement in policy making. Georgian NGOs have eagerly made use of the possibilities of the NP, but their expectations do not seem not to have been met. They had hoped the NP would revive their relations with domestic political actors and that the EU would be able to persuade Georgian government to take a more constructive stance towards them. The NP appears to have led to more intensified relations among Georgian NGOs themselves and between them and the EU. Relations with Georgian political actors do not appear to have changed under the influence of the EaP's NP.

The reluctance of Georgian government to increase its involvement in this model of governance and its persisting lack of constructive relations with NGOs show the limits of the EU's model of governance. If one of the actors involved does not participate voluntarily, the EU's model of governance loses much of its effectiveness and credibility. How the EU should entice reluctant actors to cooperate without resorting to traditional means such as conditionality remains an open question. This shows that the EU's model of governance only works when all partners are motivated to cooperate. Outside its borders, the EU loses part of its power and attractiveness and it will have to adapt to this situation in order for its mode of governance to remain credible and workable.

Conclusion

The introduction of the ENP, and subsequently the EaP, has institutionalized and intensified relations between the EU and Georgia. These policies are examples of the mechanisms through which the EU attempts to spread its typical form of governance outside its borders. This creates opportunities for NGOs: they can make use of what the ENP and EaP have to offer them to strengthen their capabilities, foster networks, or influence policy making. The ENP and EaP indeed have gradually changed EU–Georgia relations from purely bilateral to a more open method where NGOs have possibilities to be heard and to apply for funding. Looking at how this has affected Georgian NGOs however, we see that the impact of these policies remains limited. The introduction of the NP has created a new dynamic within Georgian civil society and it has strengthened ties between Georgian NGOs and the EU. Yet it has not been able to overcome existing domestic political divides showing that the EU's model of governance does not trickle though all levels, nor does it manage to involve all relevant actors.

Promoting democracy outside its borders has been at the core of the EU's different external policies and instruments. The most commonly cited example of this has been the accession process of former communist countries from Central and Eastern Europe. To induce domestic changes in the accession countries the EU relied heavily on the use of conditionality. When the EU introduced its ENP as a specific policy covering its neighbouring countries in 2003, it borrowed extensively from the previous experience of enlargement. The lack of membership perspectives, however, severely limited the usefulness and applicability of conditionality. Analysts and scholars were generally pessimistic about the chances for success for the EU to export democracy outside its borders through this policy. The external governance model applied in this research also takes into account less direct and top down mechanisms when assessing democracy promotion, such as the inclusion of NGOs in networks and institutions linked to the EaP. It shows that the EU may indeed have less impact through conditionality but that it does create favourable circumstances for NGOs to act in and, through its specific form of a network mode of governance, it still promotes democracy.

However, this chapter has shown that there are important limitations to this approach. Through the introduction of this network mode of governance the EU loses a large part of its power and right of initiative. First, it has to find the right balance between involving NGOs in policy making and the institutions of the EaP and respecting their independence. Second, The EU does not have the instruments or power to press the Georgian government to participate in these same institutions or to engage into constructive relations with civil-society actors. As a result, the inclusion of non-state actors into the ENP and EaP has been a very slow and incremental process that is still very much a work in progress. In addition to the uncooperative stance of the Georgian government, the wider results of these efforts to include NGOs into the ENP and EaP within Georgian politics or society have remained very limited. The EU's policies themselves have therefore gained democratic credibility, they appear to only have had limited impact on the democratization of Georgia itself.

References

Areshidze, I. (2007) *Democracy and Autocracy in Eurasia: Georgia in Transition*, Michigan State University Press, East Lansing, MI.

Börzel, T. (2010) *The Transformative Power of Europe Reloaded: The Limits of External Europeanization*, KFG Working Paper No. 11, February 2010, Freie Universität Berlin, Berlin.

Broers, L. (2005) After the revolution, *Central Asian Survey* 24(3), 333–350.

Delcour, L. (2011) *The Institutional Functioning of the Eastern Partnership: An Early Assessment*, Estonian Centre of Eastern Partnership, Tallinn.

De Waal, T. (2011) *Georgia's Choices*, Carnegie Endowment for International Peace, Washington, DC.

Eastern Partnership Civil Society Forum (2011) *A Strategic Roadmap for Civil Society in the Eastern Partnership*, Eastern Partnership Civil Society Forum Steering Committee.

Edwards, G. (2008) The construction of ambiguity and the limits of attraction: Europe and its Neighbourhood Policy, *Journal of European Integration* 30, 45–62.

Edwards, M. (2004) *Civil Society*, Polity Press, Cambridge.

ENPI Info Centre (2011) *€22 million for new Civil Society Facility as EU steps up Neighbourhood response*. <http://www.enpi-info.eu/main.php?id=26632&id_type=1> (accessed 23 October 2014).

European Commission (2004) *Communication from the Commission "European Neighbourhood Policy" Strategy Paper*, COM(2004) 373 final, 12 May.

European Commission (2006) *EU/Georgia Action Plan* <http://eeas.europa.eu/enp/pdf/pdf/action_plans/georgia_enp_ap_final_en.pdf> (accessed 5 December 2014)

European Commission (2008) *Eastern Partnership*, <http://eeas.europa.eu/eastern/docs/com08_823_en.pdf> (accessed 5 December 2014).

European Council and Commission (1999), Partnership and Cooperation Agreement between the European Communities and their Member States, of the one part, and Georgia, of the other part, OJ L205 of 04/08/1999 <http://ec.europa.eu/world/agreements/downloadFile.do?fullText=yes&treatyTransId=632> (accessed 23 October 2014).

Freedom House (2012) *Freedom in the World*, <https://freedomhouse.org/report/freedom-world/2012/georgia#.VIFlP0oVG70> (accessed 5 December 2014)

Freyburg, T., Lavenex, S., Schimmelfennig, F. *et al.* (2009) EU promotion of democratic governance in the neighbourhood, *Journal of European Public Policy* 16 (6), 916–934.

Gromadzki, G. (2010) *A Challenging Opportunity, The EU Plus Six – The Eastern Partnership*, Friedrich Ebert Stiftung, Berlin.

Herd, G. (2005) Colorful revolutions and the CIS, "manufactured" versus "managed" democracy? *Problems of Post-Communism* 52 (2), 3–18.

Héritier, A. (2002) *Common Goods: Reinventing European and International Governance*, Rowman & Littlefield, Lanham, MD.

Howard, M. (2002) The weakness of post communist civil society. *Journal of Democracy* 13 (1), 157–169.

Kaldor, M. and Wilke, P. (1997) *Evaluation of the PHARE and TACIS Democracy Programme 1992–1997*, ISA Consult, European Institute, Sussex University and GJW Europe, Brighton and Hamburg.

Kelly J. (2006) New wine in old wineskins: promoting reforms through the new ENP. *Journal of Common Market Studies* 44(1), 29–55.

Kohler-Koch, B. and Eising, R. (1999) *The Transformation of Governance in the European Union*, Routledge, London.

Kostanyan, H. and Nasienak, M. (2012) *Moving the EU from a Laggard to a Leader in Democracy Assistance*, CEPS, Brussels.

Lavenex, S. (2008) A governance perspective on the European neighbourhood policy: integration beyond conditionality? *Journal of European Public Policy* 15 (6), 938–955.

Lavenex, S. and Schimmelfennig, F. (2009) EU rules beyond EU borders: theorizing external governance in European politics, *Journal of European Public Policy* 16 (6), 791–812.

Lazarus, J. (2010) *Neo-liberal State Building and Western "Democracy Promotion": the Case of Georgia*. Paper presented at the Pan-European Conference on International Relations, Stockholm, Sweden, 9–11 September.

Mitchell, L. (2009) Compromising democracy: state building in Saakashvili's Georgia. *Central Asian Survey* 28 (2), 171–183.

Nodia, G. (2005) *Civil Society Development in Georgia: Achievements and Challenges*, CIPDD, Tbilisi.

Open Society Georgia Foundation/For Transparency of Public Finances (2007) *Georgia and the European Neighbourhood Policy Perspectives and Challenges*, OSFG, Tbilisi.

Pardo Sierra, O. (2011) Shaping the neighbourhood? The EU's impact on Georgia. *Europe-Asia Studies* 63 (8), 1377–1398.

President of Russia (2012) *Law Regulating the Activities of NGOs Acting as Foreign Agents*. <http://eng.kremlin.ru/news/4209> (accessed 23 October 2014).

Reporters Sans Frontières (2011) *Press Freedom Index*, <http://en.rsf.org/press-freedom-index-2011-2012,1043.html> (accessed 5 December 2014).

Rommens, T. (2008) *The European Neighbourhood Policy in the South Caucasus: Involvement of NGOs in the Democratization Process*. Paper presented at the UACES Exchanging Ideas on Europe Conference, Edinburgh, 1–3 September.

Rosenau, J. (1992) Governance, order and change in world politics, in *Governance without Government. Order and Change in World Politics* (eds J. Rosenau and E., Czempiel). Cambridge University Press, Cambridge, 1–29.

Sasse, G. (2008) The European Neighbourhood Policy: conditionality revisited for the EU's eastern neighbours. *Europe-Asia Studies* 60 (2), 295–316.

Schimmelfennig, F. and Scholtz, H. (2008) EU democracy promotion in the European neighbourhood: political conditionality, economic development and transnational exchange. *European Union Politics* 9, 187–215.

Transparency International (2011) *Corruption Perceptions Index 2011*, <http://transparency.ge/en/post/corruption-perception-index-cpi/corruption-perceptions-index-2011> (accessed 5 December 2014).

Vachudova, M. (2005) *Europe Undivided: Democracy, Leverage and Integration After Communism*, Oxford University Press, Oxford.

Wilson, J. (2010) *Colour Revolutions: The View From Moscow and Beijing*, CRASSH, Cambridge University, Cambridge.

World Bank (2012) *Ease of Doing Business in Georgia*, <http://www.doingbusiness.org/data/exploreeconomies/Georgia> (accessed 5 December 2014).

Youngs, R. (2009) Democracy promotion as external governance? *Journal of European Public Policy* 16 (6), 895–915.

Part III
(Re)Constructing Identities in a Changing World

Kevork K. Oskanian

Citizenship or Ethnicity? National Identity and Insecurity in Southern Caucasia

ABSTRACT: This chapter analyses the interaction of insecurity and conflict with the various national ideologies and identities of the three recognized South Caucasus states – Armenia, Azerbaijan Georgia – through the Copenhagen School's concept of *securitization*. The reified historiographies and resultant overlapping territorial identities within Armenia's and Azerbaijan's national ideologies are seen as locking both states in a near-existential conflict over Nagorno-Karabakh through mirroring and fundamentally incompatible security narratives. By contrast, Georgia's *civic* approach to national ideology following the Rose Revolution is seen as having offered some initial prospect for conflict resolution, at least before the 2008 war, by offering the possibility for an inclusive, multicultural Georgian identity.

KEYWORDS: South Caucasus, nationalism, security, ideology, identity, democracy, securitization theory, conflict

Introduction: National Ideology, Identity and Securitization

"Ancient hatreds": this by now discredited myth of premodern attitudes lying behind the many ethnic conflagrations that plagued the Eurasian landmass following the fall of Communism has had a remarkable staying power in the popular mind (Bowen, 1996; Kaufman, 2001; Majtorovic, 1997). What is perhaps most remarkable is its persistence within the very societies involved in those confrontations: to various degrees, Serbs, Croats, Bosnians, Kosovars, Armenians, Azeris, Georgians, Abkhaz and Ossets tend to construct their own modern wars in terms of a long-term, Manichean battle for survival spanning centuries, including times when the very concepts of "nationhood" or "ethnicity" were of little political significance.

As this chapter will argue, in the South Caucasus at least, this naturalization of ethnic hatreds is intimately linked to the nature of elite-driven postcommunist national ideology and identity and the perpetuation of the incompatible security narratives that lie at the basis of the region's conflicts. These incompatible narratives become especially salient when national ideologies are defined in *ethnic* rather than *civic* terms – a well-established distinction usually associated with the works of Hans Kohn (2008). At a fundamental level, the region's insecurities are shaped by the way its peoples define their identities and perceive their histories and, insofar as ethnic conflicts are "socially constructed", an understanding of the links between identity, historical narrative and insecurity provides an invaluable insight into the drivers of these conflicts.

The Copenhagen School's central concept, "securitization", will link these national ideologies, their identities, and the various societies' security discourses: it has, since the 1990s, become an accepted methodological tool in the analysis of a society's security narratives (Buzan *et al.*, 1998; Buzan and Wæver, 2003). As Austinian speech acts, securitizations take issues from the realm of politics into that of security, where everyday political procedures are suspended in response to existential threats to (material and ideational) "referent objects" of value. "Securitizing actors" – individuals and groups with some degree of authority over elements within a given society – make "securitizing moves", whereby such existential threats are identified and extra-ordinary measures are advocated. When relevant audiences accept these moves as valid, they become "securitizing acts" with real-world consequences (Buzan *et al.*, 1998: 21–47): as when "terrorism" is securitized as a threat in the United States and drone strikes are proposed as an extra-ordinary countermeasure; or when the Armenian minority in Nagorno-Karabakh is constructed as being under existential threat from Azerbaijan, leading to a secessionist war with Azerbaijan.

Such securitizations do not occur in a void: they are very much shaped by the social, historical and cultural specificities of the societies within which they transpire. Securitizations go far beyond the simple issues connected to *physical* survival, incorporating broader and more abstract "referent objects" as values to be protected from harm. Religious values, for instance, can elicit securitizations (Laustsen and Wæver, 2000); so can issues connected to the cultural identity of ethnic minorities; the same can be said of ideologies underpinning a state's political system (Buzan, 1993; Buzan *et al.*, 1998: 119–162). People fight and die for their religion, their "people" or "democracy" as a result. *Ideas* matter in securitizations, and this provides a crucial link between the way a given society defines itself through its national ideology, and its "security". Which values a particular state espouses, the ways it defines its own identity and that of its citizens, interact with the security narratives "out there". In constructivist terms, state ideologies, and narratives or practices of security – as expressed in these securitizations – are "mutually constitutive".

The three South Caucasian states' distinct national ideologies – as expressed in their official discourses – are inherently intertwined with the securitizations, the definitions of "threat" living in each of these three societies that underlie the regional conflicts that have haunted the region since the fall of the Soviet Union. State ideologies both *shape* and *are shaped by* the norms, values and identities that a given polity is expected to uphold and secure; and these norms, values, identities are, in turn, founded on the historical and cultural attitudes present within a given society. The extent to which state and society define themselves in civic terms, as a political community of citizens, rather than in ethnic terms, as a cultural-historical community of fate, matters: as suggested by Snyder (1993: 94), civic national identities and ideologies lend themselves more readily to compromise and adaptation to local circumstances, allowing for the inclusion of various cultural groups into the state as a collective security arrangement in defence of shared (political, civic, pluralist) values, or facilitating accommodation with citizens of other neighbouring states around shared liberal-democratic values. The latter, ethno-nationalist approach, on the other hand, tends towards a zero-sum, exclusivist logic that sees the state as the defender of a very particularist cultural, ethnic identity that, *a priori*, demands conformity to a historically fixed, reified value set, and is, as such, resistant to compromise and sensitive to external threat.

In the next three sections, I shall delve more deeply into how the national ideologies in Armenia, Azerbaijan and Georgia – as espoused by these countries' political elites - have come to shape regional security through their associated securitizations. Of particular interest will be the effect of their civic-political as opposed to ethno-nationalist content on these discourses. How have civic as opposed to ethnic definitions of national ideology and identity in these three imperfect democracies affected the insecurities constructed by elites (and counter-elites) in the South Caucasus? How have they, in turn, been shaped by the insecurities present in wider society? It is to these questions that I now turn, empirically basing myself on the official and wider discourses of security within the Armenian, Azeri and Georgian societies of the post-Soviet period.

Armenia: Between Citizenship and Ethnicity

At first glance, the question of Armenia's state ideology would seem the most straightforward, its society being the ethnically and religiously most homogenous of the three recognized states of the region. Since the expulsion of the sizeable Azeri minority during the Karabakh conflict, well over 95% of the country's population has been ethnic Armenian, with Yezidi Kurds and Molokan Russians making up most of the remainder (Republic of Armenia, 2001). Yet, from the very emergence of pro-independence stirrings in 1989, Armenia's elites were faced with a stark choice between defining their state in ethno-nationalist or civic-nationalist terms. Was Armenia going to be the homeland of *all* Armenians – including the relatively wealthy diaspora and Armenian minorities throughout the FSU – or would it define the boundaries of political inclusion/exclusion much more strictly, by becoming the state of its *resident citizens*?

Ironically, the political party that emerged from the Karabakh committees – the Armenian Pan-National Movement – chose the latter, civic variant as the newly independent state's ideology. Like all South Caucasian nationalisms, Armenian nationalism had, till then, very much been an *ethnic* affair, since its emergence in the late nineteenth century (Suny, 1993). And when it reappeared in 1980s Soviet Armenia, it very much defined the Armenians in the Armenian SSR and in the Nagorno-Karabakh Autonomous Oblast as a single "community of fate". Despite that, Levon Ter-Petrosyan and his allies came to define the Republic of Armenia in terms of its *citizens*. The first Armenian president is on the record as dismissing "[ethno]-national ideology" as a false category, and, true to form, came to challenge several ethno-nationalist taboos (Libaridian, 1999; Astourian, 2000).

One logical consequence of this emphasis on civic rather than ethnic nationalism was the at least partial disaggregation of Armenia's state interests from those of the Nagorno-Karabakh Republic (NKR) and the diaspora. Levon Ter-Petrosyan and his close advisers thus advocated unconditional relations with the Republic of Turkey, and defined the 1915 Genocide as a *moral* issue, rather than one of inter-state high politics (Libaridian, 1999, 2004). The security of Nagorno-Karabakh was seen as distinct from and subordinated to Armenia's, opening the door to concessions – outlined in Ter-Petrosyan's (1997) (in?) famous "War or Peace?" article

– that were seen as unacceptable by those in his entourage who employed an altogether different view of Armenian statehood.

By 1998, a showdown between these two interpretations of Armenia's political destiny had become inevitable. In February that year, a coalition of Karabakh war veterans and politicians originating from the enclave (including Armenia's two latest presidents) in effect forced LTP to resign in what was, in effect, a palace coup (Astourian, 2000). By that time, Ter-Petrosyan had lost much of his democratic legitimacy, through two falsified elections and one rigged constitutional referendum; public opinion was generally supportive of his removal. The new administration, led by a former president of Nagorno-Karabakh, immediately adopted a radically different ideological outlook, expanding the Republic's parameters of inclusion towards the diaspora and the enclave's Armenians.

Dual citizenship was legalized; diaspora Armenians were given the opportunity to acquire their motherland's nationality without transferring their residency. The 1915 Genocide was placed back onto Armenia's foreign policy agenda, and (except for a brief interlude during the "football diplomacy" of 2009–10), no attempts were made at increasing contacts with Turkey.[1] Official discourse stressed the commonality of interest between the Republics of Armenia and Nagorno-Karabakh and insisted on *self-determination* for the enclave as a solution to the conflict in much more explicit a manner (see Oskanian, 1998, 2005; Noyan Tapan, 2001; Public Television of Armenia, 2004; Regnum, 2008). Enmity with Azerbaijan was often reified as matter-of-fact, with former President Robert Kocharyan notably referring to the "ethnic incompatibility" of Armenians

1 "Football diplomacy" refers to an abortive attempt at creating a breakthrough in Turkish–Armenian relations in 2009–10. After several years of behind-the-scenes negotiations facilitated by the Swiss foreign ministry, both sides' heads of state attempted to prepare public opinion for an imminent thaw by attending qualification matches for the 2010 Football World Cup in each other's countries. The process culminated in the signing, in October 2009, of protocols providing for the establishment of diplomatic ties, as well as a raft of other measures aimed at normalizing broader relations between the two sides. On the Armenian side, the provision that the "historical dimension" (i.e. the 1915 massacres) be studied within a joint intergovernmental commission provoked the ire of nationalists within the country and, especially, abroad; on the Turkish side, Azerbaijan was successful in mobilizing public opinion against any weakening of Turkey's isolation of Armenia (including its long-standing economic blockade) without prior progress in the Nagorno-Karabakh negotiations. The protocols remain, as yet, unratified (Economist, 2009; Phillips, 2012).

and Azeris (as quoted in Teryan, 2003). Openly racist ideas – including the Tseghakron ideology of Garegin Njdeh, and notions of a supposed "Turkic" collective mindset – could be heard in broader societal discourse (see Lalayan, 2002a, 2002b; Ararat Center, 2009; Republican Party of Armenia, 2009).

If anything, the above indicates the ingrained nature of the securitizations emanating from and constituting Armenia's current state ideology. The "creation myth" of the current republic can be traced all the way to the 1915 Genocide and the defeat of Ottoman forces in the May 1918 battle of Sardarabad, which, in Armenian historical discourse, prevented the complete annihilation of the Armenian nation. The idea that Armenia and the Armenians have been on the verge of extinction at the hand of their Turkic "barbarian interloper" neighbours is one that permeates Armenian historiography. In that sense, 1915, 1895 and 1905 are seen as the culmination of one millennium of Turkic invasions, with little distinction between Anatolian and Azeri Turks. Following from that, the gradual disappearance of Armenians from the Azeri exclave of Nakhichevan (in 1921–89) is thus regarded as a precursor to the planned ethnic cleansing of Nagorno-Karabakh, the Armenians' last outpost against pan-Turanism (Galoian and Khudaverdian, 1988; Melkumian, 1990; Manassian, 1997).

Levon Ter-Petrosyan failed in his attempts to redefine that ideology towards a more civic form precisely because such a redefinition ran counter to the existential fears that have marked Armenian society for decades. And the role of the 1915 massacres cannot be underestimated in that regard: Armenian society views its region – particularly its Turkic neighbours – primarily through the prism of this one existential event and the persecutions that are seen to have both preceded and followed it. While a *civic* notion of national identity would undoubtedly have provided more room for accommodation and compromise – as envisaged by Levon Ter-Petrosyan and his liberal followers in the 1990s – the entrenched and intense nature of the securitizations driving Armenian insecurities clearly gave the advantage to the *ethnic* notions of community and statehood that persist to this day.

Azerbaijan: Mirroring Your Enemy

Azerbaijan's "national ideology" has been fairly stable, if complex, since the coming to power of the Aliyevs following a period of chaos immediately following independence. Azerbaijan's first postindependence President (and, as in so many Central Asian republics, its last Communist Party General Secretary), Ayaz Mutalibov, did not have sufficient time to develop a well-defined idea of "Azerbaijan". His successor, Abufaz Elchibey, was likewise in power for a mere 2 years (1992–94), although his leadership of the Popular Front had given him the opportunity to define the Azeri state primarily in *Turkic* terms. Eltchibey's foreign policy vision was turned firmly westward, and his ideology was heavily influenced by pan-Turanism, emphasizing Azerbaijan's ethno-linguistic affinity with the Turkic world, and, above all, the Republic of Turkey. This westward gaze eventually led to his ouster, in 1994, by Heidar Aliyev, whose pragmatic ideological outlook was certainly more palatable to Moscow.

The state ideology espoused since the coming to power of the elder Aliyev in 1994 has been more complex and multi-faceted than Elchybey's pan-Turanism. Contemporary Azeri identity has both ethnic and civic elements: although Azerbaijan's Turkic identity still predominates, and Kemal Ataturk's secularism does play an important inspirational role, other elements that are more specific to Azerbaijan enter the discourse as well. Firstly, Azerbaijan has maintained a distinctly *Caucasian* identity since Soviet times, as a successor state to the ancient Christian medieval kingdom of Albania (see Bunyatov, 1987; Tabrizli, 1989; Bunyatov, 1990; Alijarly, 1996; Mamedova, s.d.). Secondly, Azerbaijan's national identity has often also encompassed a historical *Iranian* aspect, leading to an increased identification with the Azeris in Iranian (or "southern Azerbaijan"). Thirdly, from a civic-nationalist perspective, Azerbaijan is often constructed, by its elites, as a tolerant multiethnic state – as opposed to Armenia's (and Armenians') perceived monoethnic intolerance (see Aliyev, 2004b, 2005b; 2005c, 2005d; Orudzhev, 2003). An intense securitization of Armenia and the Armenians interweaves neatly with almost all of the above facets of Azeri national and state ideology, but sits most uncomfortably aside these claims of tolerance and multiculturalism through the highly essentialized discourses it generates.

Azerbaijan's security concerns are intensely coloured by its loss of control over Nagorno-Karabakh, and the ethnic cleansing of areas surrounding it during 1991–94. The unresolved conflict permeates all facets of government discourse, from the National Security Concept (Republic of Azerbaijan, 2007) and the President's narratives downwards. Baku views its region and the world primarily through the lens of this ongoing issue, resulting in a national ideology constructed around the intense "othering" of Armenians as subject to an alien, incompatible political culture. This narrative – very similar to that prevalent on the ultranationalist side of the Turkish political spectrum – is replicated on a regular basis in official media and in the discourses of people and institutions of authority. While Azerbaijan's elite regularly refers to Azerbaijan's civic-nationalist aspirations, in its *practical* application, discourse remains deeply illiberal because of intense securitizations that collectively stigmatize a whole ethnos and, in so doing, almost perfectly mirror equally illiberal securitizations in Armenia.

Relations between Armenians and Azerbaijan and its predecessor states are described in terms of unending encroachment and genocide, in 1905, and 1918–20 and in 1992, culminating in an ongoing, ultimate injustice: its occupation and ethnic cleansing of Nagorno-Karabakh and 20% of Azerbaijan's territory (see Aliyev, 1998; Mamedova, 2004; Suleymanov, 2006; Aliyev, 2008; Hasanov, 2008; Hasanli, 2009). The state-sponsored, orthodox historical narrative describes Armenians as newcomers to the Caucasus, and both the Azeri president and the Azeri media perpetuate the narrative of the Armenians as interlopers by describing the Karabakh Armenians as "guests" on Azeri lands (see Aliyev, 2004a, 2004c, 2005a), who will have to accept Azerbaijan's sovereignty or emigrate (I. Aliyev, 2007; Day.az, 2009). International criticism of Azerbaijan is often – and rather conveniently for the ruling elite – ascribed to the interference of "mirovoe Armyanstvo", perhaps best translated as "world Armenianry", regardless of the source: human rights iNGOs, Western media, the foreign ministries of various states, international organizations (see Kocharli, 2004; Gasanov, 2007). The racist writings of stridently anti-Armenian authors – including the notorious Vasili Velichko – feature prominently on government websites (Republic of Azerbaijan, 2008). The destruction of the historic Armenian cemetery at Djulfa, and the recent pardoning and lionizing of Ramil Safarov – an Azeri officer convicted of murdering an Armenian co-student at a NATO language course in Budapest – also fit within this pattern (IWPR, 2006; Balayeva and Mkrtchyan, 2012; RFE-RL, 2012).

The many similarities between Armenian and Azeri discourses point to how narratives of national or state identity and perceptions of security and insecurity are tightly interlinked. While Armenia's national identity is certainly more explicitly ethnic than Azerbaijan's, the oft-stated civic, multicultural aspirations of Azerbaijan's state ideology are so coloured by its intense securitization of Armenia and Armenians so as to lose their meaning, creating an eerie similarity in the mirroring discourses of both societies. Whether it is in their mutual perceptions of encroachment and resulting massacre and injustice, the artificial and alien natures of both states and peoples, or their status as the assimilator or persecutor of minorities, both societies define each other as fundamentally incompatible. This is most apparent when one compares their narratives with those prevalent in the third state of the South Caucasus – Georgia. This state has recently adopted the most *civic* of all state ideologies, employing the most conciliatory and inclusive language towards its minorities – including the separatist Abkhaz and South Ossetians. The final section will address this, and the somewhat paradoxical fact that it was involved in *war* with its secessionist entities while the discursively much more hostile Azeris and Armenians have so far avoided a renewed hot phase of their ongoing "frozen" conflict.

Georgia: From Mystical Nationalism to Multi-Cultural Citizenship

Georgia can perhaps be described as an outlier in this sense. Its state ideology is different from both Armenia's and Azerbaijan's in that it has evolved (at least in a discursive sense) towards an explicitly civic, multicultural identity and value set, *without* the intense direct securitization of a particular ethnic group. Instead, Georgia's perceptions of threat are strongly directed towards its northern neighbour, Russia; and minorities are at most *indirectly* securitized as potential instruments of Moscow's perceived neoimperial policies in the region, rather than being seen as holders of an essentialized, entirely incompatible identity (see Republic of Georgia, 2005, 2010). The Abkhaz and Ossets are *not* in conflict with Georgia because they are somehow seen as historically and culturally prone to violent encroachment, terrorism and/or genocide; current government discourse prefers to describe these two minorities as "hijacked" by agents of the Russian Federation. The upshot of such an approach is that the intensity of mutual securitizations doesn't reach the venomous depths of those between Georgia's two neighbours.

This is quite an evolution from the earlier years of Georgia's independence. The securitization of minorities as threats was at its most intense under the presidency of Zviad Gamsakhurdia, a prominent writer to whom many contemporary authors ascribed "messianic" pretensions (Kaufman, 2001: 115; Cohen, 2004). Gamsakhurdia saw Georgia as having a unique mission within the Orthodox world, as revealed in a particularly mystical and eccentric speech delivered at TSU in 1990 (Gamsakhurdia, 1990). He also regarded Georgia's minorities as unwelcome "guests", impositions by and potential fifth columns of the Russian and Soviet states. Georgia was to become a unitary Republic, as it had been in 1918–21, and the message to minorities was that they would have to assimilate or emigrate (Jones, 1994; Nodia, 1996; Kaufman, 2001: 110; English, 2008). As is well known today, in a republic where these minorities made up well over 30% of the population, this was a recipe for disaster, eventually leading to the secession of Abkhazia and South Ossetia. The first President's authoritarian tendencies moreover led to a short but sharp civil war in 1991–92 – one that eventually brought to power the far more pragmatic Eduard Shevardnadze (Way and Levitsky, 2006).

As Georgia's president, the latter adopted a pragmatic political course, seeking some form of accommodation with Russia on the way towards reunification, while at the same time developing Georgia's relations with the West, mostly as a transit corridor for Caspian hydrocarbons. In terms of state ideology, however, Shevardnadze did not have much to offer beyond the practical necessities emanating from Georgia's difficult geopolitical position: his increasingly pro-Western stance, particularly after the failure of reunification talks with Abkhazia and South Ossetia in the early 2000s (blamed on Russian intransigence), was not accompanied by the ideological fervour that marked his successor's democratizing and liberalizing policies (see BBC Monitoring, 2000). Shevardnadze believed in the processes of *high politics* in his dealings with the outside world, rather than typically Western ideas like public diplomacy, or the notion that democracy would somehow make the Georgian state more palatable to its breakaway regions (Nodia, 2005: 47–48).

The 2003 Rose Revolution was followed by a period of relative stability that allowed Mikheil Saakashvili and his entourage to develop a state ideology that was defined precisely along these ideas: Georgia was part of *Europe*, a multicultural democracy and prospective NATO member. (By way of contrast, see BBC Monitoring, 1994; Saakashvili, 2005.) While Georgian culture did remain something of a *Leitkultur*, policymakers started approaching the country's ethnic minorities and their cultural specificity as inalienable parts of the social fabric – at least in their narratives. Alongside a State Ministry for Integration, Georgia developed a National Concept for Tolerance and Civic Integration for its Minorities that talked of their incorporation into the country's political and social life alongside the guaranteeing of their own identity (Republic of Georgia, 2009, s.d.). Georgia's superior – liberal-democratic – political and economic systems, and its accommodation of its minorities would lead the populations of Abkhazia and South Ossetia towards pressuring their *de facto* authorities towards reunification with Tbilisi (see Saakashvili, 2004a, 2004b; Saakashvili, 2008).

This "Westernization" of Georgia's national identity was, naturally, not well received in Moscow, emanating as it did from the continued intense securitization of the former imperial master as a threat to Georgian sovereignty. The conflicts between Tbilisi, Tskhinvali and Sukhumi are also primarily narrated (at least on the Georgian side) as imperial conflicts between Georgia and *Russian proxies*, rather than nationalist struggles to the death between fundamentally incompatible ethnicities, as they are in Armenia, Karabakh and Azerbaijan. To some extent, such a narrative allows for the notion that reform and political-economic progress would somehow engender a solution by providing incentives to the minorities *not* to bandwagon with that northern great power, in the absence of such fundamental incompatibilities. This line of thought seriously underestimated the intensity and staying power of those securitizations of Georgia as a "mini-empire" (Lakoba, 1995) that had driven Abkhazia and South Ossetia towards secession in the early 1990s, in addition to diverging historical narratives, especially in Abkhazia (Nodia, 1998; Anchabadze, 1999; Coppieters, 2002; Nadareishvili, 2007; Zhorzholiani *et al.* 1995: 83–96).

Early successes were registered – the removal of the thuggish Abashidze clan from Adjaria, and the emergence of Dmitri Sanakoyev as a challenger to the established pro-Russian, separatist regime in Tskhinvali (see

Peuch, 2007; Saakashvili, 2005). The latter event was particularly significant: clearly, part of the South Ossetian elite had come round to accepting the possibility of Ossetians living under Georgian rule and there is little doubt the change in discourse from Tbilisi played a role in facilitating this turn-around. A comparison with the current situation between Baku and Stepanakert/Yerevan is particularly sobering: at no point since the fall of the Soviet Union has any mainstream Armenian politician *ever* suggested the possibility of submitting to Azeri rule and neither would this presently be conceivable considering the extreme zero-sum manner in which that conflict is constructed by elites on both sides. Securitizations between the populations in South Ossetia and Georgia have lessened sufficiently for such a possibility to be considered as realistic by at least some in Tskhinvali's separatist elite.

The Abashidze and Sanakoyev episodes should, however, not be overplayed. Ajaria's population was overwhelmingly ethnically Georgian, differing mainly in its Muslim as opposed to Christian Orthodox religion (Cornell, 2002: 273–274; International Crisis Group, 2004). While Sanakoyev did break away from the separatist elite in Tskhinvali, and this schism was in itself significant, his view was very much in the minority among fellow Ossets and he soon found himself politically marginalized (Barry, 2008; Corso, 2008). The Saakashvili administration's efforts at public diplomacy through a redefined, civic notion of state identity also had little effect in Abkhazia – where securitizations of Tbilisi were historically more intense and longstanding than in South Ossetia. In any case, the August 2008 war put an end to the idea that redefined liberal/civic state or national ideologies alone would be sufficient to reunite the Georgian state – an idea that completely underestimated Russia's ability and willingness to thwart Tbilisi's march towards the West and NATO membership through the combination of a few well timed provocations and several major Georgian miscalculations.

There is no question today of either breakaway republic rejoining Georgia: confirmed in their suspicions of Tbilisi's supposedly malicious intentions, and recognized by Moscow, the elites in both *de facto* statelets view the question of reunification as irrelevant (see Interfax, 2009; s.n., 2009a, 2009b). There is, however, one important difference between Abkhazia and South Ossetia, in that the former is far more concerned about Russian absorption over the longer term than the latter. In fact, political forces in Tskhinvali have long considered the possibility of uniting with their republic's Russian, north Caucasian counterpart (see Khairullin *et al.*, 2006; Interfax, 2008; Prime-Tass, 2009). The current National Security Concept's assumption that Georgian reunification depends more on Tbilisi's relationship with Moscow than on its relationship with either Sukhumi or Tskhinvali may very well be correct.

Conclusion

The linkages between national ideology, identity and (in)security are complex – and this is fully born out in the South Caucasus. It would seem safe to say that Georgia's post-2003 national ideology is, however imperfectly, the one with the highest civic content in the region: since the Rose Revolution, Tbilisi has – in its discourses at least – adhered to a much more civic view of the state than either of its neighbours. Rhetorically, Saakashvili and leading members of the new government *usually*[2] refer to the country's numerous minorities as part of the state citizenry, rather than ethnically or culturally incompatible intruders – as Armenians and Azeris tend to construct each other. This positive view of changes since 2003 must, however, be tempered by the way pronounced policies have actually been applied in potential flashpoints within those parts of the country still under Tbilisi's control – notably the Armenian-populated region of Javakheti, where discontent still lingers. And any link between Georgia's more "civic" notion of statehood and greater security would have to contend with one gigantic elephant in the room: the August 2008 war.

Paradoxically, the regional actor with the most liberal-democratic, civically constructed identity also was the *only* one to be involved in a major armed conflict following the "freezing" of the numerous South Caucasian conflicts, in 1994. Arguably, this conflagration occurred not *because* of the nature of the securitizations between Tbilisi, Sukhumi and Tskhinvali (which, while intense, are far milder than those between Armenia and Azerbaijan), but because of pressures from the *systemic* level. Georgia's

2 Georgia's new Prime Minister did break this general pattern in remarks that were seen as disparaging the country's Armenian community, in early October 2012; he swiftly backtracked (Danielyan, 2012).

choice in favour of *liberal democracy* was just as much a choice in favour of the NATO alliance and the West, and in that sense, August 2008 had more to do with Russia's displeasure at this strategic choice, and Saakashvili's impatience, than strictly local imperatives. In terms of the self-contained societal securitizations underlying Ossetia's and Abkhazia's secession, little had changed.

Conversely, if Armenia and Azerbaijan are at peace today, this is not due to a lessening of their intense mutual securitizations or a change in their deeply incompatible ideologies and identities. In fact, the narratives and identities of both sides remain eerily symmetrical in their unrestrained mutual vitriol. Since 1998, following the defeat of the alternative civic model pushed by Ter-Petrosyan, the Armenian elite has defined its state in ethno-nationalist terms, accommodating rather than counter-acting Armenians' historical securitizations of "the Turk", securitizations that have often generated discourses of undisguised racism. On the other side of the conflict, Azerbaijan's elites have continued to intensely and indiscriminately securitize "world Armenians", again allowing for the emergence of overtly racist discourses that put a question mark over their repeated rhetorical claims to "multiethnic tolerance". Anyone glossing over these narratives of hatred marking both societies would be discounting the fact that any lasting peace and security between the belligerents would ultimately require the consent of both populations – particularly those directly affected, *within and around* Nagorno-Karabakh. And, considering recent events in addition the above, such consent will be a long time coming indeed.

References

Alijarly, S. (1996) The Republic of Azerbaijan: notes on state borders in the past and the present, in *Transcaucasian Boundaries* (eds J. F. R. Wright, S. Goldenberg and R. Schofield). London: UCL Press, 113–133.

Aliyev, H. (1998) *Decree of President of Republic of Azerbaijan about Genocide of Azerbaijani People*, <http://www.human.gov.az/?sehife=etrafli&dil=ru&sid=MTMyMjMzMTA4MTMyNjE1Mw==> (accessed 25 October 2014).

Aliyev, I. (2004a) *Interview of President of Azerbaijan Republic Ilham Aliyev for "Reuter" Agency,* <http://www.president.az/articles.php?item_id=20070810053350496&sec_id=14> (accessed 25 October 2014).

Aliyev, I. (2004b) *Speech of Azerbaijani President Ilham Aliyev at meeting at the Columbia University in New York,* <http://www.president.az/articles.php?item_id=20070813060710459&sec_id=11> (accessed 25 October 2014).

Aliyev, I. (2004c) *Speech of Azerbaijani President Ilham Aliyev at meeting in club "Chatham House",* <http://www.president.az/articles.php?item_id=20070814111242124&sec_id=11> (accessed 25 October 2014).

Aliyev, I. (2005a) *Interview of Azeri President Ilham Aliyev to Turkish Journalists,* <http://www.president.az/articles.php?item_id=20070810070009204&sec_id=14> (accessed 25 October 2014).

Aliyev, I. (2005b) *Official Reception on Behalf of President of Azerbaijan Ilham Aliyev on the Occasion of 28 May – Republican Day,* <http://www.president.az/articles.php?item_id=20070813063208583&sec_id=11> (accessed 25 October 2014)

Aliyev, I. (2005c) *Speech of President of Azerbaijan Republic Ilham Aliyev at the Meeting of Nij Settlement,* <http://www.president.az/articles.php?item_id=20070814110030455&sec_id=11> (accessed 25 October 2014).

Aliyev, I. (2005d) *Speech of President of President of Azerbaijan Republic Ilham Aliyev,* <http://www.president.az/articles.php?item_id=20070814103116081&sec_id=11> (accessed 25 October 2014).

Aliyev, I. (2007) *Greetings of President Ilham Aliyev to the People of Azerbaijan on the World Azerbaijanis Solidarity Day and the New Year,* <http://archive.president.az/print.php?item_id=20080101021742200&sec_id=135> (accessed 25 October 2014).

Aliyev, I. (2008) *Obrashchenie k Azerbaidzhanskomu Narodu v Svyazi s 31 Marta – Dnem Genotsida Azerbaidzhantsev,* <http://www.azembassy.msk.ru/events/2008/prez31.html> (accessed 24 October 2014).

Anchabadze, J. (1999) History: the modern period, in *The Abkhazians: A Handbook* (ed. G. Hewitt), Curzon Press, Richmond, pp. 132–146.

Ararat Center (2009) Activities of Ararat Center: Media Coverage, <http://blog.ararat-center.org/?p=215> - n15 (accessed 24 October 2014).

Astourian, S. H. (2000) *From Ter-Petrosian to Kocharian: Leadership Change in Armenia*, University of California, Berkeley, CA.

Balayeva, N., and Mkrtchyan, H. (2012) *Axe Murderer's Homecoming Stokes Caucasus Feud,* <http://uk.reuters.com/article/2012/09/06/uk-azerbaijan-armenia-soldier-idUKBRE88510120120906> (accessed 24 October 2014).

Barry, E. (2008) Georgia's public, and battered, face in a separatist republic. *New York Times* (1 November).

BBC Monitoring (1994) Shevardnadze Sets Out Stabilization Programme at Citizens' Union Congress. Retrieved 3 September, 2009, from Nexis UK.

BBC Monitoring (2000) Georgian President Deems Russia's Stand Towards Caucasus Security Significant. Retrieved 20 January, 2008, from Nexis UK.

Bowen, J. R. (1996) The myth of global ethnic conflict. *Journal of Democracy* 7(4), 3–14.

Bunyatov, Z. M. (ed.) (1987) *Istoricheskaia Geografiya Azerbaidzhana,* Elm, Baku.

Bunyatov, Z. M. (ed.) (1990) *Istoria Azerbaidzhana Po Dokumentam i Publikatsiyam.* Elm/Akademia Nauk Azerbaidzhanskoi SSR, Baku.

Buzan, B. (1993) Societal security, state security, and internationalisation, in *Identity, Migration and the New Security Agenda in Europe* (eds Ø. Wæver, M. Kelstrup and P. Lemaitre), Pinter, London, 41–58.

Buzan, B. and Wæver, Ø. (2003) *Regions and Powers: The Structure of International Security,* Cambridge University Press, Cambridge.

Buzan, B., Wæver, Ø., and De Wilde, J. (1998) *Security: A New Framework for Analysis,* Lynne Rienner, London.

Cohen, J. (2004) *Georgia: Changing the Guard,* <http://www.c-r.org/resources/georgia-changing-guard> (accessed 15 January 2015)

Coppieters, B. (2002) In defence of the homeland: intellectuals and the Georgian-Abkhazian xonflict, in *Secession, History and the Social Sciences* (eds B. Coppieters and M. Huysseune). Brussels: VUB Brussels University Press, 89–116.

Cornell, S. (2002) Autonomy as a source of conflict: Caucasian conflicts in theoretical perspective. *World Politics* 54(2), 245–276.

Corso, M. (2008) Georgia: unclear future for South Ossetia's pro-Tbilisi leader. *Eurasia Insight* (11 November).

Danielyan, E. (2012) Georgia's Ivanishvili in Hot Water after "Anti-Armenian Gaffe". *RFE-RL*, <http://www.azatutyun.am/content/article/24730642.html> (accessed 24 October 2014).

Day.az. (2009) Political scientist: If Karabakh Armenians want to live together with the main part of their people, let them get out of our territory and return to Armenia where they have already gained independence. *Today.Az* (18 May), from <http://www.today.az/news/politics/52244.html> (accessed 24 October 2014).

Economist (2009) Football diplomacy (3 September), <http://www.economist.com/node/14380297> (accessed 25 October 2014).

English, R. (2008) Georgia: the ignored history. *New York Review of Books* 55(17), <http://www.nybooks.com/articles/22011> (accessed 24 October 2014).

Galoian, G. A., and Khudaverdian, K. S. (eds) (1988) *Nagorniyi Karabakh: Istoricheskaya Pravka*, Izdatelstvo Akademiya Nauk Armianskoi SSR, Yerevan.

Gamsakhurdia, Z. (1990) *The Spiritual Mission of Georgia.* Lecture delivered at the Idriart Festival in Tbilisi Philharmonic Hall, 2 May 1990, <http://rustaveli.tripod.com/mission.html> (accessed 15 January 2015).

Gasanov, A. (2007) Karabakh, Nakhchevan, Dalee Vezde, Ili Kaka Protivostoyat Mirovomu Armyanstvu? *Day.az* (27 October), <http://www.day.az/print/news/politics/96141.html> (accessed 24 October 2014).

Hasanli, J. (2009) Tragicheskaya Vesna 1918 Goda. *Zerkalo* (11, 18, 25 April and 2, 9 May), <http://azeri.ru/papers/zerkalo_az/44622/> (accessed 15 January 2015)

Hasanov, A. (2008) Historical roots of the IDP crisis in Azerbaijan. *ADA Biweelky* 1(11), <http://biweekly.ada.edu.az/vol_1_no_11/Historical_roots_of_the_IDP_crisis_in_Azerbaijan.htm> (accessed 15 January 2015)

Interfax (2008) No alternative to unification of Ossetian people – North Ossetian leader. *Russia and CIS General Newswire* (6 March).

Interfax (2009) One Year on from Conflict, Uneasy Peace Prevails in the South. *Central Asia and Caucasus Business Weekly* (11 August).

International Crisis Group (2004) *Saakashvili's Ajara Success: Repeatable Elsewhere in Georgia?* International Crisis Group, Brussels.

IWPR (2006) *Azerbaijan: Famous Medieval Cemetery Vanishes*, <http://iwpr.net/print/report-news/azerbaijan-famous-medieval-cemetery-vanishes> (accessed 24 October 2014).

Jones, S. (1994) Populism in Georgia: the Gamsakhurdia phenomenon, in *Nationalism and History: The Politics of Nation Building in Post-Soviet Armenia, Azerbaijan and Georgia* (eds D. V. Schwartz and R. Panossian). University of Toronto – Centre for Russian and East European Studies, Toronto, 127–149.

Kaufman, S. J. (2001) *Modern Hatreds: The Symbolic Politics of Ethnic War*, Cornell University Press, Ithaca, NY.

Khairullin, M., Pavlikova, O., Dzhanayev, D., and Yeremjan, A. (2006) South Ossetia claims to be part of Russia. *Gazeta* (23 March).

Kocharli, T. (2004) *Armenian Deception (Historical Information)*, M-Dizayn, Baku.

Kohn, H. (2008) *The Idea of Nationalism: A Study in its Origins and Background*, Transaction Publishers, New Brunswick.

Lakoba, S. (1995) Abkhazia is Abkhazia. *Central Asian Survey* 14(1), 97–105.

Lalayan, M. (2002a) *Garegin Njdeh: Kensagrakan Aknark*, Republican Party of Armenia, Yerevan.

Lalayan, M. (2002b) *Tseghakron Sharjume: Patmutyun yev Qaghaparakhosutyun*, Republican Party of Armenia, Yerevan.

Laustsen, C. B. and Wæver, Ø. (2000) In defence of religion: sacred referent objects for securitization. *Millennium: Journal of International Studies* 29(3), 705–739.

Libaridian, G. J. (1999) *The Challenge of Statehood: Armenian Political Thinking Since Independence*, Blue Crane Books, Watertown.

Libaridian, G. J. (2004) *Modern Armenia: People, Nation, State*, Transaction Publishers, New Brunswick.

Majtorovic, S. (1997) Ancient hatreds or elite manipulation? Memory and politics in the former Yugoslavia. *World Affairs* 159(4), 170–182.

Mamedova, F. (s.d.) *Istina o Karabakhskoi Probleme*, <http://karabakh-doc.azerall.info/ru/articls/artc014.htm>.

Mamedova, K. (2004) *Khodzhaliy – Shekhidiy i Shakhidiy*, Baku.

Manassian, A. S. (1997) Gharabaghian Hakamartutyune Patmaqaghaqakan yev Iravakan Tesankyunnerits, *Gharabagh: Hakamartutyun – Hamadzaynutyun*, Haykakan Banak, Yerevan.

Melkumian, S. A. (1990) *Lernayin Gharabagh*, Luys, Yerevan.

Nadareishvili, T. (2007) *Genocide in Abkhazia*, Samoshoblo, Tbilisi.

Nodia, G. (1996) Political turmoil in Georgia and the ethnic policies of Zviad Gamsakhurdia, in *Contested Borders in the Caucasus* (ed. B. Coppieters). VUB Press, Brussels, 73–89.

Nodia, G. (1998) The conflict in Abkhazia: national projects and political circumstances, in *Georgians and Abkhazians: The Search for a Peace Settlement* (eds B. Coppieters, G. Nodia and Y. Anchabadze). Bundesinstitut für Ostwissenschaftliche und Internationale Studien, Cologne, 15–50.

Nodia, G. (2005) Georgia: dimensions of insecurity, in *Statehood and Security: Georgia after the Rose Revolution* (eds B. Coppieters and R. Legvold). American Academy of Arts and Sciences, Cambridge, 39–81.

Noyan Tapan (2001) Full text of Armenian president's Independence Day Address. Retrieved 16 June, 2009, from Lexis-Nexis.

Orudzhev, G. (2003) Azerbaijan's National Minorities Today. *Central Asia and the Caucasus*, <http://www.ca-c.org/online/2003/journal_eng/cac-04/18.orueng.shtml>.

Oskanian, V. (1998) *Address by Vartan Oskanian, Minister of Foreign Affairs of the Republic of Armenia, to the Permanent Council Meeting of the OSCE*, 8 October, <http://www.mfa.am/en/speeches/item/1998/10/08/osce/> (accessed 15 January 2015).

Oskanian, V. (2005) *Statement by Foreign Minister Vartan Oskanian in Armenian National Assembly hearings on Resolution of the Nagorno-Karabakh Issue*, <http://www.armeniaforeignministry.com/speeches/050329_vo_ana_nk.html>.

Peuch, J.-C. (2007) Caught Between Russia and Georgia, South Ossetia Rift Widens, <http://www.rferl.org/articleprintview/1079132.html> (accessed 25 October 2015).

Phillips, D. L. (2012) *Diplomatic History: The Turkey-Armenia Protocols*, Institute for the Study of Human Rights, Columbia University, New York, NY.

Prime-Tass (2009) President: South Ossetia wants to Create Union State with Russia. Retrieved 3 October, 2009, from Nexis UK.

Public Television of Armenia (2004) I am Proud to Have Fought for Karabakh, Armenian President Says. *BBC Monitoring*, 28 June.

Regnum (2008) *Recognition of Nagorno Karabakh Independence by Armenia Looks Logical and Justified: Interview with Hayk Kotanjian*, <http://www.regnum.ru/english/983635.html> (accessed 25 October 2014).

Republican Party of Armenia (2009) *Kusaktsutyan Patmutyune*, <http://www.hhk.am/hy/history/> (accessed 25 October 2014).

Republic of Armenia (2001) *Results of Census of Republic of Armenia 2001*, <http://docs.armstat.am/census/pdfs/52.pdf> (accessed 25 October 2014).

Republic of Azerbaijan (2007) *National Security Concept of the Republic of Azerbaijan*. <http://www.azembassy.org.au/uploads/docs/Azerbaijan.pdf> (accessed 15 January 2015).

Republic of Azerbaijan (2008) Bibliotheka, <http://www.mns.gov.az/publications_ru.html>.

Republic of Georgia (2005) *National Security Concept of Georgia*, <http://www.mfa.gov.ge/print.php?gg=1&sec_id=24&info_id=37&lang_id=ENG>.

Republic of Georgia (2009) *National Concept for Tolerance and Civic Integration*, <http://www.smr.gov.ge/docs/doc203.pdf> (accessed 15 January 2015).

Republic of Georgia (2010) *National Security Concept of Georgia*. Retrieved from <http://www.mfa.gov.ge/index.php?lang_id=ENG&sec_id=12> (accessed 15 January 2015).

Republic of Georgia (s.d.) *Office of the State Minister for Reintegration: Mission Statement*, http://www.smr.gov.ge/en/about_ministry.

RFE-RL (2012) *Aliyev Faces Growing Criticism for Pardon*, <http://www.rferl.org/content/aliyev-faces-growing-criticism-for-pardon/24696920.html> (accessed 25 October 2014).

s.n. (2009a) Abkhazia, S. Ossetia Will Never Be Part of Georgia. *Russia and CIS Military Weekly* (7 August).

s.n. (2009b) S. Ossetia Will Never Abandon Independence - Kokoity. *Russia and CIS Military Weekly* (7 August).

Saakashvili, M. (2004a) *Speech Delivered by President Mikheil Saakashvili at the Parade Dedicated to the Independence Day of Georgia*, <http://www.president.gov.ge/?l=E&m=0&sm=3&st=190&id=151>.

Saakashvili, M. (2004b) *Speech Delivered by the President Saakashvili at the Meeting with Members of Supreme Council of Abkhazia*, <http://www.president.gov.ge/?l=E&m=0&sm=3&st=190&id=152>.

Saakashvili, M. (2005) *Address by President Saakashvili at Independence Day Parade*, <http://www.president.gov.ge/?l=E&m=0&sm=3&st=170&id=145>.

Saakashvili, M. (2008) *The President of Georgia Addressed Abkhazian and Ossetian Population with Peace Initiative*, <http://www.president.gov.ge/?l=E&m=0&sm=3&st=30&id=2597>.

Snyder, J. (1993) Nationalism and the crisis of the post-Soviet state, in *Ethnic Conflict and International Security* (ed. M. E. Brown). Princeton University Press, Princeton, NY, 79–101.

Suleymanov, E. (2006) *Khojaly Genocide (In Documents, Facts and Foreign Press)*, A and ZS, Baku.

Suny, R. G. (1993) *Looking toward Ararat: Armenia in Modern History*, Indiana University Press, Indianapolis, IN.

Tabrizli, A. (1989). *Histoire du Daglig (Haut-) Gharabagh A La Lumière de Documents Historiques*, Association Culturelle Azerbaidjanaise, Strasbourg.

Ter-Petrosyan, L. (1997) Paterazm, te Khaghaghutyun? Lrjanalu Pahe, <http://www.levonforpresident.am/?catID=41&contID=90>.

Teryan, A. (2003) Armenian President says Armenians, Azerbaijanis "ethnically incompatible". *RFE-RL Caucasus Report*, <http://www.rferl.org/content/Article/1341802.html>.

Way, L. A. and Levitsky, S. (2006) The dynamics of autocratic coercion after the Cold War. *Communist and Post-Communist Studies* 39, 387–410.

Zhorzholiani, G., Lekishvili, S., Toidze, L. and Khoshtaria-Brosset, E. (1995) *Historic, Political and Legal Aspects of the Conflict in Abkhazia*, Georgian Academy of Sciences, Tbilisi.

Maroussia Ferry

Georgian Migrants in Turkey: Reconstruction of Gender and Family Dynamics

ABSTRACT: Drawn from a qualitative survey conducted in Kutaisi, Georgia and in Istanbul, Turkey, this chapter argues that migration tends to occupy a structural position in Georgian society. As a significant proportion of migrants are women (up to 65% in Greece and Turkey), many of whom leave behind spouses and children, it is worthwhile addressing the family and gendered outputs of migration. As Georgians enjoy particularly favourable conditions in regard to Turkish visa policies, we argue that Turkey/Georgia space has become a "circulatory territory" and that a highly gendered Turkish-Georgian "migratory system" is to be found. This generates specific behaviour patterns, norms and values that are mainly related to how to conciliate men's social role and women *de facto* autonomy.

KEYWORDS: Georgia, Turkey, circulatory migration, gender, family

Within the context of increasingly complex international migration, the particular case of mobility between Georgia and Turkey significantly exemplifies a number of important global socio-demographic and geopolitical developments. These include, in particular, the increasing feminization of labour migration (Anthias and Lazaridis, 2000; Reysoo, 2004), this being a somewhat overlooked aspect of regional integration in the Black Sea area.

The demise of the Soviet Union profoundly upset the global geopolitical balance and the frameworks of social practices and perceptions amongst people in the post-Soviet space. Within this space, the Republic of Georgia is endowed with a particularly rich experience of social and economic changes, having once been one of the most prosperous republics in the Soviet Union and quickly becoming one of the poorest after independence. For two centuries an appendage of the Russian Empire and the Soviet Union, Georgia suddenly entered the international scene in 1991. Its opening to market economy has brought about the impoverishment of the population of Georgia, while it also led to the emergence of actors that had so far been absent in the region, such as the United States and Turkey. These new actors are to be found at the political, financial, religious and business levels. But

I would rather explore the day-to-day aspect of these new links, which are created mostly through migration. Indeed, individual migration follows a path parallel to that of the geopolitical reorganization taking place in this region. Migration thus bulks large in the process known as "globalization", in a way that one could call "migration from below" (Tarrius, 2002).

Migration from the region, one may argue, was both made possible by the opening of borders and made necessary by the impoverishment of society. At any rate, it forms a privileged field of study to examine how Georgia has come to connect to neighbouring or faraway spaces, which were previously inaccessible, and how migration makes for new and regional cross-border social relations. These connections, and the mere fact of people migrating, become agents of change in Georgian social, cultural and religious ways of living; analysing these phenomena may also allow us to grasp what kinds of transformations are under way. Those changes affect economics, social organization and identities but the aim of this chapter will be to explore the family and gendered outputs of migration.

I would therefore first like to present some data concerning Georgian migration in Turkey in order to understand the process by which Georgia is newly connected to Turkey. This will be followed by a presentation of my survey results and an analysis of the gendered facet of this phenomenon. The chapter will set out the first results and some further lines of investigation drawn from an exploratory qualitative survey conducted in Kutaisi, Georgia and in Istanbul, Turkey. This survey consisted of ethnographic participant observations and interviews in a 24-family apartment block in Kutaisi and in an apartment shared by around 15 women in Istanbul.

Migration in Georgian Society

Like all countries after the collapse of the Soviet Union, Georgia underwent considerable impoverishment alongside deteriorating public services and armed conflicts on its territory. This led Georgians to begin migrating during the 1990s. Until now, these migrations have constantly increased. The latest quantified studies concerning migration were published by IOM in 2008. Between the 1989 and 2002 censuses, Georgia lost "almost 20% of its population to migration" (IOM, 2008), but this figure includes Jewish emigration to Israel and the Pontic Greek diaspora migrating to Greece. As many of the migrants are irregular and do not declare their status, it is very difficult to get a reliable figure, but all the literature about this topic stresses the significance of labour migration within Georgian society : "labor migration has become a common household survival strategy, with some estimates placing at least 1 million[1] Georgians living outside of the country" (Chelidze, 2006; IOM, 2008; Trouth Hofmann 2012: 28).

One of the most striking features of this migration is its high level of feminization. In 2002, according to the census, women represented 41% of migrants, this figure has increased and, according to some survey data, they now represent almost half of the recent migrants and around 64% of migrants to Turkey and Greece (Badurashvili, 2005; Zurabishvili and Zurabishvili, 2010; Trouth Hofmann, 2012: 119).[2] This last percentage is similar to estimates made for countries such as the Philippines where the subject of female migration has been widely studied (for example Parrenas, 2005).

When one considers that the remittances represented, for September 2011, 20% of the foreign exchange earnings of financial institutions, that around 9% of the population benefits from these remittances (Economic Policy Research Center, 2011b: 7) and that, according to the World Bank (CRRC, 2007: 17) only 38.5% of those sending remittances use bank transfers or money transfer services, the importance of the migration phenomenon for Georgian society is clear. According to Irina Badurashvili: "it is obvious that economic inputs of labor migration are extremely significant and they cannot be neglected in the analysis of social and economic situation of Georgia" (Badurashvili, 2004: 18). Consequently, it can be argued that there is a vital link between the Georgian social system and migration. Our first field survey observations also clearly reveal the importance attached to the issue of migration in everyday life, individual and familial strategies, conversations, life courses and so forth. Thus, figures and observations lead us to the statement that migration currently tends to occupy a structural position in Georgian society.

Although Turkey is not the main destination for Georgian migrants,[3] we believe that it is particularly worthwhile observing Georgian migration

1 The Georgian population being approximately 4.5 million.

2 Whereas men are still the majority migrating to Russia and the CIS countries.

3 Apart from Russia, Turkey is, nevertheless, among the top four destinations for the migrants (IOM, 2008).

to this country. This is firstly due to the particularly circular nature of this migration between Turkey and Georgia, which means that it is worthwhile making anthropological observations of the resulting mutations and patterns. Thus, according to Irina Badurashvili's (2004) survey, apart from the United States (298 US dollars sent per month and per person), Turkey is the most profitable country of immigration for Georgians: although wages are lowest there, it is the destination from which migrants send most money (US$ 194/month as against US$178 for Germany). This is due to the low cost of living in Turkey but we argue that it is also because links to the family in Georgia remain strong and generate particular economic behaviour. Secondly, this migration is interesting to observe because it is embedded within a context of relatively new and extremely significant regional exchanges that include the role played by Turkey in the Eurasian region and the dynamic of this region as a whole.

Migration in Turkey

In the Black Sea region and the Eurasian area in general, it is now well known that Turkey is the major pivotal territory: it is a significant place for exchange in the form of trading and migration but also for the transfer of political and religious ideas. This is due, firstly, to its geographical location at the gateway to Europe; secondly, its economic growth and, lastly, its migration policy. In all these respects, Turkey is situated at the exact point where the wealthy "North" and the busy reconstruction to the "East" (understood as a "new South")[4] meet one another. Consequently, Turkey plays a key role in the regional and global dynamics of population movements.

It can therefore be said that Turkey is a traditional country of emigration, an interface area for transit migrants and, more recently, a receiving country for an increasing number of migrants (Kirişci, 2008; İçduygu and Biriz Karaçay, 2012). Migration to Turkey began increasing in the beginning of the 1990s and has further increased since the early 2000's. In 1988, the total number of foreigners entering Turkey every year was around 3.4 million. This increased to 27 million in 2009 (Erder and Kaşka, 2012).

4 On this topic, see Mühlfried and Schiller (2011).

As most migrants in Turkey work illegally, most authors would stress the difficulty, if not impossibility, of establishing reliable figures.

However, it is possible to visualize the magnitude of migration through "tourist" entry statistics in Turkey. The number of migrants legally present on Turkish soil is relatively low: in 2008, there were only around 175 000. It is estimated that of the 27 million legal entries into Turkey in 2009, at least 10.5 million were represented by migrants (Erder and Kaşka, 2012). Naturally, because a large number of migrants travelling back and forth cross the border several times within the same year, this figure gives an idea of the intensity of population movements across Turkish borders rather than the actual number of migrants residing in Turkey. There have been very rough estimates, not always scientific, that migrants in a more-or-less irregular situation in Turkey represent between 150 000 and 2 million people (Erder and Kaşka, 2012).

Turkey is therefore now a country of immigration in its own right even though its migratory patterns are not the same as in Western Europe. While not being precise, these figures provide information concerning the main characteristics of migrants in Turkey. With the exception of migrants in transit, this is local, "to-and-fro" and short-term migration, mostly from neighbouring countries. It is encouraged by Turkish policies, which are liberal in terms of visas but set harsh conditions for the delivering of work permits to foreigners.[5] Erder and Kaska summarize Turkey's approach to migration as follows: "Turkey's relatively liberal border policy, its vast informal sector, extensive communal networks, unregulated migration regime and restrictive rules governing long stays for foreigners may be considered as peculiarities of the Turkish case" (Erder and Kaşka, 2012: 115).

According to most authors, the other "most striking change" (Erder and Kaska, 2012: 117) – both numerically and in terms of social representations – in Turkey's development as a country of immigration, is the massive inflow of nationals from the ex-Soviet republics. Only 4500 entered Turkey in 1988 and then, following the fall of the Soviet Union, 1.4 million in 2000 and 5.6 million in 2009 (Erder and Kaşka, 2012: 117). Nationals from the former Soviet Union accounted for 10% of entries in 1990

5 The opposite is also true as, for Kirişci, it is also the fact that these migrations are circulatory that encourages the Turkish government to be particularly liberal in terms of issuing visas to citizens from the ex-USSR and Balkan countries, unlike the policy practised with Middle Eastern countries (with the particular exceptions of Iran, Morocco and Tunisia) (Kirişci, 2008: 3–4).

(Kirişci, 2008: 2). This figure increased to 13.9% in 2000 and then reached a level of almost 21% in 2009 (Erder and Kaşka, 2012: 117). (See Figure 1 for this evolution and for the percentage of Georgian entries in it.) This particular kind of migration, entirely new on a cultural level and generating economic opportunities on both sides, inevitably became significant for social life in Turkey.

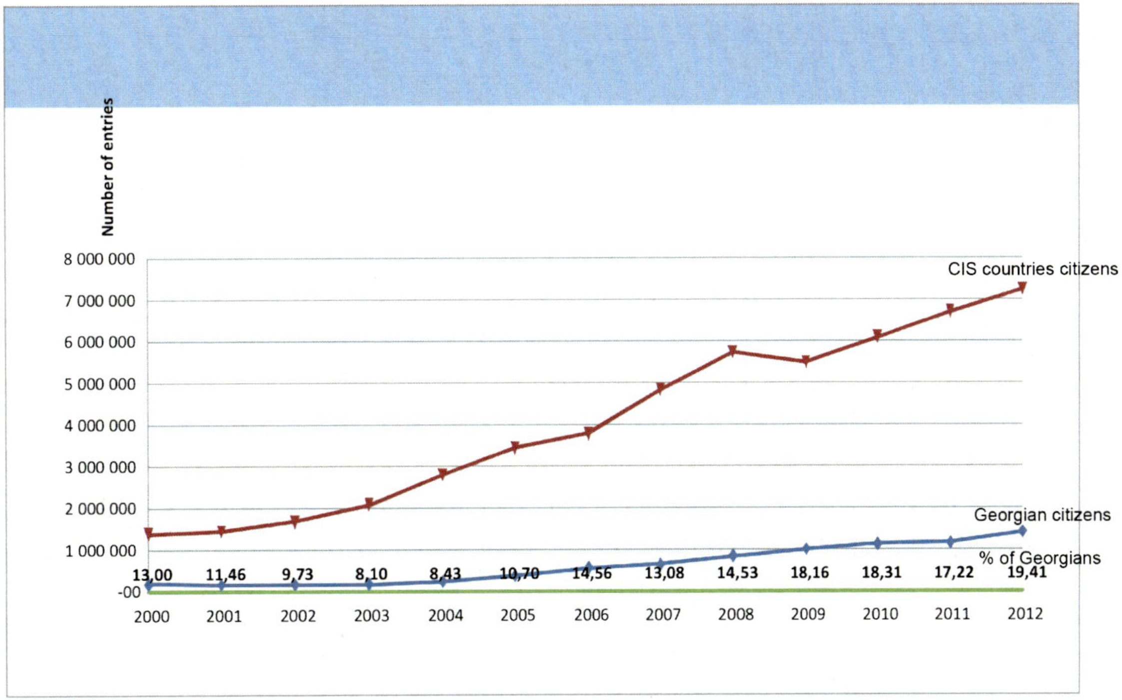

Figure 1: Tourist entries from CIS countries and Georgian citizens, 2000–12.

Source : Turkish Ministry of Tourism and Culture statistics.

The context of this migration, very briefly reviewed here, is of course, crucial in the case of Georgians in Turkey. As we will subsequently see, it is somehow paradigmatic of post-Soviet migrations in Turkey that lie somewhere "between regularity and irregularity" (Erder and Kaşka, 2012) because, although visa policies are "liberal" in Turkey, Georgians enjoy particularly favourable situation in this regard.

The Georgian–Turkish Space as a Circulatory Territory

At leadership level, Georgia and Turkey see each other as "friendly countries":[6] diplomatic relations are intense and summits and joint declarations common. Among other achievements, this cooperation led to the renovation of the Sarpi border post, the starting of the Baku–Tbilisi–Kars railway line project and the decision to make Batumi Airport a domestic airport for Turkey. It is mainly trade relations between the two countries that are seen as a priority. Bilateral trade reached US$1,104 billion in 2010, representing 16.5% of Georgia's total foreign trade, making Turkey Georgia's largest trading partner. On its website page titled "Relations between Turkey and Georgia", the Turkish Ministry of Foreign Affairs[7] comments on these good relations and mentions the "visa-free regime for tourist travel" enjoyed by the citizens of both countries.

In fact, since 2007, Georgians could legally stay for 3 months in Turkey. Georgians shared these favourable conditions with a large number of Latin American countries and, above all, with Iran and, more recently, Tunisia and Morocco. Most other nationals from the former Soviet countries are only allowed to stay for 30 days. Since February 2012 Georgians must wait for a period of three months before re-entering Turkey. However, migrants can get around this rule by paying an informal "fee" at the border and the statistics show that between the February–July period in 2011 and the same period in 2012, entries of Georgians increased by 20.17%.[8]

This liberalization of Turkey's visa policy almost coincides with the beginning of difficulties for Georgian seasonal workers and migrants in Russia that occurred in 2006 (see, among others, Mataradze and Muhlfried, 2009).

These relatively recent developments have driven an increase in the number of Georgians in Turkey. Gülay Toksöz and Çağla Ünlütürk Ulutaş, continuing the work by Atatimur (Atatimur, 2008: 121), have noted that "while the labour force profile of agencies in 2007 was composed of women from Moldova, Romania and Turkmenistan, others from Caucasian

6 At least under Mikheil Saakashvili's government.

7 See <http://www.mfa.gov.tr/relations-between-turkey-and-georgia.en.mfa> (accessed 26 October 2014).

8 According to the statistics of the Turkish Ministry of Tourism and Culture, <http://www.kultur.gov.tr/EN,36567/tourism-statistics.html> (accessed 26 October 2014).

countries, including Georgia in the first place, began increasing as from 2008"(Toksöz and Ünlütürk Ulutaş, 2012: 92). As a result, these migrants can legally reside long enough in Turkey to consider short return trips every 3 months to avoid finding themselves in an illegal situation, only the acquisition of work permits remaining irregular. The Georgian case is therefore paradigmatic because it has become possible for these "trans-migrants" to project themselves into a long-term future within this moving back and forth between Turkey and Georgia. By contrast, the 30 days permit of other former Soviet nationals means that it is almost impossible for them to make trips back to their home countries. This makes migration far more difficult. Thus, according to figures entered by nationality, it is clear that Georgia is particularly well represented: 2012 saw 1 404 882 Georgians enter Turkey, placing them in fifth position after Bulgarians and before Iranians for the first year (Table 1). When one consider the overall number of Georgians (roughly 4.5 millions), the extent of these transnational movements becomes clearer.

Table 1: Top eight nationalities entering Turkey, 2000, 2006, 2012.

2000		2006		2012	
Germany	2 277 505	Germany	3 762 469	Germany	5 028 745
United Kingdom	915 286	Russian Federation	1 853 442	Russian Federation	3 599 925
Russian Federation	677 152	United Kingdom	1 678 845	United Kingdom	2 456 519
United States	515 284	**Bulgaria**	**1 177 903**	**Bulgaria**	**1 492 073**
France	449 727	Netherlands	997 466	**Georgia**	**1 404 882**
Netherlands	439 819	**Iran**	**865 942**	Netherlands	1 273 593
Bulgaria	**381 545**	France	657 859	**Iran**	**1 186 343**
Iran	**380 819**	**Georgia**	**549 328**	France	1 032 565

Note: Entries that are probably not for tourist purposes are in bold.

Source: Turkish Ministry of Tourism and Culture statistics.

In addition to this, one should also consider the important integration of Turkish-Georgian cross-border space. First, Georgians are massively employed in the construction sector and as seasonal workers working in the tea and hazelnut plantations to be found in eastern Turkey. Here, economic interests combine with questions of identity because Kurds are

Turkish citizens and require higher wages as well as ethnically discriminated against, whereas Georgians, deemed to be "cheap and hard working" are also preferred for reasons of supposed cultural and linguistic similarities (Cigerci and Ulukan, 2010: 6; Erder and Kaşka, 2012 quoting Pelek, 2010), especially by the Laz people.[9] However, cross-border activities are not limited to the use of seasonal workers. As Kemal Kirişci noted: "Clearly, what started as circular migration in suitcase trade[10] and prostitution in the early 1990s has evolved and spread into economic activity in many sectors of the Turkish economy" (Kirişci, 2008: 5).[11] This is also true at a local level in the border region between Turkey and Georgia where many Georgians from the Batumi region are employed in small Turkish businesses, essentially for reasons of language (Cigerciand Ulukan, 2010: 6). Conversely, many Turkish construction companies employing Turkish workers are carrying out construction work in the area of Batumi, a town proving to be an attractive centre for Turks from eastern Turkey to visit for leisure and tourism and who are attracted by its casino, cheap and easily accessible alcohol and so forth.

This cross-border integration encourages the creation of links between Turkish and Georgian actors, and strengthens the opportunity for Georgian migrants to maintain a "stable" commuting relationship with Turkey, allowing them, in the words of Morokvasic (2004)[12] to truly "settle[d] in mobility". Recently, we have been able to see the beginning of something of a Georgian community[13] being formed in Turkey. For example, it is worth noting the opening[14] in 2010 of a Georgian restaurant inside Istanbul's Aksaray bus station, which serves the former Soviet Union countries and the Balkans. It was a Georgian gathering place and the decoration and quality of the food was far better than that to be found in other Georgian

9 The Laz speak a language related to Georgian and are considered ethnically close to Georgians.

10 "Suitcase trade" is a form of circular migration for the purpose of informal trading, which is mainly practiced by the former USSR population within Turkey. It involves buying small amounts of goods in a foreign country to sell them in the country of origin.

11 See also Piart (2010).

12 Even though Georgian migrants are constantly worried that the visa system could rapidly change, as it did in February 2012.

13 Taken in the least restrictive sense of the term.

14 This restaurant closed in March 2012 but another one reopened in Aksaray bus station a few weeks later.

cafeterias in the surrounding area. This is a further step towards the spatial anchoring of a group that, while creating a friendly and enhancing meeting place, also finds its own place in Istanbul's urban fabric. The opening of this restaurant was picked up by several local gastronomic blogs touting the "authenticity" of this setting where people joined together to drink, sing, fight and so forth, unlike the "touristic" Georgian restaurants to be found in the Beyoğlu district. These columns led intellectuals and executives to visit this restaurant, located right in the heart of a poor immigrant neighbourhood.

Consequently, we argue that the Turkish-Georgian space is tending to become a "circulatory territory" within the meaning given to this term by Alain Tarrius (1996): that trans-migrants use and appropriate the disparities of a territory, particularly those that are economic. This isn't done within a mental perspective structured by only two definite spaces, that is to say of a trip in one direction and then a hypothetical return, which is the rather classical pattern of postcolonial migration according to Sayad description (Sayad, 2006). In contrast, the "circulatory territory" unveils a widening of possible situations where the regularity and the flexibility of the various types of mobility shape the social environment.

While this "circulatory territory" forms part of and has a descriptive importance within the wider area of the Black Sea – with Turkey as a pivot – we feel that it is also highly significant from the Georgian point of view.

Thus, as migration tends to occupy a structural position in Georgian society, it also concerns women to a considerable extent and, since the Turkey/Georgia space has become a "circulatory territory", it can be suggested that a Turkish-Georgian "migratory system" of a highly gendered character has been established. It follows from the existence of this migration system that the family and social behaviour, as they are related to migration in Turkey, also tend to assume a certain regularity and thus generate specific behaviour patterns, norms, values and so forth. According to my informants, it would be "less prestigious" to migrate to Turkey than to Western Europe. Turkey, partly because it is predominantly Muslim, is not considered European and, unlike the West, is not seen as being an El Dorado or a place of high culture. It is also too close and too easy accessed to be a source of dreams. It is, in fact the banal, almost day-to-day nature of this migration that interests us. The study of this Georgian migration should provide information on how migration shapes lasting social relations, particularly gender relations. This takes place in a way that is somewhat different from the migration of Georgians to other countries such as Greece and Italy.

Gender Relations and Migration

Thus, to understand the links between migration and gender relations, it is necessary to try to identify the changing social context and constancies of gender relations in Georgia by not seeing them as a static environment but rather as an element relating dynamically with migration. Avenues of research and the initial results presented here come from two exploratory surveys conducted in Georgia and Turkey using the anthropological method of participant observation. Consequently, these investigations should be considered as illustrative of the migration phenomenon as it presents itself within specific social groups[15] rather than representative.

The central question highlighted by the first approaches suggested by the exploratory survey and the literature on gender relations in Georgia and the rest of the post-Soviet space highlights the tense and contradictory complexity of this situation.

In Georgia, the social differentiation of male and female roles remains very important, despite the establishment of policies promoting gender equality during the Soviet period. If, according to many authors, these policies "handed down from above" did not have a profound impact on the practices and representations in Georgia, it should nevertheless be noted that they resulted in an education among women that was almost equal to that of men as well as the massive participation of women in the labour market. In parallel with this, the role of women in Georgian society has recently undergone changes (Badurashvili, 2007; Badurashvili and al., 2008). For around the years 2000 and, more especially, since approximately 2005, the situation of women and the family has changed in Georgia under the influence (partial and complex) of Western lifestyles. For example, while the social norm of virginity before marriage is still highly present and

15 This method, known as the "snowball" method, is also justified by the fact that Georgian migrations are generally organized through informal networks. Only 10% of those interviewed by Irina Badurashvili found work by means other than their informal networks (Badurashvili, 2004: 16).

practised, it is beginning to be undermined in the capital and living with the husband's parents (also for economic reasons) is decreasing, although it still remains the situation of most young married couples. Age at marriage and first child is also increasing. However, "Westernization" continues to remain lower than in other post-Soviet countries such as Russia and Lithuania (Blum *et al.*, 2009; Aassve *et al.*, 2012). It is also worth noting a certain strengthening of religious practices among the younger generations who are the same as those influenced by the Western way of life.

The issue of gender relations in Georgia is also strongly linked to the disruption of social life after the fall of the Soviet Union. This has led to a deterioration of living standards and the social status of most families, including the affluent middle classes. In 2007, unemployment approached 40% (UNDP, 2008) and 25% of the population lived on less than US$2/day (Cigerci and Ulukan, 2010). As in most post-Soviet societies, women were more severely affected than men by poverty and their unemployment rate is slightly higher than that of men. However, most authors and our informants are willing to admit that they do not have the same reaction to this impoverishment and loss of social status. According to Zurabishvili and Zurabishvili (2010): "In the case of Tianeti [the village where they conducted their survey] we assume that women managed to adapt better to a changing economic situation than men, found new types of employment more easily than men, and felt more responsibility toward their families while men remained rather apathetic and depressed." Khomeriki (2003: 32) extends this finding to the entire country: "Women happened to be more flexible and better adapted to the new economic conditions." Without making excessive generalizations, it is possible to hypothesize that men, who identify more with their social status, would have been less able to support its loss. They would therefore have found it more difficult to work in nonprestigious sectors. This left many women with the breadwinning role[16] and this, as a chain reaction, weakened their traditional status. For example, according to Nora Dudwick (2003: 218), the difficulty of not being able to offer the traditional profuse hospitality was seen as a humiliation by men. Other authors have focused on post-Soviet male "frailty" or "emasculation"[17] and linked this to the massive and almost exclusively male

16 "... women serve as the primary breadwinners in 40% of Georgian households, although this is widely seen as a less-than-optimal situation" (Naskidashvili, 2011; Truth Hofmann, 2012: 33).

17 See Frederiksen (2011: 14) for an overview of this literature.

phenomena of alcoholism and drug addiction. The exploratory survey that I conducted in Kutaisi with 24 families living in two adjoining courtyard buildings inhabited by university professors and engineers illustrates this vividly. Among those families, five men died of heroin overdoses, three died of alcoholism, two are addicts and one of the latter became homeless. (See also UNDP, 2004.)

In addition to the exponential growth of labour demand for female workers in the West to work in the care sector, it is, according to my survey, one of the reasons that has allowed women to migrate in such large proportions. Both men and women agree that women are "better migrants" than men, because they are more "resourceful", more responsible, more reliable and, above all, faster to make savings to send as much money as possible to their families (see also Lundkvist-Houndoumadi, 2010; Zurabishvili and Zurabishvili, 2010). In many cases, it is also possible to identify causal relationships between the alcoholism and/or drug addiction of their husbands and the decision of the women to migrate. Often, the husband's death or separation from the husband represents the root cause. Of the 20 women interviewed in Istanbul,[18] a third are in this situation and, in the Kutaisi families, of the nine with a female member having migrated, seven had suffered the death, alcoholism or drug addiction of at least one family member.

Despite the important financial role, coupled with a certain degree of freedom due to geographical distance, acquired by women, the traditional perception of the distribution of social sex roles remains strong and valued (see, among others, UNDP, 2008). Margharita Lundkvist-Houndoumadi (2010) notes that, with female migration, there is a "contradiction between traditional gender expectations and actual practice" and that these practices are evolving faster than ideologies. However, we have seen that the dichotomy between fast-changing practices and conservative positions is not as clear. Conversely, there are also positions expressing a liberalization and "counter-practices" in this reaction to the destabilization of the male

18 In Turkey, the exploratory survey was essentially carried out in an apartment shared by around 15 migrant women, most of whom were working in the care sector. The apartment is located in the poor immigrant Aksaray district. I met also four isolated women in their places of work, employed by private citizens. Most of them held qualified jobs in Georgia: four were former teachers and five worked in the commercial sector. The others were administrative employees, bank employees and nurses. Only two were former housewives.

function. These aim to maintain a certain male power despite the distance and financial independence of women. Thus, it has been possible in women's networks to observe the presence of "go-between persons", often older female migrants who are friends of the family or come from the same area. They exercise a "soft" and noncoercive control by indirectly representing the male householder and the family. In Turkey, where return trips are more frequent and widely practiced, and where, as a result, the extended kinship, neighbourhood and friendship network is better maintained and livelier, the role of the "go-between" is increased.

But these "go-betweens", rather like communication technologies, could not be efficient without the complicity of the female migrants themselves. Since gender division norms are often shared and claimed by the women themselves, they would feel socially humiliated to be qualified as "immoral". This fear of acquiring a reputation for immorality is a powerful motivation for self-control, especially as the mere fact of being a migrant increases the risk of being suspected of immorality (Buckley and Trouth Hofmann, 2008). This suspicion is a lot stronger toward women migrating to Turkey where, for some, it continues to evoke the fantasy of Georgian women being kidnapped for the Sultan's harems, and most importantly that there, more than elsewhere, there is a considerable fear of women migrating for prostitution.[19] It can also be seen that a clear distinction between "good migrant" and "bad migrant" women (Lundkvist-Houndoumadi, 2010) is highly performative and limits profound changes in gender relations. We have also observed that some men stayed in Georgia and, despite being urbanized and educated, entrenched themselves in an ideological and cultural repertoire of honour in so far as all female family members are concerned, yet this honour system, in its hard conception, is considered by my informant themselves as "primitive". One might ask if the social anxiety (Linderman, 2001) caused by female migration has not led to honour becoming increasingly used as a reference. This is because it is closely linked to sexuality, an area where male control or "female self-control" is greatest. While Georgian society accepts in actual practice (while ambiguously reproving within discourses) that women can behave "like men" in

19 The recent story of the "Natashas" (see Gülçür and Ilkkaracan, 2002) remains present in people's memories and forms an integral part of the Turko-Georgian relationship. Numerous cases of human trafficking are also to be noted (IOM, 2000).

many aspects of their lives (particularly the economic aspect),[20] sexuality, and especially the issue of sexuality outside marriage, remains a fundamental taboo. Thus, the apartment shared by women surveyed in Istanbul was presented to me many times as being hermetically sealed against any male presence. Women who form a couple during the period of migration are seen as representative of "bad migrants".

But when the "forming of a couple" is not condemned but rather, on the contrary, sought and the distance brought about by migration makes it possible to take place, the concept of honour becomes more than just an idea that is discussed. For example, T., a former professor and migrant widow, told me that her life had been threatened by her son should she seek to live as a couple. We have seen that, among women migrants in Turkey, the husband was often lacking (in various ways) but that the large number of visits between the two countries maintained ties with the family. This particular migratory context, the example of T., as well as other elements found in the field, lead us to hypothesize that male authority tends to be transferred from husband to son. In a context where historical and social changes have been so rapid, it is inevitable that the generational issue is raised. Frederiksen (2011) points out that if the fragility of the male function affects all generations, it is necessary to distinguish the conditions under which it occurs in the "last Soviet generation" and in the "first post-Soviet generation".

Thus, when one aims to study the outputs of Georgian migration on the home state, one should consider that people started to migrate as their world collapsed, and, with it, their living standard, social status, values and feeling of security. Migrating has therefore to be seen as one among all survival strategies that had to be quickly invented in the 1990s (along with acquiring loans, small informal businesses and so forth). This emergency strategy lasted and stabilized to an extent but remained shaped by its history. Migration therefore has to be seen as material and symbolic violence made to Georgian society and as a very relevant way of analysing the social post-Soviet changes.

Unlike migrating to the European Union or the United States, which requires more planning and more capitalization, Turkey presents an easier and cheaper way of improving one's economic situation. Therefore, people

20 According to Mühlfried (2006: 8), quoted by Linderman (2001), for a woman to be described as being "manly" is even regarded favourably.

tend to migrate toward Turkey when they are in difficulty (Ferry, 2013). In addition, as Turkey was one of the first countries of migration from Georgia after the collapse of USSR, it became, for the Georgians, paradigmatic of this painful post-Soviet migration. While this includes the social organization and economic impacts of migration, Georgian migration to Turkey also has an interesting gender aspect. Indeed, this situation of predominantly female circulatory cross-border migration is particularly rich for examining the link between regular and independent female migration and the structure of gender relations, kinship and family in Georgia. The male function, which has already been undermined, is being even further disturbed by female migration. These women receive conflicting orders and invent practices that attempt to make compromises. The tension between interfering with and maintaining social sex roles already present in Georgian society is somewhat amplified and tested by the experience of migration in Turkey. In a sense it has become an extreme scenario that puts a patriarchal society to the test.

References

Aassve, A., Arpino, B. and Goisis, A. (2012) Grandparenting and mother's labour force participation: A comparative analysis using the generations and gender survey. *Demogaphic Research* 27(3), 53–84.

Anthias, F. and Lazaridis, G. (2000) *Gender and Migration in Southern Europe. Women on the Move*, Berg, Oxford.

Asriyan, N., Javakhishvili, D. J., Naibova, A. (2004) *Drugs situation in Southern Caucasus. Annual report, Programme of Assistance for the Prevention of Drug Abuse and Drug Trafficking in the Southern Caucasus. United Nation Development Programme,* Programme of Assistance for the Prevention of Drug Abuse and Drug Trafficking in the Southern Caucasus (SCAD Programme), Yerevan.

Atatimur, N. (2008) Reasons and Consequences of International Labor Migration of Women into Turkey: Ankara Case, M. A. Thesis, METU.

Badurashvili, I. (2004) *Determinants and Consequences of Irregular Migration in a Society under Transition. The Case of Georgia, Caucasus.*

Paper presented at the Annual meeting of the Population Association of America, Philadelphia, PA.

Badurashvili, I. (2005) *Illegal Migrants from Georgia: Labor Market Experiences and Remittance Behavior.* Proceedings of the XXV International Population Conference, Tours.

Badurashvili, I. (2007) Generational Relations and Integenerational Solidarity in Modern Georgian Society. Caucasus Research Resource Centers, *Research Paper*, Tbilisi. URL: <http://www.crrc.ge/uploads/files/publications/archive/Irina_Badurashvili_-_Eng.pdf>.

Blum, A., Lefèvre, C., Sebille, P. *et al.* (2009) La famille dans tous ces états: France, Géorgie, Lituanie, Russie. *Revue d'études comparatives Est-Ouest* 40(3–4), 5–35.

Buckley, C. and Trouth Hofmann, E. (2008) *Cultural Responses to Changing Gender Patterns of Migration in Georgia.* Proceedings of the Population Association of America Annual Meeting, New Orleans.

Chelidze, N. (2006) *Shromiti emigratisa postsabchota saqartvelodan.* [Labor migration from Post- Soviet Georgia], Lega, Tbilisi.

Cigerci U. N. and Ulukan, U. (2010) Cross-Border Labour Mobility within Georgia and Turkey. Proceedings of the Industrial Relations in Europe Conference, Oslo.

CRRC (2007) *Migration and Return in Georgia: Trends, Assessments, and Potential.* Report submitted to the Danish Refugee Council. Caucasus Research Resource Centers, Tbilisi.

Dudwick, N. (2003) No guests at our table – social fragmentation in Georgia, in *When Things Fall Apart – Qualitative Studies of Poverty in the Former Soviet Union* (eds N. Dudwick, E. Gomart and A. Marc). World Bank, Washington DC.

Economic Policy Research Center (2011a) *Employment and Unemployment trends in Georgia,* EPRC, Think Tank Fund of the Open Society Foundations, Tbilisi. URL: <http://www.osgf.ge/files/publications/2011/EPRC_Georgian_Economic_Outlook_II,_Nov_2011_ENG.pdf> (accessed 4January 2015).

Economic Policy Research Center (2011b) *The Role of Remittances in Georgian Economy,* EPRC, Think Tank Fund of the Open Society Foundations, Tbilisi. URL: <http://www.osgf.ge/files/publications/2011/Georgian_Economic_Outlook_III,_Dec_2011.pdf> (accessed 4 January 2015).

Erder, S. and Kaşka, S. (2012) Turkey in the New Migration Era: Migrants between Regularity and Irregularity, in *Turkey, Migration and the EU: Potentials, Challenges and Opportunities* (eds Seçil Paçacı Elitok and Thomas Straubhaar). Hamburg University Press, Hamburg.

Ferry, M. (2013) Female Migrants from Georgia: Profiles and Migratory Projects. *Caucasus Analytical Digest* 57, 8–10, Forschungsstelle Osteuropa, Bremen and Center for Security Studies, Zürich Research Centre for East European Studies, Bremen. URL : <www.isn.ethz.ch/Digital-Library/Publications/Detail/?ots591=0c54e3b3-1e9c-be1e-2c24-a6a8c7060233&lng=en&id=174486> (accessed 4 January 2015).

Frederiksen, M. D. (2011) Haunted by Time: Brotherhoods and Temporal Margins in the Republic of Georgia. Ph.D. Dissertation. Faculty of Humanities, University of Aarhus.

Badurashvili, I., Cheishvili, R., Kapanadze, E.,Tsiklauri, S., Sirbiladze, M. (2008) *Gender Relations in Modern Georgian Society,* United nations population fund (UNFPA) Georgian centre of population research (GCPR), Tbilisi.

Gülçür, L. and Ilkkaracan, P. (2002) The Natasha experience. *Women's Studies International Forum* 25(4), 411–421.

İçduygu, A. and Biriz Karaçay, A. (2012) Demography and migration in transition: reflections on EU-Turkey relations, in *Turkey, Migration and the EU: Potentials, Challenges and Opportunities* (eds Seçil Paçacı Elitok and Thomas Straubhaar). Hamburg University Press, Hamburg.

IOM (2000) *Irregular Migration and Trafficking in Migrants the Case of Georgia.* International Organisation for Migration Georgia, Tbilisi.

Chindea, A., Majkowska-Tomkin, M., Mattila, H., Pastor, I (2008) *Migration in Georgia: A Country Profile 2008.* International Organization for Migration, edited by Sheila Siar, Geneva.

Khomeriki, L. (2003) Gender equality in post Soviet Georgia, in *Building Democracy in Georgia. Discussion paper n°6.* International Institute for Democracy and Electoral Assistance, Stockholm.

Kirişci, K. (2008) Informal "circular migration" into Turkey: the bureaucratic and political context. *Analytic and Synthetic Notes*, 2008/21, Circular Migration Series; Political and Social Module, Robert Schuman Centre for Advanced Studies, San Domenico di Fiesole (FI): European University Institute, Florence. URL: <http://cadmus.eui.eu/bitstream/

handle/1814/8342/CARIM_AS%26N_2008_21.pdf?sequence=1> (accessed 4 January 2015).

Linderman, L. J. (2001) The gendered feast: experiencing a Georgian supra. *Anthropology of East Review* 29(2), 22–50.

Lundkvist-Houndoumadi, M. (2010) Treading on the fine line between self-sacrifice and immorality: Narratives of emigrated Georgian women. *Transcience Journal* 1(2), 50–70.

Mataradze, T. and Mühlfried, F. (2009) Leaving and being left behind: labor migration in Georgia. *Caucasus Analytical Digest* 4, 2–5.

Morokvasic, M. (2004) "Settled in mobility": engendering post-wall migration in Europe. *Feminist Review* 77, 7–25.

Mühlfried, F. (2006) Postsowjetische Feiern: Das Georgische Bankett im Wandel, in *Soviet and Post Soviet Politics and Society* (ed. Andreas Umland), ibidem-Verlag, Stuttgart.

Mühlfried, F., Schiller, F. Of Triple Winning and Simple Losing (2011) in, *The Caucasus and Central Asia, Twenty Years after Independences: Questioning the Notion of "South Countries"*, "Sudsov" programm Anr, Conference proceeding, Almaty.

Parrenas R. (2005) The gender paradox in the transnational families of Filipino migrant women. *Asian and Pacific Migration Journal* 14(3), 243–268.

Pelek, D. (2010) Seasonal Migrants Workers in Agriculture: The Cases of Ordu and Polatlı. Unpublished M.A. thesis. Bosphorus University.

Piart, L. (2010) Des mondes marchands mobiles: les commerçantes à la valise ouzbèkes, in *Dynamiques migratoires et changements sociétaux en Asie centrale* (ed. Marlène Laruelle). Éditions Pétra, Paris, 247–271.

Reysoo, F. (2004) Féminisation de la migration, in *Femmes en mouvement. Genre, migrations et nouvelle division internationale du travail* (eds Fenneke Reysoo and Christine Verschuur). Swiss National Commission for UNESCO and IUED, Berne/Geneva, 17–27.

Sayad, A. (2006) *L'immigration ou les paradoxes de l'altérité. 1. L'illusion du provisoire*, Raisons d'agir, Paris.

Sumbadze, N.(2008) *Gender and Society: Georgia. United Nation Development Programme Georgia*,Tbilisi.

Tarrius, A. (1996) Territoires circulatoires et espaces urbains. *Annales de la Recherche Urbaine* 59–60, 50–59.

Tarrius, A. (2002) *La Mondialisation par le bas: les nouveaux nomades de l'économie souterraine,* Edition Balland, Paris.

Toksöz, G. and Ünlütürk Ulutaş, Ç. (2012) Is migration feminized? A gender- and ethnicity-based review of the literature on Irregular Migration to Turkey, in *Turkey, Migration and the EU: Potentials, Challenges and Opportunities* (eds Seçil Paçacı Elitok and T. Straubhaar), Hamburg University Press, Hamburg.

Trouth Hofmann, E. (2012) "Today Everything is Backwards": Gender Ideology and Labor Migration in the Republic of Georgia. PhD. dissertation. University of Texas.

Zurabishvili, T. and Zurabishvili, T. (2010) The feminization of labor migration from Georgia: the case of Tianeti. *Laboratorium* 1, 73–83.

Part IV
Living with Protracted Conflicts

Peter Kabachnik, Beth Mitchneck and Joanna Regulska

Return or Integration? Politicizing Displacement in Georgia

ABSTRACT: Displacement in Georgia is highly politicized. By invoking inflated numbers of IDPs, failing to integrate them, or trying to discourage spontaneous return, the Georgian government's actions at times point to their use of IDPs as a political weapon. We examine the discourses and policies surrounding IDPs, including laws designed to deal with them, institutions that manage them, and political statements about IDPs, as forms of governmentality and geopower. We critically assess Georgian IDP policies and discourses, documenting the shift from solely prioritizing return to, after 2007, allowing room, alongside the rhetoric of return, for a specific understanding of integration. Our analysis highlights how, for the Georgian government, the meaning of integration is constructed in a narrow fashion, primarily understood as the provision of housing.

KEYWORDS: internally displaced persons (IDPs), Georgia, Abkhazia, displacement, governmentality, geopower, integration, return

Introduction

Displacement, and the networks, policies, and institutions that seek to govern and manage the displaced, are always politicized (Zetter, 1991; Holtzman and Nezam, 2004; Haider, 2010).[1] In Georgia, the resolution of displacement and the right of the displaced to return is highly politicized (Mundt and Ferris, 2008; Mooney, 2011). Internally displaced persons (IDPs) have been a major concern for the Georgian government and, since 1992, hundreds of legislative acts have been adopted to manage IDPs

1 Accusations of politicization are often politicized too, however (see Onlinenews.Ge, 2011). While this paper focuses on politicization of the displaced by the Georgian government, this is not meant to downplay the politicization carried out by Abkhazian, South Ossetian, and Russian authorities as well.

(Tarkhan-Mouravi, 2009; UNHCR, 2009).[2] Despite this attention, a comprehensive IDP policy was not seriously contemplated by the Georgian government until 2006, through the State Strategy document, 15 years after the first major wave of Georgian displacement ended. Until then return was the only resolution acceptable and, indeed, mentioned by most Georgian politicians. This chapter will critically assess Georgian IDP policies and discourses, documenting the shift from solely prioritizing return to constructing a specific understanding of integration, all of which impact the lives of IDPs.

We examine the discourses and policies surrounding IDPs, including laws designed to deal with them, institutions that manage them, and political statements about IDPs, as a form of governmentality (Foucault, 1991).[3] Governmentality is concerned with how governments actively produce their subjects and the "organized practices and techniques through which subjects are governed" (Bracke and Fadil, 2012: 77). This attention to IDPs, coupled with the failure or inability of the Georgian state to fully address the needs of IDPs, points to the need to examine the myriad of institutions, policies, practices and discourses that construct and constrain IDPs. Thus, labelling people as IDPs and politicizing displacement are important concerns because they place the government in a position of dominance over IDPs and IDP issues, effectively reducing IDPs voices and perspectives. These processes marginalize and exclude the displaced from their own management (Bariagaber, 1999), potentially limiting their perspectives and agency.[4] Being labelled as "displaced" by the state they are in and by the international community is a powerful form of institutionalization that actively produces these identity categories and makes them meaningful and knowable, thus making the displaced objects of analysis, accounting and control.[5] These bureaucratic practices and administrative categories help to provide common experiences that the displaced draw upon (Vetters, 2007).

2 The government's concern has encompassed both political and humanitarian issues.

3 See Rose-Redwood (2006) for a detailed examination of Foucault's notion of governmentality.

4 It should be noted that IDPs are not passive, but actively and creatively contend with their circumstances despite constraints and unequal power relations (Dunn, 2012a, 2012b; Kabachnik *et al.*, 2013).

5 There are many cases of the displaced resisting and transforming the labels that categorize them (e.g. Zetter, 1991; Owusu, 2000; Rotas, 2004; Phillips, 2011).

The Georgian government policies that are implemented to manage displacement, illustrate "geo-power", "an ensemble of technologies of power concerned with the governmental production and management of territorial space" (Ó Tuathail, 1996: 7). Thus IDPs become tools for the continuing claims of Georgian territorial integrity, as their bodies become conflated with the geobody of the national state (Kabachnik, 2012). Politicizing displacement, by, for example, President Saakashvili promising that Abkhazia will be under Georgian control soon, can shape IDPs hopes and identities (Kabachnik *et al.*, 2013), further reproducing their desire to return (Kabachnik *et al.*, 2010), which can have ramifications in terms of who they blame for their displacement (Kabachnik *et al.*, 2012), how they feel and what place-making practices they perform in their current places of residence. Internally displaced persons are further entangled with the machinations of the state and the government bureaucracy through their IDP status, which entitles them to certain resources, like monthly stipends and other benefits.

The Georgian government attempts to control, manage and politicize IDPs through various governmental processes, including categorization, counting, policies directed towards them, and parallel and segregated services and institutions created for them. These processes reveal what Dunn (2012a) has termed, an "adhocracy", where there are often unclear, competing, and improvised rules, which can lead to a "great deal of anxiety on both the part of the powerful and the powerless" (Dunn and Cons, 2014: 104). Separate institutions and policies for IDPs, like government and schools, the My House property registration programme and the disapproval of informal returnees, are all indicative of governmentality that actively politicizes displacement in order to utilize IDPs to exercise geo-power by fostering territorial claims over Abkhazia and South Ossetia, where Georgian sovereignty has been challenged and deposed by the *de facto* authorities.

We begin our discussion with an overview of how population figures are invoked to politicize and gain international attention. For the remainder of the chapter, we illustrate how the Georgian government exhibited two distinct patterns in terms of its approach towards IDPs (Mitchneck *et al.*, 2009: 1024). Prior to 2007, the focus was explicitly on return of IDPs. From 2007 on, there was marked shift, although return was still prioritized, with integration appearing on the agenda. Next, we provide an overview of the ways that displacement was politicized and local integration was hindered in Georgia prior to 2007. The examples we discuss illustrate how the government's main goal was not to integrate IDPs but to use IDPs as a tool to foster territorial claims over Abkhazia and South Ossetia (the exercise of geo-power). Then we document the shift in policy, following 2007, while still focused on return, made room for the discussion of local integration. This was a major development, as now a significant amount of attention, planning, and funding has been put towards policies of integration. Our analysis highlights how, for the Georgian government, integration is understood primarily as the provision of housing.

Governmentality and the Number Game: Counting IDPs

The official population figures of IDPs have fluctuated widely,[6] though there has been a consistent, and more realistic, downward trend in the reporting of IDP numbers.[7] Politicizing displacement makes exaggerating the amount of displaced persons more likely. Indeed, larger numbers are claimed in order to stir international sympathy for Georgia, condemnation of the separatist territories, and to acquire more international aid, while agencies dealing with IDPs pursue certain institutional objectives. Essentially, population numbers tie into the Georgian geo-power strategy because the larger the amount of displaced persons, the better their claim to territory. Therefore, it pays to review how IDP population figures have been utilized. In 1999, UNHCR statistics showed 278 500 IDPs in Georgia, and was usually rounded up to 280 000 (NRC, 2004: 33). In 2001, the Georgian government calculated the IDP population at 272 101 (266 000 of those from Abkhazia), even though the MRA extrapolated the number to be 245 700 (NRC, 2003: 31–32). Then the figures of 264 000, 257 000, and 261 000 (with 249 000 from Abkhazia) were used in 2002 (NRC, 2003: 29–30), and 260 000 in 2003 (NRC, 2004: 31). Georgian government figures, as of November 2004, listed 237 069 (224 947 from Abkhazia) or 241 000 IDPs (NRC, 2005: 36; IDMC, 2007). 247 000 IDPs are cited in the 2007 State Strategy, and many studies would use the figure of 250 000.

6 Population data for IDPs are less reliable, and more variable, than those for refugees (Mundt and Ferris, 2008).

7 An increase in numbers can appear to occur due to the fact that children of IDPs are classified as IDPs in Georgia.

The actual number of displaced in Georgia was likely to be lower, with those displaced from Abkhazia and South Ossetia at roughly 209 000 and 13 000 respectively, for a total of 222 248 (Conciliation Resources, 2009: 10; Tarkhan-Mouravi, 2009: 17; UNHCR, 2009: 6). The count of 222 248 is tabulated by the Ministry of Refugees and Accommodation (MRA), though the Georgian government has not endorsed that version. An IDP re-registration process that was conducted between April 2007–April 2008 calculated 218 858 IDPs in Georgia, of which 206 538 were from Abkhazia and the remaining 12 320 from South Ossetia (UNHCR, 2009: 10). This figure also included the 45 000–60 000 informal returnees to the Gali region (see discussion below) and the 2000 residents of the Kodori Gorge who were not displaced prior to 2008 yet were still counted as IDPs.

The variation in estimates of the IDP population size raises doubts as to the validity of these estimates and points to the difficulties in proper accounting and registration of IDPs. While official estimates of the number of IDPs in Georgia have decreased over the years, pronouncements from government officials have shown the opposite phenomenon. In March of 2010, the Georgian ambassador to Israel, Vakhtang Joashvili, used the figure of 300 000 displaced, whereas the Georgian ambassador to the United Kingdom, Giorgi Badridze stated that 350 000 people were displaced from Abkhazia (Badridze, 2010). Grigol Vashadze, the Minister of Foreign Affairs of Georgia, states that 500 000[8] were displaced in the early 1990s (Vashadze, 2009). In 2007, Saakashvili stated the improbable number of displaced numbering between 400 000 and 500 000 (BBC, 2007). Again, in 2010 and 2011, Saakashvili asserted that 500 000 were expelled from Abkhazia (Civil Georgia, 2010a; Kupunia, 2011).

While these estimates are undoubtedly inaccurate due to the fact that the entire population of Abkhazia, according to the 1989 Soviet Census, was 525 061, speaking about everyone displaced from Abkhazia, not just Georgians, can offer some increase in numbers due to the fact that most of the Jewish, Greek, Russian, and Estonian communities fled to their kin states. However, Saakashvili did not state that the displaced include IDPs in Georgia and refugees who have gone to countries like Estonia, Greece, and Israel but, in a speech given in 2008, said that the 450 000–500 000 displaced "residents of Abkhazia live in exile in their own country", an

8 He also offers a figure of 50 000 people who died during the Georgia–Abkhazia conflict. Independent assessments usually provide the figure of 10 000 killed (Amnesty International, 1998).

outright exaggeration (Civil Georgia, 2008). Currently, the official count of IDPs in Georgia is 256 103 (Mooney, 2011). This includes 238 187 IDPs displaced in the 1990s and 17 916[9] IDPs displaced during the 2008 war.

Pre-2007: Return as the Explicit Policy Goal

Initially, before 2007, the emphasis was predominantly on return.[10] Prior to 2007, local integration of IDPs proceeded at an alarmingly slow pace because integration was considered antithetical to the goal of return. The Georgian government understood local integration as detrimental to their goals as they feared that IDPs would not want to return if their living conditions were decent (Deng, 2003). Developing a policy and therefore encouraging integration of IDPs was seen as unnecessary because, according to official rhetoric, return would occur in the short term. Four key instruments of governmentality and geo-power have been critical to establishing policy: electoral policy; the establishment of the parallel Abkhaz government in exile administration and Abkhaz public schools; the refusal to encourage informal returnees to the Gali region of Abkhazia; and the My House property registration programme. All will be discussed briefly below.

IDP Electoral Policy

One of the central means by which local integration of IDPs was initially not supported by the previous Georgian government, headed by Eduard Shevardnadze, was through electoral policy. Although having the ability to vote locally and having the right to return to where one was displaced from

9 Initially, the 2008 war displaced 158 700 people but most were able to return home by October 2008.

10 Prioritizing the return of the displaced is a normative claim underpinned by a sedentarist perspective, which conflates identity and territory (Malkki, 1992). In the sedentarist and rooted logic of nationalist territorialization, the return of refugees restores the natural order. However, the focus on return is often counterproductive and even goes against the wishes of many of the displaced (Jansen, 2006).

are not incompatible, many IDPs did see it as a zero-sum game (Bagshaw, 2000).[11]

Thus local integration, for most IDPs and government officials, had been equated to the loss of the separatist territories and abandoning the right to return. Government officials did little to dispel this myth as seen through the policies they advocated and the statements they made. A Georgian government official offered the conventional wisdom on the issue by stating that promoting the local integration of IDPs would be to "effectively concede to 'ethnic cleansing'" (Mooney and Jarrah, 2004: 36). Between 2001 and 2003 these voting restrictions were struck down by Georgia's Constitutional Court.[12]

The Abkhaz Government in Exile and Abkhaz Public Schools

These parallel institutions and governmental bodies are a form of geo-power in that they seek to maintain a territorial claim and political legitimacy over space no longer under the control of Tbilisi. A wide array of institutions, such as police, schools, and hospitals, were transferred from Abkhazia and kept operating after the 1992–93 conflict, along with payments continuing to those employed there. The ethnic Georgian government officials, who had walked out of the paralyzed Abkhazian Supreme Soviet and began meeting separately prior to the outbreak of hostilities, were also kept and re-established as the Government of the Autonomous Republic of Abkhazia but usually referred to as the Abkhaz Government in Exile.

The 10 parliamentary representatives who were in place at the time of displacement had last been elected in 1992 and would remain in power indefinitely, with no elections to take place for their positions until the conflict had been solved. While this did ensure IDPs maintained a presence in government, issues important for IDPs did not necessarily make it on the agendas of the politicians representing them because IDPs had

11 Internally displaced persons could not vote in local elections, nor could they vote in electing majoritarian MPs to the Parliament (in a first-past-the-post system) (although they could vote through the proportional system) until August 2001, nearly 10 years after their displacement.

12 Similarly, it was not until 2003 that IDPs received full property rights, meaning they could then buy land without losing their IDP status, their entitlement to return and potential for property restitution (Ferris *et al.*, 2012).

no mechanism to vote them out if they did a poor job (Sumbadze and Tarkhan-Mouravi, 2003). These politician's positions were finally vacated after the parliamentary elections of 28 March 2004.

During Shevardnadze's rule, Tamaz Nadareishvili, who was openly militant towards the *de facto* Abkhazian authorities and regularly took uncompromising stances on the issue of conflict resolution, headed the Abkhazian government in exile. The Abkhaz government in exile proceeded to derail and hinder many proposals for reconciliation (Kharashvili, 2001: 235). Nadareishvili wrote several books alleging the "genocide" of Georgians at the hands of Abkhazians (Conciliation Resources, 2009: 15; e.g. Nadareishvili, 1997). He also allegedly supported militia activities in Gali (Amnesty International, 1998; Conciliation Resources, 2009: 15). He was pressured to resign and did so in January 2004 (Conciliation Resources, 2009).

Many IDPs attended IDP-only schools, run by the Abkhazian government in exile's Ministry of Education and Culture. Between 1995 and 2005, there were 45 IDP schools, officially known as Abkhaz public schools (Loughna *et al.*, 2010). Georgia has received criticism over IDP schools as another example of the failure to integrate IDPs (e.g. Greenway, 2009; Mitchneck *et al.*, 2009). When comparing IDP schools with local schools, evidence suggests that, while students did have similar levels of academic achievement, IDP schools usually had less resources and dilapidated infrastructure (Loughna *et al.*, 2010: 6). The number of IDP schools went from 45 to 24 by the middle of 2008, indicating a shift in policy, and 13 schools remain in operation today (DRC, 2010; Loughna *et al.*, 2010; IDMC, 2012). The government intended to close the schools that remained but decided to remove that stipulation from the latest version of the Action Plan based on feedback from IDPs themselves (DRC, 2010). The remaining IDP schools are to be "reverse integrated", with enrolment of the general population to continue, as most already have non-IDP students attending (DRC, 2010).

While many IDP youth have no issues in attending local schools, some IDP parents opt to send their kids to IDP schools for financial (cheaper), practical (closer), and psychological (avoid stigmatization) reasons. Another reason parents prefer IDP schools is that they want their children, many of whom do not remember or have never been to Abkhazia, to develop love and pride for their former homes. These schools instil and preserve IDP children's pride, belonging, and patriotism for Abkhazia (Scarborough *et al.*, 2006), which may forestall some connections with their current places of residence and further reproduce their desire to return.

Returnees to Gali

We can witness the government's focus on return in the negotiations as the Georgian position demands the return of all IDPs,[13] as well as in how the government contends with the IDPs who have returned to the Gali region, some seasonally, others more permanently. Whether through formal or informal means, the Georgian government has discouraged informal returnees, in part to better control IDPs and to reinforce geo-power through their claim over the territory of Abkhazia. Estimates suggest between 45 000–65 000 people have returned to the Gali region, with an additional seasonal migration of 3000 to 5000 people (ICG, 2007; Loughna *et al.*, 2010; ICG, 2008; HRW, 2011). These returnees are seen as informal and are not documented by the UNHCR as official returnees due to the Georgian government's opposition to classifying them as such.

Returnees have had to deal with harassment, crime, and insecurity at the hands of the Abkhazian authorities and organized criminal gangs but there is also ample evidence of their intimidation by Georgians as well, through posters, phone calls, violence and kidnappings (Amnesty International, 1998; NRC, 2005; ICG, 2007; Johnson, 2010; HRW, 2011). Throughout the 1990s and early 2000s, returnees to Gali felt pressured by Georgian authorities not to go back to their homes in Gali and were threatened by ostracism and were openly criticized. On 15 February 2002, Tamaz Nadareishvili referred to Gali returnees as "cowards and traitors" (Korsaia *et al.*, 2002). Reporters state that many Gali IDPs refuse to appear on camera due to fear of criticism by other IDPs and Georgian officials (Korsaia *et al.*, 2002).[14] Internally displaced persons in Gali were (and by some accounts still are) pressured not to vote or take jobs offered by the Abkhazian government. Many of these pressures were conducted by Georgian guerrilla groups, like the Forest Brothers and the White Legion, which were

13 The Abkhazian side will not even begin to discuss the fate of IDPs until their political status is acknowledged.

14 This hesitancy, mistrust, and secrecy continue today, as evidenced by unwillingness to answer questions or provide honest responses to interviewers (O'Loughlin *et al.*, 2011).

very active in the Gali region until 2004 and received both tacit and overt support from the Georgian government (Amnesty International, 1998).

The "My House" Program

In February 2006, Saakashvili issued Presidential Decree #124, which spawned the My House program (UNHCR, 2009: 30). The "Presidential Program" My House, another case of using geo-power to lay claim to the lost territories through the IDPs, consisted of identifying and registering all property claims of Georgian IDPs from Abkhazia and South Ossetia. This form of governmentality highlights the claims that IDPs have over the territories and reproduces their memories and attachments to their former homes.[15] Geographical technologies, in the form of satellite photos and GIS, were used to survey and lay claim to properties belonging to IDPs, who would be issued with certificates.

The My House programme brought the issue of property rights and restitution to the forefront for many IDPs, reproducing the IDPs' ties to Abkhazia and South Ossetia. The My House program, with so much money being spent (3 million lari) and the issuing of certificates, renewed the hopes of many IDPs that they will be able to be compensated or else be able to regain their properties. 52 615 households (49 270 from Abkhazia and 3345 from South Ossetia) had registered by October 2006 (UNHCR, 2009: 31). However, criticisms abounded stating that this program was a politicized public relations campaign offering little to IDPs of practical value (Mooney, 2011). By documenting the governmentality at work in these four main areas, we have illustrated various ways the Georgian government has highlighted return as the explicit policy goal prior to 2007.

15 This is further made clear in the My House programme website, which offers photos of Abkhazia and as the images scroll in the banner atop the page, the words "We Will Return!" and "Georgia – Will be United!" flash across the screen. See http://www.chemisakhli.gov.ge/index.php?lang_id=GEO&sec_id=1&lang_id=ENG.

2007–Present: Local Integration Finally on the Agenda

Integration

Between 2007–8, the post-Rose Revolution government began to make a remarkable turnaround by prioritizing local integration, first rhetorically (just by mentioning local integration as an important goal) and, later, through implementation of programmes to reach that goal. Integration is considered a key goal for forced migrants by the nongovernmental structures that manage and assist the displaced (UNHCR, 2006). We see integration as a "two-way process" that "involves both the newcomers and the host society and requires adaptation on the part of both parties" in employment, health, housing, education, as well as other cultural, legal, and social domains (da Lomba, 2010: 418). While definitions of integration vary (Vrecer, 2010), integration is conceptualized as best approached through a broad lens, encapsulating a wide variety of issues, for both the new arrivals and the local population. But when a government espouses policies of integration, what conception of integration are they invoking? Indeed, understandings of integration can vary widely among actors in the governance environment (Mitchneck *et al.*, 2009).

The Georgian government exhibits a pattern where integration is reduced to housing. As Mitchneck *et al.* (2009: 1030) illustrate, competing narratives of integration led to policy initiatives that expected IDP integration to "result from simply changing geographic location". Little attention has been given to probing how governments frame integration and what meanings of integration are constructed by policies and discourses (Mitchneck *et al.*, 2009). In this section, we aim to fill this gap and focus on the post-2007 strategies that indicate integration policies are being implemented and what conception of integration the Georgian government is relying on. The definition will inevitably affect policy which in turn is another instrument of governmentality to control IDPs by identifying what type of housing is legitimate and, in many cases, relocates IDPs to places the government has selected.

The State Strategy and Action Plan

The State Strategy on IDPs was developed in 2006 and ratified in February 2007. The two main goals of the strategy are, first, to return IDPs to their homes and, secondly, to integrate IDPs in their current locations in the interim period.[16] Thus the State Strategy and Action Plan are reflective of geo-power, namely retaining territorial claims through the bodies of IDPs. The government did exhibit a considerable shift with its willingness to even discuss local integration, previously a taboo topic as "temporary integration" was the key term (Sumbadze and Tarkhan-Mouravi, 2003). The State Strategy highlighted the needs to improve living conditions and prioritize local integration until return was possible. However, the Action Plan, which would entail the start of the implementation of the State Strategy policies, approved a few days before the August 2008 war, was delayed due to the conflict with Russia. It has been put into place since 2009, albeit unevenly. Despite the State Strategy's solid outline and framework of how to address the most pressing needs of IDPs (housing, social service provision, employment and training), the Georgian government has been extremely slow in designing the implementation plan. In fact, the Action Plan was revised twice since its initial delay in 2008. First it was revised to include those displaced during the 2008 war and finally approved on 28 May 2009. The Action Plan was revised yet again on 11 May 2010 to provide more transparency and better outreach to IDPs to make them more aware of their available options (Amnesty International, 2010).

The rhetoric of return still dominated even after the publication of the State Strategy (Mooney, 2011). For Saakashvili's campaign for the 5 January 2008 presidential election, he once again prioritized territorial integrity (Kabachnik, 2012), promising to return IDPs to their former homes and castigating international organizations for wanting IDPs to integrate into their local communities (Conciliation Resources, 2009: 13). The real turning point came later in 2008, as pronouncements were translated into actual practices and the implementation of the State Strategy began (Walicki, 2011). The 2008 war helped to spur, due to the millions of dollars pledged to Georgia by the international community (US$4.5 billion) the potential

16 According to the State Strategy: "1. Create conditions for dignified and safe return of IDPs. 2. Support decent living conditions for the displaced population and their participation in society."

for better prospects for local integration, while simultaneously forestalling any chances for return indefinitely (Mundt and Ferris, 2008).

It was at this time of the creation of a new wave of IDPs that the issue of local integration began to appear more frequently in government discourse. For instance, in February 2011, Saakashvili highlighted the need to improve IDPs living conditions and resettle them into their own private accommodation (Mooney, 2011).[17] In June 2012, President Saakashvili promised to provide every IDP with their own apartment before he left office (GISC, 2012). This is not only an example of politicizing IDP hopes and living conditions but it also indicates the direction of the discourse on integration and housing provision.

Overall, the government has made progress in implementing its 2007 strategy for IDPs.[18] Since 2008, the Georgian government's accomplishments include building and refurbishing housing and setting standards to guide the implementation process with the international community. This has improved the living conditions of many IDPs (IDMC, 2012: 1). The government initiated a three-phrase approach to contend with the issue of providing permanent housing for all IDPs. It was able to implement many programmes, including providing cash payments, refurbishing collective centres, and transferring ownership of public building to IDPs (Walicki, 2011; Ferris *et al.*, 2012). Unfortunately, implementation became more difficult after 2009, when international funding dried up.

Despite these developments, barriers and challenges remain. For instance, the construction of new cottages for IDPs, which was implemented by the Ministry of Interior, has been criticized for poor standards (Gvasalia, 2010; Mooney, 2011). However, the government was trying to provide more suitable homes for the displaced as quickly as possible, as there was an urgent need to ameliorate the substandard living conditions of IDPs and free up the spaces they were residing in so that they could be restored to their original functions (for example, to allow schools to reopen for students). Since the construction of these houses began very quickly after the displacement of third-wave IDPs, IDPs from the early 1990s were upset at the quick response because they remained living in dilapidated

17 Although he still mentioned that the IDP issue is not over until they can return home.

18 Government support also includes a monthly stipend of 14/11 lari (private accommodation/collective centre) per month between 2000–5, which rose to 28/22 lari per month between 2005–11. This amount needs to be supplemented by IDP families as it is not enough to cover basic needs (Mooney, 2011).

conditions. While the government did provide much-needed housing for the displaced, these 38 villages housing 17 916 IDPs from the 2008 conflict, the presumed goal of local integration remained unmet. These new villages were spatially segregated from the general population,[19] offered little to no employment opportunities and suffered from poor infrastructure, indicating that, for the government, integration was equated solely with providing housing.

At the end of 2010, the Ministry of Internally Displaced Persons from the Occupied Territories, Accommodation and Refugees of Georgia announced plans to evict IDPs from their current residence in state-owned buildings (Modebadze, 2010; Civil Georgia 2010c). This has led to multiple rounds of evictions and relocations, affecting thousands of IDPs.[20] There have been cases of failure to adhere to promises regarding compensation to evicted IDPs made half a year earlier (Civil Georgia, 2010b). Many IDPs are unhappy with the amount of the voucher they receive because it cannot offer them a similar type of apartment in the area they are being evicted from (Modebadze, 2010; Civil Georgia, 2010c). IDPs also complained of short notice, lack of information,[21] and undesirable[22] alternative housing (Amnesty International, 2011; Corso, 2011; Walicki 2011; Ferris *et al.*, 2012). These examples reveal that many IDPs feel uncomfortable and powerless at the level of spatial management and control that the government has over their lives.

The Georgian government challenges this version of events, arguing that the relocation process itself has been politicized by certain political groups (Mooney, 2011). The government cites the current poor living conditions of IDPs as justification for the relocation of IDPs to rehabilitated spaces. As of 2011, only a quarter of eligible IDPs displaced during the early 1990s have been relocated into new accommodation (Corso, 2011).[23]

19 A major contributing factor for the decision to create separate villages for IDPs was to keep people displaced from the same villages together, a preference voiced by many IDPs.

20 The latest round of evictions and relocations showed a marked improvement over the criticisms leveled at the first round (Mooney, 2011: 220).

21 In 2009–10, a hotline phone number was created and this helped IDPs with information access (Mooney, 2011).

22 IDPs are relocated to remote rural areas with few income-generating opportunities.

23 MRA officials have justified the delays due to "the cost and sheer number of people to be resettled" (Corso, 2011), as they have limited funds with which to implement programmes (IDMC, 2010).

Conclusion

In this chapter we argued that analysing the policies and tools of governmentality and geo-power used by the Georgian government reveal the narrow meaning of integration applied by the state and its institutions. This, in turn, became a part of the politicizing strategy that the Georgian government simultaneously relies upon on and constructs. This has remained an effective strategy utilized by different governments in Georgia to garner international support, both politically and financially, and to continue to maintain the doctrine of territorial integrity. Internally displaced persons become a key element in the exercise of geo-power as it is through them, in part, that the government manages space, and their displacement reinscribes the Georgian state's territorial claims.

How IDPs are being labelled, registered, and counted, how they are governed (or not) and incorporated into governmental policies and NGO and INGO activities, and how they are politicized and stigmatized by the media, politicians and the general public are important elements to examine. In our analysis of IDP governmentality, while Georgian IDP policy has shifted remarkably in the past few years to encompass policies and practices that encourage and emphasize local integration of IDPs, the spectre of return still casts its dark shadow over Georgia. Alternative approaches have been embraced and the search for durable solutions has increased dramatically recently but the government still remains focused on the right to return (Mooney, 2011: 185).

It is important to identify what understanding of integration the Georgian government employs in its policies not just because it is indicative of governmentality but also because it has dramatic repercussion for IDPs. Whether the lives of IDPs improve is predicated on the Georgian government adopting a broader conception of integration. As Mitchneck *et al.* (2009) demonstrate, the government focus on moving IDPs into private accommodation, without attention to further social and economic integration, will not be enough to integrate IDPs (see also Kurshitashvili, 2012). In addition to the provision of adequate housing, employment and income-generating activities need to be prioritized in order to diminish insecurity. The Georgian government has pledged funds for the agricultural sector but it remains unclear how IDPs will be affected (Corso, 2012). Yet, the lack of transparency of the government's budget and the Saakashvili regime's penchant for development in public space over dealing with issues such as persistent high levels of unemployment and IDP support remains a cause for concern (Corso, 2011). The picture is not entirely grim, as the MRA, despite limited funding, seems sincerely committed to achieving long-term durable solutions (Corso, 2011). If progress towards providing IDPs with the services, housing and opportunities they require to have stable lives and provide for their families continues, IDP life chances will improve. However, as we have documented, the continuation of geo-power will limit the ability of policies and practices that allow for IDP living conditions to take precedent over the rhetoric of return. With the current political shifts in the Georgian government, whether the attention to IDPs persists, and at what level, will be a fascinating question to examine over the coming years.

References

Amnesty International (1998) *Georgia: Summary of Amnesty International's Concerns*, Amnesty International, London.

Amnesty International (2010) *In the Waiting Room: Internally Displaced People in Georgia*, Amnesty International, London.

Amnesty International (2011) *Uprooted Again: Forced Evictions of the Internally Displaced Persons in Georgia*, Amnesty International, London.

Badridze, G. (2010) Georgia's olive branch. *Guardian* (5 March), <http://www.guardian.co.uk/commentisfree/2010/mar/05/georgia-russia-south-ossetia-abkhazia> (accessed 26 October 2014).

Bagshaw, S. (2000) *Internally Displaced Persons and Political Participation: The OSCE Region*, The Brookings Institution Project on Internal Displacement, Washington, DC.

Bariagaber, A. (1999) States, international organisations and the refugee: reflections on the complexity of managing the refugee crisis in the Horn of Africa. *The Journal of Modern African Studies* 37(4), 597–619.

BBC (2007) Georgia rejects Abkhazia election. *BBC News*, 5 March, <http://news.bbc.co.uk/2/hi/europe/6418229.stm> (accessed 27 October 2014).

Bracke, S. and Fadil, N. (2012) Is the headscarf oppressive or emancipatory? In *The Postcolonial Low Countries* (eds E. Boehmer and S. de Mul). Lexington Books, Lanham, MD, 73–93.

Civil Georgia (2008) President Saakashvili's televised address to Abkhazians and South Ossetians. 29 April, <http://www.civil.ge/eng/article.php?id=17723> (accessed 27 October 2014).

Civil Georgia (2010a) Abkhaz leader congratulates Yanukovych. 15 February, <http://www.civil.ge/eng/article.php?id=21985> (accessed 27 October 2014).

Civil Georgia (2010b) Ministry pledges "permanent assistance" to evicted IDPs. 31 August, <http://www.civil.ge/eng/article.php?id=22631> (accessed 27 October 2014).

Civil Georgia (2010c) Groups of IDPs Protests Against Planned Eviction. *Civil.ge*. 21 December. Online: <http://67.222.4.42/eng/article.php?id=22983> (accessed 27 October 2014).

Conciliation Resources (2009) *Out of the Margins: Securing a Voice for Internally Displaced People: Lessons from Georgia*, Conciliation Resources, London.

Corso, M. (2011) *Georgia: Making a Luxury Resort a Priority over IDPs?* 31 August, <http://www.eurasianet.org/node/64111> (accessed 27 October 2014).

Corso, M. (2012) *Georgia: War IDPs Fight Ongoing Battle with Poverty.* 8 August, <http://www.eurasianet.org/node/65764> (accessed 27 October 2014).

da Lomba, S. (2010) Legal status and refugee integration: a UK perspective. *Journal of Refugee Studies* 23(4), 415–436.

Deng, F. (2003) Hearing: internally displaced persons in the Caucasus region and Southeastern Anatolia. 10 June, <http://www.csce.gov/index.cfm?Fuseaction=ContentRecords.ViewDetail&ContentRecord_id=258&Region_id=15&Issue_id=0&ContentType=H&CFID=929232&CFTOKEN=70697758> (accessed 27 October 2014).

DRC (2010) *Final Report of the State Civic Unit: Recommendations and Conclusions*, Danish Refugee Council, Tbilisi.

Dunn, E. (2012a) The chaos of humanitarian aid: adhocracy in the Republic of Georgia. *Humanity* 3(1), 1–23.

Dunn, E. (2012b) A gift from the American people. *Iowa Review* 42(2), 37–48.

Dunn, E. and Cons, J. (2014) Aleatory sovereignty and the rule of sensitive spaces. *Antipode* 46(1), 92–109.

Ferris, E., Mooney, E. and Stark, C. (2012) From national responsibility to response – Part II: IDPs' housing, land and property rights. *TerraNullius: The Housing, Land and Property Weblog.* 22 February, <http://terra0nullius.wordpress.com/2012/02/22/from-national-responsibility-to-response-part-ii-idps-housing-land-and-property-rights/> (accessed 27 October 2014).

Foucault, M. (1991) Governmentality, in *The Foucault Effect: Studies in Governmentality* (eds G. Burchell, C. Gordon and P. Miller), University of Chicago, Chicago, 87–104.

GISC. (2012) Every IDP to have their own houses. Gender Information Network of South Caucasus. 19 June. <http://www.ginsc.net/home.php?option=article&id=22767&lang=en> (accessed 2 December 2014).

Greenway, J. (2009) *Europe's Forgotten People: Protecting the Human Rights of Long-term Displaced Persons*, Council of Europe, Strasbourg.

Gvasalia, I. (2010) *IDPs Dissatisfied with the Quality of the Rehabilitated Houses.* 10 October, <http://www.humanrights.ge/index.php?a=main&pid=12396&lang=eng> (accessed 27 October 2014).

Haider, H. (2010) The politicisation of humanitarian assistance: refugee and IDP policy in Bosnia and Herzegovina. *The Journal of Humanitarian Assistance.* 26 April, <http://sites.tufts.edu/jha/archives/700> (accessed 27 October 2014).

Holtzman, S. B. and Nezam, T. (2004) *Living in Limbo: Conflict-Induced Displacement in Europe and Central Asia*, World Bank, Washington, DC.

HRW (2011) *Living in Limbo: The Rights of Ethnic Georgians Returnees to the Gali District of Abkhazia*, Human Rights Watch, New York, NY.

ICG (2007) *Abkhazia: Ways Forward*, International Crisis Group Europe Report # 179, Tbilisi/Brussels.

ICG (2008) *Georgia and Russia: Clashing Over Abkhazia*, International Crisis Group Europe Report # 193, Tbilisi/Brussels.

IDMC (2007) *Internal Displacement: Global Overview of Trends and Developments in 2006*, Internal Displacement Monitoring Centre, Geneva.

IDMC (2010) *Georgia: Towards Durable Solutions for IDPs*, Internal Displacement Monitoring Centre, Geneva, <http://reliefweb.int/report/

georgia/georgia-towards-durable-solutions-idps-idmc-briefing-paper> (accessed 24 October 2014).

IDMC (2012) *Georgia: Partial Progress towards Durable Solutions for IDPs*, Internal Displacement Monitoring Centre, Geneva, <http://www.internal-displacement.org/assets/library/Europe/Georgia/pdf/Georgia-March-2012.pdf> (accessed 2 December 2014).

Jansen, S. (2006) The privatisation of home and hope: return, reforms and the foreign intervention in Bosnia-Herzegovina. *Dialectical Anthropology* 30, 177–199.

Johnson, C. R. (2010) Partition as a Solution to Ethnic Civil War: Statehood, Demography, and the Role of Post-War Balance of Power for Peace. Unpublished PhD dissertation. University of Maryland.

Kabachnik, P. (2012) Wounds that won't heal: cartographic anxieties and the quest for territorial integrity in Georgia. *Central Asian Survey* 31(1), 45–60.

Kabachnik, P., Grabowska, M., Regulska, J. *et al.* (2013) Traumatic masculinities: the gendered geographies of Georgian IDPs from Abkhazia. *Gender, Place, and Culture* 20(6), 773–793.

Kabachnik, P., Regulska, J. and Mitchneck, B. (2010) Where and when is home? The double displacement of Georgian IDPs from Abkhazia. *The Journal of Refugee Studies* 23(3), 315–336.

Kabachnik, P., Regulska, J., and Mitchneck, B. (2012) Displacing blame: Georgian internally displaced person perspectives of the Georgia-Abkhazia conflict. *Ethnopolitics* 11(2), 123–140.

Kharashvili, J. (2001) Georgia: coping by organising. displaced Georgians from Abkhazia, in *Caught Between Borders – Response Strategies of the Internally Displaced* (eds M. Vincent and B. Refslund Sorensen). Pluto Press, London, 227–249.

Korsaia, S., Kuparadze, M., Lomia, R. and Mirziashvili, M. (2002) *Hoping for Peace*. Studio Re. Assistance by Conciliation Resources and UNOMIG, <http://www.c-r.org/es/video-and-audio/studio-re-film-series> (accessed 27 October 2014)

Kupunia, M. (2011) Saakashvili meets Obama. 17 January. *The Messenger Online*, <http://www.messenger.com.ge/issues/2277_january_17_2011/2277_mzia.html> (accessed 27 October 2014).

Kurshitashvili, N. (2012) The impact of socially irresponsible resettlement on the livelihoods of internally displaced persons in Georgia. *Refugee Survey Quarterly* 31(2), 98–118.

Loughna, S., Bregvadze, T., and Partskhaladze, N. (2010) *Not Displaced, Out-of-Place: Education of IDP Children in Georgia*, Norwegian Refugee Council, Tbilisi.

Malkki, L. (1992) National Geographic: the rooting of peoples and the territorialization of national identity among scholars and refugees. *Cultural Anthropology* 7(1), 24–44.

Mitchneck, B., Mayorova, O., and Regulska, J. (2009) "Post"-conflict displacement: isolation and integration in Georgia. *Annals of the Association of American Geographers* 99(5), 1022–1032.

Modebadze, S. (2010) IDPs furious about potential eviction. *The Messenger Online*. 16 December, <http://www.messenger.com.ge/issues/2257_december_16_2010/2257_salome.html> (accessed 27 October 2014).

Mooney, E. (2011) From solidarity to solutions: the government response to internal displacement in Georgia, in *From Responsibility to Response: Assessing National Approaches to Internal Displacement* (eds E. Ferris, E. Mooney and C. Stark). The Brookings Institution – London School of Economics, Washington, DC, 179–229.

Mooney, E. and Jarrah, B. (2004) *The Voting Rights of Internally Displaced Persons: The OSCE Region*, The Brookings Institute-SAIS Project on Internal Displacement, Washington, DC.

Mundt, A. and Ferris, E. (2008) *Durable Solutions for IDPs in Protracted Situations: Three Case Studies*, The Brookings Institution-University of Bern, Bern.

Nadareishvili, T. (1997) *Genocide in Abkhazia*, Samshoblo, Tbilisi.

NRC (2003) *Profile of Internal Displacement: Georgia,* Norwegian Refugee Council/Global IDP Project, Geneva.

NRC (2004) *Profile of Internal Displacement: Georgia*, Norwegian Refugee Council, Geneva.

NRC (2005) *Profile of Internal Displacement: Georgia*, Norwegian Refugee Council, Geneva.

O'Loughlin, J., Kolossov, V. and Toal, G. (2011) Inside Abkhazia: a survey of attitudes in a de facto state. *Post-Soviet Affairs* 27(1), 1–36.

Onlinenews.Ge (2011) *Moscow Says UN Resolution on Georgia in Politicized Document.* 30 June, <http://www.onlinenews.ge/index.php?id=11250&lang=eng> (accessed 27 October 2014).

Ó Tuathail, G. (1996) *Critical Geopolitics: The Politics of Writing Global Space*, University of Minnesota Press, Minneapolis, MN.

Owusu, M. (2000) Reluctant refugees: Liberians in Ghana. *The Journal of the International Institute* 7(3), <http://hdl.handle.net/2027/spo.4750978.0007.302> (accessed 27 October 2014).

Phillips, M. (2011) Convenient labels, inaccurate representations: turning southern Sudanese refugees into "African-Australians". *Australasian Review of African Studies* 32(2), 57–79.

Rose-Redwood, R. S. (2006) Governmentality, geography, and the geo-coded world. *Progress in Human Geography* 30(4), 469–486.

Rotas, A. (2004) Is "refugee" art possible? *Third Text* 18(1), 51–60.

Scarborough, G., Tavartkiladze, T. and Arganashvili, A. (2006) *Rapid Assessment on the Protection and Livelihoods Situation of Internally Displaced Children and Youth Living in Collective Centers in the Republic of Georgia*, UNICEF, Tbilisi.

Sumbadze, N. and Tarkhan-Mouravi, G. (2003) *Working Paper on IDP Vulnerability and Economic Self-Reliance*, UNDP, Tbilisi.

Tarkhan-Mouravi, G. (2009) *Assessment of IDP Livelihoods in Georgia: Facts and Policies*, UNHCR and Danish Refugee Council, Tbilisi.

UNHCR (2006) Global Appeal 2007: Strategies and Programmes. United Nations High Commissioner for Refugees, UNHCR, Geneva Online: <http://reliefweb.int/sites/reliefweb.int/files/resources/1217D5273BA34A84C1257235003E8442-UNHCR-Nov2006.pdf> (accessed 27 October 2014).

UNHCR (2009) *Protection of Internally Displaced Persons in Georgia: A Gap Analysis*, UNHCR, Tbilisi.

Vashadze, G. (2009) *Georgia's Relations with Russia from 1991 to the Present*, Chatham House, London, <http://www.chathamhouse.org/sites/files/chathamhouse/15121_131009vashadze.pdf> (accessed 2 December 2014).

Vetters, L. (2007) The power of administrative categories: emerging notions of citizenship in the dived city of Mostar. *Ethnopolitics* 6(2), 187–209.

Vrecer, N. (2010) Living in Limbo: integration of forced migrants from Bosnia and Herzegovina in Slovenia. *The Journal of Refugee Studies* 23(4), 484–502.

Walicki, N. (2011) Part protracted, part progress: durable solutions for IDPs through local integration in Georgia, in *Resolving Internal Displacement: Prospects for Local Integration* (ed. E. Ferris). The Brookings Institution – London School of Economics, Washington, DC, 61–81.

Zetter, R. (1991) Labelling refugees: forming and transforming a bureaucratic identity. *Journal of Refugee Studies* 4(1), 39–62.

Giulia Prelz Oltramonti

War Economies and Protracted Conflicts: The Cases of Abkhazia and South Ossetia

ABSTRACT: This chapter looks at the role of war economies in the protraction of conflict in Abkhazia and South Ossetia from the early 1990s to 2008. It mobilizes the existing literature on boundary activation, borderlands, sanctions and the transformation of war economies to map the complexity of the two cases, while relying on extensive fieldwork to elucidate the economies of the Abkhaz and South Ossetian protracted conflicts. As a result, it unveils some of the incentives in increasing or decreasing levels of violence and protracting or ending conflict.

KEYWORDS: political economies, conflict protraction, boundary activation, Georgia, Abkhazia, South Ossetia

Introduction

This chapter focuses on the dynamics underpinning the protraction of the Abkhaz and South Ossetian conflicts between the ceasefire agreements of the early 1990s and the resumption of a full-scale conflict in 2008. The fact that both cases are protracted conflicts that cannot be considered to be resolved due to lack of a peace agreement, but that little full-intensity confrontation has occurred, is an important element of this analytical framework. These are not the only cases of no-peace, no-war protracted conflicts – ranging from neighbouring Nagorno-Karabakh to the 50-year long case of Korea – but contain enough variations within their development to allow us to observe the dynamics of separatist protracted conflicts from a new angle.

The question that I ask here – "What role did the war economies play in the protraction of the Abkhaz and South Ossetian conflicts after the establishment of ceasefire agreements in the early 1990s?" – touches upon the underlying forces that sustained this state of affairs. I start by reviewing the literature on war economies, on the issue of border activation and on sanctions and transformation of war economies. I then sketch an initial picture of the economies of the Abkhaz and South Ossetian protracted conflicts, and identify the stakeholders of the conflict economies and of the processes of boundary activation in the two cases, and proceed to address the impact of these actors on the economies of the two protracted conflicts and their significance. The empirical section of the chapter rests upon a review of governmental and nongovernmental documents and publications, and over 45 semi-structured interviews.[1]

The focus on war economies does not ignore the fact that numerous other factors contribute to the protraction of conflict and variations in levels of violence. The role of state weakness and institutional factors as stumbling blocks on the path of conflict resolution has been widely explored with regard to the Georgian cases (Coppieters*et al.*,2000), as well as the impact of political and economic shakeups, geopolitical and external influences (Baev, 1997; Lynch, 2003; Coppieters and Legvold, 2005; Cornell, 2007) and ethnicity, identity and nationalism (Matveeva, 2002). The focus on war economies does not claim the superiority of this given explanatory approach over some of the aforementioned ones; rather, it advances the case for complementarity of different approaches and fulfils the need for a better understanding of this area of enquiry.

Framing War Economies

When talking about war economies, I mean "all economic activities carried out in wartime" (Pugh and Cooper, 2004: 8). The rationale behind this approach is to investigate a key component of conflict and, in the context of this chapter, of the protraction of two conflicts after ceasefire agreements were signed in 1992, in the case of South Ossetia, and 1994, in the case of Abkhazia. This approach addresses two interrelated questions. Firstly, what were the economic motives, if any, that worked against the formal

1 The interviews with stakeholders, former officials and analysts were carried out during summer and fall 2012 in Tbilisi, Sukhum(i) and in the regions of ShidaKartli, Samegrelo and Gal(i).

resolution of conflict and the signature of peace agreements?[2] Secondly, what were the economic mechanisms that allowed the confronting parties to dodge the necessity of a formal resolution of conflict and the signature of peace agreements? I am therefore looking at the economic motivations for such protraction, as well as feasibility mechanisms. The two are closely intertwined, as motives lead to, contribute to, or support mobilization strategies, and mobilization and organization allow for motivations to be expressed through collective violence, instead of nonviolent engagement.

This circular dynamic is applicable to a number of areas – including political, social and ethnic realms – which are often strongly interconnected. For the sake of the study of conflict, the gap between disciplines is often bridged, acknowledging the complementarity of the explanatory approaches. With regard to war economies, a significant stream of literature has developed around the study of political economies of conflict, which Wennmann (2008) defines as "the study of the relationship between political and economic spheres in affecting the dynamics of armed conflict as well as the relationship between the material environment and motivations in the organisation of the use of force". While I acknowledge that war economies cannot be studied as self-standing, in an insular fashion, and are affected not only by political and geopolitical factors but also social, ethnic and religious aspects, I have decided for analytical reasons to maintain war economies as the central focus of this chapter.

On the one hand, the link between economic activity and conflict protraction in the two Georgian cases has received some scrutiny (King, 2001; Champain *et al.*,2004; Lynch, 2004), but this has mostly predated, or coincided with, the Rose Revolution and the important changes that it engendered. Other researchers have focused on more specific aspects of economic activities in Georgia, Abkhazia and South Ossetia in the 1990s and 2000s, many touching indirectly on the conflicts. They include the role of corruption (Baev, 2003), of organized crime and unsanctioned trade (Kukhianidze *et al.*,2004).

On the other hand, a significant body of literature on war economies – and political economies of war – has emerged from the investigation of conflict in other regions of the world, first introducing the link between violence and economic agendas in civil wars (Berdal and Keen, 1997; Keen,

2 As discussed later, conflict does not only allow people to pursue political goals but it has been successfully shown to be "a way of creating an alternative system of profit, power and even protection" (Keen, 1998: 11).

1998) and then dissecting the economic dimensions of conflict protraction (Keen, 2008). Two offshoots of this literature are especially relevant within the context of this chapter: the distinction between various strands of war economies (combat, shadow and coping economies), which imply different actors, motivations and incentives, organization and impacts; and the salience of borders and borderlands in conflict settings.

Let us point out that usually the normative concept of war as a state of chaos – which was successfully refuted by, among others, Berdal and Keen (1997) and Ballentine and Nitzschke (2005) – characterizes economic activity during war as criminal or illegal. It would be useful, however, to treat war economies according to the legal vacuum in which they exist, and which is characteristic of war and post-war contexts. Given these legal vacuums, not only is the focus on legality then conceptually misleading – it also undermines a sound analytical approach to the case studies. If we maintain the categorization of legal versus illegal economic activities, we are then lead to join under the same umbrella the employee of the Ministry of Defence, the one who does not take bribes, with the supplier of arms, food or services to the national army, and pitch them against a group formed by a resident of a borderland area who *smuggles* jeans or tomatoes across the border or ceasefire line to feed his family, businessmen who *smuggle* primary resources or arms to non-state combatants, and non-state combatants. While it is important to understand which actors exploit the legal vacuum, there is a more useful approach, derived from a categorization in terms of combat, shadow and coping economies, leading to a better understanding of the motivations, the incentives and the dynamics of different actors.

First, as defined by Pugh and Cooper (2004: 7–8) "combat economies include both (1) the capture of control over production and economic resources to sustain conflict and (2) economic strategies of war aimed at the disempowerment of specific groups." The main actors of such groups are combatants, members of military structures, and their political backers, whether state or non-state;[3] their key activities are varied and span from taxation and external financial support to trade, asset stripping and looting.

3 The need to move beyond a rebel-centric approach has become increasingly apparent, including a shift towards consistent analyses of the role of governments and third parties, their combatants and their military structures (Ballentine and Nitzschke, 2005: 4).

What draws them together is the motivation that drives their economic activity, namely funding the war effort or achieving military objectives.

Second, the shadow economy includes activities aimed at making a profit on the margin of conflict. These activities rely on the environment created by the war, exploiting, for example, the legal vacuum or the emergence of new borders. The rationale behind all the activities, which are extremely varied, however, is of an economic rather than a military nature. Similarly lacking a military rationale are the activities of the coping economy, whose goal is "to cope and maintain asset bases through low-risk activities, or survive through asset erosion" (Goodhand, 2003: 4).

In fact, these two last categories overlap considerably, mirroring the multiplicity of interests of some actors and the inapplicability of clear-cut distinctions between residents, elites, businessmen, military and government. The resident of the borderland area who trades in jeans or tomatoes across profitable ceasefire lines is an actor in the coping economy as long as he feeds his family, and becomes a participant of the shadow economy when he starts trading a few tons of tomatoes, adding to that remunerative gasoline and cigarettes, and accumulating a certain amount of capital out of his trade. But the question of whether there is a need to differentiate between the two is pertinent. And while it would be difficult to assert that the cleavage is absolute, there is a marked difference between the exploitation of a conflict environment and the ensuing legal vacuum, and the survival through adaptation to that very same environment.

It is also difficult to draw lines between purely combat, shadow and coping economic activities. The example of trade shows this well: trade of legal or illicit resources (gems, drugs, but also gasoline and cigarettes) may fund the war-waging effort; trade of all sorts of commodities and consumer goods are the backbone of most shadow economies; and petty trade supports, to a large extent, communities of conflict affected areas. Similarly, asset stripping is a component of all war economies but, clearly, with different aims and at different levels.

From Boundary Activation to the Salience of Borderlands

Trade across ceasefire lines – or *de facto* borders – and external *de jure* borders was one of the main components of the Abkhaz and the South Ossetian war economies, and it also allowed for some forms of foreign direct investments and some agricultural development in Abkhazia. It is therefore necessary to review the importance of boundaries and borders in conflict settings. This leads us, in turn, to examine the nature of borderlands, which allowed for the development of other components of the economies of the two protracted conflicts, namely activities that relied on the lack of territorial control by Tbilisi over Abkhazia and South Ossetia and the ensuing legal vacuum.

Generally, boundaries are the dividing lines at which something changes, which separate areas of certain rules of behaviour (Migdal, 2004). In cases of conflict, boundaries can be hardened or softened to suit various interests, a process that Tilly (2003) defined as "boundary activation". Different actors can be involved in the process of hardening or softening some boundaries, whether states or nonstate actors. What happens when a boundary is hardened or softened? While conventional liberal wisdom would affirm that, when boundaries harden, opportunities are lost, studies have shown that reality is more multifaceted, with winners and losers arising from border activation. Because of the cost for crossing borders[4] that the authorities can impose, an incentive to cross the border is created: the service of moving goods (and people) across the regulated boundary can lead to profit making. Such profit can be made by private entrepreneurs, who would pocket a margin on service fees while facilitating passage, or by authorities, which would gain from the hardening of the border but not a complete closure.

Donnan and Wilson (1999: 87) assert that "[the] existence [of borders] as barriers to movement can simultaneously create reasons to cross them." To illustrate this statement, consider that for the residents of the borderlands, commerce through dividing lines often represents one of the few ways to make a living. For the private sector, borders represent a hurdle (in

4 Defined by Donnan and Wilson (1999: 1) as "sites and symbols of power", borders are key locations where the state asserts its authority by staging border and customs posts and by limiting the flows of people and goods.

terms of logistics and finances) but also an opportunity to increase profits from additional services. For administrations and law enforcement agencies, borders are the line along which taxation can be extracted, whether officially or unofficially (i.e. bribes). Stakeholders of border systems are therefore extremely numerous and diverse.

On both sides of borders or *de facto* borders, borderlands[5] are often characterized by a weaker presence of the official authorities, due to their distance from the capital and the power that stakeholders of border systems can harness through the exploitation of opportunities created by the very existence of borders. Being areas where all opportunities created by the cleavage are exploited, borderlands often become "spaces of avoidance, where much that goes on is less than fully legal – in fact, they have a comparative advantage in illegality" (Goodhand, 2008: 234). While this is most apparent when transnational criminal networks are involved, *smuggling* also concerns residents of borderlands who make a living out of unsanctioned small trade of agricultural products, commodities or consumer goods in small quantities. This is also true for a number of other economic activities, including exploitation of natural resources, creation of monopolies within the borderlands, and use of refugees' property. A key implication is that in order to preserve this comparative advantage, stakeholders of these non-state spaces of avoidance rely on continued lack or weakness of official control and have a vested interest in the preservation of this state of affairs. Despite the potential overall positive outcomes of stable peace agreements, change is resisted by those actors that have individual stakes in the status quo, which may not be accommodated in a new framework.

Sanctions and the Transformation of War Economies

While the two main options for policymakers have traditionally been sanctions and incentives of various kinds, the support for all-encompassing economic sanctions weakened, since the early 1990s, because they were generally deemed ineffective in bringing about major changes in policy (Hufbauer *et al.*,1990: 94). Targeted sanctions, on the other hand,

5 Goodhand (2008: 193) uses the term "borderland" to indicate a "non-state space".

are intended to damage elites' interests while avoiding having a negative impact on vulnerable populations. The difficulty of such approach rests in the interconnectedness of actors and economic networks. The impact on civilian livelihoods and the fostering of what is seen as criminal behaviour were also raised as motives for discontinuing the practice of embargoes (Ballentine and Sherman, 2003: 279).

In some cases, all-encompassing sanctions proved not only ineffective but also counterproductive, generating a "rally around the flag" effect (Cortright, 2007: 392). It is extremely difficult to quantify the results of sanctions (or incentives), their "success" depends "on what goals they are measured against" (Dowty, 1994: 192). The nature of the goals that are pursued through the implementation of sanctions is crucial for their outcome. Goals have been classified in three main categories, namely behaviour change, containment and regime change (O'Sullivan, 2003); in relations to these goals, targeted sanctions have proved effective to different extents. However, there has been a tendency among policymakers to assess the effectiveness of sanctions by measure of inflicted economic pain. On the other hand, the fondness for incentives over negative sanctions grew in the 2000s. In both cases, however, the effectiveness of inducement strategies depends on sender's objectives, the nature of the recipient regime, political dynamics between sender and recipient and, crucially, the presence or absence of exogenous incentives (Cortright, 1997: 272–290; Rock, 2000). Two more factors affect the effectiveness of both sanctions and incentives. First, receivers may perceive economic pressure differently from the sender's intentions. Secondly, the ability of countries to implement them, effectively monitoring financial and commercial flows regionally. This depends on their own state capacity, in addition to neighbouring countries' policy. The failure to implement sanctions consistently alters their effectiveness, while undermining the legitimacy of the sender (Pugh and Cooper, 2004: 227–229).

While scholars and policymakers focused on how to make war less profitable, less scrutiny was devoted to how to make peace more profitable than war. A shift in that direction, initiated by Goodhand (2004), Pugh and Cooper (2004) and Pugh *et al.* (2008) was triggered by two different strands of enquiry that led to a shared perspective. On the one hand, the policy-oriented interest for economic tools of conflict transformation observed the greater effectiveness of incentives as compared to economic sanctions, and practitioners moved in that direction. On the other hand, an enquiry in the political economies of peace was a natural procession for scholars who abandoned the normative duality between peace and war and who rejected the assumption that economic transition from war to peace amounted to the restoration of the pre-war normality. Both found that, for a transition to occur and be sustainable, political economies have to be transformed, not necessarily to pre-war conditions but in order to turn stakeholders of war economies into stakeholders of peace economies.

The Economies of the Abkhaz and South Ossetian Protracted Conflicts

Zürcher *et al.* (2005) explored the possibility of applying the Collier–Hoeffler model – a quantitative analysis measuring the opportunity cost of violence (Collier and Hoeffler, 2001) – in the case of the conflicts in the Caucasus. In the end they argued that this model was not applicable in the post-Soviet Caucasus but they also noted that the "markets of violence"[6] that characterized the conflict in Georgia did not last beyond 1995, as opposed to, for example, the case of Chechnya. In fact, the economic balance that characterized the protracted conflicts in the timeframe between the ceasefire agreements of the early 1990s and 2008 differs greatly from the war economies that were created during the initial high-intensity phases of the conflicts.

While the main aim of this chapter is not to account for the economies of the high-intensity phases of the 1991–92 conflict in South Ossetia and 1992–94 conflict in Abkhazia, it is nonetheless useful to review the differences between the war economies of these periods and the economies that characterized the protraction of the conflicts after the establishment of ceasefire agreements. The intensity of violence, its use and its users did change, but with an overlap of the two periods that reached into the mid-1990s and a gradual establishment of economic systems geared towards the preservation of the status quo.

6 Markets of violence are defined as "economic areas dominated by civil wars, warlords or robbery, in which a self-perpetuating system emerges which links non-violent commodity markets with the violent acquisition of goods" (Elwert, 2003: 221).

In both cases, the bouts of high-intensity fighting during the 15-year period of conflict protraction after the signature of ceasefire agreements are few, most notably in 1998 in Abkhazia (with the expulsion of the ethnic Georgians from the Gali region) and in 2004 in South Ossetia. This is not to claim that violence as a tool of economic control disappeared from the areas under scrutiny, but that it evolved.[7] The "combat" economy category is therefore partly unsatisfactory in this context of no-peace, no-war conflict protraction. On the one hand, if we look back at the definition of combat economies, we can see that this categorization can also be broadly applicable to periods of low-intensity military confrontation within protracted conflicts. Both aspects – control over resources to pay for conflict, and disempowerment of specific group, hence economic disenfranchisement as a weapon of conflict – remain crucial aspect of the protraction of conflict even after ceasefire agreements are signed. On the other hand, the terminology of "combat" economy conveys the notion that military combat and high-intensity confrontation are implied, and fails to reflect the differences between economies of active conflict and economies of no-peace, no-war conflict protraction.

Most notably, combat economies evolved into post-combat economies according to the evolving goals of the opposing parties: first, they sustained full-fledged military confrontations, then, for Abkhazia and South Ossetia, the preservation of the status quo and the institutionalization of the *de facto* independence of the two territories. Also the components of combat economies changed considerably, shifting from the capture of economic resources during the war to pay for the war itself to employing economic strategies as tools in the protraction of conflict. Tbilisi promoted what was, for all intents and purposes, an embargo on Abkhazia, trying to use economic pressure, alongside diplomatic talks, to further its goal of reintegrating the region under Tbilisi's control. The heads of state of CIS countries agreed in 1996 on all-encompassing trade restrictions and Georgia insisted throughout the years that trade restrictions should be also respected by Turkey (not a member of the CIS). The main hurdle, however, remained that of implementation. Having no control over the Russian-Georgian border in Abkhazia, Georgia had to rely on the willingness of its northern neighbour to enforce the sanctions. Similarly, in the 1990s

7 For a journey into the complexities of defining, measuring and categorizing violence and conflict, see Cramer (2006).

it lacked the capacity to effectively patrol the Black Sea and stop maritime trade. It is only from the early 2000s onwards that it was able repeatedly to detain ships bound for Turkey and originating from Abkhazia, creating significant diplomatic rifts with its main business partner, namely Turkey. At the same time, trade restrictions did not seem to enhance the prospects for conflict resolution, leading to increasingly strained relations and distrust from the population of Abkhazia. As early as 1997, international observers pointed out that isolation brought about by the CIS-imposed trade restrictions had created additional hardship, leading to "frustration" among the local population (Security Council, 1997: 35). Tbilisi, however, soldiered on in its support for trade restrictions, notwithstanding the more generalized shift that had taken place since the early 1990s in the field of conflict resolution, away from supporting for all-encompassing economic sanctions. The rationale behind the Georgian stance was twofold. First, it considered sanctions as a mechanism to exert pressure on Abkhazia and one that had a relatively low cost, as opposed to incentives of various kinds, including financial incentives, which, especially in the early 1990s, Georgia could not afford. Second, sanctions contained an element of retaliation, which clearly emerged when various actors attempted to craft a more effective policy of boundary deactivation along the ceasefire line.

In Abkhazia, on the other hand, the newly instated *de facto* authorities encouraged the economic disempowerment of ethnic Georgians in the Gali district through violence and other means. As for the users of violence, the transition between high-intensity phases of war and post-war protraction of the unsolved conflicts saw a shift from groups of combatants with a military justification to *de facto* power ministries that found their legitimacy in the defence of the separatist entities and the consolidation of their institutions. This left plenty of scope for the proliferation of organized crime, for the exploitation of state resources for private gain and for the privatization of the use of force in borderlands, under the control of militias or local strongmen.

The evolution from combat economies to post-combat economies in Abkhazia and in South Ossetia differed but in both cases the shift in the activities carried out has mostly been from asset stripping and looting during the first post-war years, to institutionalization of pseudo-taxation on productive activities and trade, to increasing external support. The process of pseudo-taxation relied on the absence of control by the Georgian authorities over most of the territory of South Ossetia and Abkhazia, as well as the more-or-less overt decision of *de facto* authorities to exploit, or allow the exploitation of, insecurity in their Georgian-inhabited borderlands. Along the Inguri River, traders bribed the Abkhaz *de facto* border guards to get their trucks across – and this was somehow accepted as a way to pay for their salary, as they did not receive official ones in the 1990s, and received very low ones thereafter.[8] Interviews with local aid workers – both Abkhaz and Mengrelians – reveal that the *de facto* border patrol also exploited their knowledge of the terrain, showing residents where landmines were – having laid them down to start with – and then charging residents for safe passage. As they were able to control key stretches of the *de facto* border, they imposed a fee per bag of goods to be transported across. For most residents, it was nevertheless cheaper to pay this bribe along the river than to travel all the way to the one officially open bridge on the Inguri, taking into account the price of fuel and bribes to be paid at the bridge. With hazelnuts commanding a much higher price in Zugdidi than in Gali, most residents who lived within reasonable distance of the ceasefire line subjected themselves to the crossing.

In South Ossetia, businessmen trading from Russia to Georgia, or vice versa, generally paid an official fee administered by the *de facto* power ministries. *De facto* law-enforcement agencies, in return, prevented other agencies or paramilitary groups from extracting additional bribes and guaranteed a safe passage across the territory that they controlled, from the Roki tunnel to the ceasefire line (Dzhikaev and Parastaev, 2004). External support mainly came from the increasingly closer Russian ally of the two separatist *de facto* states in the 2000s; while it is difficult to assess it quantitatively, variations in direct support are at times revealed, such as, for instance, the increase in Russian contributions to the South Ossetian budget after the closure of the Ergneti market in 2004 (ICG, 2007).

Indirect external support, such as Russia's unilateral relaxation of the 1996 CIS-imposed embargo on Abkhazia in 1999, or its policy of passportization of large segments of the Abkhaz and South Ossetian populations from the 1999 onwards, had a more considerable impact on the coping economy. The passportization policy allowed residents of Abkhazia and

8 Similarly, Russian peacekeepers stationed along the Inguri were also known to partake in some of these activities (selling gasoline from their bases to gas stations in Zudgidi and participating in the trade of stolen cars). The fact that they were poorly paid and at times not paid at all is offered as a driving factor behind their activities (Kukhianidze *et al.*,2007:83–84).

South Ossetia to work in the Russian Federation, sending remittances back to the *de facto* states and contributing to their economic viability; similarly, Moscow's decision to cover pensioners' basic pensions in the *de facto* states and to provide in-kind assistance contributed to the viability of coping economies. Putin's abrogation by decree of the Russian commitment to uphold the embargo in 1999 allowed for individual crossing and trade across the Psou river between Abkhazia and Krasnodar Krai. In turn, this permitted the export of Abkhazia's small agricultural output and the beginning of a tourist industry relying on Russian holidaymakers, two noticeable sources of income for Abkhazia's cash-strapped residents (ICG, 2006).

In South Ossetia, on the other hand, a lifeline for residents came from the fact that Georgia failed to control the trade that crossed the region and that constituted most of its coping economy and its shadow economy. Given that the Georgian central government withheld from setting up customs posts along the ceasefire line between Georgia and South Ossetia, being adamant that it should be regarded as an internal administrative boundary, untaxed transit trade was South Ossetia's main economic activity between 1992 and 2004. It initially developed spontaneously at a small-scale level between Tskhinvali and Gori, operated by residents of the adjacent areas. Since 1999, however, it grew into a more structured and regulated business, where the interests of business groups and some members of the bureaucracy prevailed.[9]

Some of the stakeholders of this trade in South Ossetia and the Georgian region of Shida Kartli were clearly influential. Attempts to tax or regulate the passage of goods were resisted. As early as 1999, the Georgian government attempted to impose custom tariffs on goods entering Shida Kartli; the attempts, however, were thwarted by the high levels of corruption permeating the Georgian law enforcement bodies (Kukhianidze *et al.*,2004). A proposal was also pushed ahead under the aegis of the European Union, which would have established a joint customs regime; the South Ossetian government rejected it on the grounds that it would have curtailed its sovereignty; more realistically, such an agreement would have curtailed the scope of smuggling and future profits.

The commercial activities that constituted the shadow economy exploited both the process of boundary activation and the lack of Tbilisi's

9 For an account of the traded goods and estimates of the trade's value, see Areshidze (2002); Dzhikaev and Parastaev (2004: 201–203); Kukhianidze *et al.* (2004: 18–20).

control over its external borders. Were a peace agreement to be signed – whether in favour of South Ossetia's reintegration into Georgia, or in favour of South Ossetia's *de jure* independence – the tax-free bonanza would come to an end, and with it the competitive advantage of the South Ossetia route over the better equipped military highway that links Georgia to North Ossetia.

In Abkhazia, the shadow economy was more rooted in the exploitation of the legal vacuum than in the process of border activation – though not exclusively, as trade across the border with Russia and the ceasefire line with Georgia, and from its ports, continued to exist and became increasingly important in the 2000s (Closson, 2007; Kukhianidze*et al.*,2007). The fact that Tbilisi failed to assert its control in most of Abkhazia meant that post-Soviet privatization of state assets was carried out according to Abkhazia's rules and power politics. Actors in dominant positions within Abkhazia, which were secured by close relationships between political and economic elites, made considerable profits, controlling and/or protecting the production of agricultural and natural resources, trade and investment in large tourist complexes. These processes were closely intertwined with the political strategies employed to manage a multi-ethnic *de facto* state.

As in South Ossetia, these economic activities explain how Abkhazia had an economic viability – although minimal – that, paired with a rhetoric of siege mentality, allowed it to muddle through 15 years of conflict protraction. In both *de facto* states, smuggling allowed residents not only to make a living out of petty trade or small exports, but also to have some access to consumer goods, mostly untaxed and therefore cheaper. It is important to point out that trade flowed in more than one direction, depending on the permeability of borders and ceasefire lines, and on the prices that goods commanded in different markets. When the border between Abkhazia and Russia was closed in the 1990s, Gali residents carried items necessary for survival from Zugdidi. Consumer goods and food produce from the rest of Georgia were sold, well into the 2000s, in the markets of Sukhumi and Gagra, easing the shortages caused by the trade sanctions all over Abkhazia. This aspect rarely surfaces in Abkhaz accounts, as it would undermine the official Abkhaz position of that it is viable independent from Georgia, as well as in Georgian studies, which focus on criminal networks trading in petroleum, cigarettes, and other non-survival goods. However, if the difficulty and the cost of importing staples from Russia in the 1990s is taken into account and compared with the relative ease of crossing the Inguri, it seems likely that Abkhaz authorities restrained from better sealing the ceasefire line also because of this outcome – an inflow of necessary goods into Abkhazia – in addition to poor capacity and the larger commercial interests of a few strongmen.

The main shakeup to this state of affairs came with the change of leadership in Tbilisi and the clampdown on corruption that ensued. From December 2003 the Georgian government conducted anti-smuggling operations along the cease-fire line with South Ossetia, closed the Ergneti market and blew up some roads used for contraband. The logic behind this move was clearly stated, namely the belief that that the *de facto* regime would collapse as it was deprived of its revenues, although Tbilisi was careful to draw a line between *de facto* elites and residents of South Ossetia (Khutsidze, 2004). It offered to deliver a range of incentives, such as restoration of railway links with Tbilisi, provision of medical services, fertilizers for farmers, pensions and broadcasting in the Ossetian language on state television. Most services, however, were not delivered, either because the Georgian government failed to do so, or because the *de facto* authorities hampered their delivery. Similarly, as of 2004, the Georgian government attempted to subdue the various actors who participated in trans-ceasefire line trade to Abkhazia and to limit the volume of smuggling. These policies were borne out of two main factors: the necessity to increase its custom revenues and the belief that de facto authorities could be forced to negotiate if sources of revenue dried up.

While the Georgian budget benefited from these measures, the shadow and coping economies of the *de facto* states were severely affected, particularly in South Ossetia. It is noteworthy that the anti-smuggling operation entailed an increased presence of Georgian security forces in the areas along ceasefire lines, which were perceived as a build-up for aggression (ICG, 2004), and was subsequently very much underplayed by the Georgian side. In addition, these measures themselves were seen as tools of economic aggression and, for all intents and purposes, they were used as economic instruments of persuasion: the Georgian government decided to use the process of border activation as a tool to limit the economic resources that the opposing parties relied on in order to further their own goals. In Abkhazia the weight of trade restrictions was particularly severe in the 1990s, as a result of Russia's implementation of CIS sanctions and its own limitations on the circulation of Abkhaz residents, but in South Ossetia the key period of increasing isolation started in 2004.

In fact, since the mid-1990s the Georgian role in post-combat economies centred on various attempts to use economic leverage on the separatist regions. To varying degrees throughout the 1990s and 2000s, Tbilisi tried to exert pressure on the *de facto* authorities by allowing or impeding the economic viability of the territories that they controlled. The measures that it promoted to do so invariably affected the populations of Abkhazia and South Ossetia – including in their ability to receive support from international donors, which, channelled to the separatist regions with Tbilisi's consent, could not fund any sort of capacity-building and long-term development projects. While the successive governments of Georgia officially strove to shield civilians from the drawbacks of their economic policy towards the separatist regions, and either provided, or pledged, some support and services, mainly in the fields of education and healthcare, there was nonetheless a differentiation among the sections of the population considered more-or-less likely to support Georgian territorial integrity. Most notably, when, in 2006, Tbilisi supported the establishment of a friendly administration in South Ossetia under the leadership of Dimitri Sanakoev and parallel to the *de facto* authorities, it attempted to exploit the ethnic and political cleavages in the population of South Ossetia. It not only promoted investments and funded infrastructure in the few villages that Sanakoev's administration controlled but it further isolated the rest of South Ossetia by activating a new boundary between the two and creating hierarchies with regard to trade and provision of services.

Mapping Complexity

This overview of the Abkhaz and South Ossetian economies presents the two cases from a little-explored perspective. In fact, both cases have been generally branded "frozen conflicts" and the protracted freeze has mostly been explained through an institutionalist approach. In addition, the majority of the work carried out on wars elucidates the origins and causes of conflict at a given moment, usually at the onset, and then assumes that the same logic holds until the end. This leads to faulty analyses of the dynamics of war, as the factors affecting transitions and plateaus are overseen. This is particularly the case with regard to protracted conflicts: 20 years down the line the rhetoric usually remains the same (for example, that of reconquering ancestral lands) but most of the actors have changed, as well as, to varying extents, the geopolitical, political, economic, social, and cultural frameworks.

This research does not aim to prove the primacy of the political economic perspective in explaining every aspect of the protracted conflicts and of their developments. It aims to elucidate what the impact of the political economic factors is throughout the various phases of these two conflicts, especially through what are generally considered transitions and plateaus, as aspects that co-determine the protraction and transformation of a conflict. It elucidates some of the incentives in increasing or decreasing levels of violence and protracting or ending conflict. It also, however, provides an insight into war economies and the feasibility/ sustainability of a given state of affairs. It therefore touches upon both the "whys" and the "hows" of conflict and of its developments.

Looking at economic strategies that sustain conflict does not attempt to minimize other significant factors (political, geopolitical, territorial, identitarian) that drive conflict but, rather, complements them. When introducing the topic of this study to interviewees, I was mostly confronted with an initial dismissal of the idea, on the grounds that there were no riches or money to be made in the Abkhaz and South Ossetian cases of conflict protraction. This is profoundly untrue. There are no natural resources, such as Angola's diamonds or Afghanistan's poppies, but this research shows that the economic opportunities were many and manifold. In addition, the conditions imposed by the protraction of conflict were unavoidable for all actors involved. Residents and entrepreneurs of the areas under scrutiny had two choices: adapt to the status quo and make the best out of it, or leave. For those who stayed, there were positions of relative economic power to be attained and they were associated with strong political clout. The amount of data and anecdotes that I managed to gather from most respondents after initial hesitation attests to the importance of the economic factor, as well as its complexity.

The issue of causality necessarily arises. It is tempting to suppose a direct link between war economies and the protraction of the two conflicts in terms of a binary relationship of cause and effect. I have argued here that the relationship between the two is more complex and multifaceted. It is true that actors on all sides of the ceasefire lines exploited, or attempted to exploit, the situation dictated by the lack of conflict resolution for their own ends. Some actors, mostly partaking in shadow economies, were clearly involved in economic activities that undermined the official stances of their own parties. The most apparent example is that of Georgian authorities, which participated in cross-ceasefire lines trade, weakening Tbilisi's strategy of trade sanctions and bolstering the revenues of the separatist authorities. Aside from personal gain, however, the attainment of economic primacy in certain areas or sectors went hand-in-hand with the establishment and management of social and political positions of power. Key actors of the Abkhaz government in exile and of borderland regions used their economic clout to expand their political influence both locally and in Tbilisi. A near-monopoly over trade, or other income-generating activities, allowed Abkhaz and South Ossetian authorities to retain control and create clientele networks in the *de facto* states, as well as to rally or coerce the resident population behind the preservation of the status quo.

It is important to look at post-combat economies in the light of the different parties' objectives. While the government of Georgia tried to use economic tools to curtail the protraction of conflict, the evolution of combat economies into post-combat economies allowed the *de facto* governments of Abkhazia and South Ossetia to avoid a settlement. In fact, the status quo that was in place after the conflicts of the early 1990s suited the separatist entities to a greater extent than it suited Tbilisi. Each *de facto* government exercised control over its own territory and *de facto* borders, although to varying extents. From this perspective, a protraction of a low-intensity opposition between the two sides was very much the goal, which required the establishment of viable economies in the two regions, whether through productive and commercial activities, or through foreign support. A normative approach would address the issue of conflict protraction and the lack of conflict resolution as negative developments but it is useful to acknowledge that, for numerous parties, the protraction of low-intensity conflicts, and hence the maintenance of *de facto* independence and a legal vacuum, was a far-from-undesirable new historical development.

It is therefore impossible to advance generalizations that would establish a cause-effect link across the board. The range of actors and objectives is too vast, and their relationships should be analysed one by one. These include state and *de facto* state actors, non-state actors such as violence entrepreneurs and civilians on both sides of the divide, as well as phenomena such as cross-border trade, coping strategies, displacement and insecurity, post-Soviet transition and some of the dynamics peculiar to entities such as *de facto* states. For most of these elements there are macro, meso and micro dimensions to be taken into account. Each one of them helps us understand, on the one hand, the systems that both reap benefits from and encourage the protraction of conflicts, and on the other hand they shine a light on what it is to live through low-intensity, seemingly endless, and all-pervasive tensions. For example, coping strategies are both an indication of the ingenuity of people under duress, and of the *ad hoc* way in which this ingenuity contributes to the entrenchment of systems.

This chapter has only exposed part of the extreme complexity of the two cases. Due to space constraints, numerous aspects could not be treated, from the importance of criminal networks in shadow economies, to economic interests surrounding the Abkhaz government in exile and the local power structures in the borderlands. The developments engendered by the Rose Revolution and the impact of the successful reintegration of Adjara under Georgian control need considerably more scrutiny, as well as the role of international donors and neighbouring countries in affecting the Georgian and *de facto* states' war economies and, more narrowly, post-combat economies. It will also be necessary to include a thorough study of the economies of disempowerment, concerning long-term displaced people from Abkhazia and South Ossetia on the one hand, and disempowered populations within the *de facto* states on the other hand. While this clearly includes residents of the Gali region with IDP-status in Abkhazia, and residents of ethnic Georgian villages in South Ossetia, it also leads to a better appreciation of dynamics of power and economic control of narrow elites within the *de facto* states – whether Armenians in Abkhazia, or ousted *de facto* officials in South Ossetia.

However, this chapter set the foundations for the scrutiny of the two protracted conflicts of Abkhazia and South Ossetia from an economic perspective, which contributes in turn to a more complete understanding of the dynamics underpinning the two cases. It unveiled the complexity of the interests at play, as well as the variety of actors, their nature and their goals, and some of the mechanisms that are at their disposal to exert leverage on the opposing parties or to avoid or utilize such external pressure for their own ends. It has also shown that, while the theoretical enquiry into war economies and their transformation has been considerable since the 1990s, there are still significant theoretical gaps, especially with regard to conflict protraction. Through these two initial case studies, the chapter approached these topics, adding a new perspective complementing the existing literature.

References

Areshidze, M. (2002) Current economic causes of conflicts in Georgia, in Vaux, T. (ed.) *Strategic Conflict Assessment*. DFID, London.
Baev, P. (1997) *Russia's Policies in the Caucasus*, RIIA, London.
Baev, P. (2003) Civil wars in Georgia: corruption breeds violence, in Zürcher, C. and Koehler, J. (eds.) *Potentials of (Dis)order*. Manchester University Press, Manchester.
Ballentine, K. and Nitzschke, H. (2005) *The Political Economy of Civil War and Conflict Transformation*, Berghof Research Center for Constructive Conflict Management, Berlin.
Ballentine, K and Sherman, J. (2003) *The Political Economy of Armed Conflict: Beyond Greed and Grievance*, Lynne Rienner, Boulder, CO.
Berdal, M. and Keen, D. (1997) Violence and economic agendas in civil wars: some policy implications. *Journal of International Studies*, 26(3), 795–818
Champain, P., Klein, D. and Mirimanova, N. (2004) *From War Economies to Peace Economies in the South Caucasus*, International Alert, London.
Closson, S. (2007) State Weakness in Perspective: Trans-territorial Energy Networks in Georgia, 1993–2003. PhD thesis, LSE, London.
Collier, P. and Hoeffler, A. (2001) *Greed and Grievance in Civil War*. DECRG Project Paper, World Bank, Washington D.C.
Coppieters, B., Darchiashvili, D. and Akaba, N. (2000) *Federal Practice: Exploring Alternatives for Georgia and Abkhazia*, VUB Press, Brussels.
Coppieters, B. and Legvold, R. (2005) *Statehood and Security: Georgia after the Rose Revolution*, MIT Press, Cambridge, MA.
Cornell, S. (2007) *Georgia After the Rose Revolution: Geopolitical Predicament and Implications for US Policy*, Strategic Studies Institute, Carlisle.
Cortright, D. (1997) *The Price of Peace: Incentives and International Conflict Prevention*, Rowman & Littlefield, Oxford.

Cortright, D. (2007) The Economic Tools of Peacemaking, in Zartman, W. (ed.) *Peacemaking in International Conflict, Methods and Techniques*. Institute of Peace Press, Washington, DC.

Cramer, C. (2006) *Civil War is not a Stupid Thing*, Hurst & Co., London.

Donnan, H. and Wilson, T. (1999) *Borders: Frontiers of Identity, Nation and State*, Berg, Oxford.

Dowty, A. (1994) Sanctioning Iraq: the limits of the New World Order. *The Washington Quarterly* 17(3), 179–198

Dzhikaev, V. and Parastaev, A. (2004) Economy and conflict in South Ossetia, in Champain, P., Klein, D. and Mirimanova, N. (eds.) *From War Economies to Peace Economies*. International Alert, London.

Elwert, G. (2003) Intervention in markets of violence, in Zürcher, C. and Koehler, J. (eds.) *Potentials of (Dis)order*, Manchester University Press, Manchester.

Goodhand, J. (2003) *From War Economy to Peace Economy?* LSE Eprints, London, <http://eprints.lse.ac.uk/28364/1/Goodhand_LSERO_version.pdf> (accessed 29 October 2014).

Goodhand, J. (2004) From war economy to peace economy? *Journal of International Affairs* (special edition on international institutions and justice), 58(1), 155–175

Goodhand, J. (2008) War, peace and the places in between: why borderlands are central, in Pugh, M., Cooper, N. and Turner, M. (eds.) *Whose Peace?* Palgrave Macmillan, Basingstoke.

Hufbauer, G. C, Schott, J. J. and Elliott, K. A. (1990) *Economic Sanctions Reconsidered: History and Current Policy*, Institute for International Economics, Washington, DC.

ICG (2004) *Georgia: Avoiding War in South Oss*etia. Europe Report (No. 159). ICG, Brussels.

ICG(2006) *Abkhazia Today*. Europe Report (No. 176). ICG, Brussels.

ICG (2007) *Georgia's South Ossetia Conflict: Make Haste Slowly*. Europe Report (No. 183). ICG, Brussels.

Keen, D. (1998) *The Economic Functions of Violence in Civil Wars*. Adelphi Paper (No. 320). OUP, Oxford.

Keen, D. (2008) *Complex Emergencies*, Polity Press, Cambridge.

Khutsidze, N. (2004) Q&A with MP Giga Bokeria over South Ossetia. *Civil Georgia* (26 July).

King, C. (2001) The benefits of ethnic war: understanding Eurasia's unrecognized states. *World Politics* 53, 524–552

Kukhianidze, A., Kupatadze, A. and Gotsiridze R. (2004) *Smuggling through Abkhazia and Tskhinvali Region of Georgia*, TRACC, Tbilisi.

Kukhianidze, A., Kupatadze, A. and Gotsiridze R. (2007) Smuggling in Abkhazia and the Tskhinvali region in 2003–2004, in Shelley, L., Scott, E.R. and Latta, A. (eds.) *Organised Crime and Corruption in Georgia*. Routledge, London.

Lynch, D. (2003) *The South Caucasus: A Challenge for the EU*, ISS, Paris.

Lynch, D. (2004) *Engaging Eurasia's Separatist States: Unresolved Conflicts and De Facto States*, US Institute of Peace Press, Washington, DC.

Matveeva, A. (2002)*The South Caucasus: Nationalism, Conflict and Minorities*, Minority Rights Group, London.

Migdal, J. (2004) *Boundaries and Belonging: States and Societies in the Struggle to Shape Identities and Local Practices*, Cambridge University Press, Cambridge.

O'Sullivan, M. L. (2003) *Shrewd Sanctions: Statecraft and State Sponsors of Terrorism*, Brookings Institute Press, Washington, DC.

Prelz Oltramonti, G. (2012) Political Economy of Protracted Conflicts: Abkhazia, South Ossetia, and Violence Mitigation. *The Caucasus and Globalization*, Volume 6, Issue 1.

Prelz Oltramonti, G. (2013) Borders, De Facto Borders and Mobility Policies in Conflict Transformation: The Cases of Abkhazia and South Ossetia, in Jan Wielgohs and ArnauldLechevalier (eds.), *Borders and Border Regions in Europe*, Transcript, Bielefeld.

Pugh, M. and Cooper, N. (2004) *War Economies in a Regional Context: Challenges of Transformation*, Lynne Rienner, Boulder, CO.

Pugh, M., Cooper, N. and Turner, M. (2008) *Whose peace? Critical Perspectives on the Political Economy of Peacebuilding*, Palgrave Macmillan, Basingstoke.

Rock, S. R. (2000) *Appeasement in International Politics*, University Press Kentucky, Lexington, KY.

Security Council (1997) *Official Records. Fifty-second year. Supplement for April, May And June 1997*, United Nations, New York, NY.

Tilly, C. (2003) *The Politics of Collective Violence*, Cambridge University Press, Cambridge.

Wennmann, A. (2007) The political economy of conflict financing: a comprehensive approach beyond natural resources. *Global Governance* 13, 427–44.

Wennmann, A. (2008) *What is the Political Economy of Conflict? Delimiting a Debate on Contemporary Armed Conflict.* Paper presented at the World International Studies Conference, Geneva.

Zürcher, C., Baev, P. and Koehler, J. (2005) Civil wars in the Caucasus,in Collier, P. and Sambanis, N. (eds.) *Understanding Civil War: Evidence and Analysis.* PRIO, Washington, DC.

Minna Lundgren

Crossing the Border – An Intergenerational Study of Belonging and Temporary Return among IDPs from Abkhazia

ABSTRACT: More than 250 000 people are displaced within the borders of Georgia today. The majority of the displaced fled the armed ethnic conflicts in Abkhazia in the 1990s. The administrative boundary line between Georgia and Abkhazia has, in effect, turned into a *de facto* state border but Georgians displaced from Abkhazia have continued to cross the boundary to enter Abkhazia for longer or shorter durations. This study addresses the motives for crossing the boundary and its significance for how people understand their belonging.

KEYWORDS: Georgia, Abkhazia, internal displacement, border, belonging, home

Introduction

Worldwide, civil wars and ethnic conflicts have increased since the collapse of the Soviet Union, and have consequently caused rising numbers of refugees and internally displaced persons (IDPs) (Cohen and Deng,1998; Castells, 2003; IDMC, 2011; UNHCR 2011). Migration researchers since at least the late 1990s have emphasized that many of today's economic migrants are included in cross-border networks by maintaining extensive and regular contact across national borders but the transnational networks of forcibly displaced people have rarely been taken into account, and when their transnational relationships have been addressed, they are usually reduced to political activities (Glick Schiller, 1997; Portes, 1999; Al-Ali *et al.*, 2001; Collier, 2005; Glick Schiller *et al.*, 1995; Koser, 2007). Irrespective of the means of communication – Internet, telephone calls, letters, or physical movements – transnationalism can be interpreted as an expression of belonging both to the country of origin and the country of residence (Madsen and Van Naerssen,2003).

Common to the still few studies of transnational networking among the forcibly displaced is the fact that they all describe transnational relations over significant distances and relationships that are thus – at least mostly – maintained by indirect means of communication. This study addresses the cross-boundary activities developed by internally displaced persons (IDPs) from Abkhazia living in the area adjacent to the administrative boundary line (ABL) between Georgia and Abkhazia – in other words, IDPs who live geographically very close to their area of origin, and who, for now at least, have good opportunities to cross the ABL.[1] What motivates IDPs to cross the boundary and what is the significance of cross-boundary movement for how people understand where they belong? The generational aspect is given a central role. Most young IDPs from Abkhazia have few or no memories of their area of origin before their escape and they have thus 'inherited' their IDP status.

The movements over the boundary line can be compared to the transnational activities of economic migrants and long-distance refugees. However, Abkhazia, a former autonomous republic within the Georgian SSR, is *de jure* still a part of Georgia, and only a handful of states have recognized Abkhazia's self-proclaimed independence. But Abkhazia today functions *de facto* as an independent state and the boundary with Georgia is a *de facto* border, where legal documents are required for crossing. Hence, movement across this boundary can be compared to transnational movement. This study is therefore an important contribution not only on the motives for boundary crossings by IDPs in a particular area but also on how forcibly displaced populations maintain relations with their native areas through direct means of communication.

Method

Research on displaced persons is most often based on interviews, either with adults or with children and adolescents (Sirriyeh, 2010). Many adolescents and young adults among Georgia's displaced were forced to

1 "Administrative boundary line" (ABL), "border" and "boundary" will hereafter be used interchangeably.

leave Abkhazia when they were very young, or in some cases were born in displacement and can thus be expected to have a different connection to their home in Abkhazia than their parents. The present study of intergenerational value discrepancies between young IDPs and their parents, based on interviews with IDPs from Abkhazia living in Georgia, is therefore an important contribution to research on forcibly displaced people's cross-border activities.

The interviews were conducted in the Georgian city of Zugdidi and two nearby villages in February 2012. Most respondents were living in collective centres, a few in private accommodations. A total of 58 people (39 young people and 19 adults aged over 30) were interviewed in 31 interviews. The participants were interviewed either individually (eight interviews) or in groups of varying sizes consisting of young people (siblings, friends) or young people and adults (parents, extended family) (23 interviews).The respondents were invited to answer and discuss a number of open questions concerning their experiences of living in the border area and crossing the ABL, and their plans and thoughts about temporary visits and permanent return to Abkhazia.

Given that this essay is an exploration of a pattern of physical movement similar to transnationalism, in an area where previously there were no boundaries and to which several ethnic groups lay claim in the hopes of establishing themselves as nation-states, a brief background is called for. The results of the interviews will then be presented, and the chapter ends with some concluding remarks.

Background

The Soviet Union was constituted as a federal hierarchy with union republics, autonomous republics, autonomous oblasts, and autonomous okrugs – subnational entities with different degrees of autonomy – shared among different groups in an ethno-territorial division of space. Each unit was supposed to represent a national "homeland" for the titular population (Wheatley, 2010). When a territory was accorded autonomous status, this could be interpreted as a seal of approval from Moscow on the titular population's "right" to exist as a nation (Jackson, 2004). But the principle that each ethnic group should have its own designated territory did not necessarily mean that the titular population was in the majority in the area (Fawn and Cummings, 2001; Jackson 2004; Pelkmans 2006; Trier *et al.*, 2010). Especially in the Caucasus, an area characterized by social, cultural, and economic intermingling, the labelling of local inhabitants as belonging to one or other ethnic group did not always reflect the underlying social reality. When ethnicity became the main character of identity, other social identities such as class or clan lost importance. Numerous state policies were based on ethnic belonging; ethnic belonging was registered in passports and documents; belonging to the titular population meant preferential access to higher education and political and bureaucratic positions: the consolidation of national groups was facilitated by Soviet rule (Pelkmans, 2006).

As long as the Soviet Union existed as a strong central power that could serve as a mediator or arbitrator between the different hierarchical levels, holding the patchwork of nations together, this order worked (Matveeva, 2002; Jackson, 2004). Over and above the economic, political, and social reforms that came with the breakdown of the union and the independence of the union republics in 1991, the national elites strived to strengthen the national ties within the republics. Having gained the freedom to determine their own fate, majority peoples in the successor states sought to build modern states around dominant groups and already defined borders. Minority groups within the newly independent states were expected to go along with this development, but out of fear of losing political, economic, linguistic, and cultural status, these groups instead put forward demands for increased autonomy, and ultimately independence, often with support from Moscow (Matveeva, 2002; Pelkmans, 2006; Cheterian, 2009; Trier *et al.*, 2010). Poor Abkhazian and Ossetian integration into Georgian political structures and society also resulted in a high degree of separation from Georgian culture. When Georgia set out to gain independence, Abkhazia and South Ossetia feared for their autonomy – and they looked to Moscow as a protector, a symbol of security (Broers, 2010; Wheatley, 2010). In the years immediately following Georgian independence this led to the eruption of armed conflicts in both Abkhazia and South Ossetia and Georgia itself was plagued by a civil war that broke out when the country's first president, Zviad Gamsakhurdia, was forced from power. These conflicts and the short war with Russia in 2008 led to the forced displacement of hundreds of thousands of people. Today, more than 250 000 people are still displaced, at least one-fifth of them children and adolescents under 18 years of age (King, 2001; Svendsen, 2005; IDMC, 2009; UNHCR, 2011).

The first priority of the Georgian government has been to end this displacement by regaining control over Abkhazia and South Ossetia, and the return of IDPs to their home areas has therefore been prioritized over integration in other parts of the country (Kabachnik *et al.*, 2010). Since 2007, the government has also been working to increase the integration into local communities of IDPs who are waiting to return home (MRA, 2007); however, working for better social integration while maintaining IDPs' motivation to return requires a balance to be struck between the long term and the temporary (Tarkhan-Mouravi and Sumbadze, 2006). In Abkhazia, where the *de facto* regime proclaimed independence in 1992 and to this day still seeks to strengthen its sovereignty, there is strong opposition to the return of ethnic Georgians. Georgians accounted for 43% of the population before the 1992–93 war, so it would be difficult for the Abkhaz regime to maintain an independent Abkhazian state based on ethnicity. The IDPs have thus become a pawn in the Georgian government's pursuit of control over Abkhazia and South Ossetia (Libal, 2002; Kolstø and Blakkisrud, 2008; Trier *et al.*, 2010).

However, it is important to note the specific situation of the Gali district, where ethnic Georgians (including Megrelians, an ethnic Georgian subgroup) constituted more than 93% of the population in the 1989 all-Soviet census. The Abkhaz *de facto* government has allowed the return of the displaced prewar population to Gali, giving as its two main reasons demography and the fact that the population in Gali did not participate actively in the 1992–93 war, unlike Georgians from other parts of Abkhazia (Trier *et al.*, 2010). It is unclear how many Georgians have returned to Gali, but estimates are in the order of 45 000–65 000 (Trier *et al.*, 2010; Human Rights Watch, 2011).

Results

Zugdidi, the city where many of the interviews were held, is situated 20minutes' drive from the Inguri Bridge, which constitutes the only official border crossing between Georgia and Abkhazia. The boundary line (which follows the River Inguri) was established under the ceasefire agreement in 1994, and has evolved into a *de facto* state border since Russia and a few other states have recognized Abkhazia as an independent state.

Roughly half the respondents originated from the Gali district in southern Abkhazia. The rest came from Sukhumi (the capital), Ochamchire, or Tqvarcheli, or did not specify any one place in Abkhazia as their home. Out of the 58respondents,the vast majority – 49 people – answered that they at some point, repeatedly or regularly, had visited Abkhazia since they were first displaced. Most of them had taken unofficial routes across the boundary. In order to use the Inguri Bridge, legal Abkhaz documents are required, something that IDPs in most cases lack. Respondents stated that using "another way" or "crossing illegally" was cheaper and provided safer opportunities to bring back nuts and other agricultural products from Abkhazia. The use of unofficial routes, however, is subject to certain problems, as both Russian and Abkhazian troops are stationed along the boundary. Georgian men who participated in the1992–93 war and are suspected of participation in what in international law would be regarded as war crimes, or who are, or have been, members of a guerrilla movement, risk imprisonment if they enter Abkhazia (UNHCR, 1994; Human Rights Watch, 2011; Weiss, 2012). Men of certain ages are therefore regarded with suspicion by troops at the border crossing and along the boundary line, and for these men crossing the border can imply a significant risk (Human Rights Watch, 2011; Weiss, 2012).

One possible way to capture the motives behind why people cross the border, and also the perceptions of belongingness and the future related to these motives, is to use the information provided by respondents about how often they cross the border. Accordingly, there are different kinds of crossings: those that occur regularly, sometimes as often as every weekend; less regular, but still recurrent crossings; and, finally, occasional crossings, where people return to Abkhazia perhaps only once or twice.

Regular Crossings

Regular crossings are primarily connected with economic exchanges of various kinds. As Mirimanova and Pentikainen (2011) note, there is a continuous flow of good sin both directions across the ABL, especially nuts and other agricultural products. Women play a central role in this, since they cross more easily than men do – who might otherwise be suspected of participation in the smuggling of arms (Weiss, 2012). Apart from the requirement for legal documents, the boundary apparently has a selective permeability, with some people crossing more easily than others. The respondents described the illegal routes across the boundary as being cheaper and "better" because goods could be taken through without paying bribes. "If you use the bridge you have to pay. Otherwise, you only pay for the *marshrutka* and you cross on foot.[2] It's dangerous, but if you want to bring back the harvest, it's better. And with a family you can't afford to use the bridge", said one woman who often crossed the boundary line along with her husband and three children (Respondent7B). Several respondents in the parental generation stated that they have houses and gardens (where they grow nuts, fruit, and vegetables) in the Gali region and regularly go there to take care of these properties and any crops. Economic exchanges are seemingly an important part of these temporary returns.

However, some of the younger respondents who were studying at the university in Zugdidi also crossed the ABL every weekend. Some of them had left Abkhazia fairly recently, having spent most of their childhood in villages in Gali, and their parents and siblings were still living there. They justified their trips home by saying they wanted to see their families, and that parents often worried about them managing on their own in Zugdidi. A young boy (Respondent20A), a student at the university in Zugdidi, said that he chose to "go home on the weekends, every weekend. But I lack Abkhaz ID so I can't use the bridge, I use other roads." A young woman (Respondent2B), a second-year student, said that at weekends or as soon as she had a day off, she crossed the borderline: "When I'm at home, there's no need for words; I love my home. The Russian army stands along the boundary line, and it's always a risk to cross the border illegally. We're very afraid, yet we continue to cross this border." By both young people's accounts, they actually "live" in Abkhazia, but have to stay in Zugdidi to study, and as often as they can they cross the boundary line to go home. However, their personal safety and that of their families is something that worries them. "When you are in Abkhazia you must forget that you are Georgian. Once I had a T-shirt with a Georgian flag and my dad yelled at me that I was crazy. A boy who had a Georgian sticker on a textbook at school was beaten by the Abkhazian military" (Respondent2B). Another young

2 A *marshrutka* is a minibus running a scheduled or chartered service.

woman (Respondent 27 C), who had completed her studies a couple of years earlier, described how her parents sent her from Abkhazia to relatives outside Zugdidi when she was in her early teens, and how ever since then she had crossed the boundary line to go home and see her parents every weekend, at first so that her parents could be sure that she was doing well but now, increasingly, so she could reassure herself that her parents were coping.

Living close to the boundary and having a house in Abkhazia means that many IDPs can regularly visit and maintain contacts and relationships with their relatives, especially grandparents who live there to take care of houses and farms, but also with the Abkhazian locals. "We are close to Abkhazia and we have contacts with friends and family who live there. We also know that the Abkhaz are friendly; they are not evil. But many of our generation, who live far from Zugdidi, they do not have these contacts and do not intend to go back, or move back, in the same way as we do. We keep these contacts alive", said one girl (Respondent 5A). The respondents who talked about regular trips to Abkhazia thus testified to a life lived on both sides of the boundary line, and the importance of the opportunity to cross the boundary. One boy (Respondent 22A) spoke of how important family was to him, and how it affected his mood: "I'm happy when I'm in Abkhazia because I have many relatives there. That's the difference. I'm happier there than here. Here I'm mostly sad."

In a village outside Zugdidi, a few women were interviewed together. During the interview, a girl came into the room, and the women said that she had "come back [from Abkhazia] an hour ago". They described how most of the IDPs in the village crossed the border every weekend because their village in Abkhazia was just across the border. "We have nothing here, no jobs, nothing. All that we have today, we have brought from Abkhazia. And of course it is important that our children also know what income we have from Abkhazia", said one of the women (Respondent29C). Families bring nuts and other agricultural products from Abkhazia, which they use themselves or sell at market in Zugdidi. Crossing the ABL is thus crucial for supporting the family, as the monthly allowances for IDPs are not sufficient. This particular respondent highlighted the importance of talking about and visiting Abkhazia to show their homeland to the children: "maybe we will go back permanently one day, and maybe our generation will not be here then. But we need to talk about our traditions with our children, so that they can talk to their children. So that Abkhazia will not be forgotten and our memories not lost." To encourage the children's attachment to Abkhazia is a way to keep alive the dream of returning.

Recurrent Crossings

Some border crossings are frequent, just not as often as, say, every weekend. Crossings that take place every summer or on occasions such as deaths and funerals are referred to here as "recurrent crossings". Many of the young respondents talked about spending their summer holidays in Abkhazia in their family's house there. The summer break is not the only reason to cross the border, however, for during summer people also take care of their properties and harvest nuts and other crops. To go to Abkhazia is to lay continued claim to the ownership of the property, to highlight one's title. A 17-year-old girl (Respondent5B) said that "we have a house in Abkhazia, and a garden. We go there in the summer…But at the same time, it's not ours; it belongs to the enemy now … But I don't want to think that my parents have lost everything, and I want to take care of my father's house, his property. And take care of the wealth that I have. My wealth is my country. I want to save it and protect it." The house in Abkhazia becomes a symbol of a life different from that in Zugdidi, where life for many is characterized by a lack of normality. Despite the lack of infrastructure and personal safety, life in Abkhazia, particularly in the agricultural region of Gali, is distinguished from life in the collective centres in Zugdidi. "We have a house in Gali, not a building like here. It's a proper house" (Respondent 6A). Several young people testified to feeling similarly about the family house in Abkhazia as something positive: "I have a good feeling when I'm in my house. But when I cross the boundary and go back, it feels very hard" (Respondent31C).

Another occasion when IDPs frequently cross the boundary is to attend funerals or visit graves. The link to "those who came before us" is important. To visit the graves and attend even a distant acquaintance's funeral is a part of everyday life. Adults and adolescents alike testified to this motive for crossing the boundary. "We still have our neighbours in our village in Abkhazia. And when something happens in the village, or when somebody dies, we cross the boundary illegally and my son comes with us. So he knows Abkhazia" (Respondent9B). A young boy (Respondent31C) who had lived inAbkhaziauntil7 years before, when his father was killed, said that "my home is in Abkhazia. I go there as often as I can to visit my father's grave." One woman (Respondent3B) described how she sometimes crosses the border "to visit the cemetery where our relatives are buried ... It is important to remember relatives who came before us. It is not just about remembering; there is also a spiritual connection. It is part of our tradition to show respect for the dead." But it is difficult to arrange for IDPs who die in Zugdidi to be buried in Abkhazia. One girl (Respondent 5A) said that "I have many times seen at funerals that they pour soil from Abkhazia over the dead. Soil that a neighbour or friend has brought from Abkhazia. You wanted to return, you could not return, but on your body you still have Abkhazian soil." The difficulties experienced by those who wanted to bury their dead in Abkhazia are a cause of sorrow, as voiced by a woman (Respondent13A) who buried her mother in Zugdidi: "My father and sister are buried in Sukhumi, but my mother is buried here. She cried and cried when she understood that we could not bury her in Sukhumi." To bury someone away from their native home is understood as a symbol of a broken life course – life should start and end in the place where one belongs.

Occasional Crossings

Having a house and close relatives in the Gali region is not just a reason to return, it also provides the practical means to cross the ABL fairly frequently. The absence of a house is thus a reason not to travel to Abkhazia as often. Respondent 31A said:

> My home is there, in Abkhazia. But my house has burned down. I've been there and I feel so sad to see this place without a house. I can't go there so often, it's not possible... I have never seen my house, since it burned down. When my parents talk about it and explain what it looked like, I can't picture it in front of me. It's hard.

This was from a young boy whose parents took him to Abkhazia on a few occasions, among other reasons in order to show him the place where they had once lived.

Those who don't have houses, or who originated from Sukhumi or other areas less accessible from Georgia, spoke of single trips of a more touristic character. During the Soviet era, Abkhazia was a popular tourist destination for people from all over the Soviet Union. Some young respondents described trips to Abkhazia as pleasure trip: they talked about the seaside and holidays while their parents vividly described Abkhazian nature as exceptionally beautiful. "We went to the sea. The Black Sea is very special there. Not like in other places. The sky is beautiful. There are more natural resources. And when we were there, I discovered that I relax in a different way, better" (Respondent18B) – the sea in Abkhazia is more beautiful than in other places; the air is different; it is easier to breathe there.

The adults highlighted the fact that crossing the ABL is not only about visiting Abkhazia but also about showing the children "their homeland". One woman (Respondent 11B) stated that

> It's our duty as parents to talk to our children about Abkhazia, about everything we had, about our lives. So that they can understand and love this Abkhazia that we come from. So that they understand our love for Abkhazia. I want my children to know that we have Abkhaz relatives. They are Abkhaz, but they are our relatives. Maybe one day there will be peace between Abkhaz and Georgians. We should not hate them, they are our relatives. We have to meet them, and one day we may be able to live together.

Here again we see their reasons for talking to the children and showing them Abkhazia. The woman's daughter (Respondent 11A), having listened to her mother, said "I want to live in Abkhazia, but I don't think it's possible. Eighteen years, and we haven't been able to return. How could I think that we can return in the future? Is eighteen years not enough?"

Her mother thought for a moment, and then responded

> As a mother, my first wish is for peace and that my children are healthy and get a good education. But my heart's greatest desire is that we could return. I want my own house. I want us to live together in our house. I want my children to live in their own house. We have a terrible life here. When I say my own, I mean my house, my garden, on my street in my village. This place makes me very aggressive and stressed.

Even though this family had visited Abkhazia only once since their escape, their longing fora "normal life" was a pressing reason to cross the administrative boundary line.

Those Who Could Not Cross

It should not be concluded from the descriptions thus far that the ABL is completely open to all to cross at will, however. Any men who participated in the war or in any guerrilla movement face imprisonment if they enter the area and are found by Abkhazian or Russian forces. People who worked in government or the police also face retaliations – a risk that also encompasses their families. The respondents who had not returned even once to Abkhazia gave personal safety and the risk of violence as their main reasons and, in several cases, someone in their family had fought in the war. The testimony of people who had returned also reinforced their impression of the difficult security situation: some of these families had lost their property in Abkhazia and some, but not all, originated from Sukhumi, where it is very difficult for Georgians to travel.

One woman (Respondent 8C), who had not returned at all since her escape, said that her daughters looked at her in surprise when she talked about Abkhazia with emotion: "I want my children to see Abkhazia at least once before I die. So that they understand what Abkhazia really is." Her daughters (Respondents 8A and 8B) said that their parents' stories made them curious and they wished to go to Abkhazia to "see it". But they were quite clear that they did not want to return permanently: "Maybe I will go back, but not to live there … just to see it. When I see how my parents are so affected by this Abkhazia, I'm interested. And of course I want to go there and just see what sort of a place it is" (Respondent 8A). The older generation often emphasized memories and links to the past as a reason to return. "It's my dream, and I don't want to die without having been back once. I want to walk the streets of Sukhumi, and to feel that 'I'm in Sukhumi now'. And I don't want to die without that feeling, without having been there once" (Respondent 8C). For this woman, the loss of a happy past is hard to bear without being able to visit the place where the past played out. The younger generation, with no memories of "the good life in Abkhazia", does not have the same difficulties. One girl (Respondent 19A) remarked that "I wasn't born there, so it was easy for me, I have no memories of living there. So I wasn't sorry to go there and see that place."

Summary and Discussion

Some IDPs return to Abkhazia regularly and often; others return in the summer or for special events; still others just returned once or not at all. Some young people have thus "returned" to a place where they had never been. The frequency of their border crossings was different, as were their motives. The reasons for going into Abkhazia given in the interviews were visiting family and friends, claiming ownership and maintaining property, agriculture and harvesting, funerals, tourist trips, and nostalgia. The overwhelming majority of respondents claimed Abkhazia (alone or together with Georgia) as their homeland, and most of them had returned at least once. Border crossings and temporary returns – regular, recurrent, occasional, or even impossible – are closely linked to individual attachment to Abkhazia, to one's self-identification as being "from Abkhazia". Abkhazia is not only the geographical location but also the place of memories of the past, memories of war, and memories of escape and living in "exile".

The various motives of Georgian IDPs who chose to cross and recross the ABL can be captured schematically (see Figure 1). The main motive for temporary returns to Abkhazia is the feeling of belonging, either derived from personal experience or, in some cases, inherited. It signifies a wish to uphold some kind of continuity, to continue to belong in Abkhazia – a continuity of belonging not only upheld by temporary returns (or the desire to visit "at least once") but also by political discourse, by schoolteachers who encourage children to write about Abkhazia, and by assigning those who fled from Abkhazia the status of IDPs. Internally displaced persons, by definition, belong "somewhere else" than their current place of residence. The wish for continuity of belonging encompasses not only those who regularly, recurrently or occasionally returned, but also those who never returned.

Motives for crossing the ABL and visits to Abkhazia	Economic – property and harvest			
	Social – relatives and friends			
	Touristic trips – show to the children			
	Belonging in Abkhazia – talking to children, stories, memories			
Frequency of visits	Regular	Recurrent	Occasional	Never
Consequence for belonging	Sense of belonging decreases with no or fewer visits and contacts with Abkhazia			

Figure 1: A schematic view of motives for and consequences of boundary crossings and temporary visits to Abkhazia.]

Those who crossed the boundary regularly or recurrently gave social or economic reasons for their return: a house needs maintenance, parents need to be visited, funerals need to be attended, harvests need to be gathered in and transported to Georgia proper. Those who only occasionally crossed the ABL were often those who originated from Sukhumi, Ochamchire or Tqvarcheli, or did not have a house to go to, and therefore visited friends or relatives in Gali instead. All, in at least some aspect, claimed a historic or native belonging in Abkhazia but those of the younger generation who had yet to return even once were far less given to seeing their future as belonging in Abkhazia.

The collected interview material is too small to permit wider generalizations but the tendency among the young people is for those who do not return regularly or recurrently to show far less interest in returning permanently to Abkhazia. As one 16-year-old girl said:

> When I'm there, I love Abkhazia. But my friends are here, I was born here. That's why I love Zugdidi more than Abkhazia. My mother loves Abkhazia more than I do. When I listen to my mother, I notice that I don't have the same feelings that she has. But I understand her. She had her life there, she had her friends there, she grew up there. Her home is there. I grew up here, my friends are here. My mother talks the same way about Abkhazia. But it doesn't matter; I want to live in Zugdidi. My homeland is in Abkhazia. But my home is here. My homeland is Abkhazia because my parents were born and grew up there. But my home is here. (Respondent 18A)

Several young respondents gave similar accounts of their relationships to home and homeland. Home thus represents a place for social interaction, security, and everyday life, whereas Abkhazia is more of a historic homeland. There were also young people who expressed an uncertainty about where they belonged. "When we 'crossed' I felt that this is my own, my country, my own house. It was a good feeling", said one young girl (Respondent9A), but she went on to say that it was hard for her to say where her home was: "I was born in Abkhazia. Then we moved here, to this place. I got used to living here. And now they say that we must move to Poti. Therefore I don't know where my home is." She expressed a sense of belonging yet of rootlessness, related to the uncertainty and reluctance felt by some IDPs at being relocated to other parts of Georgia, a consequence of the government's programme to restore government buildings currently occupied by IDPs.

However, as nobody knows if and when the IDPs can return permanently to Abkhazia, one man (Respondent 15 B) questioned how long they could continue to say that they are from Abkhazia "when it's100,125 years since we fled? When we die, our personal memories of Abkhazia die. Abkhazia will be an episode in history. After many years, nobody will remember Abkhazia." Similar accounts were also reflected by other respondents:

> It's hard to know what to say to my children. But maybe I will say that they must love Abkhazia. It is our country, our homeland. But my children will not understand me, because I could not understand what and where this Abkhazia is. (Respondent 18A)

The same girl's mother (Respondent18B) agreed: "Her daughter will never understand as she understands it from me. The next generation will not know this. And they will not talk about Abkhazia. God willing, we must return before so many years have passed, before Abkhazia disappears from our memories."

Conclusions

Research on transnationalism among migrants is mainly focused on contacts that extend across continents, maintained by indirect means. In this study, however, IDPs living in a border area near to their area of origin, and the importance of their physical transitions and contacts with their homeland, are in focus. Holidays, family, property, and graves are examples of some of the more concrete motives described by the respondents. Unlike previous studies (Svendsen, 2005; UN Country Team in Georgia, 2008; Tarkhan-Mouravi 2009; Human Rights Watch, 2011), which are concerned with IDP movement across the boundary line between Georgia and Abkhazia, only a small number of respondents in this study highlight the economic importance of visits to Abkhazia. Crossing the boundary can be seen as a temporary return "home", in order to "show" the homeland to the children and encourage their attachment to and identification with Abkhazia. These temporary transitions and returns are also a symbol of the IDPs' homemaking processes. Kabachnik *et al.* (2010) identify Georgian IDPs' homemaking as "home as traveling", where "home" is situated either in a lost pastor in a future where the IDPs hope that they will have returned. "Home" thus assumes physical, temporal, and emotional dimensions. For those who had to leave their homes, "home" does not only correspond to a physical place – there is also a link to the past and to the future, where the goal, the dream, is to return (Zetter, 1999; Black, 2002). For many IDPs, however, visits to Abkhazia are also a return to a "home in the present". Several respondents witnessed to an everyday life going on in Abkhazia. Some of those who cross the boundary regularly have concrete plans to return permanently, be it as soon as they have completed their university studies or as soon as their children leave school. While waiting to return, they invest in their future home by sharing memories and returning temporarily for weekends or holidays, and not just to take care of the property, but also to strengthen ties to the homeland among those who were not born there.

The traditional view of migrants, whether they have moved voluntarily or were uprooted forcibly, is that migration is a movement in one direction; or in terms of refugee policy, a movement forward and then back again. In this study, we have seen that the cross-border movements of Georgian IDPs from Abkhazia are, in many cases, repeated and in some cases lives are lived in several places simultaneously. The younger generation of Georgian IDP shave inherited their status and are often more integrated into their "new home". Their dream of returning "home" is in many cases based on other people's images of that home. This is not particularly surprising. If younger generations to a lesser extent identify themselves as being "from Abkhazia" and show less interest in returning, one of the Georgian government's main arguments for regaining control over Abkhazia will weaken. Identification with Abkhazia and "the desire to return" is thus also a base fora political identity. Temporary visits, memories and stories from Abkhazia may in this way become a major factor in political mobilization once the generations who shave their own memories of an everyday life in Abkhazia before the war are gone.

References

Al-Ali, N., Black, R. and Koser, K. (2001) Refugees and transnationalism: the experience of Bosnians and Eritreans in Europe. *Journal of Ethnic and Migration Studies* 27(4), 615–634.

Black, R. (2002) Conceptions of "home" and the political geography of refugee repatriation: between assumption and contested reality in Bosnia-Herzegovina. *Applied Geography* 22(2), 123–138.

Broers, L. (2010) "David and Goliath" and "Georgians in the Kremlin": a post-colonial perspective on conflict in post-Soviet Georgia, in *War and Revolution in the Caucasus: Georgia Ablaze* (ed. S. F. Jones). Routledge, London, 7–26.

Castells, S. (2003) Towards a sociology of forced migration and social transformation. *Sociology* 37(1), 13–34.

Cheterian, V. (2009) The August 2008 war in Georgia: from ethnic conflict to border wars. *Central Asian Survey* 28(2), 155–170.

Cohen, R., and Deng, F. M. (eds) (1998) *The Forsaken People: Case Studies of the Internally Displaced.* Brookings Institution Press, Washington, DC.

Collier, M. (2005) *Citizens without Borders? Discussions of Transnationalism and Forced Migration*, Ninth Conference of the International Association for the Study of Forced Migration, Sao Paolo, Brazil, 9–13 January.

Fawn, R., and Cummings, S. N. (2001) Interests over norms in Western policy towards the Caucasus: how Abkhazia is no one's Kosovo. *European Security* 10(3), 84–108.

Glick Schiller, N. (1997) The situation of transnational studies. *Identities* 4(2), 155–166.

Glick Schiller, N., Basch, L., Basch, L. G. and Szanton Blanc, C. (1995) From immigrant to transmigrant: theorizing transnational migration. *Anthropological Quarterly* 68(1), 48–63.

Human Rights Watch (2011) *Living in Limbo: The Rights of Ethnic Georgian Returnees to the Gali District of Abkhazia*, Human Rights Watch, New York.

IDMC (2009) *Georgia: IDPs in Georgia Still Need Attention: A Profile of the Internal Displacement Situation*, Internal Displacement Monitoring Centre, Geneva.

IDMC (2011) *Appeal 2011*, Internal Displacement Monitoring Centre, Geneva.

Jackson, P. (2004) Ethnicity, decentralisation and the fissile state in Georgia. *Public Administration and Development* 24(1), 75–86.

Kabachnik, P., Regulska, J. and Mitchneck, B. (2010) Where and when is home? The double displacement of Georgian IDPs from Abkhazia. *Journal of Refugee Studies* 23(3), 315–336.

King, C. (2001) The benefits of ethnic war: understanding Eurasia's unrecognized states. *World Politics* 53(4), 524–552.

Kolstø, P. and Blakkisrud, H. (2008) Living with non-recognition: state- and nation-building in South Caucasian quasi-states. *Europe–Asia Studies* 60(3), 483–509.

Koser, K. (2007) Refugees, transnationalism and the state. *Journal of Ethnic and Migration Studies*33(2), 233–254.

Libal, M. (2002) Ethnic conflict in the Balkans and in the Caucasus: some general considerations. *Southeast European and Black Sea Studies* 2(2), 1–20.

Madsen, K. D., and van Naerssen, T. (2003) Migration, identity, and belonging. *Journal of Borderlands Studies* 18(1), 61–75.

Matveeva, A. (2002) *The South Caucasus: Nationalism, Conflict and Minorities*, Minority Rights Group International, London.

Mirimanova, N., and Pentikainen, O. (2011). *Regulating Trans-Ingur/i Economic Relations: Views from Two Banks*, International Alert, London.

MRA (2007) *State Strategy for Internally Displaced Persons – Persecuted. MoRA Accomodation*, Ministry of Refugees and Accomodation, Republic of Georgia, Tbilisi.

Pelkmans, M. (2006) *Defending the Border: Identity, Religion, and Modernity in the Republic of Georgia*, Cornell University Press, New York, NY.

Portes, A. (1999) Conclusions: toward a new world – the origins and effects of transnational activities. *Ethnic and Racial Studies* 22(2), 463–477.

Sirriyeh, A. (2010) Home journeys: im/mobilities in young refugee and asylum-seeking women's negotiations of home. *Childhood* 17(2), 213–227.

Svendsen, I. C. (2005) *Prospects for Return of Internally Displaced Persons (IDPs) to Abkhazia in Georgia*. Norwegian Refugee Council, Tbilisi.

Tarkhan-Mouravi, G. (2009) *Assessment of IDP Livelihoods in Georgia: Facts and Policies*, UNHCR, Tbilisi.

Tarkhan-Mouravi, G. and Sumbadze, N. (2006) The Abkhazian–Georgian conflict and the issue of internally displaced persons. *Innovation: The European Journal of Social Science Research* 19(3), 283–302.

Trier, T., Lohm, H. and Szakonyi, D. (2010) *Under Siege: Inter-Ethnic Relations in Abkhazia*, Columbia University Press, New York, NY.

UN Country Team in Georgia (2008) *UN Facilitated Review of Socioeconomic Needs in Abkhazia, Georgia: Final Report*, <http://documents.wfp.org/stellent/groups/public/documents/ena/wfp178374.pdf> (accessed 30 October 2014).

UNHCR (1994) *Quadripartite Agreement on Voluntary Return of Refugees and Displaced Persons*, <http://peacemaker.un.org/georgia-quatripartiteagreement94> (accessed 30 October 2014).

UNHCR (2011) *UNHCR Global Appeal 2011 Update*, UNHCR, Geneva, <http://www.unhcr.org/ga11/#/home> (accessed 30 October 2014).

Weiss, A. (2012) Crossing conflicting state boundaries: the Georgian–Abkhazian ceasefire line, in *Subverting Borders: Doing Research on Smuggling and Small-Scale Trade* (eds B. Bruns and J. Miggelbrink). VS Verlag für Sozialwissenschaften, Wiesbaden.

Wheatley, J. (2010) Managing ethnic diversity in Georgia: one step forward, two steps back, in *War and Revolution in the Caucasus: Georgia Ablaze* (ed. S. F. Jones), Routledge, London.

Zetter, R. (1999) Reconceptualizing the myth of return: continiuty and transition amongst the Greek-Cypriot refugees of 1974. *Journal of Refugee Studies* 12(1), 1–22.

Hanna Shelest

Foreign Policy Particularities of the *De Facto* States in the Black Sea Region

ABSTRACT: There are four separatists regions in the Black Sea area, which, at different stages of the conflicts development, have proclaimed independence – Transnistria, Nagorno-Karabakh, South Ossetia and Abkhazia. In this chapter we will analyse the mechanisms and peculiarities of the diplomatic relations of these unrecognized states. We will pay special attention to the instruments they use in negotiation, despite their non-recognized status, and we will examine how they interact with third states and whether recognition by some states adds legitimacy to the foreign policy of ex-Georgian regions. We will study the question of whether other states and international organizations can deal with these unrecognized states by traditional diplomatic means and standards or whether they need a new diplomatic approach.

KEYWORDS: unrecognized states, Transnistria, Abkhazia, South Ossetia, Nagorno-Karabakh, foreign policy analysis.

There are many examples in history when different separatist movements or ethnic groups proclaimed their independence. Most of these cases led either to war or to the full sovereignty of a new state. There are just a few examples when such proclamations resulted in a situation when there was no actual war but *de facto* states were created, which are not recognized but operate their own internal policy and foreign policy, while their final status still being under negotiation.

There are four separatist regions in the Black Sea area, which, at different stages of their conflicts development, have proclaimed independence – Transnistria, Nagorno-Karabakh, South Ossetia and Abkhazia. The Russian Federation only recognized the independence of Abkhazia and South Ossetia in 2008, after the Russian-Georgian conflict, not doing so for Transnistria.

Many authors have addressed the topic of the unrecognized states in the Black Sea region. However, most of them were particularly interested in one of three issues: the problems of self-determination (Markedonov, 2006; Graham and Horne, 2011; Byman and King, 2012; Маркедонов,

2012), conflict resolution (Caspersen and Herrberg, 2010) or relations with their "parent" states – the states from which independence is proclaimed (Kobrinskaya, 2008). Some articles are devoted to the internal development of the separatist regions. However, there is a lack of attention to the foreign policy and activity of these republics, apart from their relations with Russia and their parent states.

Moreover, these *de facto* states are usually perceived as objects rather than subjects of international relations, pretending that they are not able to conduct an independent foreign policy. However, an analysis of their current activities demonstrates that if in case of South Ossetia and Nagorno-Karabakh such a statement has a right for existence, so in case of Transnistria and Abkhazia this tendency is transforming, when unrecognized republics are striving to wider possibilities for cooperation with third parties in addition to the issues of peace negotiations, but pursue a semi-independent policy. As ability to conduct an independent foreign policy is seen as one of the obvious attributes of a sovereign state, it should become of particular interest, including unrecognized republics ability, mechanisms and tools, perception of such actions by the international community and priorities of their foreign policy.

In the opinion of D. Byman and C. King

> the real danger with phantom states is that low expectations lead to low accountability. Entities, which have no real stake in the international system, are disinclined to worry about upsetting it. For this reason alone, phantom states deserve to be moved from their position as curiosities of international affairs to being seen as a new form of state-making in an age of globalization, overlapping sovereignties, and multiple political loyalties. (Byman and King, 2012)

In this chapter we will analyse the mechanisms of the foreign relations of the unrecognized states in the Black Sea region. We will consider how they interact with third states and whether the recognition of states adds legitimacy to the foreign policy of ex-Georgian regions – whether there are any differences between their foreign policy and the foreign policy of other, unrecognized states in the Black Sea region. We will study the issue of whether other states and international organizations can deal with these unrecognized states by traditional diplomatic means, norms and standards or whether they need a new diplomatic approach towards them. We deliberately leave the issue of the peace negotiations, which have their own peculiarities both in the mechanisms used and in goals set, beyond the scope of this chapter.

State Recognition

The ability to conduct an independent foreign policy is closely connected with the problem of state recognition. The 1933 Montevideo Convention on the Rights and Duties of States set four criteria for international recognition -a state must have a permanent population, a defined territory, a government and the capacity to conduct foreign relations to receive international recognition. However, current international relations can be characterized by the tendency to delegate a part of the state sovereignty, including foreign policy, to supranational institutions, so the unambiguity of this criterion is deluding. The existence in international law of two main theories on state recognition – declaratory and constitutive – and an absence of internationally legitimized and agreed criteria to be considered as fully fledged states bring additional nuances to this situation.

Declaratory and constitutive theories of state recognition dominate current discourse in international law. According to the former, in its traditional form, a state's existence as an international legal person is independent of its recognition by existing states. Thus, when an entity satisfies the traditional criteria for statehood under customary international law – that is, as soon as it exists as a fact – this entity is a state in the sense of international law (Raic, 2002: 32). Supporters of this theory follow the Montevideo Convention, where, in Article 3, it is mentioned that "The political existence of the state is independent of recognition by the other states". This is proved indirectly by the fact that there is no rule in international law mentioning how many states should recognize the independence of the newly proclaimed state for it to be considered as a fully-fledged subject of international law.

The constitutive theory on the recognition of a state is based on the opposite thesis. The essence of it is formulated by L. Oppenheim in the following way: "International law does not say that a State is not in existence as long as it is not recognized, but it takes no notice of it before its recognition. Through recognition only and exclusively a State becomes an International Person and a subject of International law" (Oppenheim, 1905: 110). It is important to note that even the most ardent supporters of this view do not claim that recognition creates the state, as it is often suggested, since the state must, by way of necessity, exist prior to recognition. What is claimed, however, is that the act of recognition endows the already-existing state with international personality. Thus, a distinction is made between a state and an international person (Raic, 2002: 29). Without state recognition, it is impossible to imagine the membership of a state in international organizations, signing of bilateral and multilateral treaties, the conduct of foreign economic activity, and so forth. All this makes it *de facto* isolated in the world arena.

Nagorno-Karabakh and Transnistria still have not received any recognition despite the referendums on sovereignty and requests made to the international community after the Kosovo precedent. At the same time, as a result of the Russian-Georgian conflict of August 2008, Abkhazia and South Ossetia have been recognized by several states, as a result of Russian recognition and influence. Within 6 years, five countries recognized South Ossetia and Abkhazia – Russia, Nicaragua, Venezuela, Nauru and Tuvalu. In case of Abkhazia, it was announced that Vanuatu also recognized its independence in 2011; however, it was 'back-and-forward' politics, as within a month a new government of Vanuatu retracted previous decision, but then again the Ministry of Foreign Affairs of Vanuatu confirmed the recognition of Abkhazia (Transparency International, 2011). It is necessary to point out that the Minister of Foreign Affairs of Vanuatu studied at the Moscow Institute of International Relations, so had relations in Russia. There remains an issue as to why Vanuatu did not take any steps to recognize South Ossetia, as its previous acts towards these unrecognized republics had usually been conducted simultaneously. In addition, these four separatist regions have all recognized each other's independence.

Compared with the list of countries that recognized Kosovo's independence – 108 by August 2014 – the former Georgian territories have not succeeded in this respect. There are two possible explanations: either this has not been a priority of their foreign policy or Georgia's counter-policy has been more effective. It also raises the question whether it is important and necessary for Moscow, which initiated the independence process. In the opinion of Tishchenko (Тищенко, 2011), "Moscow consciously chooses small states, which cannot help Abkhazia actually provide its independence, which will help Russia to tie Abkhazia to Moscow. But Russia can raise a question of Abkhazia recognition in the United Nations based on the number of the small states, which would recognize its independence by that time." The second part of this statement is rather disputable, as even recognition by 108 UN member states does not allow Kosovo to raise the question of its membership because of the position of two permanent members of the UN Security Council – Russia and China. The United Nations also does not have a right to recognize a state but only to accept its membership, which are not identical concepts.

Mechanisms of Foreign Policy

Here we will analyse the formal elements of foreign policy activity. All four *de facto* states have their own ministries of foreign affairs. Although some functions in the security sphere are delegated to third parties – for example, to Russia in case of South Ossetia – none of them has formally delegated foreign policy functions to the Russian Federation, Armenia, or any international organization.

The existence of a ministry of foreign affairs is perceived by the unrecognized states as one of the attributes of an independent state. For example, in the opinion of the Minister of Foreign Affairs of Abkhazia, Viacheslav Chirikba, "the MFA was established on May 17, 1993 during the Georgian-Abkhazian war as an act of world announcement about the birth of the new Abkhazian state" (Ministry of Foreign Affairs of Abkhazia, 2012a).

The structures of the ministries differ from country to country depending on their foreign-policy priorities. So, in the case of Abkhazia, the reorganization of its Ministry of Foreign Affairs, completed in May 2012, "is connected with new challenges and new tasks set in Abkhazia's foreign policy" (Ministry of Foreign Affairs of Abkhazia, 2012a). There are currently nine departments: the Department of the Russian Federation, Republic of South Ossetia, CIS Countries, Transnistria and Georgia; the Department of Turkey and the Middle East; the Department of Latin America, Asia, Africa and Asia-Pacific Region; the Department of Europe, USA and Canada; the Information Department; the Legal Department; the State Protocol Department; and the Consular Service.

The Transnistrian Ministry of Foreign Affairs has a different structure, divided into the General Department of Foreign Policy; the General Department of Protocol, Legal Issues and PR; and the General Financial and Legal Department (including consular issues). So the General Department of Foreign Policy consists of the CIS Department; the Negotiations Department; the Department of Far-Abroad States and International

Organizations; and the Department of the Foreign Economic Activity (Министерство иностранных дел Приднестровской Молдавской Республики, 2012).

The Nagorno-Karabakh Ministry of Foreign Affairs is represented by: the Department of Multilateral Cooperation; Department of Bilateral Relations; Information Department; Protocol Unit; Consular Unit (Министерство иностранных дел Нагорно-Карабахской Республики, 2012a).

The South Ossetian Ministry website does not provide any information on its structure. Analysis of the South Ossetian and Nagorno-Karabakh Ministry of Foreign Affairs structures demonstrates the low intensity of their foreign policy contacts in contrast to Transnistria and Abkhazia. This is also proved by the number of visits to these regions by foreign diplomats and representatives of the international organizations and by the number of government initiatives.

Moreover, it is interesting to point out that all four websites have Russian as their first language – with options given to view them in English and local languages (Abkhazian, Ossetian, Armenian). At the same time, there are no versions in the languages of their counterparts in the conflicts (Georgian, Azeri and Romanian). However, Abkhazia adds German and Turkish versions of their website. This is indirect evidence of who is a target audience of the ministries and how much they are ready to explain their policy to the parent states.

Diplomatic Representation

With regard to diplomatic representation abroad, we can see significant difference between those two states that have received at least partial recognition and those that have not. According to the Vienna Conventions on Diplomatic Relations (1961) and on Consular Relations (1963) there are several traditional types of diplomatic representations, which are recognized according to their hierarchy, functions, immunities and credentials. Typically, they are either diplomatic missions (usually embassies) or consular posts (general consulate, consulate, consular agency). The two conventions mentioned above specify the possible functions of the respected representations and the immunities that they and their staff have. However, to open such a mission, states need to have established diplomatic relations (Article 2, Vienna Convention on Diplomatic Relations).

After the formal recognition of the independence of Abkhazia and South Ossetia, their first diplomatic relations were established, which led to the opening of official embassies. There are currently three official embassies of Abkhazia abroad – in the Russian Federation, Venezuela and South Ossetia. South Ossetia has its embassies in Russia, Venezuela, Nicaragua and Abkhazia. In these counties their diplomatic staff enjoy all immunities and privileges and are able to conduct all necessary diplomatic functions equal to those carried out by, for example, the Embassy of Ukraine or the United States in Moscow.

There are honorary consuls of Abkhazia presented in Nizhniy Novgorod (Russia), Beijing (China), San Marino and the United Kingdom. At the same time information on the UK representative is absent on the English version of the website in the "Honorary Consuls" section and was moved to the "Plenipotentiary Representatives" section. The problem is that status of the honorary consul is also defined in the Vienna Convention on Consular Relations (Chapter III). Thus, an honorary consulate cannot be opened without permission from the receiving state. So one can assume that the Ministry of Foreign Affairs of Abkhazia makes a distinction between special representatives and honorary consuls based only on the fact of the citizenship of those representatives rather than on the basic principles of international law.

Unrecognized republics introduced a special position for their diplomatic representatives in countries that had not recognized them – Plenipotentiary Representative. This status does not imply any special obligations or necessary relations with third countries. It is more a nominal title rather than that one demonstrating a special level of relations between the states. Often in case of unrecognized states, it demonstrates the specific interest of the *de facto* state in intensifying relations with a host state, presence of either diaspora or an active citizen living in this country.

Abkhazia currently has its Plenipotentiary Representatives in Bulgaria and Balkan states, Germany, Turkey, Syria, Transnistria, Greece, Italy, San Marino and Asia-Pacific Region (Ministry of Foreign Affairs of Abkhazia, 2012d).

In the case of Nagorno-Karabakh, there is a strong connection with Armenia, as most of its Representations are in countries with a strong

Armenian diaspora. As at 2012, it had permanent diplomatic representation in Armenia, Russia, the United States (concurrently in Canada), France, Australia, Lebanon and Germany (Министерство иностранных дел Нагорно-Карабахской Республики, 2012b).

Transnistria is one of the most active ones in terms of its foreign relations but at the same time has less official representations. It currently has only two official representations (embassies) abroad – in Abkhazia and South Ossetia. Until recently, Official Representations have existed in the Russian Federation and Ukraine; however they were closed by the January 2012 decrees of the president of the Transnistrian Moldovan Republic in the framework of general cost reduction with regard to international activity.

Bilateral and Multilateral Relations

Every state tries to formulate and announce the priorities and principles of its foreign policy, which are usually outlined in the Foreign Policy Doctrine or Concept of the states. Being a rather formal document, nevertheless, it brings to the attention of other members of the international community the main benchmarks and trends in the foreign activity and assists in formulation of expectations and policies. These documents are not always up to date, nor are they always adequate to the real situation; they are usually slow to be changed and some states regard them as more important than others. Nevertheless, for the unrecognized states they can act as a manifestation and an evidence of the seriousness of their foreign policy as well as proof that state recognition is not the only priority.

Only Transnistria's foreign policy has been formalized in this way – in its 2005 Foreign Policy Concept. In 2012, a new Concept was presented for a public discussion. One of the differences between two documents is that there is a greater concentration, in the more recent one, on the possible participation in integration processes in Eurasia, initiated by Russia, such as the Customs Union, Eurasian Economic Union, etc. (Article 3). The second difference is the inclusion of a paragraph on the continuity of the current peacekeeping format (controlled by the Russian Federation), which was totally absent in the 2005 version.

Bilateral Relations

There are three directions of the bilateral relations of the *de facto* states: relations with each other, cooperation with the Russian Federation and contacts with neighbour states. Relations with parent states are characterized more by the need to continue peace negotiations than by the desire to conduct normal political and economic dialogue. Relations with other states are usually characterized by sporadic diplomatic visits, either within the peace initiatives, in connection with humanitarian assistance or confidence-building measures, or, less often, as a reconnaissance visits. The legal framework is also presented only in the relations between each other or with the Russian Federation and Armenia. The only exception is the "Agreement on trade, economic, scientific, and cultural cooperation between Transnistria and Odessa region (Ukraine)" signed in July 1998 and the same Agreement with the Vinnitsa region (Ukraine), signed in August 1997.

The relations between unrecognized states are the most active and strive for classical interaction between the states. The most dynamic contacts are between Abkhazia and Transnistria, as well as between former Georgian territories. Nagorno-Karabakh is the most passive among them, preferring to coordinate relations with Armenia rather than other states.

Coming back to Abkhazia, serious agreements between Sukhumi and Moscow were signed only after the formal recognition of its independence. So, in September 2008, the Agreement on Friendship, Cooperation and Mutual Assistance between the Republic of Abkhazia and the Russian Federation was signed, followed by the Agreement on joint efforts in the field of protection of the state border of the Republic of Abkhazia (30 April 2009) and the Agreement on Cooperation and Mutual Assistance in Customs Affairs (16 October 2010).

Military cooperation has always been among the priorities in the relations between these two states and this is demonstrated by the agreement on cooperation in the military field of 15 September 2009 and the Agreement on a joint Russian base on the territory of the Republic of Abkhazia (17 February 2010) (Ministry of Foreign Affairs of Abkhazia, 2012b). At the same time no similar document exists in the relations of the Russian Federation and Transnistria, which are limited to protocols and communiques after working meetings and multilateral agreements within the peace process.

Bilateral relations with Nicaragua are another example demonstrating the development of formal relations. As for now General Agreement on Friendship and Cooperation between the Republic of Abkhazia and the Republic of Nicaragua has been signed, as well as an Agreement on trade and economic cooperation, an Agreement on mutual visa-free travel for citizens of the Republic of Abkhazia and citizens of the Republic of Nicaragua, a Framework Agreement on merchant shipping and a Framework Agreement on air communication(Ministry of Foreign Affairs of Abkhazia, 2012b).

Morefrequent visits are observed to Abkhazia and Transnistria, which are paid by the representatives of international organizations, including the UN, the EU, OSCE and the Council of Europe, in addition to the diplomatic representatives accredited in the respected parent-states. Reciprocal visits of the representatives of the unrecognized states are usually held unofficially, even though they are well publicized in the *de facto* states. In April 2012 the delegation of the Ministry of Foreign Affairs of Abkhazia made statements about a successful visit to Italy and San Marino, even mentioning that "25 of the60 deputies of the supreme legislative body of San Marino made a statement about the need to recognize Abkhazia" (Ministry of Foreign Affairs of Abkhazia, 2012a). However San Marino's Foreign Affairs Secretary, AntonellaMularoni officially said that San Marino doesn't recognize Abkhazia independence and confirmed her support for Georgia (San Marino, 2012).

Visits to foreign states are usually connected with cultural issues (as happened with the Abkhazian delegation visit to the Turkish province of Duzdce in June 2012, where they participated in the arrangements devoted to the celebration of the twentieth anniversary of the establishment of the Abkhazian cultural centre in the city of Duzdce). Typically, such visits are presented as great successes of Abkhazian diplomacy even if they do not have any effect on the further development of the relations or lead to formal recognition.

International actors display some interest in interacting with unrecognized territories; they are occupied with the search for a formula to allow possible engagement and cooperation with governments and societies of the new state entities. Such interest is mainly increasing due to the fact that the unrecognized states have become special factors in their regions, controlling quite large, sometimes strategically important, lands, possessing substantial military and economic potential, and being capable of developing in conditions with limited opportunities (Mayilian, 2012).

Multilateral Relations

The multilateral relations of the unrecognized states are usually presented in two dimensions: (i) peace and final status negotiations and (ii) participation in specific international organizations. Sometimes *de facto* states use the format of the peace negotiations not to reach the final resolution of a conflict or a settlement of the particular issue in the bilateral relations with the parent state but to demonstrate their positions – "to send messages of the view of the Abkhaz side to the world community" (Ministry of Foreign Affairs of Abkhazia, 2012a) in the absence of appropriate channels of communication between their respected governments and the third states.

The first organization that the unrecognized states of the Black Sea region sought to join was the Unrepresented Nations and Peoples Organization (UNPO). It is an international organization which members are "indigenous peoples, minorities, and unrecognized or occupied territories who have joined together to protect and promote their human and cultural rights, to preserve their environments, and to find nonviolent solutions to conflicts which affect them" (UNPO, 2012). It currently consists of 41 unrepresented nations and peoples. Abkhazia became a member in 1991. Others have not paid enough attention to the work of this organization and the mechanisms for communication with international community that it presents, preferring cooperation within a small circle of the post-Soviet counterparts.

The first organization that was created by the *de facto* states in the Black Sea region was the Commonwealth of Unrecognized States, which, in Russian, has a similar abbreviation to the Commonwealth of the Independent States, sometimes called the CIS-2. The Union of Unrecognized states was created in 1992, where in addition to four post-Soviet territories, Srpska Krajina (Croatia) and Republika Srpska (Bosnia and Herzegovina) were members. The last two withdrew their membership in 1995 after settling their conflicts with the parent states and losing status of "unrecognized". Transnistria, Nagorno-Karabakh, South Ossetia and Abkhazia renewed the organization's activity in 2000 by establishing a Foreign Ministers Council. Rules of Procedures were signed later and the Organization changed its title to the Commonwealth. However, we can regard this organization more as a forum rather than a real institution.

In 2006, the Presidents of Transnistria, Abkhazia and South Ossetia signed the Joint Declaration on Creation of the Community "For Democracy and Peoples Rights". This organization lost the participation of Nagorno-Karabakh, which for the previous several years had concentrated more on Armenia with no real interest in the joint efforts of the unrecognized states. Very often this organization is referred as a successor of the Commonwealth of Unrecognized States. One of the new feature that this agreement had was the creation of joint peacekeeping forces (Совместное заявление, 2006), which has never been realized. Analysis of the latest activities and news within the Community demonstrates that Transnistria is mostly interested in its further development. Organizations has been working sporadically, almost ceased activities in 2008 with the recognition of independence of Abkhazia and South Ossetia, but reminded about itself in 2014 with the Statement of the Parliamentary Assemble of the Community "For Democracy and Peoples Rights" condemning policy of the Ukrainian Government, humanitarian situation in Ukraine and so called blockade of Transnistria (Сообщество, 2014).

The development of relations within these organizations shows that it has been more a reaction to the creation of GUAM and Commonwealth of the Democratic Choice by their parent-states rather than real aspiration of the fully-fledged cooperation.

Visa Policy

Visa policy is also one of the elements of the foreign policy of a country as it demonstrates the level of relations between the states and also their openness. The four *de facto* states of the Black Sea region have different entry policies.

Abkhazia introduced visas after proclaiming independence in 2008. With the absence of consular representatives recognized in other countries, applicants have to send the required documents via email to receive permission, and within three days upon arrival to receive a real visa at the Consular department of the MFA. At the same time, citizens of the following states do not need a visa to enter Abkhazia: Azerbaijan, Armenia, Belarus, Vanuatu, Venezuela, Kazakhstan, Kirgizstan, Moldova, Nauru, Nicaragua, Transnistria, the Russian Federation, Tajikistan, Turkmenistan, Ukraine, Uzbekistan, South Ossetia (Ministry of Foreign Affairs of Abkhazia, 2012f). This list concurs with the list of the CIS states plus those who have recognized Abkhazian independence.

South Ossetia has decided not to introduce any visas for foreigners; however, they need to inform the Ministry of Foreign Affairs of South Ossetia three days in advance and to obtain formal permission (Ministry of Foreign Affairs of South Ossetia, 2012).

The entry policy of the Nagorno-Karabakh republic is more complicated. Foreigners need a visa to enter the *de facto* state, which they can receive only at the Representation of the Nagorno-Karabakh Republic in Armenia, and in exceptional cases at the Ministry of Foreign Affairs in Stepanakert (Nagorno-Karabakh). Usually it takes several days to receive a visa (Ministry of Foreign Affairs of Nagorno-Karabakh Republic, 2012).

Transnistria has not introduced any visa policy for foreigners. However most of them prefer to bypass its territory in case travelling from Moldova to Ukraine to escape additional checks or not being allowed to pass its territory.

In their turn foreign states need to formulate their visa policy towards unrecognized states. In case of South Ossetia and Abkhazia, Georgia has introduced a so-called "neutral" passport for foreign travelling, which is recognized by Western states. However, the Abkhaz side stated that the refusal of some Western countries to issue visas to Abkhaz and South Ossetian citizens on the basis of the Russian passports "was a gross violation of the provisions of the Universal Declaration of Human Rights, concerning freedom of movement rights, and that the imposed introduction of the Georgian 'neutral passports' for the citizens of Abkhazia and the South Ossetia was an unlawful interference into the internal affairs of these sovereign states" (Ministry of Foreign Affairs of Abkhazia, 2012c). The opinion of Abkhaz government was that "Residents of Abkhazia have their Abkhaz national passports which meet all international standards as well as a universally recognized passport of the Russian Federation" (Ministry of the Foreign Affairs of Abkhazia, 2012e).

Most of the citizens of Transnistria use one of the three passports for foreign trips: Ukrainian, Russian or Moldovan. As some of the citizens can simultaneously have several foreign passports, they normally use whichever is more suitable for entering the particular country of destination.

Thus, we can conclude that the recognition status of the *de facto* states in the Black Sea region has a significant influence on their ability to conduct their foreign policy activities. Although these states strive to find alternative means of communication with the international community, they also try to secure traditional methods of diplomatic interaction. The visits of their representatives to foreign states may be mostly not welcome but the *de facto* states are always open for the visits of the foreign diplomatic representatives to their respective territories.

The current foreign policy of Abkhazia, South Ossetia, Nagorno-Karabakh and Transnistria can be characterized by their attempts to use traditional mechanisms of fully recognized states, such as the establishment of a Ministry of Foreign Affairs or opening of special representations; however their "unrecognized" status means that they are unable to use all the tools that highly depend on the establishment of formal diplomatic relations, which are impossible without official recognition. Hence, the partial recognition of South Ossetia and Abkhazia demonstrates a shift in relations with these states. At the same time, all four states regard the state recognition issue and relations with the Russian Federation and Armenia as priorities, dealing with other states more in terms of the peace process or reconnaissance with their current affairs, without discussion of perspectives and possibilities of bilateral relations until the final resolution of their status.

One can argue about whether recognition is the ultimate goal of the foreign policy of the unrecognized states, when all foreign interactions directly or indirectly aim to ensure further formal recognition. If in certain periods in history this can be seen as an objective of all their activities, after almost 20 years of their *de facto* situation, the foreign policies of the four unrecognized Black Sea states seek to diversify goals, when recognition aspirations are holding along with the daily foreign interactions between each other, with neighbour states or possible donors (international organizations or third states).

Multilateral activities are limited to peace talks and to contacts with the close circle of states alike. While for internal consumption, the foreign activities of the four states are mostly presented as those of independent, fully fledged, legitimate states, so in their external relations *de facto* states endeavour to act in the framework of existing international norms, such as the Vienna Conventions, or to limit their activities to the regional level of contacts. While work towards recognition or settling their final political status, as well as interactions with the parent states and mediators, remains a priority, unwillingness to stay in isolation forces them to look for additional ways to communicate with the world.

References

Byman, D. and King, C. (2012) The mystery of phantom states. *The Washington Quarterly* 35(3), 43–57.

Caspersen, N. and Herrberg, A. (2010) *Engaging Unrecognised States in Conflict Resolution: An Opportunity or Challenge for the EU?* International Crisis Group, <http://www.initiativeforpeacebuilding.eu/pdf/1012CMI.pdf> (accessed 1 December 2014).

Graham, B. A. T. and Horne, B. (2011) Unrecognized states: a theory of self-determination and foreign influence. *APSA 2011 Annual Meeting Paper*, <http://ssrn.com/abstract=1900411> (accessed 1 November 2014).

Kobrinskaya, I. (2008) "Unrecognized states" in Russia's domestic and foreign policy. *PONARS Eurasia Memo*, No. 10.

Markedonov, S. (2006) Unrecognized geopolitics. *Russia in Global Affairs* 4(1), 68–79.

Mayilian, M. (2012) *Recognized and Unrecognized States: Formula of Interrelations*, <http://theanalyticon.com/?p=1489&lang=en> (accessed 1 November 2014).

Ministry of Foreign Affairs of Abkhazia (2012a) *May 17 is the Birthday of the MFA of Abkhazia*, <http://mfaapsny.org/en/information/index.php?ELEMENT_ID=132> (accessed 1 November 2014).

Ministry of Foreign Affairs of Abkhazia (2012b) *International Agreements*, <http://mfaapsny.org/en/policy/agreements.php> (accessed 1 November 2014).

Ministry of Foreign Affairs of Abkhazia (2012c) *On the 20th Round of the Geneva Discussions on Security and Stability in the South Caucasus*, <http://mfaapsny.org/en/information/index.php?ELEMENT_ID=247> (accessed 1 November 2014).

Ministry of Foreign Affairs of Abkhazia (2012d) *Representatives of Abkhazia,* <http://mfaapsny.org/en/policy/representative.php> (accessed 1 November 2014).

Ministry of the Foreign Affairs of Abkhazia (2012e) *Statement by the Foreign Ministry of the Republic of Abkhazia,* <http://mfaapsny.org/en/information/index.php?ELEMENT_ID=221> (accessed 1 November 2014).

Ministry of Foreign Affairs of Abkhazia (2012f) *Visa Information,* <http://mfaapsny.org/council/visa.php> (accessed 1 November 2014).

Ministry of Foreign Affairs of Nagorno-Karabakh Republic (2012) *The Procedure of Foreign Citizens' Entry to the NKR,*<http://www.nkr.am/en/the-procedure-of-foreign-citizens-entry-to-the-nkr/92/> (accessed 1 November 2014).

Ministry of Foreign Affairs of South Ossetia (2012) *Procedure of the Entry to the Territory of the Republic of South Ossetia,* <http://mfa-rso.su/taxonomy/term/13> (accessed 1 November 2014).

Oppenheim, L. F. L. (1905) *International Law*, Vol. 1,Longmans, Green and Co, New York.

Raic, D. (2002) *Statehood and the Law of Self Determination,* Kluwer Law International, The Hague.

San Marino, il governo non riconosce l'Abkhazia come Stato indipendente (2012) *San Marino Fixing*,<http://www.sanmarinofixing.com/smfixing/san-marino/7602-san-marino-il-governo-non-riconosce-labkhazia-come-stato-indipendente.html> (accessed 1 November 2014).

UNPO (2012) *About UNPO,* <http://www.unpo.org/section/2> (accessed 1 November 2014).

Transparency International (2011) *Vanuatu press release on recognition of Abkhazia,* <http://transparency.ge/en/node/1321> (accessed 1 November 2014).

Маркедонов С. (2012) Де-факто образования постсоветского пространства: двадцать лет государственного строительства. *Аналитические доклады Института Кавказа*, №5. Институт Кавказа.

Министерство иностранных дел Приднестровской Молдавской Республики (2012) *Структура Министерства иностранных дел Приднестровской Молдавской Республики*,<http://mfa-pmr.org/index.php?newsid=298> (accessed 1 November 20124).

Министерство иностранных дел Нагорно-Карабахской Республики (2012a) *Структура Министерства иностранных дел Нагорно-Карабахской Республики*, <http://www.nkr.am/ru/nkr-mfa-structure/115/> (accessed 1 November 2014).

Министерство иностранных дел Нагорно-Карабахской Республики (2012b) *Постоянные представительства*, <http://www.nkr.am/ru/permanent-representations/104/> (accessed 1 November 2014).

Совместное Заявление Президентов Республики Абхазия, Приднестровской Молдавской Республики и Республики Южная Осетия (2006) *«ОЛЬВИЯ-ПРЕСС»*, <http://www.olvia.idknet.com/ol85-06-06.htm> (accessed 1 December 2014).

Сообщество «За демократию и права народов» осудило деятельность киевских властей (2014)*ИА REGNUM*, <http://www.regnum.ru/news/polit/1805254> (accessed 1 December 2014).

Тищенко, М. (2011) Вот и верь после этого людям. *Lenta.ru*, <http://lenta.ru/articles/2011/06/20/fail/> (accessed 1 November 2014).

Part V
The Politics and Economics of Energy

Fabio Indeo

Azerbaijan's Role in the Euroasiatic Energy Chessboard: Geopolitical and Strategic Perspectives

ABSTRACT: The availability of huge hydrocarbon reserves in Azerbaijan and its geographic position as a strategic "energy bridge" between East and West have contributed to enhance its geopolitical centrality in the regional energy chessboard. These conditions could allow Azerbaijan to successfully play both roles of energy supplier and energy hub in the "East–West" corridor in the near future. Baku is currently developing several pipeline projects, such as the EU Southern Gas Corridor and the Trans-Anatolia Gas Pipeline. Nevertheless, potential regional instability linked to the unsolved Caspian status, strained relations with neighbours and the obligatory Georgian export energy route could seriously hinder this Azeri geopolitical ambition.

KEYWORDS: energy diversification, Azerbaijan, Southern Gas Corridor, European Union, Trans-Caspian corridor, Russia

Introduction

The presence on its territory of huge oil and gas reserves and its location as a kind of "energy bridge" between Caspian energy resources and European markets represent two main geopolitical factors that have enhanced the strategic relevance of Azerbaijan in the regional and international scenario.

These conditions have attracted several energy projects that have aimed to cross Azerbaijan or to use Azeri oil and gas reserves through pipelines and liquefied natural gas (LNG) transport options: the most famous is the EU Southern Corridor (which includes pipeline projects like Nabucco, TAP, ITGI, White Stream) among others like the Azerbaijan–Georgia–Romania–Hungary Interconnector (AGRI) or the recent Trans-Anatolia Gas Pipeline Project, which stress the rising importance of this Caucasian state.

Starting from an analysis and comparison of Azerbaijan's and the EU's energy diversification strategy goals, the aim of this chapter is to evaluate whether Azerbaijan could play both roles of energy supplier and energy hub in the "East–West" corridor in the near future, and which geopolitical, strategic and economic gains it could obtain. As a matter of fact, its geographic position and energy reserves allow Azerbaijan successfully to play a multivector policy in the regional energy scenario – aimed to deal with different geopolitical state-actors in order to maximize strategic and economic gains - considering that:

- Azerbaijan is a strategic key partner for EU, assisting the latter to implement its energy security strategy focused on the diversification of export routes;
- Azerbaijan could be a relevant geopolitical partner in the Russian energy strategy, aimed to preserve EU dependence on Russian gas by hindering the realization of the Southern Corridor;
- Azerbaijan is the obligatory route for Central Asian states (mainly Kazakhstan and Turkmenistan), which aim to deliver their oil and gas exports to the Western and European markets: as a matter of fact, a precondition for a full implementation of the Southern Corridor is Turkmen–Azeri appeasement.

Nevertheless, potential regional instability linked to the unresolved Caspian status, strained relations with Armenia, Russia and Iran and the obligatory Georgian export energy route, could seriously hinder this Azeri geopolitical ambition.

Azerbaijan's Diversification Strategy of Energy Exports between Geopolitical Issues and EU Energy Needs

Thanks to its strategic geographic position and huge oil and gas reserves, Azerbaijan has become a significant regional and international player on the international energy chessboard, which legitimates its role as transit country and energy supplier for the route defined as the "East–West" corridor.

Since the implosion of the Soviet Union in 1991 and the national independence of the post-Soviet states the promotion of a westward energy route – allowing the transport of Caspian oil and gas to the EU markets bypassing Russian and Iranian territory – has represented an ambitious and multifaceted strategic card to play, both for external geopolitical actors (mainly the European Union and United States) and the new Caucasian and Central Asian independent states.

On the one hand, a westward energy export route could be regarded as a tool to strengthen the political sovereignty and economic independence from Moscow of Azerbaijan and the post-Soviet states (Jonson, 2001: 16–19). On the other hand, the huge hydrocarbon reserves located in the Caspian basin clearly appear as the main attraction driving powerful external geopolitical players to focus their strategic interests and goals on the area; according to the International Energy Agency, there are 48 billion barrels of proven oil reserves in the Caspian region, whereas gas reserves are estimated at 13 trillion cubic metres (tcm), 7% of the world's total proven natural gas reserves (International Energy Agency, 2010: 499–500, 524–525).

If the US markets are too far to benefit from the Caspian energy, redirecting the Caspian hydrocarbons towards European markets could represent a relevant option for the EU's strategy of diversifying routes and supplies and strengthening its energy security by means of reducing dependency on the Russian energy imports.

The Ukraine–Russia gas disputes of 2006 and 2009, and Belarus in 2007, regarding the gas price and transit fees – which caused disruption in Russian gas supplies to European countries – dangerously stressed Europe's vulnerability because of its dependence on imported Russian gas, pushing the EU 27 to develop new alternative pipelines oriented to the European markets and bypassing Russian territories and Gazprom's control.

Furthermore, according to the different scenarios forecasting future levels of natural gas demand and supply (European Commission's Directorate-General for Energy 2010; International Energy Agency, 2010; United States Energy Information Administration, 2010), EU natural-gas demand will rise to range between 470 and 650 billion cubic metres (bcm) in 2030: with domestic production estimated to cover less than 20% of the EU's projected gas consumption, the EU import requirements are likely to reach a level of 370 to 580 bcm by the end of 2030 (Institut für Europäische Politik, 2011: 13–35).

In order to reduce these serious threats to its energy security situation, the EU has planned to promote the realization of an energy "East–West" corridor, conceived as a framework of infrastructures known as the Trans-Caspian Oil and Gas Transport System, which aims to channel hydrocarbons from Azerbaijan and Central Asian energy-rich countries (Turkmenistan, Kazakhstan and Uzbekistan) in a westward direction to the European markets.

The implementation of this alternative energy route has allowed Azerbaijan to become a strategic player, mainly because of its centrality in connection with the EU energy-route diversification plans and benefiting from other relevant assets that enhance its position.

Firstly, from a geographic-geopolitical perspective, Azerbaijan is an obligatory route for energy corridors transporting Caspian resources planned to bypass Russian and Iranian territory: as a matter of fact, the 1979 US sanctions on Iran and the international opposition to Teheran's decision to develop a nuclear policy have hindered any attempt to exploit an Iranian energy route (potentially shorter and easier to realize) or to import Iranian hydrocarbons. Moreover, the ecological and security concerns that have given rise to a need to reduce oil-tanker traffic through the Bosporus and the Dardanelles straits have contributed to a rise in Azerbaijan's importance as an alternative transit route and strategic hub for Caspian energy exports.

Secondly, the availability of huge oil and gas reserves has allowed Azerbaijan to become a potential supplier country of this "East–West" corridor: according to British Petroleum's 2013 *Statistical Review of World Energy,* Azerbaijan's proven reserves of gas amount to 0.9 tcm (0.5% of the world's total proven natural gas reserves) while Baku also holds 7000 million barrels of proved oil reserves (0.4% of the world total of proven oil reserves) (British Petroleum, 2013: 6, 20). Following the projections for the newly discovered gas fields (ACG Deep, Absheron, Umid and Shafag-Asiman), Azeri gas reserves could easily double and reach 2.5 tcm (Ismayilov, 2012), enhancing Baku's ambitions to play both roles (transit and supplier country) within the EU strategy of diversification.

Furthermore, Azerbaijan could benefit from another strategic advantage linked to its geographic position: unlike Turkmenistan and Kazakhstan, Azeri energy exports don't have to cross the Caspian Sea in order to reach Western markets. If tanker transport could solve the problems for Central Asian oil exports, the unsolved legal status of the Caspian basin and the political rivalry of the five littoral states have set back, until now, the completion of a Trans-Caspian Gas Pipeline (TCGP).

In addition to these strategic *atouts,* since its national independence the Azerbaijani republic has adopted a profitable multiple pipeline strategy in the energy sector, aimed to diversify its export options while lessening Russia's traditional role as a transit country for Caspian energy suppliers – which has clearly enhanced its position as strategic bridge linking Caspian resources and EU markets with profitable gains for both (Badalyan, 2011: 3).

Consequently, Azerbaijan rejected the possibility of using the existing Russian-oriented pipeline by realizing two new export routes: a northern route from Baku to the Russian Black Sea port of Novorossiisk (completed in 1997, with a capacity of 100 000 barrels of oil per day) and a Western route from Baku to Georgia's Black Sea coast of Supsa (completed in 1999, with a capacity of 120 000 barrels per day). The Baku-Supsa pipeline marked the beginning of reorienting Azeri energy exports away from Russia and created the first alternative route bypassing Russian territory for Caspian energy exports (Bagirov, 2001: 190–194).

In 2006 thecompletion of the Baku–Tbilisi–Ceyhan (BTC) oil pipeline and the Baku–Tbilisi–Erzurum (BTE, also known as the South Caucasus Pipeline, SCP) gas pipeline have represented the first concrete steps to implement the "East–West" corridor (Nuriyev, 2008: 159–160). Both these pieces of infrastructure have a strong geopolitical impact: the BTC (with a capacity of 1.2 million barrels per day) must be conceived as a potential realization of the Trans-Caspian oil corridor, because Kazakhstan and Turkmenistan also commit themselves to channel oil in this project (respectively with 53 million tonnes per year since 2006 and 2.52 million tonnes in 2012), transported by tankers through the Caspian Sea (Azernews, 2013). Even if the BTE has a limited capacity (about 6–8 bcm per year), this pipeline is the first gas export route that bypasses Russian territory, engendering hopes for the future realization of a wider TCGP (Cornell, Tsereteli and Socor,2005).

Through these initiatives Baku has strongly demonstrated, to the EU, its commitment to implement an alternative energy corridor from the Caspian basin, delivering its oil and gas and hosting on its territory the first trunk of the export route.

Azerbaijan's Role in the Southern Gas Corridor: Strategic Gains

The diversification of export energy routes is essential for a supplier country because it ensures energy security while avoiding total dependence on a single export route. To achieve this strategic goal, Azerbaijan has also agreed to sell a limited part of its gas (1–3 bcm) to Russia, preferring to maintain open all export routes and economically lucrative opportunities.

The convergence of interests between Azerbaijan and EU focused on the energy diversification concept has set up the Caucasian republic in the role of a key partner for the EU, in order to achieve its energy security through the implementation of the Southern Gas Corridor (SGC).

In addition to its strategic geographic position as a feasible transit route for the SGC, Azerbaijan also appears to be the only supplier country that could concretely fill this energy corridor with its gas reserves: according to the estimates, Shah Deniz gas field alone – which until now has been the only identified source to supply the SGC – holds reserves of 1 tcm (BP, 2013). In 2030 the Azeri production of gas should reach 55 bcm: considering a forecasted domestic consumption of 14.5 bcm, Baku could hypothetically commit to export 35 to 40 bcm of gas (International Energy Agency, 2010: 526–530; 2011:165).

In recent years Baku has undertaken three fundamental steps aimed to support the SGC: in January 2011 Azeri President Aliyev signed, with the President of the European Commission, Barroso, a Joint Declaration on the Southern Gas Corridor, which commits Azerbaijan to deliver 10 bcm of gas per year to the EU markets (European Commission, 2011a); in September 2011 Azerbaijan agreed to allow EU to adopt a mandate to negotiate a legally binding treaty between the EU, Azerbaijan and Turkmenistan to build a Trans-Caspian Pipeline System (European Commission 2011b). This initiative represents a political institutionalization of the energy dialogue, aimed to reach the necessary bilateral arrangements between Azerbaijan and Turkmenistan in order to legally solve their border disputes concerning the Caspian offshore energy fields.

The third crucial step was the so-called Izmir Agreement of October 2011, based on the bilateral agreement between Azerbaijan and the Shah Deniz producers with Turkey for the delivery and transit of Azeri gas to Turkey and onward to European Union territory (Socor, 2011).

We can observe that the Southern Gas Corridor is structured in a multitude of pipeline projects, which in some cases are competing with each other (Institut für Europäische Politik, 2011: 11): the Nabucco pipeline is the most famous but there are also the Turkey–Greece–Italy Interconnector (ITGI), the Trans-Adriatic Pipeline (TAP), the White Stream and the AGRI. All these projects shared the goal of transporting Azeri gas to the European markets through a southern route and bypassing Russian territory and control, even if the potential implementation of White Stream and the AGRI could also open a western route crossing the Black Sea.

The ITGI pipeline consists of the interconnector between Turkey and Greece, which is already operational, and the planned extensions to Italy (the Interconnector Greece–Italy pipeline, IGI) and Bulgaria (the Interconnector Greece-Bulgaria, IGB); this project will be fully operational in 2017 and should deliver 10 bcm of Azeri gas. However, in February 2012 Shah Deniz Consortium excluded the ITGI project from those being considered to deliver Azeri gas to Europe, *de facto* postponing its potential inclusion in the SGG (Natural Gas Europe, 2012).

The TAP (which was until June 2013 in direct competition with Nabucco West in order to transport the Azeri gas extracted from the Shah Deniz Phase 2 of development) is planned to have a capacity of 10 to 20 bcm of gas and to cross Greece, Albania and the Adriatic Sea on the way to Italy. The TAP consortium has also planned to realize additional trunks connecting the TAP to the proposed Ionian–Adriatic pipeline (which is intended to supply gas to the Western Balkans) and to Bulgaria, through the completion of the Greece–Bulgaria interconnector (Trans-Adriatic Pipeline, 2013).

For the European Commission Nabucco represents the "the flagship project of the diversification efforts of the EU for our security of supply", even if several hurdles have postponed its completion until now: the lack of a EU shared energy strategy, the unsolved Caspian legal status – which hampers the realization of an energy corridor between the two shores of Caspian Sea, preventing the inclusion of Central Asiangas suppliers (mainly Turkmenistan) in this project -, the lack of gas suppliers – with the exception of Azerbaijan – able to meet the planned capacity of 31 bcm per year, the competition with the Russian-backed South Stream project, and growing financial costs. The potential strategic relevance of Nabucco's original version was based on its planned capacity, three time bigger than the other proposed routes of the SGC, such as ITGI or TAP. The original project foresaw a route running from Turkey to the European gas hub of Baumgarten in Austria, via Bulgaria, Romania, and Hungary (Baev and Øverland, 2010: 1075–1090).

The White Stream is an unclear project to build a Georgia–Ukraine–EU gas pipeline – with an offshore route linking Georgian port of Supsa and Romanian port of Constanta – to transport 8 bcm of Azeri gas supplying Romania as well as the European markets.

The AGRI represents one of the main and more interesting options for the export of Azeri gas: it could be the first LNG project in the Black Sea, with a planned capacity of 7 bcm, which should later be upgraded to 20 bcm. Together with White Stream, these projects have a strategic rationale for the Azeri energy diversification policy because they represent an alternative export corridor compared with the southern route, which also bypasses both Russian and Turkish territory (EurActiv, 2010). Ukraine also expressed the will to be involved in the project, planning the completion of a LNG terminal in Odessa, which could give rise to additional geopolitical issues involving the Russian–Ukrainian relations (80% of Russian gas exports to Europe crosses Ukraine territory). The potential participation of Turkmenistan in the AGRI project as a gas supplier could transform this route into one of the main gas supply routes to the EU, also downplaying the energy-bridge role played by Turkey. However the huge costs of this project (4.5 billion euros just to develop an initial capacity of 8 bcm) could discourage international and regional energy companies from financing the AGRI's completion (AGRI, 2013). Moreover, at present the AGRI project appears as a potential competitor to the SGC, mainly because it relies on the same volume of Azeri gas extracted from the Shah Deniz Phase 2 of development, which is already committed to fuel the TAP project: consequently, the potential implementation of the AGRI interconnector will depend on a future increase in Azeri gas exports in a westward direction.

Baku's commitment to feed these projects with its own gas will legitimate its strategic position towards European attempts at energy diversification.

Furthermore, the regional scenario has suddenly changed following the Azeri–Turkish agreement to complete the Trans-Anatolia Gas Pipeline (TANAP): in December 2011 the two parties signed a Memorandum of Understanding, and in June 2012 they signed the intergovernmental agreement to complete this pipeline.

This planned pipeline will be operational in 2017–18 (when Shah Deniz Phase Two of production comes on stream), with an initial capacity of 16–17 bcm, of which 10 bcm will be delivered to EU markets and 6 bcm to the Turkish market: the TANAP consortium foresees a rising capacity aimed to reach 30 bcm in 2026 and 60 bcm after 2030, even if this ambitious output could be reached only with the participation of Turkmenistan and other suppliers like Kazakhstan and potentially Uzbekistan (Trans Anatolia Natural Gas Pipeline, 2013; Cutler, 2012). The South Caucasus Pipeline (also known as Baku–Tbilisi–Erzurum) will be the connecting link between Azerbaijan and the TANAP, after upgrading its capacity from its current level of 7 bcm to 23 bcm per year by 2017.

The TANAP represents a feasible opportunity for Azerbaijan to play both the roles of transit country and of supplier country within the SGC, also benefiting from several economic, political and strategic gains. Moreover Baku will also play a third important role, as financial investor in this infrastructure, committing huge revenues obtained through oil exports in order to realize a strategic export route that allows it to diversify Azeri economic gains. As the consortium's partners will finance the pipeline's construction in proportion to their respective stakes, Azerbaijan will become the pipeline's main owner, through which Baku will sell its gas, produced in Shah Deniz.

Furthermore, Azerbaijan would collect transit fees from other gas producers and shippers that would use this pipeline, such as Turkmenistan and Kazakhstan: their future involvement and commitment in the full implementation of the Trans-Caspian Pipeline will be necessary in order to expand the TANAP's capacity (Socor, 2012a). As a matter of fact, as in the case of oil exports, Azerbaijan could also easily exploit its role as transit country on the gas energy chessboard: in 2011, Azerbaijan earned \$53 million from the transit of oil from Kazakhstan and \$12.8 million from oil coming from Turkmenistan, supplies destined to fuel the BTC pipeline (Abbasov, 2012).

In geopolitical terms, Azerbaijan makes its strategic contribution by directly helping the EU to achieve its energy security goals though the diversification of export routes and supplies: the Azeri commitment to finance and build its own pipeline, fuelling it with its own gas and selling it to the European markets, shows the political will of Baku to cooperate with Brussels. Like the BTC, the TANAP is also a strategic project for both Baku and Brussels, because it was conceived to transport gas out of Russian control through a pipeline exclusively dedicated to Caspian hydrocarbons.

In the EU perspective, the launch of the TANAP has led to substantial rethinking of the original Nabucco project in order to revitalize the SGC: the Nabucco consortium decided to reconfigure its project for a new role, as a European continuation of the TANAP project, proposing a shortened version of the "EU flagship project".

In June 2012 the newly dubbed Nabucco West was selected (2 days after the signature of the Azerbaijan–Turkey intergovernmental agreement) as a potential route to deliver Caspian gas in Central Europe, which will concretely allow Azeri gas to reach EU markets. Meanwhile, in February 2012 the Shah Deniz producers also chose the Trans-Adriatic Pipeline project as the TANAP's potential south-western extension (Muradova, 2012).

On 28 June 2013, the Shah Deniz consortium finally selected the Trans-Adriatic Pipeline project as the main export energy corridor for the Azeri gas to Europe, temporarily freezing the Nabucco West project. The development of the TAP project represents the first concrete step in realizing the Southern Energy Corridor, strongly highlighting the enhancement of the energy cooperation between EU and Azerbaijan. However, the choice of the Shah Deniz gas producers consortium – in which British Petroleum and Norway's Statoil are the main shareholders with 25.5% each – between TAP and Nabucco West was profoundly influenced by a sort of "neogeopolitic energy game", involving companies supporting different projects and having different economic and energy goals: Statoil supports the TAP project also because it holds 42.5% of the stakes within the TAP consortium, while SOCAR privileged Nabucco West, further showing its political support to the "EU flagship project" (Eurasianet, 2013).

Considering the EU supply diversification goals, TAP appears an antistrategic project compared to Nabucco West, mainly because it will divert gas supplies away from countries that strongly depend on Gazprom's monopoly (Central and South-East European countries such as Bulgaria, Hungary, Austria): the Italian market (as well as Switzerland) is highly diversified and amply supplied, and it could also benefit from the LNG option (Socor, 2012b).

Moreover, TAP's planned capacity (maximum 20 bcm) could not fully satisfy Azeri export ambitions, pushing Baku to support alternative gas export routes to deliver additional volumes of gas to the markets, due to the expected increase in national production over the next years.

The availability of BP, Statoil and Total to acquire a combined 29% in the TANAP must be interpreted as a significant step of the producers to politically and economically support the realization of this project, which should enhance Azerbaijan's role on the energy chessboard (New Europe, 2012).

Geopolitical Hindrances in the Regional Scenario

Notwithstanding the TANAP's implementation, growing interest from the international energy companies and external political actors in the Azeri resources, some factors linked to the regional scenario could seriously hinder Azerbaijan's ambition to become a strategic supplier and transit country for the EU.

Azeri opportunities to export in a westward direction depend to a large extent on transit through Georgia, both though a pipeline and LNG. This shows Azerbaijan's potential vulnerability and the lack of diversification of its energy routes: this obligatory Georgian export route exposes the national energy sector to serious threats of interruption of export supplies in case of Georgia's political instability. This happened in 2008 when, following the Russia–Georgia war (involving Ossetia and Abkhazia), Azeri oil and gas flows through the BTC and BTE pipelines were temporarily blocked (Tsereteli, 2009).

In addition to this geographical hindrance, Russian geopolitical and energy ambitions and the unsolved Caspian legal status are two other issues that could set back Azerbaijan's strategy in the energy sector.

Since 2009 Russia developed an energy partnership with Azerbaijan, aimed to acquire 1.5 bcm of gas per year but this amount doubled following a new deal signed on January 2012 (Azernews, 2012). This gas is channelled into the existent Gazi–Magomed–Mozdok pipeline, which potentially represents an additional option of diversification export oriented to the north, bypassing Georgian and Turkish territory. Gazprom has periodically proposed its intention to purchase all Azeri gas destined to export, for two main reasons: firstly, to obtain a reliable and closer energy source in order to fill the South Stream pipeline project, which should deliver 63 bcm of gas per year to EU markets by 2015.

Secondly, the real Russian goal is to prevent the completion of the Trans-Caspian gas corridor and a Turkmenistan's involvement, setting back the building of the so-called "missing link" (a subsea pipeline) between the two shores of the Caspian Sea. As mentioned above, the full implementation of the TANAP project will depend on the commitment of Turkmen gas, in order to enhance the pipeline's capacity over 30 bcm of gas per year. Russia is trying to prevent the planned East–West Turkmen pipeline – with a capacity of 30–40 bcm of gas – from fuelling the TCGP, offering to purchase growing volumes of Turkmen gas, which would be also diverted to fuel the South Stream project.

The completion of the TCGP as well as the implementation of the TANAP undermines the Russian export plans economically: as a matter of fact, 30 bcm of the gas delivered to the EU markets (through the SGC) will represent one-third of Gazprom's lucrative business based on Europe's strong dependence on Russian gas imports (Fitzpatrick, 2011).

Consequently, Azerbaijan seeks to avoid a hard approach toward Russia. It also takes security issues into consideration: Baku fears Moscow's future position in the Armenian–Azeri frozen conflict over Nagorno-Karabakh, because Armenia is a strong military ally of Russia and both are partners in the Collective Security Treaty Organization (CSTO). In terms of the CSTO's mechanism Russia would intervene on Armenia's side in the case of a war with Azerbaijan over Karabakh (Kucera, 2011). Azeri-Armenian relations have progressively worsened in recent years, due to the increasing defence spending of both countries, which could potentially lead to a dangerous military confrontation, triggered by provocative gestures of both sides (International Crisis Group, 2013).

Tense bilateral relations between Azerbaijan and Turkmenistan are another issue that could damage Azeri energy ambitions: until 1991 Baku and Ashgabat both claimed ownership of three Caspian oilfields, even if currently two of these – the Azeri field (Omar to Turkmenistan) and the Chirag/Osman – represent the main source of oil-wealth for Azerbaijan.

The third disputed oilfield, Kyapaz/Serdar, frequently exacerbates tensions between these two countries: in June 2012 Azerbaijan diplomatically reacted against Turkmen attempts to undertake geological exploration on Kyapaz/Serdar, which were perceived by the Azeri Foreign Ministry as a clear violation of the 2008 agreement, within which the two Caspian states agreed to suspend all explorations or work activities on the disputed field until all issues on the division of the seabed are resolved (Aliyev, 2012).

Following the 2010 Caspian summit, Azerbaijan and Turkmenistan share a common position concerning the possibility of building an underwater Caspian pipeline with the agreement of the nations directly involved. However, the further implementation of this bilateral energy cooperation is prevented by the opposition of Russia and Iran, which privilege consensus among all the littoral states and could exercise their right to veto for all Caspian pipeline energy projects.

Despite negotiations on a Trilateral Agreement to realize the Trans-Caspian-Pipeline that are currently ongoing – through EU tripartite meetings – Turkmen president Berdymukhammedov continues to postpone the decision to commit volumes of national gas to the implementation of this energy corridor: during the visit of EU energy commissioner Günther Oettinger to Azerbaijan and Turkmenistan in September 2012, the Turkmen President stressed the relevance of the TSCP for the national aims of energy diversification, but he avoided clearly and openly supporting the project (Geropoulos, 2012).

Furthermore, the Azeri and Turkmen decision to hold military naval exercises in the Caspian Sea will not contribute to softening bilateral relations, but will worsen the regional scenario: as some analysts noted (Peyrouse and Laruelle, 2009: 17–35; Kucera, 2012), in recent years the five Caspian littoral states have been increasingly involved in a "militarization race" aimed at strengthening their navies and defence capacities, drawing up a dangerous scenario of instability and threats to security, which could delay energy projects in the Caspian basin. For Turkmenistan these exercises represented the first military naval manoeuvres in its history. Azerbaijan military naval exercises were openly focused on the protection of "Oil and Gas Fields, Platforms, and Export Pipelines" from a terrorist attack but also on preventing dangerous threats within the Caspian area, mainly coming from the Iranian side (Aliyev, 2012).

Tense relations with Iran could also set back Azerbaijan's key energy role. In addition to the historical rivalry linked to nationalistic and territorial claims and religious differences between the two states, other geopolitical factors exacerbate the reciprocal mistrust. On the one hand, Iran fears that Azerbaijan could support and facilitate joint American and Israeli military action against Teheran, particularly following Baku's decision to buy military equipment – anti aircraft missiles and drones – from

Israel, weapons that could be also used in regional disputes; on the other hand, Azerbaijan worries that Iranian destabilizing actions could threaten the internal stability of its secular regime. These tensions fuel a condition of instability in the Caspian region, which will prevent the development of the planned energy projects and the exploitation of the offshore fields located in the disputed territorial waters, a scenario that favours Russia's energy interests in the area (Shlapentokh, 2012).

Following TANAP's intergovernmental agreement, Turkish–Azeri political relations and energy cooperation appear to be at the highest level, overcoming past disagreements on gas prices: at present both countries have the geopolitical opportunity to become a strategic bridge for the alternative energy corridors to the EU. However, Russia's energy interests could weaken Azeri–Turkish relations, considering that Turkey is strongly dependent on Russia's gas imports, through the Balkan route and the Blue Stream pipeline (which links Russia to Turkey across the Black Sea, with a transport capacity of 16 bcm): in 2012 Turkey imported 34.9 bcm of gas by pipeline, 24.3 bcm of which was delivered by Gazprom (BP 2013).

Consequently Russia is seeking to strengthen its energy cooperation with Turkey – through a proposal to enhance Blue Stream's capacity – in order to make the Azeri gas option less attractive: in 2011, Russia obtained Ankara's agreement to build the planned South Stream pipeline through Turkey's Black Sea exclusive economic zone, aimed to compete with the EU's Southern Corridor.

At present, the unsolved Caspian legal status and Russian energy interests are substantially freezing the achievement of a win-win appeasement with Turkmenistan, a strategic precondition for a full implementation of the SGC.

Conclusion

European Union dependence on imported natural gas is expected to rise in the near future. In this scenario, the strategy of route and supply diversification will become the main geopolitical EU foreign-policy goal. Thanks to its geographic position and to the political decision to commit its gas reserves in a westward energy route direction, Azerbaijan could soon become a key partner for the EU, helping it to enhance its energy security. However, Azerbaijan will successfully achieve its ambition to play this double strategic role of energy hub and supplier only if there is internal and regional stability and security.

The risk of instability linked to an "Arab spring" scenario is a threat to be considered, even if in 2011 the Azeri authorities were able to prevent it. In the regional scenario, the traditionally tense relations with Iran and Armenia and the growing militarization race of all five Caspian littoral states will not help the Azeri strategy, contributing to a perceived condition of instability and intraregional rivalry that could hinder the development of energy projects in the Caspian basin.

The preservation of good political relations and cooperation with Turkey and Georgia represents a key factor in Azeri foreign policy because these are inevitable transit countries for its westward energy deliveries. In the Azeri strategic perspective, it is fundamental to preserve the cooperation with Turkey, which represents the main feasible energy route to reach European markets, allowing Baku to reinforce relations with a powerful geopolitical player in the regional context.

However, the implementation of the TANAP and, to a lesser extent, the AGRI projects will negatively affect Russian energy interests in the region, pushing Moscow to enhance its presence in the Caspian-Caucasus region in order to balance this situation. Azerbaijan wants to avoid a cooling of relations with Russia, even if the failed negotiations to prolong the Russian lease of the Azeri Gabala radar station would introduce another element of tension in the geopolitical regional scenario.

The Azeri–Turkmen tensions regarding Kyapaz/Serdar seem to suffice to postpone the completion of the TCGP, progressively downplaying Azeri energy ambitions: in 2030, without Turkmen gas supplies, Azerbaijan could not fill the TANAP planned capacity of 60 bcm, reducing the strategic relevance of its supplier and transit role with regards to the EU energy needs. Nonetheless, even a TANAP pipeline of reduced capacity and carrying only Azeri gas will represent a success for Azerbaijan's export diversification strategy, allowing Baku to fuel lucrative European markets through the future rise of national production and exports.

References

Abbasov, S. (2012) Azerbaijan: possible Iran sanctions offer Baku no golden energy opportunity. *Eurasianet*, <www.eurasianet.org/node/64923> (accessed 3 November 2014).

AGRI (2013) *AGRI. The First LNG Project to be Developed in the Black Sea. Project Overview*, <http://www.agrilng.com/agrilng/Home/DescrierеProiect> (accessed 3 November 2014).

Aliyev, K. M. (2012) Neighborhood challenge: Outlook for Caspian security from Azerbaijan. *New Europe Online*, <http://www.neurope.eu/blog/neighborhood-challenge-outlook-caspian-security-azerbaijan-0> (accessed 3 November 2014).

Anar, V. (2012) Azerbaijan-Turkmenistan relations: shattered brotherhood. *Eurasia Daily Monitor* 9(122), <http://www.jamestown.org/programs/edm/single/?tx_ttnews[tt_news]=39548&cHash=6a125c6590a825caa7aeac2f8b821080> (accessed 3 November 2014).

Azernews (2012) Russia's Gazprom to double Azerbaijan gas imports. *Azernews*, <http://www.azernews.az/oil_and_gas/40570.html> (accessed 3 November 2014).

Azernews (2013) BTC transports over 7.4m ton of Turkmen oil. *Azernews*, <http://www.news.az/articles/economy/81061> (accessed 3 November 2014).

Badalyan, L. (2011) Interlinked energy supply and security challenges in the South Caucasus. *Caucasus Analytical Digest* 33, 3.

Baev, P. K. and Øverland, I. (2010) The South Stream versus Nabucco pipeline race: geopolitical and economic (ir)rationales and political stakes in mega-projects. *International Affairs* 86(5), 1075–1090.

Bagirov, S. (2001) Azerbaijan's strategic choice in the Caspian Sea, in *The Security of the Caspian Region* (ed. G. Chufrin), Oxford University Press/SIPRI, Oxford, 190–194.

British Petroleum (2013) BP Statistical Review of World Energy 2013, 6,20, <http://www.bp.com/content/dam/bp/pdf/statistical-review/statistical_review_of_world_energy_2013.pdf> (accessed 29 December 2014).

British Petroleum (2013) *Shah Deniz,* <http://www.bp.com/productlanding.do?categoryId=9006668&contentId=7078987> (accessed 3 November 2014).

Cornell, S. E., Tsereteli, M. and Socor, V.(2005) Geostrategic implications of the Baku-Tbilisi-Ceyhan pipeline, in *The Baku-Tbilisi-Ceyhan Pipeline: Oil Window to the Wes.* (ed. F. S. Starr and S. E. Cornell), Central Asia-Caucasus Institute and Silk Road Studies Program, Washington, 18–24, 31–36.

Cutler, R. (2012) Azerbaijan and Turkey tilt towards new "Trans-Anatolian" natural gas pipeline. *Central Asia-Caucasus Institute Analyst,* <http://www.cacianalyst.org/?q=node/5720> (accessed 3 November 2014).

EurActiv (2010) Europe's southern gas corridor. The great pipeline race. *Euractiv,* <http://www.euractiv.com/energy/europe-s-southern-gas-corridor-great-pipeline-race-linksdossier-498558> (accessed 29 December 2014).

Eurasianet (2013) Consortium turns down Nabucco West pipeline. *Eurasianet,* <http://www.eurasianet.org/node/67185> (accessed 3 November 2014).

European Commission (2010) *EU Energy Trends to 2030 (Update 2009),* Publications Office of the European Union, Luxembourg.

European Commission (2011a) *Joint Declaration on the Southern Gas Corridor,* <http://ec.europa.eu/energy/infrastructure/strategy/doc/2011_01_13_joint_declaration_southern_corridor.pdf> (accessed 3 November 2014).

European Commission (2011b) *EU Starts Negotiations on Caspian Pipeline to bring Gas to Europe,* press release, IP/11/1023. European Commission, Brussels.

Fitzpatrick, C. A. (2011) Turkmenistan weekly roundup. *Eurasianet,* <http://www.eurasianet.org/node/64477> (accessed 3 November 2014).

Geropoulos, K. (2012) EU bets on gas from Azerbaijan, Turkmenistan for Trans-Caspian pipe. *New Europe Online,* <http://www.neurope.eu/article/eu-bets-gas-azerbaijan-turkmenistan-trans-caspian-pipe> (accessed 14 November 2012).

Institut für Europäische Politik (2011) *Europe's Energy Future: Natural Gas Supply between Geopolitics and the Markets,* Institut für Europäische Politik, Berlin, 11, 13–35.

International Crisis Group (2013) Armenia and Azerbaijan: a season of risks. *ICG Europe Briefing* No. 71, <http://www.crisisgroup.org/~/media/Files/europe/caucasus/b071-armenia-and-azerbaijan-a-season-of-risks.pdf> (accessed 3 November 2014).

International Energy Agency (2010) *World Energy Outlook 2010,* OECD/IEA, Paris, 499–530.

International Energy Agency (2011) *World Energy Outlook 2011,* OECD/IEA, Paris, 165.

Ismayilov, E. (2012) Azerbaijan's estimated gas reserves exceed 2.5 trillion cubic meters. *Trend Az,* <http://en.trend.az/capital/energy/2036361.html> (accessed 3 November 2014).

Jonson, L. (2001) The new geopolitical situation in the Caspian region, in *The Security of the Caspian Region* (ed. G. Chufrin), Oxford University Press/SIPRI, Oxford, 16–19.

Kucera, J. (2011) Russia's credibility and its military sales to Azerbaijan. *Eurasianet,* <http://www.eurasianet.org/node/64085> (accessed 3 November 2014).

Kucera, J. (2012) The great Caspian arms race. *Foreign Policy,* <http://www.foreignpolicy.com/articles/2012/06/22/the_great_caspian_arms_race?page=0,0> (accessed 3 November 2014).

Muradova, M. (2012) Azerbaijan favors Trans-Anatolian pipeline and Nabucco West. *Central Asia and Caucasus Institute Analyst,* <http://www.cacianalyst.org/?q=node/5816> (accessed 14 November 2014).

Natural Gas Europe (2012) ITGI loses out to TAP in Shah Deniz bid. *Natural Gas Europe,* <http://www.naturalgaseurope.com/itgi-dropped-from-southern-corridor-race> (accessed 14 November 2014).

New Europe (2012) BP, Statoil and Total buy into TANAP gas pipeline. *New Europe,* <http://www.neurope.eu/article/socar-bp-statoil-and-total-buy-tanap-gas-pipe> (accessed 14 November 2014).

Nuriyev, E. (2008) Azerbaijan and the European Union: new landmarks of strategic partnership in the South Caucasus-Caspian basin. *Southeast European and Black Sea Studies* 8(2), 159–160.

Peyrouse, S. and Laruelle, M. (2009) The Militarization of the Caspian Sea: "great games" and "small games" over the Caspian Fleets. *The China and Eurasia Forum Quarterly* 2(7), 17–35.

Socor, V. (2011) Azerbaijan and its gas consortium partners sign agreements with Turkey. *Eurasia Daily Monitor* 8(201), <http://www.jamestown.org/single/?no_cache=1&tx_ttnews[tt_news]=38603&tx_ttnews[backPid]=7&cHash=6bc581ad046414cd-39c92f5db174f9fc> (accessed 3 November 2014).

Socor, V. (2012a) Direct road to Europe: Azerbaijan's trans-Anatolia gas pipeline. *Eurasia Daily Monitor* 9(2), <http://www.jamestown.org/single/?no_cache=1&tx_ttnews[tt_news]=38834> (accessed 3 November 2014).

Socor, V. (2012b) Trans-Anatolia, Nabucco-West pipeline projects: an optimal fit. *Eurasia Daily Monitor* 9(62), <http://www.jamestown.org/single/?no_cache=1&tx_ttnews[tt_news]=39189> (accessed 3 November 2014).

Trans Adriatic Pipeline (2013) *Trans Adriatic Pipeline. Route,* <http://www.trans-adriatic-pipeline.com/en/tap-project/route/> (accessed 3 November 2014).

Trans Anatolia Natural Gas Pipeline (2013) *TANAP Project, the Silk Road of Energy, Has Been Signed,* <http://www.tanap.com/en/the-energy-of-the-future-is-ready.aspx> (accessed 14 November 2014).

Tsereteli, M. (2009) *The Impact of Russia-Georgia War on the South Caucasus Transportation Corridor,* The Jamestown Foundation, Washington, DC.

United States Energy Information Administration (2010) *International Energy Outlook 2010,* DOE/EIA, Washington, DC.

Sybilla Wege

The Black Sea Region as a Strategic Energy Corridor: International Dynamics of Cooperation and Competition

ABSTRACT: The Black Sea region plays a key role in the transport of fossil energy sources from the Caspian basin to Europe. As a transport hub for oil and natural gas the region stands in the centre of competing national interests due to its geographical position. While the EUis seeking to diversify its energy sources through new gas pipeline routes to the Caspian area, Russiais actively undermining these efforts in order to hold and extend its position as Europe's chief supplier of natural gas. This article examines the competitive behaviour between the EU and the Russian Federation towards pipeline projects in the Black Sea region. The goal of this study is to analyse the likelihood of upcoming cooperation between the two major protagonists.

KEYWORDS: Black Sea Region, energy corridor, international pipeline, strategy

Introduction

The Black Sea Region plays a more important role than its geographical dimensions might suggest. It connects Europe to Central Asia, the Caspian and the Middle Eastern states. The wider Black Sea Region includes the littoral states of the Black Sea,[1] Moldova and the Southern Caucasus countries of Armenia, Azerbaijan and Georgia.[2] Due to its geographical location, the region plays a key role for the international transport of fossil energy sources to Europe from the Caspian area, which holds substantial amounts of the world's oil and gas reserves (Karbuz, 2010). The Caspian basin comprises Russia, Azerbaijan, Kazakhstan, Turkmenistan and Iran

1 Bulgaria, Romania, Ukraine, Russia, Georgia and Turkey.

2 Hereafter the Black Sea Region and the wider Black Sea Region will be used as synonyms.

and is, after the Persian Gulf, the second most important region in term of oil and gas resources (Žulinskij, 2006). Moreover, there are high hopes that the exploration and development of additional fields in Turkmenistan, Kazakhstan and Azerbaijan will increase the potential value of the region.

Most hydrocarbon transit routes from the Caspian region cross the Black Sea Region to arrive downstream in Europe. The region plays a crucial role as an energy corridor for the future energy market (Karbuz, 2010). The competition over different pipeline projects in recent years reflects its importance not only to Europe and Russia but also to other global powers. Initially, the major contenders were Russia, on one hand, struggling to consolidate its sphere of influence in the post-Soviet states and to hold a tight control over it stable and advantageous gas supplies, and, on the other hand, the European Union and the United States, seeking to construct transit routes to ensure access to Caspian resources without reliance on the Russian pipeline network (Cornell and Nilsson, 2008: 28). In the meantime further countries, such as China and India, have also set their focus on the Caspian Region, primarily motivated by the high dependence of their rapid economic growth on a stable access to energy supplies (Koolaee and Imani-Kalesar, 2010: 86).

The Caspian states are all connected to the former Soviet pipeline system and enable Russia to hold a complete monopoly over all transit routes to Europe, supplying oil and gas from other countries at the border for further distribution. The control of the pipeline routes is just as important for the actors involved as the resources they transport. However, since 2006, Europe has been able to import oil directly from Azerbaijan bypassing Russian territory through the Baku–Tbilisi–Ceyhan pipeline. The building of the 1768 km-long line, with a capacity of 1 million barrels per day, constitutes a strategic milestone and represents a first step toward providing oil from Caspian countries directly to Europe (Cornell, Tsereteli and Socor, 2005: 17). On the other side, in terms of natural gas supplies a monopoly is still in place. After many years of speculation about possible gas pipelines to be built over this crossroad to Europe, three competing projects are currently being considered, namely the Russian South Stream pipeline and two other European options, either the Nabucco West pipeline or the Trans-Adriatic-Pipeline (Pflüger, 2012: 1). At least, the European option will be connected with the Turkish–AzeriTrans–Anatolian Pipeline (TANAP).

The Black Sea region is also relevant in terms of regional and international security. The region faces multiple challenges, most notably due to competing interests of its nation states, the ongoing transformation of former communist countries and so-called "frozen conflicts". The Black Sea region comprises 11 states with a variety of ethnic backgrounds and spheres of influence. Bulgaria and Romania are members of NATO and members of the European Union. Ukraine is "split" between the West and Russia. Georgia leans towards the West but borders on Russia's soft underbelly. Turkey and Russia vacillate between East and West, pulled in different directions by national interests and national pride, particularly the unresolved, long-running, unsteady disputes in Georgia and Moldova and between Armenia and Azerbaijan (Shelest, 2009: 1).

This chapter discusses Russian and European interests in the Black Sea region, directly linked to their stated energy strategies, in order to reflect how these objectives and tactics have shaped the current landscape of competing pipeline projects. The chapter argues that the European Union has not succeeded with the "Southern Corridor" as a supply diversification strategy. It has rather triggered a Russian response that proved to be more a political and reactive solution than an economics-driven one. It shows that one cannot speak of cooperation but, rather, of a competitive pattern that generates more burdens than mutual gains.

Russia's Interests in the Black Sea Region

The Russian Federation is a major player in the world energy markets. It possesses the world's largest reserve of natural gas, the second largest of coal, and the eighth largest of crude oil (EIA, 2012). Russia's proven natural gas reserves are 44.6 tcm, which comes to over a quarter of the world's proven resources. After the United States, Russia is currently the world's second largest extractor of gas with an annual production of 607 bcm (BP, 2012: 20), and the largest exporter of natural gas and oil. In 2011, the volume of exported gas was more than 200 bcm, of which the largest share (150 bcm) was directed to European markets (Gazprom, 2012b).

The Russian gas industry is dominated by OAO Gazprom, a publicly traded company in which the government holds a majority stake of 51%.

Gazprom owns about half of Russia's proven gas reserves and all the main gas processing facilities in the country (Gazprom, 2012a). It has the exclusive right to control all of Russia's natural gas pipelines and its exports (Gazprom Export, 2012).

Energy exports are the backbone of the Russian economy and have been its major growth driver in recent years. They contribute more than 40% of the Federal budget revenues and represent 70% of the country's total exports (Solanko, 2011: 20). At the very outset of Putin's presidency in 2000, the new government made a clear commitment to re-establish itself as a major regional, even global, political actor, and to use its energy policy for the strategic development of the country (Arakelyan and Kanet, 2012: 265). In this context, the government has pursued policies of nationalizing energy assets while limiting access by international energy companies, providing a clear comparative advantage for Russian companies. Gazprom controls gas purchases and deliveries from the post-Soviet countries to the outside world. Russia's intention is to maintain tight control over how gas from the Caspian region is sold to Europe and Asia.

The complete ownership of all the gas distribution networks to Europe grants Russia immense bargaining power with its suppliers, as well as market power at the end-consumer level. It enables Russia to procure energy supplies from the former Soviet states at relatively low prices and to export to Europe at higher rates and for hard currency. In this context, the export monopoly of Gazprom represents the fundamental prerequisite for the dual pricing policy of Russia, differentiating between national and international end consumers (Winrow, 2005: 91). In 2011, the gas export prices to Western Europe were 4.1 times higher than those for the Russian market (Gazprom, 2012b).

For the reasons mentioned above, the Black Sea region represents a zone of Russian "strategic interests". Thus, the government's focus is to restrict political and economic competition from the former Soviet republics of Central Asia and the Caucasus (Finon and Locatelli, 2007: 5), keeping its advantageous monopolistic position and dominant power.

EU Interests in the Black Sea Region

The EU member states are the world's largest energy importer, sourcing more than half of their energy supply from outside the Union. According to official statistics, EU imports in 2011 covered 84% of their oil needs and 64% of their gas consumption (European Council, 2011: 1). For the next few decades, the EU is expected to become even more dependent on gas imports as its own relatively small resources – mainly located in the North Sea – are depleting. In the recent past, some national policy decisions have also contributed to a probable increase of the EU's dependency on natural gas imports. Thus, the German agreement of April 2011 on phasing out nuclear power by 2022, after the Fukushima nuclear disaster in Japan, as well as the French decision to prohibit shale gas drilling, underpin the expectation of a rapid rise of natural gas imports (Belkin *et al.*, 2012: 5). However, whether there will be a rapid rise in German gas consumption is yet to be seen. According to the European Commission, the share of gas imports should pass the 80% mark by 2030.

Natural gas plays a crucial role in the EU's current energy mix. It comprises about 25% of the EU's primary energy consumption, and the figure is expected to be even higher by 2030 (Eurostat, 2011: 9) whereas its domestic energy production – out of which nowadays nuclear power comprises the largest share (30%) – has been steadily declining since 2002 (European Council, 2011: 1).

Currently, the EU sources around 35% of its natural gas and 30% of its oil needs from Russia (European Commission, 2011b: 1). Different EU member states resort to natural gas to a various extents in terms of import levels and supply sources. Some large natural gas consumers, such as Spain, do not import any Russian gas, but obtain it mostly from Algeria through the Maghreb–Europe Gas Pipeline (BP, 2012: 28). Germany, on the other hand, as the second biggest natural gas consumer in the EU, relies for almost 40% of its imports on Russia (BP, 2012: 28). Moreover, countries such as Finland and the new member states in the East, due to geographic constraints, are virtually captive consumers of Russian gas(EurActiv, 2011).

Certainly, the acquisition of Gazprom's majority shares by the government in 2005 (Gazprom, 2007: 80) and the resulting centralization of the energy sector in Russia led to initial worries in the EU with regard to its energy security. Episodes such as the unexpected suspension of gas delivery from Russia to Europe in the years 2006 and 2009, or the danger of a possible attack on the pipelines during the Georgia war in 2008, have acted as a "wake-up call" for the need for alternative transport conduits (European Commission, 2011a: 5). As a matter of fact almost 80% of Russian natural gas exports to Europe flow via pipelines through Ukraine, Belarus and Moldova (Stern, 2006: 2). For instance, the conflict between Russia and Ukraine in 2009 has resulted in significant reductions of pressure in the pipelines from Gazprom, affecting the supply of many EU member states.

In short, the limited domestic gas supply along with the expectation of higher demand levels have called for a stronger mechanism to secure new, diversified and safe supply routes (European Commission, 2011a: 7) to Europe. In this respect, an energy strategy was elaborated by the European Commission in 2011 based on the principles of diversification of sources, transport routes and mechanisms together with the building of reliable partnerships with suppliers, transit and consumer countries (European Commission, 2011a).

Despite efforts to pursue a cohesive EU-wide energy security policy, what one could observe in the last years has been rather a pursuit of policies of "economic nationalism", where the commercial interests of the strongest economic powers override the common EU energy security interests (Henry, 2010: 2). So far, the member states have been unable to agree on a common strategy and to carry out a common policy. This has been due primarily to major differences between the interests of individual EU member states and consequently to their diverging approaches to Russia (Caneva, 2011). On one hand, EU countries as Germany; Italy and France consider Russia as an important and trustworthy strategic partner; on the other hand the new EU member states such as Poland or Czech Republic "have experienced firsthand the Russian use of energy disruption for political ends" (Henry, 2010: 14). As an example for the differences within the Union one could mention the Nord Stream gas pipeline, inaugurated in 2011 and linking Germany directly with Siberia's natural gas reserves through the Baltic Sea. Since its birth, the project has been subject to harsh criticism, because the Baltic countries and Poland interpreted the pipeline as a politically motivated strategy that turned out to be rather a bilateral agreement rather than a common European project (Whist, 2008: 19).

The Black Sea Competing Pipeline Landscape

Europe's increasing anxiety over its dependence on Russian natural gas imports has led to the development of the so-called "Southern Corridor", representing the EUs most promising solution (De Jong, 2012: 1; Sartori, 2012: 3) and highest energy security priority (Commission of the European Communities, 2008: 4). After many failed initiatives, its most prominent and realistic pipeline projects were the Nabucco West pipeline and the Trans-Adriatic Pipeline (TAP). A decision to choose between the two projects was announced by mid-2013. In June 2013, the Consortium of the Shah Deniz II gas field chose the Trans-Adriatic Pipeline to bring the gas from Turkey to Italy. Up to the Turkish border, the Trans-Anatolian gas pipeline (TANAP) will deliver gas produced from the Azerbaijani fields of Shah Deniz.

The Nabucco pipeline is the European endeavour to connect the world's richest gas regions to the European consumer markets. Although it has the strong support of the European Union, the project was proposed by Nabucco Gas Pipeline International GmbH, a joint venture between five European energy commercial companies: RWE (Germany), FGSZ (Hungary), OMV (Austria), Transgaz (Romania), the Bulgarian Energy Holding (Bulgaria), and Turkey's state owned Botaş.

The initial version of the planned pipeline, currently labelled Nabucco Classic, was signed in June 2002 and was supposed to run from Turkey via Bulgaria, Romania and Hungary to Austria at a total length of 3893 km (European Commission 2013: 1). Since the agreement signed by Turkey and Azerbaijan in 2011 on the construction of the Trans-Anatolian Gas Pipeline (TANAP), bringing gas from the Shah Deniz II field to Turkey, the Nabucco project was reduced to a shorter version, namely Nabucco West. The latter begins at the Bulgarian–Turkish border and should transport to Austria fewer gas quantities than the original plans, with a total length of 1300 kilometres (RWE 2012). Although the planned supply of 10–23 bcm per annum represent no more than 10% of the EU gas imports and 2% of its yearly consumption, the pipeline could deliver gas to the European countries which currently have the lowest levels of diversification.

The weakest point in the Nabucco pipeline refers to the question of gas supplies. One of the most probable sources for the project is the gas field Shah Deniz II, from whose expected additional production only 10 bcm supply has been assured to Europe (Cutler, 2012), starting from 2017/2018 (Razayeva and Tsakiris, 2012: 17). So far no other additional sourcing partners to fill the pipeline with the remaining volumes are in place. For the time being gas-rich Turkmenistan could not stand as a possible partner for the European Union, sourcing gas via a trans-Caspian pipeline to Azerbaijan. Russia and Iran have been successfully using the dispute over the yet-unsettled juridical status of the Caspian Sea as a practical instrument to veto Western involvement in the region preventing the construction of an infrastructure venue crossing the sea. Furthermore, due to the EU sanctions against Iran as well as the unresolved political situation in Northern Iraq, a bilateral agreement with either of these potential suppliers is at the moment unforeseeable (Katzman, 2010: 5).

The Trans-Adriatic Pipeline (TAP), as a proposed project, will transport natural gas from Azerbaijan via Greece and Albania to Italy's southern coast and further into Western Europe. The pipeline offers the shortest gas transit route of all the pipeline projects planned in the Southern Gas Corridor (TAP, 2012) so far. The pipeline is expected to carry up to 20 bcm gas per year. However, the project suffers from the same sourcing problems as in the Nabucco pipeline, only having 10 bcm *de facto* secured from Azerbaijan.

The planning process of the TAP AG as a joint venture company between EGL (42.5%), Statoil (42.5%) and E.ON (15%) started in 2003. In July 2013, TAP's shareholding consisted of BP (20%), SOCAR (20%), Statoil (20%), Fluxys (16%), Total (10%), E.ON (9%) and Axpo (5%). The pipeline would be ready to transport natural gas from the Caspian region as soon as the Shah Deniz II field in Azerbaijan starts production. The project costs are estimated to be around 1.5 billion dollars.

The South Stream pipeline is Russia's response to Europe's Southern Corridor. It is a gas pipeline planned to transport Russian natural gas under the Black Sea to Europe. According to Gazprom, the planned route is to start from the Russian Black Sea coast and run offshore to Bulgaria and further to northern Italy through Serbia, Hungary, Slovenia, and Austria (Gazprom, 2012c). After crossing the Black Sea, the pipeline should go onshore via two branches, crossing at least six countries, totalling between 1600 and 2500 km overland (Gazprom, 2011a: 5; Gazprom, 2012c). However, a final investment decision concerning bypassing countries and endpoints is still to be made (Gazprom, 2012d). The pipeline projection is to carry up to 63 bcm of natural gas per annum and to have its first supplies in 2015 (Gazprom, 2012c).

As officially announced by Gazprom, the project aims to meet Europe's additional demand for gas (South Stream, 2012a) and therefore to strengthen European energy security. Moreover, as already referred in the Russian Energy Strategy 2030, the South Stream pipeline represents one of the country's most "important strategic energy infrastructure projects" (Ministry of Energy of the Russian Federation, 2010: 61) and is seen as a chance to diversify natural gas routes away from transit countries such as Ukraine and Belarus. Additionally, it enables the direct supply of energy resources to European end-users (South Stream, 2012a).

For the completion of this EUR 15 billion gas project (South Stream, 2012b), Gazprom has formalized bilateral agreements on several country sections, strategically differentiated by offshore and onshore portions of the pipeline. For the 900 km underwater section of the pipeline running under the Black Sea, an international consortium was created between Gazprom and Western companies. Gazprom has 50% participation in the so-called South Stream Transport AG followed by Eni (20%) with the remainder split between Germany's Wintershall Holding and France's EDF group. For the largest and remaining portion of the pipeline, namely the onshore section, Gazprom has already built joint ventures, together with national energy companies, with the majority of shares in its hands (Kazmin, 2009: 24; Gazprom Export, 2012). For instance, at the end of 2010 the following joint companies were incorporated to implement the pipeline project: the South Stream Serbia AG (Gazprom 51%, Srbijagas 49%), the South Stream Hungary ZRT (Gazprom 50%, the Hungarian Development Bank MFB 50%) and the South Stream Bulgaria AD (Gazprom 50%, the Bulgarian Energy Holding 50%) (Gazprom, 2012c).

Indeed, regardless of the cooperation arrangements in place, Gazprom is the sole gas supplier for the project and is in control of design, construction and operation in each country section. It also holds commercial control of the project. Together with each participant country, the costs for the pipeline construction are supposed to be shared by Gazprom roughly on a 50–50 basis (Socor, 2012). For host countries that cannot financially afford to participate, such as Bulgaria, Gazprom will step in and finance the country's share in order to guarantee the completion of the project (Mazurkevich, 2012).

Analysts argue that the realization of this project could also represent an instrument to maintain political and economic leverage over Europe. South Stream would enable Russian influence to expand in Southern Europe, while Nord Stream pipeline permits the connection to Germany and northern Europe (Baran, 2008: iii).

Unlike the Nord Stream pipeline project on the Baltic Sea, which has at least some amount of Russian gas resources exclusively dedicated to it (at least in the planning), South Stream has had, until now, no known resource backup in Russia or elsewhere. As described by the South Stream consortium, "it is incorrect to say that South Stream is linked to any particular field" (South Stream, 2012c). Further, due to stagnant gas production and the aging fields currently in operation, Russia has been unable to identify any internal gas reserves to supply the proposed South Stream system. Analysts argue that the pipeline would only shift some gas volumes from the Ukrainian transit routes into South Stream, although far from meeting South Stream's declared future capacity (Baran, 2008: iii).

As a reactive project to Nabucco, Russia's effort in pulling over potential European suppliers such as Kazakhstan, Turkmenistan and Uzbekistan some years ago, through long-term contracts, had marked the government's first strategic steps (Gazprom, 2009). Recently, the so-far pro-European state and supporter of Nabucco, Azerbaijan, has also made a commitment in signing a gas-supply treaty of 3 bcm to Russia (Gazprom, 2011b). At a first glance, such measures seem to be highly cost intensive; on a long-term basis they have significant implications and fulfil geo-strategic purposes towards the Caspian and Black Sea area (Pop, 2008).

Conclusion

The mutually interdependent energy relationship between, on one side, the EU as the world's largest energy importer, with its objective of reducing dependence on one sole source of supply, and, on the other side, energy giant Russia, with its ambition to secure its predominant position over transit routes and supplies, has created a "dynamic game" of competition and bilateral partnerships over possible pipeline routes.

By reviewing recent strategic actions and reactions taken by the EU for the construction of alternative pipeline scenarios, one could mention that it has not yet acted as a consistent and homogeneous player with regards to the European Commission's energy strategy. European Union countries still negotiate individually and also often divergently, resulting therefore in different outcomes for different states.

In retrospect, Europe's idea of the "Southern Corridor" as an option to secure the EU's supply has so far largely been a failure because only 2% of its yearly annual gas consumption is guaranteed. No other supply partners have been pulled in and therefore the original plan to build a transport conduit independent of Russian control has not yet been put in place. Nevertheless, if Nabucco West or TAP is finally chosen, the Southern Corridor could still play a strategic role for Europe, even though a quite modest one, by transiting and supplying Bulgaria and Greece – countries that currently depend almost 100% on Russia's Gazprom.

In contrast to Russia, the EU has also been incapable of combining "its political vision with the properly considered financial means" for the realization of the Southern Corridor (Dudau, 2012: 9). The projects turned out to be primarily driven by commercial interests. The Southern Corridor has been shaped and influenced to a great extent by the interests of private investors and large-scale companies acting under constraints set by Russia.

In the foreseeable future, a likely scenario is a further increase of European dependence on Russian fossil sources, regardless of the completion of TAP. Upcoming cooperation between Russia and one united EU with regard to pipeline projects is not in sight. Europe's intention to secure its energy supply by diversifying sources will further stimulate Russian strategic actions to reach individual EU states through bilateral agreements, be it at the consumer level or the transit level, creating a landscape of further competing pipelines. Russia, with the strict pursuit of its strategic goals, will preserve its position of domination in the Caspian Region and will further take advantage of divided European interests.

In the long term, new developments in the natural gas markets, such as the production of shale gas, could change the relationship between Europe and Russia. This may offer a number of advantages for Europe: lower natural gas prices, more readily available gas on the European market and adding diversity to the EU's gas supplies. But, taking into account environmental considerations in contrast to the traditional methods of production and transportation, it still requires a lot of time and investment.

References

Arakelyan, L. A. and Kanet, R. E. (2012) Russian energy policy in the South Caucasus, in *Russia and Its Near Neighbours: Identity, Interests and Foreign Policy* (eds M. R. Freire and R. E. Kanet), Macmillan, Basingstoke, 265–286.

Baran, Z. (2008) Security Aspects of the South Stream Project. *Center for Eurasian Policy Hudson Institute,* <http://www.europarl.europa.eu/RegData/etudes/note/join/2008/388962/EXPO-AFET_NT(2008)388962_EN.pdf> (accessed 22 December 2014).

Ratner, M., Belkin, P, Nichol, J. and Woehrel, S. (2012) Europe's energy security: options and challenges to natural gas supply diversification. *CRS Report* 13(3), <http://www.fas.org/sgp/crs/row/R42405.pdf> (accessed 3 November 2014).

BP (2012) *BP Statistical Review of World Energy,* <http://www.bp.com/content/dam/bp/pdf/Statistical-Review-2012/statistical_review_of_world_energy_2012.pdf> (accessed 22 December 2014).

Caneva, S. (2011) EU–Russia energy relations: lack of unity in the union. *E-International Relations* 7(3), <http://www.e-ir.info/2011/03/07/eu-russia-energy-relations-lack-of-unity-in-the-union/> (accessed 3 November 2014).

Commission of the European Communities (2008) *Second Strategic Energy Review. An EU Energy Security and Solidarity Action Plan,* <http://eur-lex.europa.eu/LexUriServ/LexUriServ.do?uri=COM:2008:0781:FIN:EN:PDF> (accessed 3 November 2014).

Commission on the Black Sea (2010) *A 2020 Vision for the Black Sea Region,* <http://www.ctsp.vt.edu/publications/data/a%202020%20vision%20for%20the%20black%20sea.pdf> (accessed 22 December 2014).

Cornell, S. E. and Nilsson, N. (eds) (2008) Europe's Energy Security: Gazprom's Dominance and Caspian Supply Alternatives, *Central Asia-Caucasus Institute and Silk Road Studies Program*, Washington, DC, <http://www.isdp.eu/images/stories/isdp-main-pdf/2008_cornell-nilsson_europes-energy-security.pdf> (accessed 3 November 2014).

Cornell, S. E., Tsereteli, M. and Socor, V. (2005) Geostrategic implications of the Baku-Tiblisi-Ceyhan pipeline, in *The Baku-Tbilisi-Ceyhan Pipeline: Oil Window to the West* (ed. S. F. Starr and S. E. Cornell), Central

Asia-Caucasus Institute and Silk Road Studies Program, Washington, DC, 17–38, <http://www.isn.ethz.ch/Digital-Library/Publications/Detail/?id=110791> (accessed 3 November 2014).

Cutler, R. (2012) Nabucco West in pipeline final. *Central Asia*, No. 7, <http://www.atimes.com/atimes/Central_Asia/NG07Ag01.html> (accessed 3 November 2014).

De Jong, S. (2012) Europe's southern gas corridor: Central Asia and the EU's drive towards energy diversification. *EU-GRASP Policy Brief* 8(3), <http://i.unu.edu/media/unu.edu/publication/27192/Europes-Southern-Gas-Corridor-Central-Asia-and-the-EUs-Drive-Towards-Energy-Diversification.pdf> (accessed 22 December 2014).

Dudau, R. (2012) The Shah Deniz end game and the plights of the Southern Corridor. *Caucasus International*2(2), 93–108.

EIA (2012) *Countries Russia. Overview Data,*<http://www.eia.gov/countries/country-data.cfm?fips=RS> (accessed 3 November 2014).

EurActiv (2011) *Europe Switches to Gas*, <http://www.euractiv.com/energy/europe-switches-gas> (accessed 22 December 2014).

European Commission (2000) *Green Paper. Towards a European Strategy for the Security of Energy Supply*, <http://ec.europa.eu/energy/green-paper-energy-supply/doc/green_paper_energy_supply_en.pdf> (accessed 3 November 2014).

European Commission (2011a) *Energy 2020. A Strategy for Competitive, Sustainable and Secure Energy*, <http://ec.europa.eu/energy/publications/doc/2011_energy2020_en.pdf> (accessed 3 November 2014).

European Commission (2011b) *Statistics and Market Observatory for Energy. Monthly and Cumulated Crude Oil Imports*, <http://ec.europa.eu/energy/observatory/oil/import_export_en.htm> (accessed 3 November 2014).

European Commission (2013)*Gas interconnection. Gas Bridge between Asian & Europe.* <http://ec.europa.eu/energy/eepr/projects/files/gas-interconnections-and-reverse-flow/nabucco_en.pdf> (accessed 22 December 2014).

European Council (2011) *EU Energy Policy*, <http://www.european-council.europa.eu/media/171257/ec04.02.2011-factsheet-energy-pol_finaldg.en.pdf> (accessed 3 November 2014).

Eurostat (2011) *European Commission. Consumption of Energy,* <http://epp.eurostat.ec.europa.eu/statistics_explained/index.php/Consumption_of_energy> (accessed 3 November 2014).

Finon, D. and Locatelli, C. (2007) *Russian and European Gas Interdependence. Can Market Forces Balance Out Geopolitics?* LEPII 01, <http://halshs.archives-ouvertes.fr/docs/00/12/96/18/PDF/Cahier41bis.pdf> (accessed 3 November 2014).

Gazprom (2007) *Annual Report 2007,* <http://www.gazprom.com/f/posts/75/910228/1annual_eng_2007.pdf> (accessed 22 December 2014).

Gazprom (2009) *Gazprom Delegation Visits Turkmenistan.* Gazprom Press Center, 22 December 2009, <http://www.gazprom.com/press/news/2009/december/article73501/> (accessed 3 November 2014).

Gazprom (2011a) *South Stream. Energizing Europe,* Brussels <http://gazprom.com/f/posts/85/290063/presentation.pdf> (accessed 3 November 2014).

Gazprom (2011b) Gazprom to increase Azerbaijani gas purchase to 3 bcm in 2012. Gazprom Press Center, <http://www.gazprom.com/press/news/2011/december/article125849/> (accessed 3 November 2014).

Gazprom (2012a) *About Gazprom,* <http://www.gazprom.com/about/> (accessed 4 November 2014).

Gazprom (2012b) *Gazprom in Foreign Markets,* <http://www.gazprom-questions.ru/en/foreign-markets/> (accessed 22 December 2014).

Gazprom (2012c) *South Stream. Significance,* <http://www.gazprom.com/about/production/projects/pipelines/south-stream/> (accessed 4 November 2014).

Gazprom (2012d) Board of Directors request to adopt final investment decision on South Stream before year end. Gazprom Press Center, <http://gazprom.com/press/news/2012/may/article135750/> (accessed 4 November 2014).

Gazprom Export (2012) *South Stream,* <http://www.gazpromexport.ru/en/projects/6/> (accessed 4 November 2014).

Henry, H. (2010) The EU's energy security dilemma with Russia. *POLIS Journal*4, <http://www.polis.leeds.ac.uk/assets/files/students/student-journal/ma-winter-10/helen-e.pdf> (accessed 4 November 2014).

Karbuz, S. (2010) Losing the energy battle: how and why the US and EU need to engage the Black Sea region. *Journal of Energy Security,* <http://www.ensec.org/index.php?option=com_content&view=article

&id=255:losing-the-battle-why-and-how-the-united-states-and-europe-need-to-engage-the-black-sea-region&catid=108:energysecuritycontent&Itemid=365> (accessed 4 November 2014).

Katzman, K. (2010) *Iran Sanctions.* Congressional Research Service, <http://fpc.state.gov/documents/organization/141587.pdf> (accessed 4 November 2014).

Kazmin, R. (2009) South Stream. *European Energy Review7*, <http://www.europeanenergyreview.eu/data/docs/eer11/EER11-5-SouthStream.pdf> (accessed 4 November 2014).

Koolaee, E. and Imani-Kalesar, M. (2010) India's Energy Security Strategy Towards the Caspian Sea Region,*Central Asia-Caucasus Institute and Silk Road Studies Program,* Washington, DC.

Mazurkevich, A. (2012) *Gazprom to Finance Bulgarian South Stream,* RIA Novosti, Moscow, <http://en.rian.ru/business/20120609/173936233.html> (accessed 4 November 2014).

Ministry of Energy of the Russian Federation (2003) *The Summary of the Energy Strategy of Russia for the Period of up to 2020,* <http://ec.europa.eu/energy/russia/events/doc/2003_strategy_2020_en.pdf> (accessed 4 November 2014).

Ministry of Energy of the Russian Federation (2010) *Energy Strategy of Russia for the Period of up to 2030,* <http://www.energystrategy.ru/projects/docs/ES-2030_(Eng).pdf> (accessed 14 November 2014).

Pflüger, F. (2012) The Southern Gas corridor: reaching the home stretch. *European Energy Review, January 12.*

Pop, V. (2008) Energy security: South Stream vs. Nabucco gas pipelines. *Southeast European Times,* <http://www.setimes.com/cocoon/setimes/xhtml/en_GB/features/setimes/features/2008/02/14/feature-02> (accessed 4 November 2014).

Razayeva, G. and Tsakiris, T. (2012) *Strategic Imperative. SAM Review. Azerbaijani Gas Strategy and the EU's Southern Corridor,* <http://www.eliamep.gr/wp-content/uploads/2012/08/tsakiris.pdf> (accessed 4 November 2014).

RWE (2012)*Nabucco consortium welcomes decision on Shah Deniz II,* <http://www.rwe.com/web/cms/de/37110/rwe/presse-news/pressemitteilungen/pressemitteilungen/?pmid=4008077> (accessed 22 December 2014).

Sargsyan, S. (2012) *Trans-Caspian Gas Pipeline: Goals, Problems and Risks.* Noravank Foundation, <http://noravank.am/eng/articles/detail.php?ELEMENT_ID=6564> (accessed 4 November 2014).

Sartori, N. (2012) *The European Commission's Policy towards the Southern Gas Corridor: Between National Interests and Economic Fundamentals.* Instituto Affari Internaizionali. IAI Working Paper No. 1, <http://www.iai.it/pdf/DocIAI/iaiwp1201.pdf> (accessed 4 November 2014).

Shelest, H. (2009) *Threats to the National and European Security in the Black Sea Region: Comparison of the Black Sea Synergy and Reality.* Presentation on the General Assembly of the CPMR Balkan and Black Sea Commission (BBSRC) held in Odessa, <http://www.balkansblacksea.org/pub/news/31_108_prsentation_hanna_shelest.pdf> (accessed 4 November 2014).

Sianko, N. (2012) The European Union and Russia: an energy dialogue. *ISG International,* <http://www.rieas.gr/images/energy25.pdf> (accessed 22 December 2014).

Socor, V. (2012) South Stream: a project with changeable geography. *Eurasia Daily Monitor* 9 (143), <http://www.jamestown.org/single/?no_cache=1&tx_ttnews%5Btt_news%5D=39686&tx_ttnews%5BbackPid%5D=7&cHash=f86991047df7918bd8f6b5959fbe8cf2> (accessed 4 November 2014).

Solanko, L. (2011) *Why Energy Efficiency is Vitally Important for Russia,* Economics of Energy and. Environmental Policy. First Quarter 2011, 19–22.

South Stream (2012a) *Project significance,* <http://www.south-stream.info/pipeline/significance/> (accessed 30December 2014).

South Stream (2012b) *South Stream is estimated to cost EUR 15.5 Billion,* <http://www.south-stream.info/press/news/news-item/south-stream-is-estimated-to-cost-eur-155-billion-1/> (accessed 30 December 2014).

South Stream (2012c) *Five Questions about South Stream,* <http://www.south-stream.info/press/faq/> (accessed 30 December 2014).

TAP (2012) *Trans Adriatic Pipeline Route,*<http://www.trans-adriatic-pipeline.com/en/tap-project/route/> (accessed: 4 November 2014).

Whist, B. S. (2008) Nord Stream: Not just a pipeline. An analysis of the political debates in the Baltic Sea region regarding the planned gas pipeline from Russia to Germany. *FNI Report* No. 15, <http://www.fni.no/doc&pdf/FNI-R1508.pdf> (accessed 4 November 2014).

Stern, J. (2006) The Russian-Ukrainian gas crisis of January 2006. *Oxford Institute for Energy Studies*, <http://www.oxfordenergy.org/wpcms/wp-content/uploads/2011/01/Jan2006-RussiaUkraineGasCrisis-JonathanStern.pdf> (accessed 22December 2014).

Winrow, G. M. (2005) *Energy Security in the Black Sea-Caspian Region. Perceptions*, <http://sam.gov.tr/wp-content/uploads/2012/01/Winrow.pdf> (accessed 4 November 2014).

Žulinskij, M. G. (2006) Geopolitika Kaspijskogo regiona. *Geografija* No. 2006/96, <http://geo.1september.ru/article.php?ID=200600306> (accessed 22December 2014).

Oana Poiană

Regional Cooperation and National Preferences in the Black Sea Region: A Zero-Sum Game Perpetuated by Energy Insecurity?

ABSTRACT: This chapter takes a snapshot of the current geopolitical setting in the Black Sea region by observing the regional dynamics in recent years. It also aims to determine whether the Black Sea littoral states proceeded to an inward focus pursuing their national interests instead of actively participating in regional cooperation projects during this time frame and what the major reasons behind their actions are. It uses two dimensions of analysis: the general involvement of these states in regional cooperation schemes and their regional cooperation in the energy sector. Particular emphasis is placed on the energy sector due to its great capacity to influence overall cooperation in the region.

KEY WORDS: Black Sea region, European Union, regional cooperation, national interest, energy security

Introduction

After decades of acknowledging, affirming and reaffirming the indisputable strategic significance of the Black Sea region and the importance of finding an inclusive policy that would serve not only the interests of the regional states but also the interests of the external actors involved in the region, no effective policy could be identified despite a series of achievements. Moreover, the region has been caught in a perpetual deadlock, fighting to balance between a deeply rooted Soviet legacy and the Western magnetism, each Black Sea state having a different position on the axis between these two major poles. Currently, the main regional representatives of the two poles in the region (the EU and Russia) are both undergoing profound systemic transformations meant to improve their status in world affairs and offer new incentives for extending their sphere of influence in the Black Sea area. Although, both actors have recognized the imperatives of change considering the deteriorating economic situation worldwide, the paths they have chosen are significantly divergent. The European Union is directing itself towards a relatively uncertain future by evolving into a federation of nation-states, but Russia adopts a more conservative stance, seeking to restore its past grandeur by attempting to create the Eurasian Union, which redraws the older contour of the Soviet Union.

In the light of these considerations, a widespread discontent over the evolution of the Black Sea regionalization process can be observed at the moment among academics and policymakers alike. The fact that more than 6 years have passed since the European Commission released its last report on the implementation of the Black Sea Synergy and more than 3 years since the European Parliament called for the adoption of an EU strategy on the Black Sea without developing it, represents probably the best evidence that supports these concerns. Yet, regional issues of the Black Sea region "are not waiting peacefully for the European Commission to put pen to paper", as was argued by Ungureanu (2012) in a recent debate, nor do they remain unaffected by the growing economic crisis. Perhaps, it is now, more than ever, important to establish clearly what it is possible and what it is not in terms of Black Sea regional cooperation.

To do so we have to look into the past in order to analyse the interaction records between the Black Sea states and identify the causal mechanisms that built up the current state of affairs. This chapter therefore aims to assess the level of willingness to engage constructively in regional cooperation initiatives within the Black Sea region as opposed to a more reluctant type of Black Sea partnership that uses other forms of cooperation for promoting national preferences. In this respect, the study uses two dimensions of analysis. The first dimension examines the level of implication in regional schemes of cooperation that aimed to enhance cooperation in a wide range of sectors (economic, security, environmental, maritime), while the second focuses on regional cooperation in the energy sector considering it as an essential driver of the Black Sea regional cooperation. The position of each Black Sea littoral country would be examined considering the already mentioned dimensions of analysis in correlation with the following corresponding indicators presented in Table 1.

Table 1: Dimensions of analysis and indicators.

	Dimensions of analysis	*Regional cooperation*	*National preferences*
1.	**Implication in regional schemes of cooperation**	Number of relevant, unambiguous participations and memberships. Number of initiatives created by a state in order to become a key regional actor, assuming a leading role in the region.	Ambiguous position in various initiatives, vague commitments as a result of exposure to different levels of conditionality. Development of bilateral agreements as opposed to regional initiatives involvement. Valorization (exploitation), politicization and trading of their geographic location. Blocking initiatives that do not comply with their own interests.
2.	**Regional cooperation in the energy sector**	Integration into the regional energy market. Consistent energy security strategy. Signing protocols. Improving energy infrastructure. Overall convergence with regional energy security policies.	Volatility of energy partnerships (shifting alliances, involvement in competing pipeline projects). National energy dependency and vulnerability assessment considering their status – recipient, provider or transit countries.

Acknowledging the fact that a country that follows its national preferences does not necessary exclude or neglect regional cooperation and that this cannot be seen as a zero-sum game, the study will attempt to reflect also the affinity of a country to one direction and in the same time the level of willingness to embrace the other. Using manly qualitative research instruments (document and discourse analysis), the chapter will assess the position of the Black Sea littoral countries[1] pertaining to the two dimensions of analysis. After completing this stage of research we would obtain a comprehensible view of the current regional state of affairs that emphasizes the major issues the European Union should take into consideration

1 For the purpose of this study, the term "Black Sea region" is used to refer to the six littoral states, namely Bulgaria, Georgia, Romania, Russia, Turkey and Ukraine.

when formulating a new strategy for the Black Sea Region. The chosen time frame of the study represents a period characterized by the emergence and development of "second wave" regionalism (pre- and post- EU enlargement) (Cottey, 2009: 4), which also covers the energy crisisdetermined by the 2006 and 2009 and 2014 gas disruptions between Ukraine and Russia. Thus, this time frame allows us to observe potential patterns of regional cooperation and the eventual transformation of national preferences succeeding major regional events.

Involvement in Regional Schemes of Cooperation

Judging by the great number of Black Sea regional groupings, organizations, institutions, projects and various other initiatives, one would expect to encounter a region with an exceptional system of cooperation based on perfectly functioning economic and political partnerships. Obviously, this is not the case if we perform an in depth empirical analyse of the actual situation of the Black Sea regional cooperation. A fresh examination of the Black Sea littoral countries involvement in regional cooperation schemes since the mid-2000s can be observed in Table 2 but behind these figures lie a whole range of issues that have characterized the interactions between the states and also multiple levels of conditionality that have traced the boundaries of regional cooperation. Apart from the already listed schemes of regional cooperation, the Black Sea states have also concluded numerous bilateral, agreements and alliances in different sectors creating an intricate system of interdependences which at times has generated confusion and even hampered the implementation of a more integrated regional cooperation.

Table 2: Regional cooperation schemes.

Year	*REGIONAL SCHEMES OF COOPERATION*	*Bulgaria*	*Georgia*	*Romania*	*Russia*	*Turkey*	*Ukraine*
2001	Black Sea Naval Cooperation Task Group (BLACKSEAFOR)	✓	✓	✓	✓	✓	✓
2001	The Danube Black Sea Task Force (DABLAS)	✓	✓	✓	✓	✓	✓
2001	South Caucasus Anti-Drugs (SCAD) Programme		✓				
2004	International Federation for Sustainable Development and Fight Against Poverty in the Mediterranean-Black Sea (FISPMED)	✓	✓	✓	✓	✓	✓
2004	The Baku Initiative	✓	✓	✓		✓	✓
2004	Operation Black Sea Harmony			✓	✓	✓	✓
2005	Community of Democratic Choice (CDC)		✓	✓			✓
2005	Kyiv Initiative		✓				✓
2006	Black Sea Forum	✓	✓	✓		✓	✓
2007	Black Sea Synergy	✓	✓	✓	✓	✓	✓
2007	The German Marshall Fund / Black Sea Trust for Regional Cooperation (BST)	✓	✓	✓	✓	✓	✓
2007	Union of Black Sea and Caspian Confederation of Enterprises (UBCCCE)	✓	✓	✓		✓	✓
2007	The Black Sea Basin Joint Operational Programme	✓	✓	✓		✓	✓
2008	Black Sea Euroregion	✓	✓	✓			
2008	Regional Cooperation Council (RCC)	✓		✓		✓	

Year	*REGIONAL SCHEMES OF COOPERATION*	*Bulgaria*	*Georgia*	*Roma-nia*	*Russia*	*Turkey*	*Ukraine*
2008	Black Sea NGO Forum	✓	✓	✓	✓	✓	✓
2008	The Black Sea Peacebuilding Platform		✓	✓	✓	✓	✓
2009	Eastern Partnership		✓				✓
2009	Eastern Partnership Civil Society Forum		✓				✓
2009	The Black Sea Peacebuilding Network		✓		✓	✓	✓
2009	Black Sea Energy and Economic Forum- inaugural	✓	✓	✓	✓	✓	✓
2010	Black Sea Renewable Energy Forum	✓		✓		✓	✓
2010	Black Sea Economic Forum- inaugural	✓	✓	✓	✓	✓	✓
2011	Southeast European Law Enforcement Center (SELEC)- former SECI	✓		✓		✓	
Total	24	16(0)	20 (0)	19(4)	11 (0)	18(2)	20 (1)

● Overlaping initiatives; ● Assuming initiative

In this context, it is highly difficult to draw any valid conclusion regarding the level of involvement only by interpreting the data included in Table 15.2. However, these figures offer the possibility of identifying certain trends of cooperation if correlated with a case-specific analysis. Thus, if we take Bulgaria's case we can observe that since the mid-2000s it has been involved in 16 forms of cooperation and assumed a leading role along with Romania and Greece in the implementation of the Black Sea Synergy. Examining the table, we can identify an ascending level of cooperation between 2006–8, which coincides with increased EU interest in the Black Sea region and can be explained by Bulgaria's prior EU accession preparations and the following responsibilities attached to its membership. Although it was involved in cooperation schemes covering a wide range of areas (security, energy, economy) its role did not impede cooperation, nor did it significantly contribute to its enhancement. Overall, Bulgaria's national preferences were well reflected in its agenda towards the Black Sea region. The EU and NATO membership have undoubtedly affected its relations with Turkey and Russia but Bulgaria succeeded in balancing its actions by adopting a rather cautious engagement. According to Lessenski (2007: 52), one of the most important future challenges of Bulgaria would be to find a way "to accommodate its intensive energy cooperation with Russia with its moral responsibility to help reforms in Georgia." Recently, Bulgaria has taken ambitious steps towards decreasing its high dependence on Russian energy imports and has significantly improved its energy transport infrastructure by building interconnectors with its neighbouring countries. Following these favourable developments, Bulgaria can find a balancing act and support Georgia's reform agenda without jeopardizing its energy cooperation with Russia. However, after EU accession, Bulgaria appears to be a rather inert country in terms of regional cooperation and support. It is hard to tell whether its current stance represents a "strategic inertia" or a temporary lack of strategy.

Since the mid-2000s, Georgia has been the most affected Black Sea state, being exposed to various transformations as a result of the 2003 coloured revolution and the 2008 war. Despite these turbulent circumstances, Georgia has one of the highest scores in regional cooperation, participating in 20 Black Sea cooperation schemes. One of the most fervent supporters of EU involvement in the region and aspiring to NATO membership, Georgia became involved in all the regional cooperation schemes initiated by the EU, being at times more confident concerning EU's implication in the Black Sea regional cooperation than the EU itself (Manoli, 2010: 16). Suffering from internal political instability and dealing with a weakening economy, Georgia is, at the same time, struggling to calibrate its actions to avoid future confrontations with Russia. In this sense, it has recently signalled a revival of military cooperation with Russia under the framework of the BLACKSEAFOR (naval security organization) after a long-term absence (Gorenburg, 2011). Following the 2012 parliamentary elections, Georgia was expected to further improve its relations with Russia in several sectors but not at the expense of jeopardizing NATO accession. One of the most prominent Georgian involvements in regional cooperation was the constant engagement in CDC (Community of Democratic Choice), a fact that reflects its commitment to good governance and recognizes the importance of cooperation for supporting the democratic reform (Kulick and Yakobashvili, 2008: 32). Overall, Georgia lacked the necessary resources to assume initiative and had a rather reactionary engagement throughout the time but its presence in a large number of initiatives confirms its willingness for cooperation and supports the region-building process.

Unlike its east-coast neighbour, Romania participated in 19 cooperation schemes during this time frame and has been a pioneer in assuming various initiatives. Its keen interest in enhancing Black Sea regional cooperation increased significantly after it gained EU membership and further developed under the Black Sea Synergy framework. Before EU accession, Romania promoted only one initiative, namely the Black Sea Forum, which was criticized for being "a rather modest proposal" (Anghelescu, 2011: 123), which lost momentum as it was received with an obvious lack of enthusiasm in the region, especially by Turkey, which considered it to be a challenge to its own desire to acquire the leadership of regional initiatives (King, 2008: 98). Because Romania initiated the Black Sea Forum and the Black Sea Euroregion, it was criticized for following its own Black Sea policy while promoting the Black Sea Synergy (Delcour and Manoli, 2010: 13). However, as an EU member, Romania was the first to implement concrete projects in the environmental sector fulfilling its responsibility as it was ascribed by the EU Black Sea Synergy. In this respect it organized, in 2010, the Black Sea Renewable Energy Forum and elaborated the Black Sea Environment Partnership expressing its hope that soon Bulgaria and Greece will implement and coordinate their energy and transport partnerships as well (Băsescu, 2012). Despite its very proactive role, Romania's cooperation initiatives did not produce the expected results, mainly because they were insufficiently supported by the Romanian political elite (following elections) and by its regional partners. One of the main opponents of Romania's initiatives was Russia, which was present only at the Black Sea NGO Forum in 2008. Russia's reluctance could be partially explained by its constant rejection of any Western involvement in the region. After being an EU and NATO member for a considerable amount of time, Romanian's regional initiatives are being automatically perceived as countering Russian regional influence and its regional interests as diametrically opposed to those of Russia. Adding to this, the historical events (the Transnistrian "frozen conflict" and the dispute over the confiscated Romanian treasure) together with Romania's ambition to diminish its dependency on Russian energy imports have definitely intensified the dividing lines between the two countries.

A brief analysis of Russia's involvement in the Black Sea regional cooperation schemes in recent years shows that, even though formal participation can be found in several cases, there is a lack of engagement in actual relevant multilateral forms of cooperation. It is important to mention that not all of the 24 regional schemes of cooperation were conceived to include Russia within their framework; some of them were purposely created to enhance further integration in the EU eastern neighbourhood and some of them emerged as a reaction to Russian hard power actions. According to Kuzio (2008: 2), the creation of GUAM could be perceived as a reaction to the separatism promoted by Russia in the post-Soviet era which maintained the "frozen conflicts" of Azerbaijan, Moldova and Georgia. Another factor that united these four countries was the Russian military presence on their territory (Russian troops in Moldova and Georgia and the Russian Black Sea Fleet in Crimea). When Ukraine and Georgia were officially encouraged to seek NATO membership in 2008, Russia adopted a more aggressive position towards them and their issues related to separatism and energy dependency (Arbatova, 2008: 31). In addition to this, Russia expressed reservations regarding the Concept Paper of the Baku initiative and refused to involve itself in this initiative. Moreover, as a sign of its discontent, Russia participated only as an observer at the conference that followed in 2006 (Morata and Sandoval, 2012: 144). Russia was not very enthusiastic about the creation of the Community for Democratic Choice either. President Putin refused to participate during the forum but instead sent an embassy official to the event. The Russian press reacted strongly to this initiative, which was perceived in Moscow as an opportunity to encourage Georgian and Ukrainian rapprochement with the West and thus considered as an attempt to weaken Russia's influence in the Black Sea region (Peuch, 2005). Russia also declined the invitation to participate at the Black Sea Forum. As was expected, Russia asked to be represented on diplomatic level, sending the Russian ambassador to participate just as an observer (Jagharian, 2006). Russian reluctance or noninvolvement towards Black Sea initiatives continued in the following years and all the forums and initiatives declined by Russia had a very short life, fading into oblivion shortly after their initiation. Out of the six Black Sea littoral states, Russia has the lowest score on participation in regional cooperation schemes (11) but this tells nothing about its actual power as a leading regional actor. Its strong regional influence is a consequence of acting along the lines of a very pragmatic foreign policy that favours bilateral forms of cooperation instead of multilateral or regional ones. Although, since the mid-2000s, it had no intention to initiate a Black Sea regional cooperation framework that would involve all the Black Sea states, Russia reacted to various initiatives, either by expressing its clear disagreement, or by accepting a passive membership. In time it became evident that Russia is not willing to consider regionalism as a potential means to serve its national strategic interests.

One of the most consistent littoral states and probably the oldest promoter of the Black Sea regional cooperation and institutionalization, Turkey has sought to maintain its pivotal role as a Black Sea actor by advancing various schemes of regional cooperation. However, since the mid-2000s, Turkey has participated in only 18 regional cooperation schemes and had little success in initiating new multilateral forms of regional cooperation. Although the creation of the Organisation of Black Sea Economic Cooperation (BSEC) could not be included in our analysis (given the chosen time frame of the study), it is worth mentioning it not only for its longevity and its contribution to the regional cooperation development but also for emphasizing Turkey's strong commitment to establishing concrete, meaningful and inclusive forms of regional cooperation. Other important Turkish contributions aimed to assure regional stability by improving military cooperation took the form of the BLACKSEAFOR and the Black Sea Harmony Operation (Wilson, 2006: 4). These two initiatives represented notable achievements in maintaining regional peace and Russian adherence to them confirmed the importance of Turkey as a catalyst for enhancing a closer cooperation between the riparian states. On the other hand, the presence of Russia in every regional framework supported by Turkey (sometimes at the expense of excluding important extraregional actors) supports the maintaining of Turkey's regional leadership (Triantaphyllou, 2007: 228).

In 2009 Turkey also came with a proposal to create a political umbrella for incorporating already existing military cooperation and announced its intention to create a Black Sea Defence Ministerial Process,[2] which planned to replicate the Southeast European Defence Ministerial Process (Manoli, 2011: 4). The fact that Russia fully supported this proposal has brought suspicion among regional internal and external actors. Russia's cooperation record over the last decade also reveals an interesting trend that supports the hypothesis of a Turkish-Russain rapprochement. Although Russia got involved in the Black Sea Synergy, its lack of support and its insistence on maintaining the Synergy on an equal basis with BSEC was perceived as a deliberate act of obstructing its potential (Delcour and Manoli, 2010: 6) On the contrary, Russia participated in all the initiatives put forward by Turkey and was a constant supporter of the BSEC since its launching. As stated in *Today's Zaman* (Akkan, 2012), Turkey's relations with Russia in the field of energy, trade and tourism are expected to improve even further now that Vladimir Putin returned to office. Given the increasing affinity between the two countries, Turkey decided to take "a 'neutral' position in the undeclared competition between Russia and the West" within the Black Sea region (Özbay, 2011: 45). Its slow track towards EU membership and its exclusion from the EU's newly crafted Eastern Partnership initiative has undoubtedly caused Turkish frustration, which entitles us to question its future loyalty to the EU's Black Sea initiatives.

Ukraine represents another Black Sea country that has adopted an indeterminate stance between Russia and EU. This could be observed in 2010 when President Yanukovych stressed Ukraine's commitment to continuing the negotiations for the Association Agreement with EU, while only several months after, decided to extend the stay of the Russian Black Sea Fleet in Sevastopol for another 25 years in exchange of a 10-year discount for its energy supplies exports (Gnedina and Sleptsova, 2012: 2). Similarly, in May 2013, President Yanukovych signed a memorandum with the Eurasian Economic, Commission which was perceived in Russia as a clear

2 This initiative was not included in the list of regional cooperation schemes due to insufficient information regarding its evolution. The project was expected to be discussed at a High Level Meeting in Ankara in 2009 but the Black Sea littoral countries (excepting Russia) were reluctant to implement it.

sign of Ukraine's intention to join the Eurasian Economic Union (Kudelia, 2013). Subsequently, Yanukovych asserted in a public discourse that "European standards are the demand of time" and expressed his confidence that Ukraine will sign the Association Agreement at the EU summit in Lithuania on November 2013 (Yanukovych, 2013). Yanukovych´s last moment decision to reject EU's offer at Vilnius, triggered mass pro-European demonstrations and represented the catalyst of the following Crimean crisis.

This type of ambivalence reflects Ukraine's unsynchronized foreign policy goals which undermine its credibility both externally and regionally. Its Black Sea policy over this time frame can be characterized as being "sporadic, spontaneous and very often reactionary than proactive" (Shelest, 2011: 114). As a result, Ukraine participated in 20 regional cooperation schemes but its commitments were vague, especially for those initiatives that included a potentially dominant Russia (Delcour and Manoli, 2010: 11). Thus, it can be speculated that the 2006 and 2009 Russian energy cut-offs led Ukraine to adopt a more cautious approach towards its eastern neighbour. Consequently, the decision to keep open the option of joining the Customs Union while insisting on the European integration track was regarded as an act of political slyness that ensured Ukraine's "survival". Nevertheless, as it has been already proven by the Crimean crisis, this double trajectory strategy will not represent an option for Ukraine, as the country is approaching a momentous choice. Recently, the International Black Sea Economic Forum was organized under the auspices of the Ukrainian president and can be regarded both as a revitalization of the Ukrainian interest towards the region and as an attempt to set itself clear and unambiguous foreign policy goals.

At a rhetorical level, there is evidently a strong willingness for cooperation among the Black Sea states and over the last years this commitment to cooperation was stressed on numerous occasions. However, none of the six Black Sea states could fully match their words with deeds. The fact that little progress has been made in terms of regional cooperation is not entirely their fault but is rather the result of a series of systemic constraints. The EU has also contributed to regional fragmentation by supporting sectoral and bilateral cooperation and by engaging differently with the regional states. This compartmentalized strategy has deepened the regional discrepancies that, in turn, caused the states to practise a double game strategy which did not favour the regional integration. Interpreting the numbers, Romania stands out as the country with the highest number of initiatives and a high commitment for promoting EU's policy in the region. Despite its efforts, very few of its initiatives materialized. At the opposite pole stands Russia with the lowest score both for participation in the existing regional forms of cooperation and for taking initiative to create new ones. The other Black Sea states sent ambivalent signals and had cautiously approached the multilateral forms of cooperation because they were not willing to sacrifice their long-lasting bilateral forms of cooperation that secured their national interests.

Regional Cooperation in the Energy Sector

Many studies directly or indirectly reduce the entire Black Sea deadlock to an energy security dilemma and there are sufficient arguments to validate this assumption. The general scarcity of energy resources has shaped the interactions between this region and the rest of the world and interactions between Black Sea countries themselves. As Helm (2007: 1) stated, lately "energy policy replaced to a large extent the foreign policy of the states." Currently, energy-related issues are the most challenging ones for the world affairs and the current situation of the Black Sea region strongly reflects it. Most of the Black Sea countries are involved in international energy projects with different statuses. There are supplying countries (their status offers them a competitive advantage, being more powerful and able to negotiate their interests), transit countries (which struggle to promote their energy projects in order to enhance their role in the region) and consumer countries (which fight to find the best option that would decrease their dependence on imported oil and gas). Moreover, the region itself plays both the role of an energy supplying area considering the recently discovered gas deposits on its territory and the role of a transit route for energy projects that aim to transport gas from the Caspian Sea to Europe. We will now analyse the national energy policies for each Black Sea littoral country taking into consideration their status, their level of energy dependency, their involvement in energy projects and their reliability as energy cooperation partners.

Among the Black Sea countries, Bulgaria was the most affected by the 2009 gas disruption due to its poor system of pipeline connections that did not allow it to receive energy supplies from other sources (Schmidt-Felzmann, 2011). Ever since, Bulgaria has been striving to reduce its 100% dependency on Russian gas and sought to create alternative routes to avoid potential similar crisis. In this respect, Bulgaria has received financial help from the European Commission and has recently started to work on a pipeline connection with Romania that is expected to be fully operational by 2013 (Focus Information Agency, 2012). Moreover, after Romania and Turkey announced the discovery of gas deposits on their Black Sea coasts, Bulgaria also began to conduct exploration, hoping for similar results.

Bulgaria is both an energy recipient and an energy-transit country. As a recipient country, it represents one of the Europe's largest energy consuming countries relaying mostly on imports from Russia. However, as a transit country, Bulgaria has the opportunity to strengthen its bargaining potential by virtue of its strategic location. Its latest actions in the energy field have confirmed that Bulgaria took this opportunity and simultaneously participated in energy projects that were initiated by Russia and also in those supported by the EU. Specifically, Bulgaria supports the implementation of the Russian South Stream pipeline project, which was supposed to transport Russian gas under the Black Sea to the Bulgarian coast. In this regard, it has signed several memoranda with Gazprom containing technical and financial details of its implementation and obtained, in exchange, an 11% discount on Russian gas prices (Daborowski, 2012). On the other hand, Bulgaria also decided to support the EU-backed Nabucco pipeline project, which aimed to diversify the European gas supplies and thus reduce the Russian energy monopoly (Schmidt-Felzmann, 2011: 577). Out of the two competing pipeline projects, South Stream has definitely made significant progress during the last years due to President Putin's strong commitment to accelerate its construction. As a consequence of the EU's recent decisions to introduce new requirements concerning the access to energy networks, Bulgaria agreed to start the construction of the project on its territory at the beginning of June 2013 (Novinite, 2013). However, the project seems to have stalled because a precondition of its initiation is that it receives derogation from the European Commission allowing exemption from the rules of the Third Energy Package (Stoyanov, 2013). Meanwhile, the rationale for constructing this pipeline has disappeared given the fact that the competing pipeline project, Nabucco is no longer considered a viable option. As a confirmation, in December 2014 the Russian president officially announced the decision to abandon South Stream. In recent years, Nabucco has faced numerous setbacks and experienced financial issues, and it was constantly criticized concerning its ability to supply the planned volume of gas. As a result, the Nabucco Consortium has prepared an alternative technical design (Nabucco West) that had a much shorter rout in comparison with the one that was initially planned. However, in June 2013, Shah Deniz Consortium selected the Trans-Adriatic Pipeline (TAP) to deliver natural gas from the Shah Deniz II gas field in Azerbaijan via the Trans-Anatolian natural gas pipeline (TANAP) instead of selecting Nabucco West project (British Petroleum, 2013). Although the main European diversification plan has failed, Bulgaria continues its diversification and technical upgrade strategy by announcing the completion of all the interconnectors with Greece (IGB), Romania (IBR), Serbia (IBS) and Turkey (IBT) by the end of 2015 (*Natural Gas Europe*, 2013).

Georgia represents another Black Sea country that is highly dependent on oil and gas imports. Although 98% of its energy resources are imported, Georgian territory represents the link between Azerbaijan and Turkey and an important route for the demanding EU markets. It currently hosts "three pipeline outlets to western markets from the Caspian basin" (Energy Charter, 2012). In 2006 Georgia together with Turkey and Azerbaijan constructed the Baku–Tbilisi–Ceyhan (BTC) oil pipeline and in 2007 the same countries completed a natural gas pipeline, called the South Caucasus Pipeline (SCP). In 2010, Georgia also signed a memorandum of understanding with Azerbaijan and Romania in order to construct the Azerbaijan–Georgia–Romania Interconnector (AGRI), which will transport liquefied natural gas from Azerbaijan to Romania. Although this project was not an energy strategy priority for the last years, a recent announcement made at the second Annual Balkan Oil and Gas Summit reveals that the AGRI project is expected to be created as soon as possible, now that Romania has lost all hope of implementing Nabucco (*Natural Gas Europe*, 2013). Lately, Georgia has signalled a desire to extend its role as an energy transit nation and announced its intention to construct two East–West pipeline sections, planning the implementation of a Georgian Trans-Caucasian corridor for Caspian exports (Daly, 2013). According to its Action Plan with EU, one of Georgia's priorities is to "continue cooperation in the Energy, Transport and Science and Technological development fields in the context of the EU/Black Sea/Caspian littoral states and neighbouring countries initiatives" (EU–Georgia Action Plan, 2006). Yet, the 2008 Russia–Georgia war has caused negative repercussion for the Georgian energy supply traffic from Azerbaijan to Europe (BTC suffered a terrorist attack) emphasizing, once again, the strong regional impact of Russia not only in the energy field but also concerning security matters. Since Georgia has signed the Association Agreement with the EU in 2014 and announced its aspiration of receiving the Membership Action Plan to join NATO, it is expected that Russia will soon apply pressure either by affecting trade cooperation (imposing embargos on Georgian products) or by attempting to violate its territorial integrity as it did in June 2013 when it decided to extend the border line between South Ossetia and Georgia and grab 1,000 feet of Georgian land (Cecire, 2013). Fortunately, Georgia decided in 2007 to start purchasing gas exclusively from Azerbaijan, thus avoiding any potential energy security threats coming from Russia.

Although Romania has domestic reserves both of oil and gas, it relies mainly on Russian imports and it has to guarantee its energy security seeking diversification (European Bank for Reconstruction and Development, 2012). As such, Romania has been a strong supporter of the Nabucco pipeline which planned to transport natural gas from Turkey to Austria crossing its territory but also the Hungarian and the Bulgarian one. Now that the long-planned Nabucco has failed, Romania has to reformulate its energy strategy and accelerate the implementation of AGRI. As one energy expert highlighted, "there has probably never been in the past 23 years a stronger deception in terms of Romania's energy security than the Nabucco debacle" (Pachiu, 2013). Recently, the Romanian President, Traian Băsescu, publicly assumed responsibility for wagering everything on Nabucco and refusing any involvement in the South Stream project, but underlined the fact that Romania would not abandon its energy independence goal (Băsescu, 2013). Although the energy independence plan may seem too ambitious, Romania has rapidly developed its renewable energy sector and it is "the largest producer of oil and gas in Central Europe, holding five percent of Europe's proven oil reserves and 1.2 percent of the proven gas reserves" (Assenova, 2013). Moreover, in 2012 Romania discovered a natural gas deposit on its Black Sea waters that could cover its needs for 20 years and would allow it to offer gas to Moldova through the newly constructed interconnector Iasi-Ungheni. ExxonMobil and Omv-Petrom are currently working on creating the technological structures of exploitation and the transportation system of the gas reserves to the shore. Taking into consideration that Romania pays one of the highest prices in the region for its Russian gas imports, energy independence for 20 years would have positive economic effects for the country and would improve its standing in relation to Russia (Molnar, 2012).

Out of the six Black Sea littoral countries, Russia is definitely the most significant energy actor in the region, having the greatest natural gas reserves in the world and being in the top 10 countries with the largest oil reserves. As the holder of such large natural gas resources, Russia is also an exporting leader, securing more that 40% of the global gas export (BP Statistical Review, 2012). Additionally, Russian control over pipelines and resources has offered it a great political leverage within the region and worldwide. In addition, Russian was able to obstruct any alternative that the EU could find for reducing its dependency on its energy supplies. Other transport corridors that aim to transport energy resources from the Caspian basin also rely on Russian downstream pipeline infrastructure (Henderson and Weaver, 2010: 139–150). Instead of supporting a European energy integrated space in the Black Sea region, Russia crafted its energy policies in order to serve its own national interests, in particular, those of becoming an energy superpower by dominating European and Eurasian markets. However, for the last 2 years, these energy markets proved to be very dynamic and in the future Russia will probably have to adjust its energy policies to new regulations and accept new price-setting systems in order to preserve its dominant position. According to Umbach (2013), Azerbaijan's growing gas exports to European and Turkish markets as well as the newly discovered offshore gas resources in Romania, Bulgaria and the Mediterranean Sea, represent a serious concern for Russia, which now faces a reduction in European gas demand. Since the mid-2000s, the EU share of Russia's total gas sales profit has fallen from 60% to 40% and this trend is expected to continue considering the rapidly changing conditions within the current energy markets. The national governments in the Black Sea region still have a high level of resilience given the long-term energy cooperation and the strong network of bilateral agreements that have been established with Russia but its unstable pricing system and its reluctance to create a liberal and transparent energy market might not be an option for it in the near future.

The only Black Sea country that has clear bargaining potential seems to be Turkey, which succeeded in reducing the Russian monopoly over the external transport routes by transporting Azerbaijan oil and natural gas through the Baku–Tbilisi–Ceyhan pipeline. Turkey also represented the link between Middle East energy supplies and the European market, given its strategic importance for the Nabucco pipeline project (Tanrisever, 2012: 17). Considering these strategic developments, Turkey has declared its willingness to become an energy hub that would contribute to European energy supply diversification. Furthermore, the recently discovered gas reserves on the Turkish Black Sea coast represent an impetus for action regarding further exploration. Given this context, it can be argued that a closer energy partnership with Turkey can represent the deciding factor that will shape future energy cooperation in the Black Sea region and will determine the success or failure of any energy strategy envisioned by the two main regional power poles, namely Russia and EU. Yet, recent Turkish actions in the energy field indicate a change of priorities. This is explained by the fact that approximately 65% of Turkish gas import is still provided by Russia through the Blue Stream pipeline constructed under the Black Sea (Tanrisever, 2012: 15). In December 2014, president Putin agreed to increase gas exports to Turkey by 3 billion cubic meters and granted Turkey a 6 percent discount on the price of that gas (Albayrak, 2014). Excepting several price disputes in 2012, its collaboration with Russia in the energy sector was productive and gradually, the Russian-Turkish rapprochement has become evident, especially after Turkey agreed to permit South Stream to cross its territorial waters. In exchange, Russia agreed to construct the first Turkish nuclear power plant (Resneck, 2012).

However, Russia had long-running gas pricing disputes with Ukraine, which led to the 2006 and 2009 disruptions. Since then, Ukraine has been constantly seeking diversification but is currently still relying exclusively on Russian supplies. Although Ukraine has benefited from lower prices on oil and gas exports from Russia, Russia continues to press Ukraine by insisting to impose prices that are 50% higher than the prices paid by other Russian costumers. Its plan is to entirely control the Ukrainian gas system including its storage facilities (Hranovsky *et al.*, 2011: 16). Adding to this, Russia stated that a reduction on the price would be conditional on Ukraine's membership of the customs union (Åslund, 2012). However, Ukraine does not seem very enthusiastic about joining the customs union, mainly because in the past Russia has shown that its foreign trade policy has been often influenced by its changing political priorities. (Gnedina and Sleptsova, 2012: 15). Although before his disappearance, Yanukovych succeeded to sign a deal with the Russian president which bought 15bn$ of

Ukrainian debt and reduced the price of Russian gas supplies by one third (Walker, 3013), in June 2014 Ukraine experienced another gas disruption due to a price dispute which was temporarily solved in October 2014 when Russia agreed to continue delivering gas to Ukraine for the winter.

As a result of the Russian-imposed conditionality and the anticompetitive behaviour of Gazprom, the European Commission has launched an investigation concerning the potential monopolistic actions of Russia's Gazprom, which is suspected of obstructing competition in the Central-Eastern European energy markets. Yet Moscow continues to deny such accusations and perceives the investigation as an EU attempt to obtain a reduction of the gas price in order to improve its economic situation. As a reaction, the Russian President has recently signed a decree that prohibits Gazprom from offering further discounts to its foreign customers without being priory approved by the Russian government (Voice of Russia, 2012).

Hence, we can observe that regional cooperation trends in the energy sector are also worrying because Russia occupies the highest position in the regional supply chain, while the remaining littoral countries are all mainly recipient countries that struggle to squeeze between the energy projects promoted by Russia and those supported by the EU. Given this context, we cannot talk about regional energy cooperation but rather about Russian political pressure to comply with its norms on its own terms. Taking into consideration the unfortunate gas cutoffs in 2006, 2009 and 2014, the EU's plan of creating a new energy architectural environment would have to include a set of common norms that will ensure a high level of predictability and reliability. The investigation of Gazprom together with the regulations provided by the Third Energy Package may represent a first step for strengthening the EU's regulatory power but this can still be interpreted as a counterbalancing action that leaves little space for genuine cooperation in the energy sector. According to this logic, the more the EU expands its normative space, the more Russia contracts its own. Consequently, EU enlargement and NATO enlargement have enabled Russia to justify its zero-sum view of politics (Sherr, 2012: 18), its Crimean invasion and its new military doctrine.

Conclusion

After the latest round of EU enlargement there were great expectations regarding the initiation of a sustainable regionalization strategy for the Black Sea region that would strongly impact the regional cooperation between the Black Sea states creating a sense of unity and stability within the region. Unfortunately, the cumulative effects of the declining European economy and the worsening political situation have blocked further integration causing a certain "enlargement fatigue". Moreover, although it was expected that the Black Sea states will automatically gravitate towards the EU (except for Russia), this did not happened, mainly because there were other regional actors promoting divergent security agendas (Vasilyan, 2010: 88–93). The EU planned to project its soft power in the region, choosing to play a mediator role and act as a unifying element but avoided identifying a clear form of engagement with Russia. The EU-Russia Partnership and Cooperation Agreement did not prevent Russia from countering the EU's attempt to develop a regional framework for cooperation in the Black Sea region. Russia's interference caused Black Sea regional cooperation to stall. The EU's rhetoric of solidarity had no power over Russian energy threats, which leave little space for genuine regional cooperation. Russia obstructed the majority of the regional cooperation schemes and maintained a tense climate within the region by contributing to a clash of interests in the energy sector.

Having declared the Black Sea region as an area of utmost importance for their strategic interests, both the EU and Russia are expected to continue developing very different agendas as an expression of their incompatible approaches. Hence the fact that today the Black Sea region is one of the most problematic areas in terms of cooperation and one of the most vulnerable areas concerning the potential future escalation of violent conflicts does not come as a surprise. Taking into consideration recent events in the Black Sea region, there are very few reasons for an optimistic outlook regarding an improvement in regional cooperation. The ongoing economic crisis has strongly impacted the EU, which is now primarily preoccupied with its economic consolidation and it is expected to concentrate its actions on this direction rather than concern itself with further integration or the adoption of a new Black Sea strategy. Consequently, major positive transformations within the region are highly improbable at the moment, at least until the economic and political situation becomes more stable.

The question at hand is not whether the Black Sea states have a genuine interest in engaging constructively in regional cooperation schemes but whether they are allowed to do so. Deciding what kind of regionalization process should be implemented in the Black Sea area cannot be the task of a single actor (the EU or Russia) and the experience of recent years has clearly confirmed this. It is the unique interplay between regional and external actors that decides what kind of regionalism it can accommodate. However, the fact that the Black Sea countries are able to compartmentalize their differences and cooperate on a bilateral level proves that regional cooperation in the Black Sea area cannot be such an abstract idea. An EU-Russia rapprochement would definitely represent the catalyst of a more integrated Black Sea regional cooperation. Unfortunately given the new geopolitical architecture within the region and the recent western sanctions imposed to Russia, it is very difficult to envision significant improvements in the EU-Russia relationship.

References

Akkan, F. (2012) Bilateral ties between Turkey, and Russia likely to improve under Putin's presidency. *Today's Zaman*, <http://www.todayszaman.com/national_bilateral-ties-between-turkey-russia-likely-to-improve-under-putins-presidency_273900.html> (accessed 20 September 2014).

Albayrak, A. (2014) Turkey's gas deals with Russia raise concerns of dependency. *Today's Zaman*, <http://www.todayszaman.com/national_tur keys-gas-deals-with-russia-raise-concerns-of-dependency_365960.htl> (accessed 7 December 2014).

Anghelescu, I. (2011) New Eastern Perspectives? A critical analysis of Romania's relations with Moldova, Ukraine and the Black Sea Region. *Perspectives* 19(2), 123–142.

Arbatova, N. A. (2008) Regional cooperation in the Black Sea area in the context of EU-Russia relations. *Xenophon Paper* 5, 25–36.

Åslund, A. (2012) Putin's bad-neighbour policy. *Project Syndicate*, <http://www.project-syndicate.org/commentary/putin-s-bad-neighbor-policy-by-anders--slund> (accessed 5 November 2014).

Assenova, M. (2013) *Bulgaria and Romania: Pursuing Energy Security in a Changing Environment.* Centre for European Policy Analysis, <http://cepa.org/content/bulgaria-and-romania-pursuing-energy-security-changing-environment> (accessed 5 November 2014).

Băsescu, T. (2012) *Presidential Discourse during the Opening of the BSEC Summit in Istanbul*, <http://www.agerpres.ro/politica/2012/06/26/basescu-la-ocemn-romania-este-foarte-angajata-in-concretizarea-magistralelor-maritime-ale-marii-negre-19-31-33,> (accessed 19 September 2013).

Băsescu, T. (2013) Television broadcast, <http://www.capital.ro/detalii-articole/stiri/basescu-nu-exista-miza-mai-mare-decat-independenta-energetica-a-romaniei-187087.html> (accessed 5 November 2014).

BP Statistical Review of World Energy (2012), <http://www.bp.com/content/dam/bp/pdf/Statistical-Review-2012/statistical_review_of_world_energy_2012.pdf> (accessed: 19 September 2013).

British Petroleum (2013), *Shah Deniz targets Italian and Southeastern European gas markets through Trans Adriatic Pipeline*, <http://www.bp.com/en/global/corporate/press/press-releases/shah-deniz-targets-italian-and-southeastern-european-gas-markets.html> (accessed: 19 September 2013).

Cecire, M. (2013) *Russia-Georgia Normalization Hits a Plateau*, <http://www.worldpoliticsreview.com/articles/13036/russia-georgia-normalization-hits-a-plateau?goback=%2Egde_4660379_member_252637307#%21> (accessed 5 November 2014).

Ciută, F. (2008) Region? Why region? Security, hermeneutics, and the making of the Black Sea Region. *Geopolitics* 13(1), 12–147.

Cottey, A. (2009) Subregional cooperation in Europe: an assessment. Regional integration and global governance papers, Working Paper, Collage of Europe and the Comparative Regional Integration Studies Programme of the United Nations University, vol. 3, 1–24. Cited in Manoli, P. (2012) *The Dynamics of Black Sea Subregionalism*, Ashgate, Aldershot.

Daborowski, T. (2012) Bulgaria: a demonstration of the multi-dimensional nature of the energy policy. Analyses, *Center for Eastern Studies*,

<http://www.osw.waw.pl/en/publikacje/analyses/2012-09-05/bulgaria-a-demonstration-multi-dimensional-nature-energy-policy>.

Daly, J. (2013) *Georgia Seeks Expanded Role as Caspian Energy Corridor,* <http://oilprice.com/Energy/Crude-Oil/Georgia-Seeks-Expanded-Role-as-Caspian-Energy-Corridor.html> (accessed 5 November 2014).

Delcour, Laure & Manoli, Panagiota (2010) *The EU's Black Sea Synergy: Results and Possible Ways Forward.* European Parliament, Directorate-General for External Policies, European Parliament.

Energy Charter (2012) *Georgia: In-Depth Energy Efficiency Review,* <http://www.encharter.org/fileadmin/user_upload/Publications/Georgia_EE_2012_ENG.pdf>.

EU-Georgia Action Plan (2006). <http://eeas.europa.eu/enp/pdf/pdf/action_plans/georgia_enp_ap_final_en.pdf>.

European Bank for Reconstruction and Development (2012) *Strategy for Romania,* <http://www.ebrd.com/downloads/country/strategy/romania.pdf> (accessed 5 November 2014).

Focus Information Agency (2012) *Bulgaria Starts Work on Gas Interconnector with Romania,* <http://ua-energy.org/en/post/23360> (accessed 5 November 2014).

Gnedina, E. and Sleptsova, E. (2012) *Eschewing Choice*: Ukraine's Strategy on Russia and the EU. CEPS Working Document No.360, January 2012, 1–21. <http://aei.pitt.edu/33337/1/WD360_Gnedina_%26_Sleptsova_on_Ukraine.pdf> (accessed 5 November 2014).

Gorenburg, D. (2011) Ten years of BlackSeaFor: a partial assessment. *Bosphorus Naval News Online,* <http://turkishnavy.net/2011/05/12/ten-years-of-blackseafor-a-partial-assessment/> (accessed 5 November 2014).

Helm, D. (2007) *The New Energy Paradigm,* Oxford University Press, New York.

Henderson, K. and Weaver C (2010) *The Black Sea Region and EU Policy: The Challenge of Divergent Agendas,* Ashgate, Aldershot.

Hranovsky, V. and Nanivska, V. (2011) New Foreign Policy: Ukraine has a plan. *Policy Studies* 1(2), 5–70.

Jagharian, T. (2006) *No Russian Officials at the Black Sea Summit,* <http://www.armeniandiaspora.com/showthread.php?52012-No-Russian-Officials-At-Black-Sea-Summit> (accessed 5 November 2014).

King, C. (2008) *The Wider Black Sea Region in the 21st Century*, Center for Transatlantic Relations, Washington, DC.

Kudelia, S. (2013) *The Price of Brotherly Love: What Will Russia Lose From Integrating Ukraine?* Policy Memo, PONARS Eurasia, <http://www.ponarseurasia.org/memo/price-brotherly-love-what-will-russia-lose-integrating-ukraine> (accessed 5 November 2014).

Kulick, J. and Yakobashvili, T. (2008) Georgia and the wider Black Sea, in *The Wider Black Sea Region in the 21st Century* (eds. Hamilton, Daniel and Mangott, Gerhard), Center for Transatlantic Relations, Washington, DC, 23–51.

Kuzio, T. (2008) *GUAM as a Regional and Security Organisation*, <http://www.taraskuzio.net/conferences2_files/GUAM_Azerbaijan.pdf> (accessed 5 November 2014).

Lessenski, M. (2007) The Black Sea Cooperation: An Outlook from Bulgaria. *Xenophon Paper* 2(4), 51–165.

Manoli, P. (2010) Reinvigorating Black Sea Cooperation: A policy Discussion, Policy Report, *Commission on the Black Sea*, Gutersloh, 3, 7–40.

Manoli, P. (2011) Black Sea Regionalism in perspective. *Neighbourhood Policy Paper* 2, 1–10. <http://www.khas.edu.tr/cms/abaum/dosyalar/files/NeighbourhoodPolicyPaper%2802%29%281%29.pdf> (accessed 5 November 2014).

Molnar, S. (2012) *Black Sea Discovery Could Cover Romania's Natural gas Needs for 20 Years*, <http://www.naturalgaseurope.com/romania-black-sea-gas-exxon-mobil-omv-petrom-domino> (accessed 5 November 2014).

Morata, F. and Sandoval, I. (2012) *European Energy Policy. An Environmental Approach*, Edward Elgar, Cheltenham.

Natural Gas Europe (2013) *Black Sea Rising*, <http://www.naturalgaseurope.com/black-sea-oil-gas> (accessed 5 November 2014).

Novinite (2013) *Nabucco Construction in Bulgaria to be Launched in 2013*, <http://www.novinite.com/view_news.php?id=146730> (accessed 5 November 2014).

Özbay, F. (2011) The relations between Turkey and Russia in the 2000s. *Perceptions Journal of International Affairs* 16(3), 1–172.

Pachiu, Laurentiu (2013) *Some Enquiries on Romania's Post Nabucco Energy Policies*, <http://www.naturalgaseurope.com/pachiu-analysis-romania-post-nabucco-energy-policy> (accessed 5 November 2014).

Peuch, J.-C. (2005) *Ukraine: Regional Leaders Set Up Community of Democratic Choice*, <http://www.rferl.org/content/article/1063461.html> (accessed 5 November 2014).

Resneck, J. (2012) New energy between Cold War foes Turkey, Russia, *Washington Times*, <http://www.washingtontimes.com/news/2012/sep/3/new-energy-between-cold-war-foes-turkey-russia/?page=all> (accessed 5 November 2014).

Reuters (2013) *Russian PM Plays Down Talk of Gas Wars, Warns Ukraine on EU*, <http://www.reuters.com/article/2013/11/01/russia-medvedev-ukraine-idUSL5N0IL4P220131101> (accessed 5 November 2014).

Schmidt-Felzmann, A. (2011) EU member states' energy relations with Russia: conflicting approaches to securing natural gas supplies. *Geopolitics* 16(3), 574–599.

Shelest, H. (2011) The Black Sea region a security challenge for Ukraine. *Turkish Policy Quarterly* 10(3), 113–120.

Sherr, J. (2012) Gas power politics. *The World Today* (October and November), 18–21.

Stoyanov, V. (2013) *Dissecting the Prospects for South Stream Beyond the Media Hype*, <http://www.naturalgaseurope.com/prospects-south-stream-beyond-media-hype> (accessed 5 November 2014).

Tanrisever, O. F. (2012) Turkey and Russia in the Black Sea region: dynamics of cooperation and conflict. *Black Sea Discussion Paper Series* 1, 1–26.

Triantaphyllou, D. (2007) Energy Security and Common Foreign and Security Policy (CFSP): the wider Black Sea area context. *Southeast European and Black Sea Studies* 7(2), 289–302.

Umbach, F. (2013) *Russia's Hold Europe's Gas Market is Changing Rapidly*, <http://www.worldreview.info/content/russias-hold-europes-gas-market-changing-rapidly?goback=%2Egde_1973625_member_273788571#%21> (accessed 5 November 2014).

Ungureanu, T. (2012) *Black Sea Strategy Debate*, 17 April, Strasbourg, <http://www.europarl.europa.eu/sides/getDoc.do?pubRef=-//EP//TEXT+CRE+20120417+ITEM-018+DOC+XML+V0//NL> (accessed 18 September 2014).

Vasilyan, S. (2010) A cacophony: the EU's security policy towards the South Caucasus, in *The Black Sea Region and EU Policy: The Challenge of Divergent Agendas* (eds K. *Henderson and C. Weaver*). Ashgate, Aldershot, 87–104.

Voice of Russia (2012) European Commission vs Gazprom: action-counteraction, <http://english.ruvr.ru/2012_09_11/European-Commission-vs-Gazprom-action-counteraction/> (accessed 5 November 2014).

Walker S. (2013) Vladimir Putin offers Ukraine financial incentives to stick with Russia, *The Guardian,* <http://www.theguardian.com/world/2013/dec/17/ukraine-russia-leaders-talks-kremlin-loan-deal> (accessed 5 November 2014).

Wilson, R. (2006). U.S. Policy in the Black Sea Region. *Turkish Policy Quarterly* 5 (2), 11–15.

Yanukovych, V. (2013) *President: European Integration is Construction of Europe in Ukraine,* <http://thessalonici.mfa.gov.ua/en/news/news-from-ukraine/603-viktor-janukovich-jevrointegracijace-budivnictvo-jevropi-v-ukrajini> (accessed 20 September 2014).

Slawomir Raszewski

States over Markets? Development of a Turkish Gas Hub and its Effects on Regional Energy and Security

ABSTRACT: A long period of neoliberal discourse regarding energy matters in Europe has significantly altered the logic and narratives underpinning the issue of energy markets and supply security. Drawing on a range of international political economy perspectives, this chapter's argument is twofold. Firstly, featuring the case study of Turkey, it argues that state participation in delivering energy-supply security in the Black Sea and the Caucasus (BSC) region has been unrivalled. Secondly, it argues that, for a state to deliver patterns of enhanced interdependency that lead to energy security regionally, measures including market regulation would need to be involved to ensure the development of an energy market. As the period of neoliberal discourse regarding energy in Europe continues, in Turkey the state role in the field of energy supply security and transit is being further strengthened with implications for energy and security within the BSC region.

KEYWORDS: energy security, energy market liberalization, Turkey, gas hub, energy diplomacy, EU energy policy, energy supply dependence, BOTAŞ

The State of Play in International Energy

Neoliberal energy security discourse is rooted in the concept of sustainable development that was first introduced into public policy debate in the 1980s to link the then-unfolding environmental politics with economic development. Since its emergence, this discourse has occurred in three underpinning issue areas: (i) social, (ii) economic and (iii) environmental. Owing to the emerging discourse's normative strength, these three issue areas have been widely applied to public policy and management of hydrocarbon energy in the EU, which is an energy-consuming region. In Europe, the signing of the Maastricht Treaty in 1992 allowed not only for the creation of a single market but, crucially, for recognizing the three issue areas as drivers of the Community's energy policy. Indeed, the three pillared "energy security" objectives that were introduced through the Treaty of Amsterdam paved the way for EU's energy policy. As set out in that Treaty, the objectives included the security of supply, aimed at minimizing risks and impacts of possible supply disruptions; competitive energy markets, to ensure that energy supply was available at low cost for producers and consumers, in order to contribute to industrial competitiveness and wider social policy objectives; and finally, maintaining environmental sustainability (Directorate-General for Energy, 1999: 8).

Sanctioned by the Treaties of Maastricht and Amsterdam as the internal energy policy, the three issue areas also became a hallmark of the Community's involvement with external partners in the field of international energy relations (Belyi, 2008).

For most of the period since the mid-1990s, energy policy in the EU has been presented and analysed through the lenses of liberalism and realism, rather than the postinstitutional theory of energy governance. This is illustrated by the case EU-Russia energy relations (Stern, 2002; Konoplyanik, 2008). With focus on the role of rules globally, energy governance represents an attempt to hedge realist and liberal approaches to energy by building a framework to address empirical problems encountered both by energy producers and consumers (Bressand, 2010; Raszewski, 2012a).

The "golden triangle" of energy security, comprising competitiveness, security of supply, and environmental concerns, has been the "standard" signpost of involvement with external partners for the EU. Internal energy rules have also been subject to externalization efforts to ensure that the EU energy rationale encapsulates jurisdictions beyond the EU (Keating, 2012: 93). As the nature of European energy governance evolved, the debate over values and norms underpinning trade in energy resurfaced abruptly: European Union-Russia energy relations' stumbling block so far has been as to whether gas should be treated as a market commodity, a polemical stance that Brussels defends, or, perhaps, as a special type of inherently strategic natural resource, as Moscow tends to treat it. Energy has also been perceived as strategic by state actors in the BSC region, particularly policies aimed at supply security and diversification of transit routes.

As the energy producer-consumer debate continues, more focus has been put on the political economy of energy transit. Nevertheless, discussions that followed have mainly reflected geopolitical aspects of real or perceived rivalry between energy liberalism and energy realism embodied by EU–Russia energy relations. Rather than focusing on the political economy of energy the discussion has been arguably distorted by "Great Game-type commentary", which largely represented voices of interest groups and energy lobby perspectives (Baev and Øverland, 2010: 1076). As the discussion has been heavily politicized, the most important aspect of energy security policy – the transit of energy that "guarantees energy security" (Haghighi, 2008: 462) – is yet to be addressed.

Explaining Turkey's Role in the Development of the Energy Trade

The transit of natural gas has grown in importance as the single most problematic matter in energy relations between the EU and Russia since the mid-1990s, with Ukraine becoming the most important hotspot in the process. Attributed to differences in energy security values, rather than patterns of energy governance, the policy divergence between the EU and Russia has opened up new opportunities for Turkey and, more broadly, for the BSC region. As in the case of Russia, the EU's energy policy aimed at the institutional harmonization of its own energy laws and policies with those of Turkey through the Energy Community Treaty (ECOT) framework. This move has been resisted by Ankara, which instead has sought policy alternatives. In the ECOT context, Brussels conditioned Turkey's making "full use of its potential" towards becoming "a major energy transit hub" (Solana, 2006: 3) upon acceptance of bilateral relations with the EU and making the Turkish energy laws harmonious with the energy laws of the EU. The careful wording of Turkey's role as an "energy transit hub" as outlined by the EU clearly reflected a reluctance on the part of the Commission and the Higher Representative to put all of their eggs into one basket with respect to energy diversification (Raszewski, 2012b: 125). Turkey has resisted this and Brussels' attempts to export energy consumers' norms to its own jurisdiction as it would have imposed EU norms on Ankara without Turkey being actually a part of the Community. Simultaneously, Turkey has taken bold steps to enhance its central role as an energy security guarantor in the development of the gas trade between the East and the West of the Eurasian continent. One option has been a policy that aims at facilitating a hub-based gas trade in Turkey but without harmonization of its laws with the EU. While geographic location has been the most common referent to validate Turkey's claim for playing the role (Barysch, 2007: 2; Triantaphyllou, 2007: 297), challenges still remain.

A gas hub refers to a point – physical or virtual – where several interconnecting pipelines meet and are supplemented by nearby gas storage facilities (Energy Charter Secretariat, 2007: 231). Such a physical point provides customers, shippers and gas marketers primarily with receipt and delivery access to the pipelines that facilitate transportation between these points. As a virtual point it offers a legal framework that allows that movement and/or transfer of gas ownership (Tobin, 2003: 1–2). With a favourable political geography of Turkey (Cohen, 2011: 217) stretching between the BSC and EU regions, the gas hub concept may be even more appealing as it would sanction enhancement of competition in a pan-European energy trade by supplying new volumes of natural gas.

Nevertheless, following the impact of liquefied natural gas (LNG) supplies from Qatar available in Western Europe on a spot market basis, a transition is under way in the gas market and involves a shift from long-term contracts to hub-traded short-term contracts based on gas-trade relations that have been the defining feature of gas markets in Europe since 2009 (Stern and Rogers, 2011: 7). On the other hand, though, with the economics of the trading hubs of continental Europe – such as the Central European Gas Hub (CEGH) at Baumgarten, Austria or Belgium's Zeebrugge and Punto di Scambio Virtuale in Italy – still low in market liquidity, there are good prospects for a Turkish gas hub in what is emerging as an East–West gas-trade structure. The question remains whether Turkey is prepared to take this opportunity and extend the existing map of trading points while adding up to a more liquid trade in gas?

In the context of energy transit and trade, Roberts (2004) focuses on the geopolitical and strategic importance of Turkey as a transit state, while pointing out political and security issues that may inhibit Ankara's aspiration of turning itself into a gas-trading state. As opposed to Roberts, Winrow (2009) explicitly refers to the gas hub notion remaining uncertain with regard to prospects for an emerging Turkish gas hub as long as current security and political obstacles remain unresolved. An opposing view on the rationale, feasibility and operationalization of the new gas market developments is offered by Finon and Locatelli (2008), who essentially uphold a stance that states play the key role in oil and gas industry through long-term contracts and energy geopolitics, arguing for leaving energy security to major buyers and sellers instead. Nevertheless, the bottom line is that the major theoretical and analytical approaches to Turkey's role in developing a gas hub reflect the concerns of external players and are associated either with energy supply or energy transit security. Owing to the two dominant discourses on energy security – the EU focus on markets on the one hand, and Russia's take on energy geopolitics on the other – Turkish energy policy identity and narratives underpinning it, has been heavily contextualized around development of a gas hub.

Striving for "Energy Security" Relevance: The Odd Case of Turkey

Turkey is stretched between energy producers and exporters to the east and energy consumers and importers to the west. Turkey's neighbouring regions to the east are nonliberalized energy-trade complexes, whereas to the west mainly liberalized, market-based patterns of energy trade thrive. The energy-rich regions to the east are mainly autocratic regimes, with state capitalist organization prevailing as a form of governance. To Turkey's west, the predominant socio-economic form of organization includes pluralistic democracies with energy governance structures organized around institutions (Özdemir and Raszewski, 2012: 7). Correljé and van der Linde draw on the two opposing concepts of "Market and Institutions" (MI) and "Regions and Empires" (RE) when discussing energy security relations between the EU and its eastern neighbourhood. "Market and Institutions" is conceptualized as a "continuation and intensification of the international system based on multilateral relations and a globalization of markets" whereas by RE they refer to "the break-up of the international system into competing blocks, which may engage in rivalry over the control of energy resources and markets" (Correljé and van der Linde, 2006: 533). "Market and Institutions" and harmonization of its energy law with that of the EU-orchestrated framework of the Energy Treaty would have benefited multilateral energy relations and globalization or, at least, the de-regionalization of the Eurasian gas trade embodied by the EU–Russia gas trade.

The major regional project aimed at ensuring the physical exchange of gas from the east has been the Nabucco pipeline. It would, at the same time, convert Turkey into a transit corridor without prospects of becoming a gas-trading hub between East and West. For this reason Ankara has resisted EU's liberal ECOT framework while the Turkish government has been careful in exercising its energy transit powers under the Nabucco Intergovernmental Agreement (IGA), signed in July 2009. In the Nabucco context it is not surprising that the IGA did little to promote political agreement between the MI and RE. Instead, it has meticulously addressed technical issues, postponing and possibly disabling Ankara's decision to ratify it.[1] It demonstrates Ankara's reluctance to join the EU-led gas-trade structures, as they do not guarantee breaking dependence on Turkey's energy-rich eastern neighbourhood epitomized by the RE concept. Favouring energy geopolitics, post-Nabucco arrangements with regards to gas trade and transit have heavily gravitated towards states. A memorandum of understanding signed between the governments of Azerbaijan and Turkey in December 2011 to construct the Trans-Anatolia Natural Gas Pipeline (TANAP) opened a new chapter in regional energy security. The TANAP consortium, comprising the State Oil Company of Azerbaijan (SOCAR) and the Petroleum Pipeline Corporation of Turkey (BOTAŞ) seeks to complete the project that will link the developed Shah Deniz phase 2 gas field in Azerbaijan. Routed via Georgia and Turkey, the TANAP project is worth 7 billion USD and, when completed in 2019, is expected to pipe 16 billion cubic metres (bcm) of Azeri gas to European markets (Kashi, 2013). The TANAP is scalable and aims to deliver 16 bcm in 2020 with further capacity increases in 2023 and 2026 of 23 bcm and 31 bcm respectively. The pipeline project, in Turkish Prime Minister Erdoğan's words, is not just for the sake of strengthening Turkish-Azerbaijani energy relations but, particularly, for enhancing EU energy supply security (TANAP website). Contributing to Europe's energy security is one of four principal aims of Turkish Energy Strategy (TES) with the three others including diversifying supplies, increasing its share of renewables and increasing energy efficiency. Aiming to become the tenth largest economy by 2023, the energy factor may become a serious challenge as Turkey's energy use is expected to increase dramatically from 114 million tonnes of oil equivalent (mtoe)

1 Author's elite interview with a Senior Gas Industry Representative and a former energy advisor to the Turkish Government. Ankara, Turkey, July 2010.

in 2011 to 218 mtoe in 2023 (Acar, 2013: 5). The backbone of the EU policy on energy – market liberalization – is absent from the four policy areas aimed at enhancing energy security of Turkey. These developments underscore the feasibility of the Turkish state-owned vision of a gas hub that rest on energy geopolitics and, owing to state-owned energy industry involvement, rely on long-term contracts to create a stronger bond between energy buyers and sellers (Finon and Locatelli, 2008).

On the other hand the RE concept suggests continuation of the long-term contractual energy trade with its major gas supplier, Russia, which has been advancing in the last decade. This has significantly undermined Turkey's balance of trade and payments, which has been a headache for past and present Ministers for Energy and Natural Resources, with the cumulative cost of the "take or pay" contracted gas from Iran and Russia reaching 4.2 billion USD in 2009 (Finanstrend, 2009). The alternative that has been on the table is a state-championed gas hub that would be under control of the state-owned gas monopoly, BOTAŞ, through a separate legal entity to be exclusively involved in functional and legal gas transactions. With the focus on virtual rather than purely physical characteristics of a gas hub, the new role Turkey seeks to acquire reminds us of Rosecrance's idea of a trading state in which security is overridden by trade priorities. Drawing on the Turkish example, in a trading state a range of actors "participate in foreign policy-making or diplomatic games and … the interests and priorities of these actors are quite different from those of traditional foreign policy-makers of Turkey" (Kirişci, 2009: 33).

State-Owned Energy Security

A "one-size-fits-all" definition of energy supply security does not exist and, as such, supply security has to be considered from at least two time-based perspectives: short-term and long-term supply. The long-term energy supply security is about investment adequacy in natural gas infrastructure such as physical transport pipelines, which enable energy supply that is efficient and delivered at reasonable and stable prices (Lévêque, Glachant, Barquín *et al.*, 2010: 5–6). The short-term energy security refers to adequate energy crisis facilities, in particular significant storage capacities to be used at times of technical and non-technical shortages (Stern, 2006: 24). Possessing domestic sources of energy is yet another "selling point" in a gas-hub policy, ensuring a level of trade liquidity uncharacteristic of Turkey. With its power sector dependent on gas and a very modest indigenous resource base of their own, Turkey's natural gas production stood at 1 bcm in 2009 with the country relying on imports in more than 98 percent of its gas needs (International Energy Agency, 2009: 67).

At the crossroads between MI and RE, Turkey's energy diplomacy aims at creating both a physical and a virtual "centre of gravity" in the international hub-based gas trade, which would be state controlled. The emergence of a hub-based energy trade in Turkey may be viewed as consistent with Turkey's ambition to progress from the periphery of the two storylines of MI and RE to the centre of Eurasian gas relations. Ankara's policy has been elaborated with reference to the existing and planned physical infrastructure and its attractive geographical location as the two sole advantages. While Turkey's position in this respect is advantageous on a number of accounts, there are challenges too.

Whereas the physical aspects of creating a centre of gas gravity has been extensively reported on and written about, it is worthwhile looking into the nonphysical part of the story. Competitiveness and the reasonable maturity of the gas market make the gas-hub idea conceivable. For the concept to be achievable in a near future, a number of issues have to be addressed, from regulatory authority to short-term energy security.

Responsibility, in terms of reforming Turkey's natural gas sector, was assumed by the Energy Market Regulatory Authority (EMRA) following the enactment of the Natural Gas Market Law no. 4646 in May 2001, and was expanded to include natural gas, oil and liquefied petroleum gas (International Energy Agency, 2009: 19). Despite Law no. 4628 designating EMRA as "the sole authority" for regulating Turkey's energy market, a vertical separation in the gas market has to yet occur (Çetin and Oguz, 2007: 3859). Unbundling and elimination of the market monopolistic structure of the state-owned vertically integrated gas utility, BOTAŞ was never initiated as envisaged by the law. By enactment of Law 4646, the state national champion, BOTAŞ, was legally subordinated to market forces. Nevertheless, the provision has yet to materialize to functionally separate "physical" and "virtual" functions of the gas industry to ensure the supply, trade and storage functions are operated by individual BOTAŞ-owned companies.

The discontinuation of the unbundling and deceleration in energy-sector liberalization resulted in a limited involvement of EMRA, which, in the face of the post-2006 shift to security and strategy rather than to law and economics, remained rather a peripheral institution within the political sector of Turkish energy policy.

Yet, functionally non liberalized energy markets are common among the EU member states. For that matter, while legally unbundled, neighbouring Bulgaria has been referred to as having "zero actual liberalization" in the energy sector despite the government's energy strategy dating back to 2008 (Nitzov *et al.*, 2012: 6). Fragmented policy on energy coupled with a complex regulatory and energy security objectives are yet to bring fruit in this EU member state that is 100% dependent on imported gas from Russia.

Low-institutionalized, Bulgaria's natural gas sector relies on a single public supplier, Bulgargaz EAD, which is a fully-owned subsidiary of the 100% government-owned Bulgarian Energy Holding (BEH), responsible for gas imports from subsidiaries of Gazprom and intermediaries (Nitzov *et al.*, 2012: 2).

Turkey's aspiration to become a gas hub coincides with its gas market's exposure to so-called take-or-pay contracts for piped gas. These are long-term, usually 20-to-30 year contractual arrangements in which the contracting party commits to purchase a given amount of natural gas from a provider, which has to be paid for no matter if consumed, without a resale option. The price in the take-or-pay contracts is determined by indexation to a gas substitute, usually crude or other refined products. While providing security of demand to the seller, this type of contract puts the price risk on the consumer and may result in overcapacity.

Gas supply to the Turkish gas market is saturated with long-term contracts, which may be viewed as a challenge to the creation of a virtual gas trading hub. Over three-quarters of all natural gas imported by the monopoly BOTAŞ rests on this type of contractual obligation. Russia supplies 57.95%, Iran 18.64% and Azerbaijan 8.67% of piped gas (Stratfor, 2012). These unbalanced gas relations have had effects on gas import contingency in the past and have been coupled with insufficient gas storage facilities following the commissioning of the Blue Stream gas pipeline (Özdemir, 2007: 135).

Oversaturation with long-term contracts has negative effects on development of energy policy alternatives. While Sofia could, in theory, benefit from interconnections to Turkey as well as other countries in the Balkans (in particular Greece and Romania), overreliance on two parallel gas pipelines from Russia via Ukraine, Moldova and Romania confines Bulgaria's gas system to a lack of flexibility and supply security.

Previously signed take-or-pay supply contracts envisaged consumption peaking at 55 bcm and 84 bcm in 2010 and 2020 respectively, whereas in 2009 actual consumption was merely 33 bcm. With 22 bcm of annual overcapacity and available underground gas storage for 2.1 bcm only, gas contingency turned out to be erroneous.[2] Turkey's troublesome long-term supply security has been coupled with inadequate risk management in the event of a short-term gas supply crisis. As a NATO member, Ankara has been unable to fulfil its short-term supply security obligation of 3 months' supply minimum, and the country's energy complex also has insufficient storage facilities (Shaffer, 2006: 97). Investment in a natural gas grid and storage capacity is under way, although rather slowly. Turkey was even incentivized to explore gas storage options in the Ukraine while getting its own underground gas storage facilities – the North Marmara and the Değirmenköy Underground Natural Gas Storage facilities – onto the agenda (Oğan, 2006; Oğan and Aytekin, 2002: 69). The Tuz Gölü underground storage, a World Bank project that has been in discussion for several years now, has yet to be built (Today's Zaman, 2011).

Turkey is emerging as a one of the fastest growing economies in the world with a staggering 9% and 8.5% economic growth in 2010 and 2011 respectively (Dombey, 2012). Owing to its energy security stand, further growth and a sustainable development of its energy sector may be put under stress. Allowing for the virtual gas hub while catering for energy security actions relying on the Turkish Derivatives Exchange may be an advantageous way forward.

The long-term, contract-led gas market in Turkey has attracted attention from major gas producers from Azerbaijan, Russia and Qatar, who have sought cooperation opportunities that may harbinger further prospects for the gas hub project. As implementation of the Third Energy Package within the EU jurisdictions continues, companies such as Gazprom were prohibited from acquiring a 50% stakes in the CEGH at Baumgarten, Austria. This has been viewed as a window of opportunity for Russian energy players in accommodating their interests in liberalizing the Turkish

2 Author's elite interview with a senior energy expert. Ankara, Turkey, July 2010.

energy market, where Russian capital seems to be welcome (**Özdemir** and Raszewski, 2012: 19). Recent examples include downstream deals between Bosforus Gaz and Prima Energy Trading LLC, a Gazprom subsidiary, as well as Avrasya Gaz, a Gazprombank subsidiary (Ersoy, 2012). As much as Ankara's aspiration to become a centre of energy trade may sound appealing from the point of view of enhancing energy security in the BSC region, the very unbalanced gas relations between Turkey and her key energy suppliers may seriously challenge the feasibility of a regional energy security architecture. As Ankara, Baku and Tbilisi continue strengthening state ownership and their management role in large-scale energy projects, regional security architecture remains unchanged.

The Way Forward

From Russia to the countries of the Caspian, the Middle East and the Mediterranean, Turkey is located in close vicinity to major gas-producing regions. Middle Eastern gas reserves are closer to the European markets than those of Russia, and Turkey is the natural conduit for these resources between Asia and Europe while being an important energy market in its own right. Change in the political economy of energy trade and the shifting balance of power in the international system creates a window of opportunity for Turkey's gas-hub policy to transform the country into a "centre" by 2023 (Öğütçü, 2012). In the long term, by using this advantage, there is a potential for Turkey to form a gas hub and contribute to the sustainable development of gas trade regionally. But the current state-centric discourse and the focus on geopolitics may be insufficient to achieve the ambition of turning Turkey into a trading state and a centre of gravity in the natural gas trade. Owing to the specificity of the piped gas trade which is often subject to a great deal of politicization, Turkey's aspiration to become a gas hub may need to be examined from a wider, regional perspective, which involves perspectives from the BSC region in addition to the European context. Just as with energy consuming and producing regions, where diversification of energy supply and energy demand play a key role in policy making, in Turkey a focus on the energy security of its physical and virtual trade also needs guarantees by way of infrastructure, in addition to a robust microeconomic and legal basis. The National Balancing Point concept will be introduced in the Network Industry Code and state-owned BOTAŞ is pending restructuring to allow for the concept to be accommodated but the legal basis, in terms of a new energy transit law that draws on experience achieved elsewhere, could be a much more advanced.

References

Acar, O. (2013) *Turkey's 2023 Vision: An Evaluation from the Energy Perspective*. Presentation at seminar titled "Turkey's Energy Strategy Under Pressure: Domestic Bets and Regional Constraints" organized by the French Institute of International Relations on 2 July 2013 in Paris.

Baev, P. K. and Øverland, I. (2010) The South Stream versus Nabucco pipeline race: geopolitical and economic (ir)rationalities and political stakes mega-projects. *International Affairs* 86(5), 1075–1090.

Barysch, K. (2007) Turkey's role in European energy security. *Centre for European Reform Essays*, 12 December 2007. <http://www.cer.org.uk/sites/default/files/publications/attachments/pdf/2011/essay_turkey_energy_12dec07-1381.pdf> (accessed 5 November 2014).

Belyi, A. V. (2008) EU external energy policies: a paradox of integration, in *Europe's Global Role: External Policies of the European Union* (ed. J. Orbie), Ashgate, Aldershot.

Bressand, A. (2010) The future of producer-consumer cooperation: a policy perspective, in *Global Energy Governance: New Rules of the Game* (eds A. Goldthau and J. M. Witte), Brookings, Washington, DC.

Çetin, T. and Oguz (2007) The reform in the Turkish natural gas market: a critical evaluation. *Energy Policy* 35(8), 3856–3867.

Cohen, S. B. (2011) Turkey's emergence as a geopolitical power broker. *Eurasian Geography and Economics* 52(2), 217–227.

Correljé, A. and van der Linde, C. (2006) Energy supply security and geopolitics: a European perspective. *Energy Policy* 34(5), 532–543.

Directorate-General for Energy (1999) Energy in Europe: economic foundations for energy policy. *The Shared Analysis Project* (special issue,

December), <http://ec.europa.eu/energy/library/executive_sum.pdf> (accessed 5 November 2014).

Dombey, D. (2012) Turkish boom belies slower growth. *The Financial Times* (2 April). <http://www.ft.com/cms/s/0/cbf9019e-7cdb-11e1-a676-00144feab49a.html#axzz27CTRsPSm> (accessed 5 November 2014).

Energy Charter Secretariat (2007) *Putting a Price on Energy: International Pricing Mechanisms for Oil and Gas.* Brussels: Energy Charter Secretariat, <http://www.encharter.org/fileadmin/user_upload/document/Oil_and_Gas_Pricing_2007_ENG.pdf> (accessed 6 November 2014).

Ersoy, E. (2012) Gazprombank unit to buy 26% of trader Avrasya, Turkey board says. *Bloomberg,* 3 January, <http://www.bloomberg.com/news/2012-01-03/gazprombank-unit-to-buy-26-of-trader-avrasya-turkey-board-says.html> (accessed 6 November 2014).

Finanstrend (2009) BOTAŞ Genel Müdürü Saltuk Düzyol görevinden ayrıldı. *Finanstrend* (2 October), <http://www.finanstrend.com/haber/37856/botas-gm-saltuk-duzyol-gorevinden-ayrildi> (accessed 6 November 2014).

Finon, D. and Locatelli, C. (2008) Russian and European gas interdependence: could contractual trade channel geopolitics? *Energy Policy* 36(1), 423–442.

Haghighi, S. S. (2008) Energy security and the division of competences between the European Community and its member states. *European Law Journal* 14(4), 461–482.

International Energy Agency (2009) *Energy Policies of IEA Countries: Turkey 2009 Review,* IEA, Paris. <http://www.iea.org/publications/free publications/publication/turkey2009.pdf> (accessed 28 December 2014).

Kashi, D. (2013) 'The Trans-Anatolian Gas Pipeline (TANAP) will help move natural gas to Europe through Turkey from Azerbaijan's natural gas reserves', *International Business Times* (16 August), <http://www.ibtimes.com/trans-anatolian-gas-pipeline-tanap-will-help-move-nat ural-gas-europe-through-turkey-azerbaijans> (accessed 6 November 2014).

Keating, M. F. (2012) Re-thinking EU energy security: the utility of global best practices for successful transnational energy governance, in *Dynamics of Energy Governance in Europe and Russia* (eds C. Kuzemko,

A. V. Belyi, A. Goldthau and M. F. Keating), Palgrave Macmillan, Basingstoke.

Kirişci, K. (2009) The transformation of Turkish foreign policy: the rise of the trading state. *New Perspectives on Turkey* 40, 29–57.

Konoplyanik, A. (2008) Regulating energy relations: acquis or energy charter? In *Pipelines, Politics and Power* (ed. K. Barysch), Centre for European Reform, London.

Lévêque, F., Glachant, J-M., Barquín, J. *et al.* (2010) *Security of Energy Supply in Europe: Natural Gas, Nuclear and Hydrogen*, Edward Elgar, Cheltenham.

Nitzov, B., Stefanov, R., Nikolova, V. and Hristov, D. (2012) *The Energy Sector of Bulgaria*, Atlantic Council Issue Brief, Washington, DC.

Oğan, S. (2006) Mavi Akım: Türk–Rus İlişkilerinde Mavi Bağımlılık. *TÜRKSAM*.<http://www.turksam.org/tr/makale-detay/548-mavi-akim-turk-rus-iliskilerinde-mavi-bagimlilik> (accessed: 28 December 2014).

Oğan, S. and Aytekin, İ. (2002) Mavi Akım: Türk–Rus İlişkilerinde Mavi Bağımlılık. *Stratejik Analiz* 3(32), 66–70.

Öğütçü, M. (2012) Letter from Istanbul. Prepared for Qatar's Quantum 20 February 2012. The European Geopolitical Forum. <http://gpf-europe.com/forum/?blog=external_relations&id=111> (accessed: 28 December 2014).

Özdemir, V. (2007) The Blue Stream natural gas pipeline: implications on energy security and foreign policy. *Journal of Central Asian and Caucasian Studies* 2(3), 135–148.

Özdemir, V. and Raszewski, S. (2012) States over Markets? Development of a Turkish Gas Hub and its Effects on Sustainable Market Development. Unpublished paper presented at International Conference titled "Sustainable Development in the Energy Sector", co-organized by the Centre for Energy, Petroleum and Mineral Law and Policy and the Moscow Higher School of Economics. Perm, Russia, 17–19 April 2012.

Raszewski, S. (2012a) Security and economics of energy in Eastern Europe, in *Dynamics of Energy Governance in Europe and Russia* (eds C. Kuzemko, A. V. Belyi, A. Goldthau and M. F. Keating), Palgrave Macmillan, Basingstoke.

Raszewski, S. (2012b) European Union Energy Policy and the Black Sea/Caspian Region: Between Security Community and Security Complex? PhD thesis. University of Leeds.

Roberts, J. (2004) The Turkish Gate: energy transit and security issues. *Turkish Policy Quarterly* 3(4), 17–19.

Shaffer, B. (2006) Turkey's energy policies in a tight global energy market. *Insight Turkey* 8(2), 97–104.

Solana, J. (2006) *An External Policy to Serve Europe's Energy Interests.* Paper from Commission/SG/HR for the European Council S160/06, <http://www.consilium.europa.eu/ueDocs/cms_Data/docs/pressdata/EN/reports/90082.pdf> (accessed 6 November 2014).

Stern, J. (2002) *Security of European Natural Gas Supplies: The Impact of Import Dependence and Liberalization*, Royal Institute of International Affairs, London.

Stern, J. (2006) The new security environment for European gas: worsening geopolitics and increasing global competition for LNG. Oxford Institute for Energy Studies NG 15, October. <http://www.oxfordenergy.org/wpcms/wp-content/uploads/2010/11/NG15-TheNewSecuirtyEnvironmentForEuropeanGasWorseningGeopoliticsandIncreasingGlobalCompetitionforLNG-JonathanStern-2006.pdf> (accessed: 28 December 2014).

Stern, J. and Rogers, H. (2011) The transition to hub-based gas pricing in continental Europe. Oxford Institute for Energy Studies NG 49, March. <http://www.oxfordenergy.org/wpcms/wp-content/uploads/2011/03/NG49.pdf> (accessed: 28 December 2014).

Stratfor (2012) Turkey's natural gas imports 2011. *Stratfor Global Intelligence* (20 March), <http://www.stratfor.com/image/turkeys-natural-gas-imports-2011> (accessed 6 November 2014).

TANAP website (2014) *Trans Anadolu Doğal Gaz Boru Hattı Projesi*, <http://www.tanap.com/tanap-nedir> (accessed: 28 December 2014).

Tobin, J. (2003) *Natural Gas Market Centers and Hubs: A 2003 Update.* Energy Information Administration, <http://www.eia.gov/pub/oil_gas/natural_gas/feature_articles/2003/market_hubs/mkthubs03.pdf> (accessed 6 November 2014).

Today's Zaman (2011) Turkey, China ink deal to build Tuz Gölü gas storage. *Today's Zaman*, 29 November. <http://www.todayszaman.

com/business_turkey-china-ink-deal-to-build-tuz-golu-gas-storage_264299.html> (accessed: 28 December 2014).

Triantaphyllou, D. (2007) Energy Security and Common Foreign and Security Policy (CFSP): the wider Black Sea area context. *Southeast European and Black Sea Studies* 7(2), 289–302.

Winrow, M. G. (2009) Problems and prospects for the "Fourth Corridor": the positions and role of Turkey in gas transit to Europe. Oxford Institute for Energy Studies NG 30, June. <http://www.oxfordenergy.org/wpcms/wp-content/uploads/2010/11/NG30-ProblemsandProspectsForTheFourthCorridorThePositionandRoleofTurkeyinGasTransitToEurope-GarethWinrow2009.pdf> (accessed: 28 December 2014).

Nikoloz Sumbadze

The New Gas Era: Shaping Energy Policy in the South Caucasus Region

ABSTRACT: The shale gas revolution had important consequences for the global energy industry. Shale gas is considered to be a promising source of energy to satisfy growing energy demand, increase energy security, generate economic benefits and reduce the carbon footprint. Discoveries and technological advances in shale gas industry have led to cheaper gas production and lower gas prices, decoupled from oil prices. Shale gas deposits are mostly found in emerging markets, creating a potential for import-dependent countries to improve their energy security. Considering the attitude to and knowledge of shale gas development in the United States and the EU, this chapter shows the potential impact of shale gas on South Caucasus region and its energy policy and its future gas market development.

KEYWORDS: South Caucasus, shale gas, natural gas markets, hydraulic fracturing, energy policy

Introduction

Until quite recently nobody anticipated that shale gas would become a major rival of other energy sources and an energy "game changer" worldwide. Discoveries of massive shale gas reserves together with technological advances made it economically viable for large-scale production and more attractive to the business sector. Starting from the boom in the United States, the shale gas revolution has significant implications for international gas markets and has created huge uncertainties throughout the energy mix.

Many international energy agencies and organizations have studied shale gas developments and have produced numerous recommendations. Their findings show the significance of the huge reserves and the trade-off between environmental protection and economic growth. According to recent analyses, global conventional[1] natural gas resources are equivalent to 120 years of consumption. Adding proven shale gas reserves can sustain natural gas production over 250 years (IEA, 2011).

A recently released report by the US Energy Information Administration (EIA) estimated that shale gas resources within 41 countries amounted to 7229 TCF (trillion cubic feet), whereas conventional gas reserves are only 3157 TCF (EIA, 2013b). However, shale gas reserves and production always tend to increase as more wells are drilled and additional capacity is found. Globally, 45% of the total estimated natural gas resources are in shale formations. While the EIA projects that global gas demand will be more than doubled between 2010 to 2035 years, shale gas will make up about 32% of the total supply compared to 14% in recent years (EIA, 2012). Considering these projections, continued shale gas discoveries, together with growing production, can contribute to depressing natural gas prices further in the future.

In contrast to the global oil market, natural gas is traded at a regional level and is differentiated among marketplaces. They are divided into three categories based on price mechanisms:

- Competitive gas markets with spot prices characterized by sophisticated financial instruments and the interaction between large numbers of buyers and sellers.
- Oil-indexed gas markets where price is directly linked to oil prices. This market is characterized by a limited number of market participants.
- Government-regulated gas markets, where price is mandated by the government.

Differences among the price mechanisms within regions are due to local geographical factors and gas reserve capacities. Traditionally, natural gas is

1 Natural gas can be found in conventional and unconventional forms whereas shale gas is found in unconventional forms. The main difference between these two forms of natural gas is that shale gas extraction is kept under the ground and the cost is associated with its extraction. Conventional gas is easily extractable because it is mostly found in multiple, relatively small, spongy zones. However, extraction of shale gas requires additional special processes known as horizontal drilling and hydraulic fracturing (fracking) while it remains tightly trapped in shale rocks. Water, sand and chemicals are injected into the well with high pressure and gas is released after fracking the shale rocks.

transported through pipelines and liquefied natural gas (LNG) form. However both forms require high capital expenditure and long-term contracts between producers and consumers. The tendency to globalize the natural gas market will require additional transportation routes to be developed for the interregional gas trade. Gas pricing may dictate its global perspectives because low gas prices can strongly influence fuel choice in the future. Clearly, shale gas may lead to stable and lower gas prices and become a genuine player for transferring regional gas markets to a global level.

The main drivers of natural gas demand in the future will include access to supply, the level of economic activity, the competitiveness of gas against other forms of energy, changes in technology and government policies (IEA, 2011). One problem attributed to natural gas is that demand is price inelastic in the short term whereas demand becomes elastic in the long term. In the absence of a substitute, it takes several years for the economy to adjust gas consumption behaviour in response to higher prices. In the future, the electricity, transport and residential sectors will have major implications for gas demand. Hopefully, lower gas prices would make power generation cheaper and gas-fired vehicles economically viable from a long-term perspective.

The potential of shale gas as a more abundant and relatively low-cost energy source promises more affordable energy and stable prices. The effect of shale gas has been to decouple the price of gas from oil and move toward market-oriented spot prices in the United States. When evaluating its future prospects, several factors must be taken into consideration. The supply of shale gas will depend on the returns on investment. It will also require properly developed pipelines and other distribution facilities to support transportation and trade across the world. However, shale gas demand will be reflected by natural gas price developments. Currently, prices are low and tend to drop even further. Whether natural gas prices drop or increase will largely depend on whether there will be a sufficient stream of revenue to maintain production of shale gas. In this respect, well developed regulatory support from the government for private companies will be crucial if they are to engage in large-scale activities. Easy access to permits and license for production and subsidies can be additional incentives for them to explore and develop new shale gas reserves. Environmental factors are another potential risk affecting shale gas perspectives. Recent public concerns related to health-and-safety issues demonstrate important resistance from society. Finally, shale gas can have geopolitical implications. It may change energy markets and change gas importer countries to exporter countries. This will affect energy security and consequently change political relationship between countries.

Considering the recent boom in the shale gas industry as a potential source of economic development and prosperity, the formation of complex energy policies and market conditions is required in the coming decades. Currently, many laws and regulations affecting the energy sector remain unchanged. However, it is clear that some existing laws have to follow recent gas-market developments and new legislation should be implemented to support market activities in the near future. The South Caucasus, as a region for energy transit, is an area of vital interest for the development of energy transit routes by a large number of energy players. Europe is trying to diversify its energy supply through the South Caucasus region to ensure the security of its gas supply and to avoid dependence on major monopoly players, which might be tempted to use their monopoly position for political gains. Shale gas development will have core implications on the region's future energy policy development and geopolitical challenges. This chapter analyses potential impacts of shale gas on regional gas-market developments, international gas pipeline projects in the South Caucasus region and how renewable energy sources and electricity prices in the region will be affected by international gas-market developments.

United States versus European Shale Gas Markets

The recent shale gas revolution in the United States played a major role in changing the natural gas market in recent years. The net impact was to unlock vast quantities of untapped gas, which was previously locked into insufficiently porous rock formations. The net result was an explosive growth in shale gas production. Consequently, shale-driven gas prices fell to a yearly average of 2.77 USD/MMBtu (million metric British thermal units) in 2012 while the price of natural gas in 2011 was on average 4 USD/MMBtu, based on Henry Hub.[2] On the other hand, wholesale gas prices in

2 Henry Hub Natural Gas Spot Price, United States Energy Information Administration, <www.eia.org>.

the United States are less than a quarter of the current price of gas in the United Kingdom and Europe. Asian counties, mostly depending on imported gas, pay four times more than US prices.

Uncertain energy prices and the increased importance of self-sufficiency demonstrates the potential for the shale gas revolution to continue in the United States. The United States mostly relies on traditional fossil fuels because they are less expensive and they are abundant. Therefore, shale gas production in the United States can play a key role in its energy mix. In 2012, the United States consumed more natural gas than it produced. Although domestic gas demand is increasing, lower gas prices make the United States less attractive for imports and conversely more attractive for exports. According to EIA, the United States is projected to become a net exporter of natural gas by 2020. Shale gas production, which is anticipated to grow by 113% from 2011 to 2040, is the greatest contributor to natural gas production growth, which in turn is anticipated to increase gas exports by 17.7% per year from 2020 to 2040 (EIA, 2013a). A number of LNG import terminals have already converted to export terminals and several LNG facilities are awaiting permits. The country's shale gas industry is market oriented and sufficient regulations are in place for its proper functioning. However, there is still a lack of pipeline, terminal and storage facilities to hold and transport shale gas to the customer base. On the other hand, shale gas is receiving attention from environmentalists and the public, which may lead to tighter government regulations regarding land access, water usage and hydraulic fracturing. Adding more regulation and the engagement of federal government in the industry may increase the cost of production and lower the level of production.

Shale gas is a divisive issue in Europe. The existence of substantial shale gas reserves makes Europe focus on the development of the shale gas industry with the aim of reducing its dependence on imported gas. However, there are a wide range of economic, regulatory and environmental issues that cast doubt on the prospects of shale gas. Furthermore, high production costs and low margins reduce investment incentives for starting up. Uncertainties in the regulatory framework and a lack of experience and infrastructure also create risks for shale gas companies in terms of long-term economic viability.

Europe has been the largest natural gas consumer and importer for decades. In recent years its gas production has reduced while its import dependency increased. Today, natural gas amounts to 24% of Europe's primary energy consumption and this figure is expected to increase to about 35% by 2030. Analyses show that Europe's energy policy and possible bans on shale gas development will increase its dependence on natural gas imports so that by 2030 more than 80% of the EU's gas requirements will be covered by imported natural gas.[3]

The main differences between the US and European shale gas markets relate to political, physical, social and economic matters. Political influence on the US shale gas industry is relatively low. Dominated by small companies, shale gas exploration and production takes place without political control but with attention given to natural energy security. In contrast to the United States, political support varies by country in Europe and is basically driven by domestic and regional energy security issues. Shale gas in the United States can be found in unpopulated areas, generally in deserts. In addition, the United States has a long history of technological experience in exploration and the production of shale gas together with properly developed pipeline networks. In Europe, which is densely populated, shale gas production becomes more difficult because it requires more sophisticated technological solutions. For example, shale gas production in Poland costs three times as much as in the United States (Pfeifer, 2012). Furthermore, less developed transportation routes and vulnerability to groundwater delay shale gas development in many European countries. In terms of economics, the US gas market is competitive and a lot of sellers and buyers can easily trade gas and benefit from price transparency. Incentive to become a net exporter will dictate whether there is a further increase in shale gas exploration. In the United States, exploration is conducted initially by smaller private companies and undertaken later by big companies, which engage in production. Landowners' property rights create additional financial incentives for private owners. In the United States, all mineral rights are owned by individual land owners so they have an incentive to sell their royalties. In Europe, shale gas exploration and production activities are performed by national oil and gas companies. At the same time, existing land property rights do not stimulate private companies to engage in shale gas operations because even if land is privately owned, the natural resources located beneath the ground are owned by the state.

Generally, Europe is an oil-indexed gas market where a few big sellers play a dominant role in the market. Gas prices are high but their

3 Eurogas, <www.eurogas.org>.

transparency tends to be low. Shale gas is publicly accepted in almost all US states. There is only a little public resistance, which is eliminated through establishing new regulations and requirements for shale gas drilling. Compared to the United States, there is less tolerance of the industry from the public varied across countries in Europe. Some countries have banned shale gas production and are very strict. In this respect, Europe needs to create policy guidance based on US experience in order to estimate potential benefits and costs of shale gas. It is clear that cost of shale gas extraction will be higher in Europe than in the United States. Without specific policy support it is unlikely that European shale gas will be cheap as in the United States and undercut Russia's oil-indexed gas imports. Thus, shale gas does not look like a game changer for Europe.

The South Caucasus Energy Outlook

The South Caucasus region was always treated as a strategic place where geopolitical interests of the United States, Russia, Europe, the Middle East and Central Asia converge. After the collapse of the Soviet Union, the South Caucasian countries gained independence and started a gradual transformation towards democracy. It is obvious that countries share a common vision in specific areas but they perceive geopolitical threats and gains differently and these differences are reflected in their foreign-policy priorities.

The energy sector is one of the strategic areas for the South Caucasus countries. While the energy policies of these countries are not similar, they are oriented to reap economic benefits from the use of local energy resources and to utilize the transit potential of their favourable geostrategic locations. Georgia has clearly declared its policy to integrate into European institutions. Its priority is to liberalize the energy market and integrate it into the regional and European energy markets. Armenia sees its position in the region differently. Although it seeks to maintain a balance in its relationships with Europe and Russia, it has been overdependent on Russia and basically integrated in all regional organizations led by Russia. The driving force of Azerbaijan's energy policy is its huge oil and gas reserves.

Revenues from oil and gas production and its importance as a supplier for Europe make it the fastest growing economy in the South Caucasus region.

The South Caucasus countries can be divided into energy-rich countries, transit countries and countries with no involvement in either energy or transit. Georgia is mostly rich in hydro resources. According to official estimates, Georgia utilizes only 18% of its hydro resources whereas its potential capacity in terms of electricity production is estimated to be 15 000 MW.[4] Today 75% to 80% of its total electricity consumption is generated by hydropower plants (HPPs) and only 20% to 25% by gas-fired thermal power plants (TPPs).[5] In terms of gas potential, Georgia has limited resources. Generally, gas demand is covered by imported gas whereas domestic gas production has an insignificant share. In 2012, Georgia imported 1920 million m^3 out of which 36% was used for TPPs for electricity generation, 27% for the residential sector and 37% for commercial sector.[6] Clearly, today Georgia is a net energy importer and a possible growth in demand in the future must be satisfied through imported resources because domestic fossil fuel resources are limited.

Most imported gas in Georgia comes from Azerbaijan, supplemented by Russian gas. However, its advantageous geographical location is used for gas transit from the Caspian region to Europe. Hence, Georgia receives transit fees for gas pipelines crossing Georgian territory. Gas transit in Georgian territory is conducted by the South Caucasus Pipeline (SCP) and the North South Gas Pipeline (NSGP). The SCP, also known as the Shah Deniz Pipeline, has a capacity of 20 BCM and transports gas from Azerbaijan to Turkey. Georgia receives a transit fee amounting to 5% of the actual volume of the transported gas. Assuming full utilization of the pipeline, Georgia can receive 1 BCM of natural gas every year. Georgia also has the right to purchase a maximum amount of 0.5 BCM of gas annually at a discounted price, starting from 55 USD per 1000 m^3 in 2006 with an increase of 1.5% per year. On the other hand, the NSMGP can transport 12 BCM of natural gas from Russia to Armenia. Georgia receives about 10% of its total transported gas from this pipeline.[7]

Azerbaijan's electricity generation is dominated by natural gas. In 2012, gas-fired TPPs generated 84% of total electricity consumption while

4 Ministry of Energy of Georgia, <www.energy.gov.ge>.
5 Electricity system commercial operator (ESCO), <www.esco.ge>.
6 Ministry of Energy of Georgia, <www.energy.gov.ge>.
7 Georgian Oil and Gas Corporation, <www.gogc.ge>.

only 16% came from hydropower plants. On the other hand, Azerbaijan is rich with oil and gas reserves, taking an important role in international oil and gas pipeline projects as one of the major gas suppliers. Its gas reserves are estimated to be 0.9 trillion m^3 while its R/P ratio is 57.1.[8, 9]. Huge gas reserves and a subsidized domestic supply have translated into a slow growth in domestic demand and utilization of the country's potential in international gas projects.[10]

The electricity sector in Armenia is divided into three generation sources: nuclear, TPPs and HPPs. The share of nuclear in electricity generation is 30% to 40%, whereas the share of TPPs is 30% to 35% and the remaining 20% to 35% is distributed to HPPs.[11] Moreover, Armenia's gas supply comes mostly from Russia and it is estimated that Russia controls nearly 80% of its energy system (Cecire, 2011). Like Georgia, Armenia has also very limited fossil-fuel resources.

The South Caucasus countries find themselves with a high degree of physical dependence on neighbouring countries for gas supply. While energy markets in these countries are relatively small, they definitely need to diversify gas supply, support infrastructure development and apply new technologies for gas storage. Moreover, harmonization with European competitive market principles is crucial. At present, the South Caucasus countries are treated as strategic transit routes for natural gas transportation. Transit fees are mostly used for the operation and maintenance of these pipelines. Therefore, transit fees cannot guarantee security of supply or provide a solution for the problem of infrastructure, either in the short term or the long term.

On the one hand, huge oil and gas reserves exist in the Caspian and Middle Eastern region. On the other hand, there is a large market for, and demand for, energy sources from Europe and even Turkey. The South Caucasus region, as the shortest transit route between these supply and demand regions, can be considered for the establishment of energy trading centre. Establishing an energy trading centre in the South Caucasus region

8 The R/P ratio is a reserves-to-production ratio, which means that if the remaining reserves at the end of any year are divided by the production in that year, the result is the length of time (years) that those remaining reserves would last if production were to continue at that rate.

9 BP (2013).

10 The State Statistical Committee of Azerbaijan, <www.stat.gov.az>.

11 Ministry of Energy and Natural Resources of Armenia, <www.minenergy.am>.

may increase investments for the development of additional transit routes and infrastructure that will guarantee a substantial stream of revenues for the countries in this region. However it will require a very reliable physical infrastructure, financial instruments and legislation to promote commercial trading, which has to be developed.

The Role of Europe and Russia in the South Caucasus Region

Traditionally, the South Caucasus region was influenced by the various political and economic interests of Europe and Russia. More specifically, countries from South Caucasus were linked to Europe's and Russia's strategic economic and energy policies and this affected their development. Due to its geopolitical location, there is growing competition between Russia and Europe to take control over the region's energy resources and infrastructure, in order to realize competing pipeline projects.

In the coming decades, the demand for natural gas in Europe will increase substantially. While natural gas reserves are being exhausted, Europe will most probably need to import it. The development of the shale gas industry may contribute to satisfying the rising gas demand in Europe. However, its contribution will remain on a small scale and substitute only a small proportion of imported gas. In order to meet the increasing demand, Europe will need to look into additional natural gas import options. Today, Europe imports only a small amount of natural gas in LNG form. The largest share of its gas import is delivered through Russia, while Europe also imports gas from Norway and North Africa. Europe also tries to diversify its supply sources and plans to set up a Southern Gas Corridor. The new path will carry natural gas from the Caspian and Middle Eastern regions to Europe. Several pipeline projects of the Southern Gas Corridor have already been developed, whereas prospective gas pipeline projects such as the Trans-Adriatic Pipeline (TAP), Trans Anatolian Natural Gas Pipeline (TANAP),the Azerbaijan–Georgia–Romania Interconnector (AGRI), South Caucasus Pipeline expansion plan and White Stream are intended to ensure diversification of supply routes and sources in order to decrease its dependence on imported gas import from politically sensitive regions.

Considering the huge natural gas reserves in the Caspian and Middle Eastern regions, only a small part of the reserves will be available for the Southern Gas Corridor in the near future. The politically difficult relationship between Europe and Iran has cancelled the Nabucco pipeline project negotiations and has made the transport of Qatar gas to Europe using the Iranian pipeline network unrealistic. In this respect, Azerbaijan remains the preferred choice for Europe. Azerbaijan's Shah Deniz gas field, in its second stage, will produce 16 BCM of natural gas. However, less than 10 BCM will be used for export to the EU. Residual gas will be transported to Turkey and secured for only one of the Southern Gas Corridor projects. Consequently, Azerbaijan has an important role in the Southern Gas Corridor. Moreover, Azerbaijan can be a future transit path for gas deliveries from Turkmenistan. On the other hand, Georgia also plays a key role as a transit country en route to Europe for the Southern Gas Corridor. Armenia is the only country from the South Caucasus region that does not play a direct role in the Southern Gas Corridor.

Apart from the Southern Energy Corridor, Europe has started various political initiatives in the South Caucasus region, such as the European Neighbourhood Policy (ENP) and the Eastern Partnership. However, energy policy still plays a key role in the relations of Europe and the South Caucasus countries. In general, Europe has not developed a common domestic and foreign energy policy with regard to South Caucasus. Its policy should not only focus on the role of the region as a transit corridor for oil and natural gas delivery but also represent a broader approach also dealing with the development of democracy, economy, trade and transparency.

For many years, Russian power and influence in the South Caucasus region has been increasing. Securing its dominant position, Russia's energy resources and energy policy play a central role in its strategy and foreign relations. Today, Russian state-owned companies are actively involved in most strategic industries across the South Caucasus, including the electricity and gas sector. Furthermore, Russia remains one of the most important trading partners for the three states. In the future, Russia can only benefit from its huge energy resources. However, its resources must be delivered to consumption centres in the international energy market, implying that the development of new transit infrastructure is required. Realizing the role of South Caucasus in facilitating the transit of oil and gas from Caspian region to international markets without the need to rely on Russia, Russia has already implemented several large-scale energy projects aiming to increase the transit capacity for Russian gas and oil to Europe, including North and South Stream.

Along with its huge conventional gas reserves, estimated at 1688 TCM, Russia's proven shale gas reserves amount to 285 TCM.[12] From Russia's point of view, the shale gas revolution is only American propaganda and a source of financial manipulation. Even though Russia is rich with shale gas resources, it could take a century before shale gas is produced there. It has sufficient reserves of natural gas and their cost-effectiveness will lead to Russia maintaining a competitive position in the international gas markets.[13]

In fact, Europe still remains highly dependent on Russian gas. Shale gas threatens Russian dominance over the region. While France and Bulgaria have banned shale gas production, several European countries are seeking to engage in sizable production and investment in the industry. The main markets are concentrated in Poland, Romania and Ukraine and development of the shale gas business can eliminate Russia's influence on Europe (WEC, 2011). Russia and its state-owned gas company, Gazprom, see shale gas as a potential main rival to its conventional gas production and supply in the future. Currently, the European gas market is a main driving force of Gazprom's profit and production volumes. By developing new pipeline projects in the region, Russia expects to keep European gas demand and prices high. However, considering new market realities, Gazprom has agreed to review existing contracts and introduce a spot component into contracts with its large consumers. Gazprom particularly negotiates with those countries where shale gas reserves are available, although these contracts are long term, oil linked and based on the take-or-pay principle. Shale gas development will sustain low spot prices, which reduces Gazprom's sales in Europe. Therefore, declining gas demand and prices in Europe will push Russia to turn its attention to the fast-growing Asian markets.

Russia's dominant role will also affect shale gas development in the South Caucasus region. Russia is aggressively pushing forward its gas-pipeline projects, aiming to sustain its role in Europe's natural gas supply. It has long-term gas contracts with countries from the region, locking them into high gas prices. Although countries are increasingly interested in shale gas

12 EIA, 2013.

13 RT, <http://rt.com/business/medvedev-gazprom-shale-russia-947/> (accessed 7 November 2014).

developments, shale gas operations can potentially be started only after long-term gas contracts have expired.

Prospects for Shale gas in the South Caucasus: Issues and Opportunities

The rising importance of shale gas in the United States and Europe could affect the South Caucasus region in the future. While the natural gas market is characterized by oil-indexed and long-term contracts, shale gas developments in this region seem to have an even longer time perspective than in Europe. In general, there is weak government interest and support in shale gas operations, resulting in a lack of exploration activities. Only a few pre-feasibility studies have been conducted in the two countries with the help of international organizations. Even though several potential shale reserves are found in Georgia, further research and analyses are needed to approve precise potential of Georgian shale gas reserves. In addition, market regulatory and infrastructure reviews are required to verify its economic viability. Today, preliminary rough estimates indicate that Georgia's shale gas potential can be comparable to most successful shale gas plays in the United States (WEG, 2010).

Preliminary assessments suggest that Armenia's shale gas potential is small. However, Armenia is continuing to carry out assessments and technical studies of its resources with the United States, including investigations of its shale gas potential. On the other hand, shale exploration presents an opportunity for Armenia to reduce reliance on foreign energy. Increased domestic energy sources can also help to offset an ongoing rise in natural gas prices. Exploration of Armenia's shale reserves may discover that they are not commercially viable, which will reduce Armenia's ability to remake its energy policy. However, shale offers Armenia the prospect of economic growth and would increase its geopolitical options (Cecire, 2011). Shale gas development will be challenging for conventional gas from Azerbaijan as LNG comes into the international market game. As an owner of huge reserves, Azerbaijan will have to take aggressive steps to compete with shale gas in the future. Still, Azerbaijan aims to enter and become one of the major players in European gas market after 2017. Based on the US example, where it took a minimum of 5 years to launch shale gas production, Azerbaijan believes that it will take more than 5 years for Europe, even using American experience (NGE, 2012).

There are several substantial benefits that can be gained from shale gas production for South Caucasus countries. First, it can be a promising fossil fuel that will satisfy their growing energy demand. Armenia and Georgia are largely dependent on imported conventional gas from their neighbouring countries. Depletion of their reserves in the future needs to be replaced either with other energy resources or shale gas, as projected global energy demand will increase by about 30% by 2040 and natural gas will become a major energy source, with a 60% increase in demand from 2010 to 2040. On the other hand, demand for coal will decline because energy demand tends to shift to less carbon-intensive energy sources (ExxonMobil, 2012). Following global trends, the electricity and transport sectors will be main contributors in the South Caucasus countries and they will drive growth in natural gas consumption. Future growth in electricity demand will require addition of new capacity. Building new TPPs could be the optimal decision, taking into account future trends in natural gas developments. Compared to any other fossil fuel, natural gas is becoming a cheaper energy source and it produces the lowest greenhouse gas (GHG) emissions. Shale gas production in the south Caucasus countries can satisfy the natural gas demand for TPPs and reduce the carbon footprint. Another benefit of shale gas is its influence in reducing energy dependence in these countries. Further exploration of shale gas resources and the development of the shale gas industry in the South Caucasus countries can promise substantial shale gas production to balance their energy demand based on local gas production.

The South Caucasus countries may also reap direct and indirect economic benefits by developing the shale gas industry. It can maximize companies' profits but also create wealth for these nations. Direct financial benefits could include government revenues and various types of taxes paid by shale gas companies. Clearly, these taxes will vary depending on the legislation in each country. For instance, the economic contribution of shale gas in 2010 amounted to 18.6 billion USD in government tax revenues in the United States and this amount is projected to increase to 57 billion USD by 2035. Based on a cumulative distribution of tax revenues, the shale gas industry will generate more than 933 billion USD over the year of 2037 (IHS Global Insight, 2011). In addition, indirect benefits are related to new job creation, the development of new industries and low and stable gas prices, which, in turn, will make a positive economic contribution. In 2010, more than 600 000 jobs came from the shale gas industry. Moreover, it has been projected that it will support a total of over 1.6 million jobs across the United States by 2035 (IHS Global Insight, 2011). Shale gas-driven low gas prices will contribute to reduced electricity generation costs and residential tariffs, which will stimulate economic growth and industrial activity in the South Caucasus countries. But a boom in economic activities might increase GHG emission from shale gas, higher than the existing projections. In addition to its economic benefits, the developing shale gas industry may assist Georgia, Armenia and Azerbaijan to meet their GHG emission targets in future. Additional indirect benefits could be associated with the development and sale of gas-fired vehicles. The best example is the United States, where natural gas is becoming widely used in the transport sector.

While fossil fuels are used extensively in electricity generation, shale gas can produce electricity efficiently compared to other fossil fuels. There are concerns that shale gas can substitute not only coal but also renewables. Expectations from cheap shale gas could prevent development of relatively expensive renewables but, due to uncertainties in the global gas market, the shale gas revolution could fail to provide cheap gas. By that time it might be rather late to return to renewable sources as a climate-change-oriented solution. However, a number of experts considers shale gas as a "transition" fuel in the movement from high carbon-emitting energy sources towards clean and zero-emission renewable sources.

Considering the experiences of the United States and Europe, shale gas development in the South Caucasus countries could be opposed by local communities and environmentalists due to the environmental risks of hydraulic fracturing processes. Fracturing involves radioactive materials and heavy metals, which may be harmful for the environment and dangerous for health. A high level of resistance form the public might negatively affect shale gas development in the region. Chemicals used in fracturing operations may leak into underground water reservoirs and ultimately pollute drinking water. Proper regulation is required to minimize groundwater contamination risks. However, a number of studies have revealed that this risk has been overstated and poor well completion is the main contributor to environmental problems, rather than fracturing itself (MIT, 2011). Shale gas can also be a geological hazard, resulting in explosions and increased seismic activity. In some circumstances, shale gas can leak from a well or landfill and induce property damage or threaten people's health. A large volume of water is required for shale gas extraction. It may increase municipal water management risks in water-restricted or high-demand areas where water is intensively used in the residential sector. Another risk can arise from storing large volumes of chemicals at the shale gas site together with liquid and solid waste produced during drilling and fracturing. This can lead to increased erosion of soil, pits on well sites and contamination of surface water. Finally, the environmental impact on biodiversity is another concern for public. Shale gas drilling activities may have a harmful impact on wildlife and habitats.

Conclusion

Several conclusions can be drawn from the above analysis. The shale gas revolution has dramatically changed natural gas markets. The United States can be seen as an innovator of technological advances that have resulted in shale gas becoming a game changer in the global energy market. Compared to other fossil fuels it causes less pollution and is cheap. The recent decoupling of natural gas prices from oil prices indicates an interest by many countries in using cheap energy sources in industrial activities. With its high dependence on Russian gas, Europe is interested in exploiting its shale gas potential with the aim of improving its energy security and diversifying its energy supplies. However, environmental risks, regulatory issues and lack of infrastructure make shale gas a long-term project.

The South Caucasus region, as a focal point of energy transit, has led to interest from big energy players in the market. There are few assessments related to shale gas potential in the region. While natural gas constitutes a high proportion of their energy mix, shale gas may eliminate countries' dependency on foreign energy and may affect their energy policy. There is a need for further research and assessments together with a desire on the part of governments to initiate shale gas production in this region. Regulated gas markets in combination with long-term contracts make shale gas development a long-term vision and challenge for the South Caucasus region, rather than a current issue.

References

BP (2013) *Statistical Review of World Energy,* British Petroleum, <http://www.bp.com/content/dam/bp/pdf/statistical-review/statistical_review_of_world_energy_2013.pdf> (accessed 7 November 2014).

Cecire M. (2011) Shale gas reserves could widen Armenia's horizons. *World Political Review* (8 September).

EIA (2012) *Annual Energy Outlook 2012 with Projections to 2035,* US Energy Information Administration, Washington, DC.

EIA (2013a) *Annual Energy Outlook 2013,* US Energy Information Administration, Washington, DC.

EIA (2013b) *Technically Recoverable Shale Oil and Shale Gas Resources: An Assessment of 137 Shale Formations in 41 Countries Outside the United States,* US Energy Information Administration, Washington, DC.

Exxon Mobil (2012) *2012 The Outlook for Energy: A View to 2040,*<http://www.wec-france.org/DocumentsPDF/rapports/RapportEXXONMOBIL.pdf>.

IEA (2011) *Are We Entering a Golden Age of Gas?* Special Report. International Energy Administration, Paris.

IHS Global Insight (2011) *The Economic and Employment Contributions of Shale Gas in the United States,* IHS Global Insight, Washington, DC.

MIT (2011) *The Future of Natural Gas,* Massachusetts Institute of Technology, <https://mitei.mit.edu/system/files/NaturalGas_Report.pdf>.

NGE (2012).*The Southern Gas Corridor: Competition is the Best for Everyone, Natural Gas Europe,* <http://www.naturalgaseurope.com/gulmira-rzayeva-azerbaijan-southern-corridor> (accessed 7 November 2014).

Pfeifer, S. (2012) Finds that form a bedrock of hope. *Financial Times* (22 April).

WEC (2011) *Survey of Energy Resources: Shale Gas – What's New?* World Energy Council, London.

WEG (2010) *Potential for Shale Gas in Georgia: Preliminary Study for Feasibility Analysis of Shale Gas Exploration in Georgia,* World Experience of Georgia, Tbilisi.

Christoph H. Stefes and Ghia Nodia

Concluding Thoughts

The last pages of this volume are Janus-faced. On one hand, they will situate the contributions of this volume in the broader research agenda on the South Caucasus of recent years. On the other hand, we look ahead and highlight research lacunae and fruitful venues for further social science work on Armenia, Azerbaijan and Georgia. Although the entire region does not comprise more than fifteen million people, it provides social scientists with a fascinating laboratory of societies that have laboured for almost 25 years with the quadruple challenge of building new political systems and economies as well as states and nations (Kuzio, 2001).

A review of articles published in three popular area studies journals (*Europe-Asia Studies, Post-Soviet Affairs*, and *Communist and Post-Communist Studies*) between 2004 and 2014 reveals that the South Caucasus has enjoyed considerable scholarly attention. Roughly 40 articles have been published that focus on one or more countries of the region. That is almost one-fifth of all articles published in these three journals since 2004. This overrepresentation of the region, given its size, is good news. On the downside, the research agenda is narrow, focused on Georgia, and very much influenced by current events. Of the 40 articles, more than 10 articles focus exclusively on Georgia and in the vast majority of articles with multiple case studies, Georgia figures prominently. The same level of attention is not given to Armenia, not to mention Azerbaijan, which is analysed in just six articles (single-case *and* multiple-case studies).

It also appears that current events significantly shape the research agenda. Not counting coverage of the Russia–Georgia War of 2008, 11 articles focus on ethnic minorities and ethnic conflict in the South Caucasus. Another seven articles analyse different aspects of the Russia–Georgia War and another five studies discuss the causes and consequences of the Colour Revolutions, especially the Georgian Rose Revolution of 2003. Somewhat surprising, given the limited role that the EU plays in this region, is the interest in EU-South Caucasus relations – especially, EU-Georgia relations, which is the focus of six articles. The remaining articles analyse state-building and governance issues (four) local politics (two) welfare politics (two) as well as gender relations, regime dynamics and foreign-policy making (each one). Research topics that were once prominent in the field of post-Soviet transitions have now largely disappeared. For instance, research on civil society, political values, the political economy of market transitions and public policies (with the exception of social policy) is missing.

The contributions in this volume do partially mirror the general research foci of scholars working on the South Caucasus, but they also go well beyond it. Ethnic identity, relations and conflict figure prominently in this volume (see the chapters by Kabachnik, Lundgren, Oltramonti, Oskanian, and Shelest). These chapters still make an important contribution, though. The focus is much less on the origins of ethnic conflict in the South Caucasus but much more on the current status of frozen conflicts and *de facto* states and the kinds of impact that this situation has on identity formation, economic development, foreign policy development and so forth. While it might be politically incorrect to ascribe any sovereignty to the three *de facto* states of the South Caucasus, it is still worthwhile analysing them as political systems *sui generis,* following the tradition of Charles King (2001) and Dov Lynch (2004).

Research on the influence of external democracy assistance is also presented in this volume (Rommens and Zielys) as well as an analysis of the causes of the Color Revolutions (Rahmetov) and studies of welfare politics and gender relations (McMullaugh and Ferry, respectively). A research area that is well covered in this volume, but not so much in the regional studies journals mentioned above, is energy politics and economics (Indeo, Poiana, Raszewski, Sumbadze, and Wege). That said, energy and geopolitics in the Caspian region remains a research topic that enjoys prominent coverage among students of international relations (Dekmejian and Simonian, 2003; Weaver 2011; Kubicek 2013).

To redirect our attention from the past to the future, we begin our discussion of fruitful venues for future research with the one contribution to this volume not mentioned so far. Sichinava takes recent Georgian elections seriously. In other words, he considers Georgian elections as meaningful institutions for voters' expressions of preferences. Indeed, among the three South Caucasian countries, Georgia has made the most progress towards free and fair elections. While the future of Georgia's democracy can be assessed only with cautious optimism, it is not too early to apply bread-and-butter models of Western psephology to the analysis of Georgian elections and test how far they can travel (not far, as Sichinava points out). And while we are at it we should also expand the analysis to the study of party politics, which is much more informed by theoretical frameworks applied to democracies than to authoritarian regimes. The same holds true for the study of civil society, which, unfortunately, appears to have gone out of vogue. Yet in Georgia we see an interesting development of the structures of cooperation and confrontation between Georgia's nongovernmental organizations and government, indicating a maturation of state-society relations. A comparison with Georgia's neighbours would help us to identify the driving forces of this process – for example, Western influence, democratization and cultural traits (Ishkanian 2008, Muskhelishvili and Jorjoliani 2009; Falkenhain 2014). A comparison across space and across time would also allow us to test arguments about the possible influence of the EU on the region. The recent signing of the EU-Georgia Association Agreement should, in principle, increase the EU's leverage on Georgia and accelerate political and economic liberalization. In contrast, Azerbaijan and Armenia, which in 2013 even reversed its pro-Western course (Giragosian, 2014), remain at arm's length to the EU. Western-induced liberalization is therefore unlikely in these countries.

Armenia and Azerbaijan are interesting cases with which to investigate the mechanism that leads to the (in)stability of (semi)authoritarian regimes, a topic that has gained prominence in political science since the seminal study of Barbara Geddes (1999). While much quantitative work has been produced (de Mesquita and Smith, 2011; Svolic, 2012; Tanneberg *et al.*, 2013), in-depth case studies are few and far between (Magaloni, 2008; Pepinski, 2009). Yet McMullaugh (in this volume) already raises important questions for future research. Even though oil resources make it easier for authoritarian rulers to stay in power (Smith, 2004), why has the Azerbaijani leadership decided to benefit the elite and not the people? Other rentier states such as Saudi Arabia spread the wealth much wider and thereby legitimize their nondemocratic regimes. Even more fascinating is the case of Armenia. Deprived of valuable natural resources, Armenia's semiauthoritarian regime has shown remarkable resilience, even in the face of mass protests. How can we explain the loyalty of the "guys with guns and money"? What explains the weakness of Armenia's opposition? To what degree do informal institutions of corruption and clientelism explain the coherence of Armenia's economic and political elite (Stefes,

2006)? While looking inside the inner circles of authoritarian rule is no easy task, it is a worthwhile endeavour, allowing us to test the sometimes far-fetched claims that scholars of authoritarian regime survival have made in their quantitative studies.

Almost a quarter of a century after the collapse of communism, social scientists will also study the political economy of market liberalization in new places. While the politics of economic transition was a rich area of research during the 1990s (Kaufmann and Siegelbaum, 1996; Hellman, 1998; Bunce, 1999), the politics of economic transitions has not sparked much scholarly interest in more recent years, which holds especially true for the South Caucasus. Yet the economies of the South Caucasus are still in transition and the divergent paths that these countries have taken – from a late "shock therapy" in Georgia after 2003, to inert liberalization in Armenia, to a frozen economic transition in Azerbaijan – raise many interesting research questions (Papava, 2009). What explains the choice of transitions that political elites in these three countries have taken? To what degree have economic policies been derailed by severe governance problems in these countries? How successful has liberalization been for the South Caucasian economies? Standard theories do not seem to provide satisfying answers to these questions (Stefes and Wooden, 2009).

Even more glaring is the absence of comparative studies that assess the social and political consequences that economic transitions have had on the Armenian, Georgian, and Azerbaijani societies.[1] For instance, even though a small middle class appears to be emerging, it is also true that, after the collapse of Communism, wealth became increasingly concentrated in all three countries while poverty rates have been slowly declining in recent years. The gap between rich and poor is therefore continuously widening. This gap becomes readily apparent when travelling through the South Caucasus. While the three capitals witness increasing gentrification, with property values and rents shooting through the roofs, the rural areas are falling further behind. How will these social and economic stratifications within the urban areas and between the urban and rural areas affect future political and economic transitions? Will the emerging middle class be able to press for further liberalization, as many scholars seem to hope, or does social and economic inequality harbour so much potential for social unrest that political instability will undermine any further political and

1 We owe this observation to our colleague Stephen Jones.

economic reforms? How will the political, economic and social interests of the underprivileged strata be organized and channelled into the political processes? Will neopatrimonial structures be able to contain social powder kegs? And to what degree does regime type matter for the political impact of social and economic stratifications?

In general, social, economic, and political transitions in the countries of the South Caucasus take place at very different speeds and these asynchronous developments contain considerable potential for societal conflict. In particular, the role of religious organizations may be an important indicator to look at. Georgia is an important exception among formerly Communist countries where the surge in religiosity did not coincide with the short period of the post-Communist transition, but has continued as a steady trend ever since independence (Zviadadze, 2014). Here, religious organizations vocally and sometimes even violently oppose the seeping in of Western norms that are blamed for accelerating moral decay and the loss of national identity, and try to influence the outcome of political competition. While at present Azerbaijan is usually considered a rather secular country, it may be on the way to follow the trajectory of autocratic regimes where radical Islam develops into the most powerful social force balancing the domination of secular autocracy, but also trends of societal Westernization (Hadjy-zadeh, 2011). Comparative studies of the role of religion in the South Caucasus are still rather rare yet interest in this issue will most likely rise.

Given the manifold challenges South Caucasian societies will experience in the coming decades, there is a need for policy-oriented studies that are less inspired by theoretical debates than by the search for feasible solutions to pressing problems. For example, since the Soviet welfare system was largely dismantled and no alternative has been created in its stead, the public education, health, and retirement systems (to name just a few) lack funding, institutions, and expertise. And when governments attempt to address the problems through new policies, citizens are suspicious, unwilling to support new measures, and sometimes willing to take to the streets in opposition to these new policies. In Armenia, recent pension reforms sparked mass protests, as citizens suspected that planned pension contributions would be diverted to other programmes or simply embezzled (Arakelyan, 2014). Decades of corruption and mismanagement have left poor prospects for good governance even if the abuse of public office declined, as public and private actors view each other with suspicion. How contentious state-society relations can be transformed into partnerships for the formulation and implementation of much needed policy reforms deserves the attention of social scientists.

In short, this volume has made a small contribution to a wider research agenda on the South Caucasus. The studies presented here have put a new spin on popular research topics, such as ethnic conflict and the role of Western powers in the South Caucasus, and addressed less-discussed issues (e.g. changing gender relations, elections, and the social and economic costs of protracted ethnic conflicts). There is little doubt that much more research needs to be done to understand the manifold facets of social, political, and economic transitions. The good news is that a new generation of young social scientists inside and outside of the South Caucasus has the skills and the scholarly curiosity to engage new research topics.

References

Arakelyan, L. (2014) *Mass Protest Movement Against Armenian Pension Reform,* Institute for War & Peace Reporting, <http://iwpr.net/report-news/mass-protest-movement-against-armenian-pension-re form> (accessed 8 November 2014).

Bunce, V. (1999) The political economy of postsocialism. *Slavic Review* 58(4), 756–793.

Dekmejian, R. H. and Simonian, H. H. (2003) *Troubled Waters. The Geopolitics of the Caspian Region*, I. B. Tauris, London.

De Mesquita, B. B. and Smith, A. (2011) *The Dictator's Handbook*, Public Affairs, New York.

Falkenhain, M. (2014) *Straightjackets or Arenas? NGOs in the Institutions of Competitive Authoritarian Regimes.* Paper presented at the 11th International Conference of the International Society for Third-Sector Research, Muenster, 22–25 July 2014.

Giragosian, R. (2014) *Armenia's Surprising U-Turn.* European Council on Foreign Relations Policy Memo, <http://www.ecfr.eu/page/-/ECFR99_ARMENIA_MEMO_AW.pdf> (accessed 8 November 2014).

Hadjiy-zadeh, H. (2011) *Islam and Religious Freedom in Independent Azerbaijan: Analytical reviews, Essays and Sociological Research on*

Religiosity in Newly Independent Azerbaijan, Lambert Academic Publishing, Saarbrücken.
Hellman, J. S. (1998) Winners take all: the politics of partial reform in post-communist transitions. *World Politics* 50(2), 203–234.
Ishkanian, A. (2008) *Democracy Building and Civil Society in Post-Soviet Armenia*, Routledge, London.
Kaufmann, D. and Siegelbaum, P. (1996) Privatization and corruption in transition economies. *Journal of International Affairs* 50(2), 419–458.
King, C. (2001) The benefits of ethnic war: understanding Eurasia's unrecognized states. *World Politics* 53(4), 524–552.
Kubicek, P. (2013) Energy politics and geopolitical competition in the Caspian Basin. *Journal of Eurasian Studies* 4, 171–180.
Kuzio, T. (2001) Transition in post-communist states: triple or quadruple? *Politics* 21(3), 168–177.
Lynch, D. (2004) *Engaging Eurasia's Separatist States: Unresolved Conflicts and de Facto State*, United States Institute of Peace Press, Washington, DC.
Magaloni, B. (2008) *Voting for Autocracy: Hegemonic Party Survival and its Demise in Mexico*, Cambridge University Press, New York, NY.
Muskhelishvili, M. and Jorjoliani, G. (2009) Georgia's ongoing struggle for a better future continued: democracy promotion through civil society development. *Democratization* 16(4), 682–708.
Papava, V. (2009) Georgia's economy: post-revolutionary development and post-war difficulties. *Central Asian Survey* 22(2), 199–213.
Pepinski, T. B. (2009) *Economic Crises and the Breakdown of Authoritarian Regimes: Indonesia and Malaysia in Comparative Perspective*, Cambridge University Press, New York, NY.
Smith, B. (2004). Oil Wealth and Regime Survival in the Developing World, 1960–1999. *American Journal of Political Science* 48(2), 232–246.
Stefes, C. H. (2006) *Understanding Post-Soviet Transitions. Corruption, Collusion and Clientelism*, Palgrave Macmillan, New York, NY.
Stefes, C. H. and Wooden, A. E. (2009) Tempting two fates: the theoretical foundations for understanding Central Eurasian transitions, in *The Politics of Transition in Central Asia and the Caucasus* (eds. A. E. Wooden and C. H. Stefes), Routledge, New York, NY, 3–29.
Svolic, M. (2012) *The Politics of Authoritarian Rule*, Cambridge University Press, New York, NY.

Tanneberg, D., Merkel, W. and Stefes, C. H. (2013) Hard times and regime failure. Autocratic responses to economic downturns. *Contemporary Politics* 19(1), 115–129.

Weaver, C. (2011) Black Sea regional security: present multipolarity and future possibilities. *European Security* 20(1), 1–19.

Zviadadze S (2014) *Religion und Politik in Georgien*, Verlag Dr Kovač, Hamburg.

Notes on Contributors

Maroussia Ferry is a PhD candidate at École des Hautes Études en Sciences Sociale (EHESS), Paris and a fellow at the French Institute for Demographic Studies (INED). She is currently conducting anthropological fieldwork in Georgia and Turkey, investigating how the feminization of migration affects post-Soviet Georgia, with a focus on the Turkish case.

Fabio Indeo holds a PhD in geopolitics. Currently he is external research fellow in geopolitics at the University of Camerino (Italy), visiting research associate at the Center for Energy Governance and Security (EGS) of Hanyang University (South Korea) and lecturer on "Conflicts and energy resources" at the University of Roma Tre, Italy. His research field focuses on the geopolitics of Caucasus and Central Asia: energy security and diversification strategy; geopolitics of pipelines and of energy transport routes; the external influences of Russia, European Union, United States and China; Afghanistan and regional security. In 2013 he published The decline of the Nabucco Project: a geopolitical defeat for the EU, in *EGS Global Energy Monitor* 1(7), pp. 1–3.

Peter Kabachnik, PhD, is an associate professor of geography in the Department of Political Science and Global Affairs at the College of Staten Island, The City University of New York (CUNY) and a member of the graduate faculty in the Earth and Environmental Sciences Program at The Graduate Center, The City University of New York (CUNY). He is a political and cultural geographer whose interests lie in the way that people interact with places, and the interplay between place, mobility, and identity more generally. He is currently working on a research project examining post-Soviet memory, personality cults and the memorialized landscape in Georgia, focusing on contemporary understandings of Stalin. Using Georgian IDPs as a case study, he also focuses on geographies of displacement, or the various ways that people are affected by, and deal with, the harsh circumstances surrounding the need to leave one's home. Some of the themes that Dr Kabachnik examines in this project are: how IDPs conceptualize home, by examining how they think about their former homes in Abkhazia and the way they live in their current living spaces; the geopolitical factors that shape the discourses that fuel the conflict and how changing gender roles create a perceived challenge to dominant masculinities.

MINNA LUNDGREN is a doctoral student in sociology at the Department of Social Sciences at Mid Sweden University. Her research interests include human rights in post-conflict settings, social vulnerability and forced migration in the former Soviet republics. In her doctoral research project she focuses on experiences of protracted displacement among Georgian IDPs (internally displaced persons) from Abkhazia.

MARCY MCCULLAUGH received a PhD in political science from the University of California at Berkeley in August 2013. Her dissertation focused on redistributive social spending in mineral-rich authoritarian regimes, using the cases of Russia, Kazakhstan and Azerbaijan.

BETH MITCHNECK is a professor of geography at the University of Arizona. She is a human geographer with research interests in migration, particularly human displacement in Eurasia, and how space and place interface with social interaction patterns and ultimately human security. Beth has published on migration, governance, and social networks. She is currently researching displacement in Georgia and international migration in Russia.

GHIA NODIA is Professor of Political Science and Director of the International School of Caucasus Studies at Ilia State University in Tbilisi, Georgia. He is also the founder of the Caucasus Institute for Peace, Democracy and Development (CIPDD), an independent public policy think tank based in Tbilisi, which he has led (with a short interruption) since 1992. He has published extensively on two sets of topics: regional security, state building and democratization in the Caucasus, and theories of nationalism and democratic transition in the post-Cold War context. He has been involved in pro-democracy advocacy efforts in Georgia and internationally, and has been a frequent participant in international congresses and conferences on related topics.

KEVORK OSKANIAN is a visiting lecturer at the University of Westminster and a Research Associate at the Foreign Policy Centre, London. He received his PhD from the London School of Economics, and has formerly coedited the *Millennium Journal of International Studies,* as well as *After Liberalism?* – a volume on the future of liberalism in international relations. His latest work – *Fear, Weakness and Power in the Post-Soviet South Caucasus* – is a monograph on regional security in that part of the former Soviet Union.

OANA POIANĂ is a PhD candidate in international relations at Babes-Bolyai University, Faculty of European Studies, Cluj-Napoca, Romania. She conducted research at Central European University in Budapest (Hungary) and Otto von Guericke University in Magdeburg (Germany). Her research interests focus on European energy security, regionalization in the wider Black Sea Area, Eurasian politics and EU foreign policy.

GIULIA PRELZ OLTRAMONTI is a teaching and research assistant at the Université libre de Bruxelles. She holds a BA in European social and political studies from University College London and a MA in conflict, security and development from King's College London. Her research interests cover political economies of conflict protraction, and the role of borders in conflict transformation. Recent publications include a chapter on borders, de facto borders and mobility policies in conflict transformation in *Borders and Border Regions in Europe*, edited by Wielgohs and Lechevalier (2013), and an article on political economies and conflict mitigation in *The Caucasus and Globalization* (2012).

ANVAR RAHMETOV holds a PhD in political science from the IMT Lucca Institute for Advanced Studies in Lucca, Italy. He has been on research visits to Central European University (Hungary), Harvard's Davis Center for Russian and Eurasian Studies (United States) and WZB – Berlin Social Science Research Centre (Germany). His research interests lie in the workings of soft authoritarian regimes, protest politics and business-politics nexuses in the post-Soviet countries. He is now based in Tashkent and works for an international organization.

SLAWOMIR RASZEWSKI is research associate in the European Centre for Energy and Resource Security, Department of War Studies, King's College

London. Dr Raszewski was previously a research associate in the Centre for International Minerals and Energy Law, University of Queensland, Australia, and a visiting scholar in the Faculty of Political Sciences, University of Ankara, Turkey. Dr Raszewski holds his PhD from the University of Leeds (UK) and his research interests focus on security studies and energy politics.

Joanna Regulska is a professor of Women's and Gender Studies, and Geography, at Rutgers, the State University of New Jersey. Her research concentrates on women's agency, political activism, grassroots mobilization, and the construction of political spaces by women within a context of regime change and post-conflict environment. Her work has also focused on gender dimensions of European integration and on the eastern enlargement of the European Union. Her current multi-year NSF funded research examines everyday practices and livelihood strategies of Internally Displaced Persons (IDPs) in Georgia. She is especially interested in understanding how women engage in transformative practices as political subjects and agents of social change under flexible and ever-changing conditions where instability and unpredictability become a norm. Joanna has published extensively on women's political identity, women's movement, and political and economic transformations in Europe and the Caucasus.

Thijs Rommens is an affiliated researcher at the Leuven Institute for the Study of International Politics and European affairs (LINES) at the University of Leuven, Belgium. He is currently working on his PhD on the impact of the EU's Eastern Partnership on NGOs in Georgia. For this research he conducted multiple research stays in Georgian think tanks and universities. His research interests include Europeanization, democracy support and civil society development, with a specific focus on the South Caucasus.

Hanna Shelest, PhD, is a senior researcher at the National Institute for Strategic Studies, Odessa Branch, Ukraine. Her research interests include conflict resolution, mediation and security in the Wider Black Sea, Balkans and Middle East regions, unrecognized states and the foreign policy of Ukraine. She has more than 50 academic and more than 100 media articles published in Ukraine, Russia, Moldova, Georgia, Sweden, Turkey, Azerbaijan, Lithuania, Romania, and so forth.

David Sichinava is a PhD candidate at the Department of Human Geography, Tbilisi State University. His research interests include political geography with focus on elections, urban geography, internal displacement in Georgia and socio-spatial modelling using geographic information systems (GIS).

Christoph H. Stefes is Associate Professor for Comparative European and Post-Soviet Studies at the University of Colorado Denver. He is a visiting scholar at the Wissenschaftszentrum Berlin für Sozialforschung (Social Science Research Center Berlin) where he investigates the conditions of stability of autocratic regimes. He specializes in the successor states of the Soviet Union in the South Caucasus and Central Asia. His research focuses on governance and the detrimental consequences of corruption in this region. In addition, he serves as a senior fellow at the Ecologic Institute Berlin, analyzing societal conflicts caused by climate change.

Nikoloz Sumbadze is a PhD student in economic policy at Tbilisi State University, chief specialist of Electricity Department at Georgian National Energy and Water Supply Regulatory Commission (GNERC) and a visiting lecturer at the School of Business and Management, Grigol Robakidze University. His research interests include energy policy, energy security, power markets, energy trading, sectoral economics, renewable energy, energy efficiency and sustainable development with a focus on the EU and South Caucasus countries.

Sybilla Wege has a degree in Slavic studies with a qualification in business administration at the University of Mannheim in Germany and is currently enrolled as an external PhD student in the Department of Political Science at the University of Mannheim. Her thesis examines Russian foreign energy policy and Russia's economic ambitions in the Caspian region with regard to the international gas market. She has worked as a business consultant for various municipal energy suppliers across Germany, focusing on portfolio and operational process optimization. Currently, she is working as a team leader in the procurement of energy and natural gas at an energy holding company specializing in supplying gas and electrical power. Her function involves mainly the strategic management of product offers, short- and mid-term gas procurement, and portfolio risk analysis and evaluation.

Povilas Žielys is an affiliated member of the Institute of International Relations and Political Science, Vilnius University (Lithuania). He has taught at Vilnius University and General Jonas Žemaitis Lithuanian Military Academy. His research interest is democratization processes in Eastern Europe and the South Caucasus.

INTERDISCIPLINARY STUDIES ON CENTRAL AND EASTERN EUROPE

Edited by
Christian Giordano, Nicolas Hayoz & Jens Herlth

This series focuses on the political, economic and cultural changes in Eastern Europe and the former Soviet Union. It offers a platform for inter-disciplinary research on this multifaceted part of the world. The focus lies mainly on current and recent developments in societies and political systems; but research on cultural and historical backgrounds has its place here, too. The range of disciplines includes political science, history, and social anthropology, but also philosophy, cultural studies, and literary criticism. The articles are written in English.

Band 1 Nicolas Hayoz & Andrej N. Lushnycky (eds)
Ukraine at a Crossroads.
269 pp. 2005.
ISBN 3-03910-468-3, US-ISBN 0-8204-7157-7

Band 2 Nicolas Hayoz, Leszek Jesień & Wim van Meurs (eds)
Enlarged EU – Enlarged Neighbourhood.
Perspectives of the European Neighbourhood Policy.
392 pp. 2005.
ISBN 3-03910-624-4, US-ISBN 0-8204-7167-4

Band 3 Nicolas Hayoz & Simon Hug (eds)
Tax Evasion, Trust, and State Capacities.
How good is Tax Moral in Central and Eastern Europe.
379 pp. 2007.
ISBN 978-3-03910-651-6, US-ISBN 978-0-8204-7168-6

Band 4 Andrej N. Lushnycky & Mykola Riabchuk (eds)
Ukraine on its Meandering Path Between East and West.
Interdisciplinary Studies on Central and Eastern Europe.
210 pp. 2009.
ISBN 978-3-03911-607-2

Band 5 Leonidas Donskis (ed.)
A Litmus Test Case of Modernity.
Examining Modern Sensibilities and the Public Domain in the Baltic States at the Turn of the Century.
314 pp. 2009.
ISBN 978-3-0343-0335-4

Band 6 Marta Dyczok & Oxana Gaman-Golutvina (eds)
Media, Democracy and Freedom.
The Post-Communist Experience.
246 pp. 2009.
ISBN 978-3-0343-0311-8

Band 7 Josette Baer (ed.)
From Post-Communism toward the Third Millenium.
Aspects of Political and Economic Development in Eastern and South-Eastern Europe from 2000–2005.
272 pp. 2011.
ISBN 978-3-03911-773-4

Band 8 Galina Michaleva & Andrey Ryabov (eds)
Russian Challenges.
Between Freedom and Energy.
240 pp. 2011.
ISBN 978-3-0343-0529-7

Band 9 Nicolas Hayoz, Leszek Jesień & Daniela Koleva (eds)
20 Years after the Collapse of Communism.
Expectations, achievements and disillusions of 1989.
679 pp. 2011.
ISBN 978-3-0343-0538-9

Band 10 Claire Gordon, Marko Kmezic & Jasmina Opardija (eds)
Stagnation and Drift in the Western Balkans.
The Challenges of Political, Economic and Social Change.
325 pp. 2013.
ISBN 978-3-0343-1152-6

Band 11 Christian Giordano & Nicolas Hayoz (eds)
Informality in Eastern Europe.
Structures, Political Cultures and Social Practices.
490 pp. 2013.
ISBN 978-3-0343-1455-8

Band 12 Forthcoming

Band 13 Viktor Stepanenko & Yaroslav Pylynskyi (eds)
Ukraine after the Euromaidan.
Challenges and Hopes.
271 pp. 2015.
ISBN 978-3-0343-1626-2

Band 14 Ghia Nodia and Christoph H. Stefes
Security, Democracy and Development.
In the Southern Caucasus and the Black Sea Region.
380 pp. 2015.
ISBN 978-3-0343-1300-1